Reluctant Allies

Reluctant Allies

German-Japanese Naval Relations in World War II

Hans-Joachim Krug, Yōichi Hirama,
Berthold J. Sander-Nagashima, and Axel Niestlé

Coordinated by Berthold J. Sander-Nagashima

Naval Institute Press
Annapolis, Maryland

Naval Institute Press
291 Wood Road
Annapolis, MD 21402

This book has been brought to publication with the generous assistance of Edward S. and Joyce I. Miller

The authors wish to acknowledge the work of Dr. Berthold Sander-Nagashima, who served as the coordinating editor for this volume. Without his able assistance, this book could not have been published.

Library of Congress Cataloging-in-Publication Data

Reluctant allies : German-Japanese naval relations in World War II / Hans-Joachim Krug . . . [et al.].

   p. cm.

   Includes bibliographical references and index.

   ISBN 1-55750-465-2 (alk. paper)

   1. World War, 1939–1945—Naval operations, German. 2. World War, 1939–1945—Naval operations, Japanese. 3. Germany. Kriegsmarine—History—World War, 1939–1945. 4. Japan. Kaigun—History—World War, 1939–1945. 5. Germany—Military relations—Japan. 6. Japan—Military relations—Germany. I. Krug, Hans-Joachim.

D770.R45 2001

940.54'5943—dc21

                                 2001031259

Printed in the United States of America on acid-free paper ∞

08 07 06 05 04 03 02 01   9 8 7 6 5 4 3 2

First printing

WHAT IS PAST IS PROLOGUE.

Shakespeare, *The Tempest.*

Inscribed at the entrance to the
National Archives, Washington, D.C.

Contents

Preface

On 28 September 1944, from the Central Atlantic, the German submarine U-219 headed southwest on a transport mission to Southeast Asia. She was loaded to her maximum capacity with advanced technical equipment for Germany's ally, Japan. By radio message she received orders to replenish U-1062, returning from Penang at 11°51'N, 34°45'W. However, the rendezvous position had been compromised by Allied code breaking. The U.S. Escort Carrier Group, TG 47.1, reinforced by TG 22.1, was already waiting in that vicinity for the German submarines when they attempted contact.

As darkness fell, the surfaced U-219 was attacked by an airplane from escort carrier (CVE) *Tripoli*. She managed to shoot down the attacker and submerge. But after crash diving she was quickly localized and persistently attacked with torpedoes and depth charges for nearly three consecutive days.

As U-219 attempted to report the engagement by radio to German Submarine Command, the submarine was again depth-charged and bombed from the air. Forced to submerge, she survived innumerable antisubmarine warfare (ASW) attacks. She stayed submerged for sixty-nine consecutive hours, finally escaping with tolerable damage. During the same encounter U-1062 was lost in action.

As far as I know, the U-219's was the longest submerged run of any conventional German submarine. It was possible only because the commanding officer, by mere chance, found a salinity layer on which the boat could drift with engines and nearly all machinery turned off, utilizing the absolute minimum of battery power. However, the CO_2 content of the breathing air had risen to ten times the tolerance level. When the sub finally had to surface, it emerged in the middle of a sandstorm blowing out from the African coast. The storm precluded a radar echo and kept TG 41.7 from regaining contact.

Commencing in October 1942, after operating along the African west coast and around the Cape of Good Hope, German submarines had also begun to penetrate into the Indian Ocean. In September 1944 I was a first lieutenant, serving as executive officer of U-219, her destination being this operations theater. When she reached port on 12 December 1944 it was at Tanjung Priok on Java. Because the repair facilities at Priok were very poor, U-219 was still loading badly needed raw materials for transport back to Europe when Germany capitulated to the Allies.

For the supply missions between Europe and the Far East, for which German and Italian surface cargo vessels had initially been used, quite a number of German, Italian, and Japanese submarines were employed from the middle of 1943 to the very end of the war. Aside from their transport missions, the German U-boats also routinely performed combat missions while in or en route to the Indian Ocean.

Relatively little has been published thus far about the naval cooperation between the German and the Japanese navies during World War II. From my personal experiences during the war, augmented by extensive studies of historical sources and my tour of duty as the German military attaché to Japan from 1969 to 1973, I felt obliged to try to preserve this aspect of maritime warfare for historical study.

During my assignment in Japan, I had close contacts with a number of Japanese naval officers, who, during their service in the Imperial Japanese Navy, had themselves acquired experience with German-Japanese naval cooperation. We were fortunate enough to also find in Rear Adm. (Ret.) Yōichi Hirama, as Japanese co-author, a former naval officer who had worked on similar topics during his service with the Japanese Maritime Self-Defense Force (JMSDF) and had established himself also as a historian and professor of military history.

During his active naval service, Admiral Hirama served as a staff member of the Intelligence Department of the Japanese Maritime Staff Office of Tokyo. His task there was intelligence exchange with the foreign military attachés stationed in Tokyo. At that time he first came to know me. When I went to Japan in preparation for this book after my retirement, I invited Dr. Hirama to join me and write about the Japanese aspects of German-Japanese naval cooperation. Admiral Hirama, then retired, consented. After tours of duty at the Japanese National Institute for Defense Studies (Military History) and as professor for military history at the National Defense Academy, he was especially suited for this task.

Admiral Hirama agreed that the subject of German-Japanese relations during World War II would be valuable for future research, especially for naval history. The subject has not been covered very thoroughly so far. And, as German and Japanese are not read very extensively worldwide, we decided to write this book together in English.

Details on the German-Japanese alliance from the mid-thirties until 1945 and the wartime exchange of materials and personnel between the two countries are covered by the authors Cdr. Berthold J. Sander-Nagashima and Dr. Axel Niestlé, who kindly made their results on these topics available for inclusion in this publication. It should be noted that the aforementioned authors are solely responsible only for their respective parts of the book.

As our book will show, interests among the Axis partners did not fully coincide and collided in many instances. For many reasons the efforts of the tripartite powers did not lead to successful cooperation. There were differences of strategic goals not only between the nations but also between the different national services. The Indian Ocean was the only theater in which Japanese and German strategies could have practically and effectively been made to match. The opportunity was missed because the partners could not coordinate or synchronize their national interests. To benefit from their history, however, it is well worthwhile to study their failure and the mechanisms that caused it.

This book was written by four authors. Part 1 contains the text of Captain GNY (Ret.) Krug and Rear Admiral JMSDF (Ret.) Hirama. Parts 2 and 4 are the work of Commander GNY Dr. Sander-Nagashima. Part 3 was written by Dr. Niestlé. Thus it represents a mixture of German and Japanese viewpoints. It demonstrates that there are, among the authors, many different approaches to the topic, just as different navies handle similar tasks in different ways, and we have kept those differences in mind. These four authors come from three different nations and two different generations. One wrote with the experience and know-how of the participant, the others mainly from a historian's view. We hope that these varying perspectives will be more revealing than one viewpoint alone. We used primary Japanese, German, and Allied sources and extensive literature to reach a truthful account of the time, which we hope will serve future historians well.

Even as these events by now have drifted back into the past, along with the distress they caused the nations involved, it is worthwhile to scrutinize the reasons for the failure of the naval cooperation between Germany and Japan. Experience gained from looking back into the past, appropriately evaluated, may benefit our future. As the inscription at one entrance to the United States National Archives building states, "The heritage of the past is the seed that brings forth the harvest of the future."

We dedicate this book to all naval personnel who have consecrated their devotion, even their lives, to their countries in fulfilling their duty.

HANS-JOACHIM KRUG AND HIRAMA YŌICHI

Acknowledgments

Being the only German naval officer who saw active naval service in Asia twice—once with the German submarine force during World War II and the second time as German military attaché to Japan in the seventies—I felt strongly compelled to write this book about the German-Japanese maritime cooperation during World War II. My idea was to work on this topic in collaboration with Japanese experts. During my second assignment in Japan, I had close contacts with a number of Japanese naval officers, who had experience with German-Japanese naval cooperation during their service in the Imperial Japanese Navy. When I mentioned the project to Admiral Uchida Kazutomi, the former JMSDF Chief of Staff, himself author of a number of recognized naval publications, he brought me into contact with Japanese naval historians. I also looked for personal expertise in the *Berlin-kai*, a circle of members of the wartime Japanese embassy at Berlin, and among former officers who had seen service in the Japanese submarine bases in the Indian Ocean.

I was fortunate enough to find in Rear Adm. (Ret.) Hirama Yōichi, our Japanese co-author, a naval officer who, following his service in the JMSDF, has worked on similar topics as a historian and professor with the Japanese National Institute for Defense Studies.

Commander GNY Dr. Sander-Nagashima kindly made available the research results of his dissertation on of German-Japanese naval relations, and he provided most of the primary sources for the research. He also took responsibility for editing the manuscript, a difficult and time-consuming task that took him away from his other work for quite some time. His knowledge of Japanese and English also proved invaluable to our project. Without his considerable effort and devotion to detail, this book would never have been published. We are greatful for his work on our behalf.

Dr. Axel Niestlé kindly provided the results of his extensive research in the field of German U-boat warfare and the exchange of materiel and personnel between Germany and Japan during World War II.

I am especially grateful for the information I acquired from Rear Adm. Ishiki Toshio, Rear Adm.(Ret.) Fuji Nobuyuki, Capt.(Ret.) Terashima Satoru, Cdr.(Ret.) Sakai Susumu, and Cdr.(Ret.) Torisu Kennosuke, as well as Mr. Komine Yoshimitsu of the Yasukuni Shrine War Museum.

Of the *Berlin-kai* members I am especially obliged to two former naval attachés in Berlin, the late Rear Adm. Kojima Hideo and Vice Adm. Taniguchi Yasumarō. Of great help to me also were historians Capt. Tomi Ichirō, Shōji Jun'ichirō, Ōki Takeshi, and Maj. Gen.(Ret.) Goda Yutaka, such officials as Rear Adm. Sato Kenzo, and such enthusiasts as Kajimoto Yoshiaki. I must also acknowledge Banzai Yoshimasa, my interpreter of long standing. Contacts with former Japanese submariners yielded essential insider knowledge.

Capt. Douglas M. Sherburne, USN (Ret.), kindly initiated my first contacts with the publisher and with the U.S. Naval Historical Center and the National Archives. Bernard F. Cavalcante and Kathleen Lloyd of the former and Harry Riley of the latter were especially helpful with my researches.

Edward S. Miller, the author of *War Plan Orange,* whom Rear Admiral Hirama knew from research work in Japan, played a very special role in the making of this project. Not only was he kind enough to scrutinize the manuscripts of Admiral Hirama and me and to provide us with valuable advice; he also introduced me to the Suitland Branch of the National Archives and above all, made this publication possible by generously funding it. All four authors gratefully thank him for this decisive help.

Worldwide correspondence with experts with pertinent knowledge—from Lt. Cdr. David M. Stevens, RAN, and the Municipal Council of Penang Island, to Rear Adm. Antonio Severi of the Ufficio Storico of the Italian navy, Capt.(Ret.) Claude Huan (French navy), and Gus Britton of the British Submarine Museum—helped to improve our competence.

Furthermore, the privately run German U-boat Archive at Cuxhaven with its director Horst Bredow, the Militärgeschichtliches Forschungsamt (MGFA) at Potsdam and the Bundesarchiv-Militärarchiv at Freiburg were also reviewed for suitable material.

I had the opportunity to talk to the late Adm.(Ret.) Paul Wenneker, the former *Deutscher Admiral Ostasien* (German Admiral, East Asia), his chief of staff's daughter Maria Freitag, his aide Lt. Cdr. Heinz Priesmeier, and his secretary Ingeborg Krag, as well as the former German *Chef im Südraum* (Chief, Southern Area) commander, Wilhelm Dommes. I also interviewed the following former commanding officers from U-boats that operated in Asian waters: Vice Adm.(Ret.) Kurt Freiwald, Capt.(Ret.) Otto Herwartz, Cdr.(Ret.) Jürgen Oesten, and the civilian exchange engineer Heinrich Foders; they allowed me to go through some of their papers. Very helpful also were former personnel of the German auxiliary cruisers lost in Asian waters, who still meet regularly. Most helpful were Wilhelm Osterfeld, Jürgen Herr, Günter Klare, and Heinz Trinkaus. After losing their ships, they served in German shore installations in Japan and Southeast Asian bases. Lt. Cdr. Konrad Hoppe, former base commander of Surabaya, and Lt. Herbert Schrein and my classmate Lt. Ulrich Horn, both former auxiliary cruiser aviators, also belong in this category.

I owe encouragement also to authors, writing about related topics, with whom I have corresponded: Thilo Bode, Hans-Joachim Braun, Dr. John W. M. Chapman, Prof. Dr. Joachim Glaubitz, Dr. Gerhard Krebs, Dr. Erich Pauer, Dr. Werner Rahn (Captain, GNY), Dr. Theo Sommer, and many others. The opportunity to check the English translation of documents against Dr. Chapman's translation in his publication, *The Price of Admiralty,* relying on his expertise, was of great help. Mr. Sven Pfahlert finally took upon his shoulders a large part of the arduous work of translation.

The list would become too long if I mentioned everyone who supported us in some way while preparing and writing our texts. I would like to thank my co-authors for their collaboration and especially my wife, Charlotte, for the many years of patience and indulgence with which she tolerated my endeavor.

HANS-JOACHIM KRUG

Chronology

1902
30 Jan.   Anglo-Japanese Alliance

1919
28 Jun.   Versailles Peace Treaty signed

1922
6 Feb.   Washington Naval Conference

1926
9 Aug.   Germany admitted into League of Nations

1930
21 Jan.   London Naval Disarmament Conference

1932
1 Mar.   Japan proclaims Empire of Manchukuo
25 Jun.   Soviet-Polish Nonaggression Pact

1933
27 Mar.   Japan resigns from League of Nations
14 Oct.   Germany resigns from League of Nations
16 Nov.   United States reestablishes diplomatic relations with Soviet Union

1934
26 Jan.   German-Polish Nonaggression Pact

1935

16 Mar. Germany reestablishes compulsory military service
18 Jun. British-German Fleet Agreement
 1 Aug. Rear Admiral Dönitz commander, German submarine force

1936

25 Oct. Berlin-Rome Axis
25 Nov. German-Japanese Anti-Comintern Pact
31 Dec. Japan revokes Washington Naval Agreement

1937

 7 Jul. Beginning of Sino-Japanese war
21 Aug. Sino-Soviet Nonaggression Pact
 6 Nov. Italy joins Anti-Comintern Pact
11 Dec. Italy resigns from League of Nations

1938

11 Mar. Austria annexed by Germany (*Anschluss*)
   May   Japanese and Soviet troops clash at Ussuri
23 Jun. German military adviser staff leaves China
29 Sept. German–Western Powers Munich Agreement
 1 Oct. Germany occupies Sudetenland region of Czechoslovakia
 3 Nov. Japan proclaims "New Order" for Eastern Asia

1939

16 Mar. Germany occupies rest of Czechoslovakia
31 Mar. British warranty declaration for Poland
15 Apr. Parts of U.S. Fleet transferred from Atlantic to San Diego
28 Apr. Germany renounces German-British Fleet Agreement,
         German-Polish Nonaggression Pact, and Munich Agreement
22 May   German-Italian Steel Pact
24 Jul. Anglo-Japanese Tientsin Agreement
26 Jul. United States cancels trade agreement with Japan
23 Aug. German-Soviet Nonaggression Pact
 1 Sept. Germany attacks Poland
 3 Sept. England and France declare war on Germany
16 Sept. Japanese-Soviet cease-fire, Nomonhan
17 Sept. Soviet invasion into eastern Poland
 8 Dec. Japan rejects German request for submarines

1940
Japanese code "Purple" broken
Mar.   United States offers $20 million loan to China
Apr.   U.S. Pacific Fleet transferred from San Diego to Hawaii
9 Apr.   Germany invades Denmark and Norway ("*Weserübung*")
10 May   Germany attacks the Netherlands, Belgium, and France
12 May   Japan declares neutrality in European war
Jun.   German air force main code broken
9 Jun.   Begin German auxiliary cruiser operations in Indian Ocean
22 Jun.   French-German cease-fire
Aug.   Italian submarines transferred to Atlantic
17 Aug.   German Armed Forces High Command proclaims total
blockade on Great Britain
Sept.   Italian offensive from Libya toward Egypt
2 Sept.   U.S.– British naval lend-lease contract
23 Sept.   Japan occupies northern Indochina
24 Sept.   Royal Navy raid on French fleet at Dakar
27 Sept.   Tripartite Pact signed
11 Nov.   TS *Automedon* papers captured in Bengal Gulf
Dec.   British counterattack on Benghasi and Tobruk

1941
11 Jan.   German submarines to operate off West Africa
Feb.   Formation of German Afrikakorps
22 Feb.   German CA *Admiral Scheer* off Seychelles
Mar.   Afrikakorps reconquers Cyrenaica
4 Mar.   Last Italian submarine leaves Eritrea
16 Mar.   British forces invade Italian Somalia and Eritrea
3 Apr.   First blockade-runner arrives from Japan
13 Apr.   Japanese-Soviet Neutrality Pact concluded
8 May   German naval code "Home Waters" compromised
22 Jun.   Germany attacks Soviet Union
28 Jun.   German counterattack crosses Egyptian border
27 Jul.   Japan occupies southern Indochina
1 Aug.   U.S. scrap-iron and oil embargo for Japan
14 Aug.   Atlantic Charter proclaimed
6 Nov.   First German blockade-runner arrives Japan
7 Dec.   Japanese attack on Pearl Harbor
8 Dec.   United States and United Kingdom declare war on Japan

10 Dec. Japanese forces land on northern Malaya
10 Dec. U.K. BB *Prince of Wales,* BC *Repulse* sunk
         Japanese forces land in Philippines and Guam
         Germany and Italy declare war on United States
16 Dec. Japanese forces land on northern Borneo
25 Dec. Japanese forces conquer Hong Kong

1942
Jan.   Japanese 4th Submarine Squadron based in Penang (later 5th and 8th)
11 Jan.   Japanese forces invade Netherlands Indies
18 Jan.   German-Italian-Japanese [Tripartite] Military Agreement
24 Jan.   Japanese take Balik Papan oil fields
 1 Feb.   German navy changes code (the fourth Enigma rotor)
14 Feb.   Japanese parachute landing, eastern Sumatra
15 Feb.   Singapore capitulates
16 Feb.   Japanese carrier raid on Port Darwin
27 Feb.   Battle of the Java Sea
 9 Mar.   Netherlands forces capitulate at Batavia (Jakarta)
 5 Apr.   Japanese carrier raid on Ceylon
May   Japanese submarines off East African coast
          Japanese 8th Submarine Group formed at Penang
 5 May   British fleet landing on Madagascar
 8 May   Corregidor surrender
5–7 Jun. Battle of Midway
28 Jun.   Beginning of Soviet summer offensive
21 Jul.   Japanese forces land on eastern New Guinea
 7 Aug.   U.S. landing on Guadalcanal
 8 Aug.   First Solomons sea battle
24 Aug.   Second Solomons sea battle
 1 Sept. Japanese 8th Submarine Group based in Penang
          Some Japan submarines withdrawn from Indian Ocean
24 Sept. German Caucasus thrust fails
Oct.   German submarine operation "Eisbär" (Polar Bear)
          off South Africa
30 Oct.   German submarine code "Triton" compromised
Nov.   German submarine operation "Eisbär II"
 8 Nov.   U.S. and British landing at French North Africa

18 Nov. German-Japanese Economic Agreement
22 Nov. German Sixth Army encircled at Stalingrad

1943

14 Jan. Casablanca Conference
30 Jan. Grand Admiral Dönitz is commander in chief, German navy
Feb. Japan begins withdrawal from Guadalcanal
Feb. German submarine operation, "Seehund" (Seal)
2 Feb. German forces in Stalingrad capitulate
9 Mar. German submarines independently to Africa's southeast coast
May Italian submarines leave Bordeaux for Indian Ocean
13 May German North Africa forces capitulate
23 May Suspension of the Battle of the Atlantic
Jun. German submarine operation "Monsun (Monsoon) I"
1 Jun. Penang, Singapore, Jakarta operational as German naval bases
27 Jun. Sea transfer of Subdhas Chandra Bose, U-180 to I-29
1 Jul. Blockade-runner service discontinued
10 Jul. Allied landing on Sicily
Sept. German submarine operation, "Monsun II"
German submarine operations from Penang
8 Sept. Italian capitulation
23 Sept. Italian Südraum submarines enter German navy
Oct. German attaché code Tokyo "Bertok" broken
17 Oct. Last German raider sunk off Japanese coast
26 Dec. Last blockade-runner arrives from Japan
Teheran Conference

1944

Jan. German submarines independently to Indian Ocean
Feb. British Eastern Fleet buildup
Carrier raids begin on Japanese bases
May German submarine operations from Penang
Jun. Only two submarines return to German realm loaded with cargo
6 Jun. Allied invasion in Normandy (Operation Overlord)
12 Jun. U.S. forces land on Saipan
17 Jul. Tōjō cabinet resigns in Japan
20 Oct. U.S. forces land on Leyte

1945

20 Feb.	8th Submarine Group disbanded
Apr.	Four returning submarine cargoes lost to Allies
21 Apr.	Last German Südraum submarine mission
30 Apr.	Suicide of Hitler
7 May	German capitulation to Western Powers
10 May	German Südraum submarines handed over to IJN
20 Jun.	Okinawa captured
6 Aug.	First atomic bomb on Hiroshima
8 Aug.	Soviet Union declares war on Japan
9 Aug.	Second atomic bomb dropped on Nagasaki
15 Aug.	Japanese capitulation
5 Sept.	British forces land in Singapore
12 Sept.	Japanese capitulation, Southeast Asia area

PART 1

German and Japanese Naval Conceptions and Operations

1

A Short History

Japan's relations with Germany, like its relations with other Western nations, officially began only a few years before the Meiji Restoration in 1867.

The arrival of Commodore Perry and his "Black Ships" into Tokyo Bay in 1854 opened Japanese ports to the world.[1] That same year, the United States led the Western powers in signing trade agreements with Japan, to be followed the next year by Russia, England, France, and the Netherlands.[2] Portugal negotiated its own treaty five years later. Russia had already sent warships to Japan, commanded by Admiral Putjatin.

These were landmark developments, because Japan had been closed to foreign trade since the mid-seventeenth century. Although always headed nominally by an emperor, Japan had been ruled for two and a half centuries (1601–1867) by shoguns (the equivalent of commanders in chief of the armed forces)—specifically, by a series of Tokugawa shogunates. An early Tokugawa (Iemitsu) had in 1641 expelled all foreigners except the "Germans"—actually, the Dutch, who were technically German until the end of the Thirty Years' War—and the Chinese, and accorded the exceptions only very limited trading privileges. But by the latter half of the nineteenth century the shogunate had weakened. Internal and external pressures to open Japanese ports to international trade finally brought the barriers down.[3]

At the time of the Meiji Restoration, that is, the point at which Japan became a modern nation, the Second German Empire did not yet exist. What did exist was the so-called *Deutscher Zollverein* (German Customs Union), consisting of German coastal states interested in overseas trade. One of its members was Prussia, which sent an East Asia expedition to Japan, China, and Siam in 1860 to learn more about those countries and explore the possibilities for concluding some form of trade agreement with them. The expedition sailed three Prussian warships under the flag of the diplomat Count Friedrich zu Eulenburg.[4] They arrived in Tokyo Bay on 4 September 1860. On 24 January 1861, a "shipping, trade, and friendship" treaty was signed by Japan and Prussia. The Tennō (emperor) would not ratify the treaty until almost two years after the Prussian consulate was established at Yokohama in 1883.

By then the twenty-five relatively independent German principalities would have formed in 1871 a federation, the Second German Empire, ready to deal as a unity with the Island Empire in diplomacy, in trade, and, eventually, in war.

MILITARY RELATIONS

Interactions between Japan and Germany in military matters, sporadic as they were, go back even further than commerce. Hans Wolfgang Braun, a German gunner in the service of the Dutch East India Company, came to Hirado via Amsterdam and Batavia (Jakarta). One of the mortars he constructed (with an 1,800-foot range) for the shogun's military government in 1639 can still be seen at the Military Museum Yasakuni Shrine, Tokyo.

When Japan was opened to foreigners again during the Meiji Restoration, Sgt. Carl Koeppen organized and trained a small army for the local lord of the Wakayama prefecture. It was disbanded in 1871, however, after only a year and a half.

After the Restoration, the modern Imperial Japanese Army was established after the French model and trained by French instructors. In 1885, several years after the German victory in the 1870–71 Franco-Prussian War, the Japanese general Duke Katsura succeeded in having Prussian major Jacob Meckel appointed as an instructor at the newly established Imperial Army War College.[5] He was appointed at the request of Japanese War Minister Ōyama, on a visit to Germany, to provide an officer of appropriate background for this duty. The later Brigadier General Meckel, a noted disciple of the famous Field Marshal Count von Moltke, was nominated and served at the Japanese War College for three years. During his assignment he initiated a number of reforms and was highly noted for his work.[6] Even as late as during the Russo-Japanese War, victorious Japanese commanders stated, in cables to him, that they had partly owed their victories to his guidance.[7]

This recognition is particularly noteworthy because German-Japanese relations had deteriorated considerably since the Peace Treaty of Shimonoseki, which was signed after the Sino-Japanese War ended in 1885. During this time, Germany, in concert with Russia and France, had taken action to deprive Japan of the Liaotung Peninsula, which it had occupied during the war with China. Emperor William II, enthroned since 1888, had coined the slogan of the "Yellow Peril." Moreover, Germany was the only foreign power that did not send any military observers to witness the fighting, and the German emperor had, at the outset of the Russo-Japanese War, openly placed his sympathy with Russia.[8]

MARITIME RELATIONS

Maritime relations between Germany and Japan began with the Meiji Restoration. In 1869, when in Northern Honshu dissident local lords fought the imperial government, they used the side-wheel frigate *Kaiten,* formerly the *Danzig,* which they had bought from Prussia. The *Kaiten* was used in the battle of Miyako Bay to shell and ram the French-built ironclad *Kotetsu,* the former Confederate *Stonewall Jackson,* which the imperial government had acquired via obscure channels after the collapse of the Confederacy.[9]

During the Russo-Japanese War, a German-built armored cruiser fought in the Japanese line in the decisive Battle of Tsushima. The ninety-eight-hundred-ton battleship *Yakumo* was delivered in 1901 by the German Vulkan Shipyard at Stettin.

After the establishment of colonies in the Pacific between 1884 and 1900 and until World War I, the German Empire maintained a cruiser squadron in the Western Pacific.[10] Until its relocation to Tsingtao in 1902, a German naval hospital was maintained in support of the East-Asia Squadron on the Bluff at Yokohama.

EXCHANGE OF COMMERCE AND TECHNOLOGY

The commercial and technical exchange between Germany and Japan derived from the original Prussian-Japanese Trade Treaty, which had gradually been extended to the North German Federation in 1867 and the German Customs and Trade Association in 1869.[11] Germany, like the other industrialized nations, assisted the new Japanese government in the establishment of basic industry. One of the first enterprises was the Gutehoffnungshuette steel mill constructed by the Germans at Yawata in 1901. Other renowned companies followed suit with similar projects, such as the Mannesmann steel tube factory and the large Siemens-Schuckert electrical plant in 1905. A new trade and shipping treaty, including a customs agreement, was concluded in 1911.

JAPAN AGAINST GERMANY

Since the first Japanese industry was founded under government control, it was only natural that, from the very beginning, close links existed between German-inspired industry and the armed forces, especially the Imperial Japanese Navy (IJN) and its construction program. However, these links were shaken by a bribery scandal in 1913 that toppled the administration of former Navy Minister Adm. Yamamoto Gombei. Despite comparable involvement on the part of British arms producers, the scandal supposedly had some influence in the Japanese decision to enter World War I as an enemy of Germany. Such an anti-German alignment conflicted with the intentions of Japanese naval officers who, like Yamamoto, had trained with the German navy.[12]

German-Japanese relations and Japanese public opinion regarding Germany had already deteriorated, years before the bribery scandal, as a result of the maladroit German intervention regarding the Liaotung Peninsula in 1895. After the pro-German premierships of Ito and Katsura, Prime Minister Okuma (who assumed office after the death of Katsura in 1913) and his foreign minister, Katō, shifted their allegiance toward England.

Soon after the beginning of World War I, Great Britain asked Japan for assistance in eliminating German naval forces in Chinese waters, based on its alliance of 1902.[13] On 15 August 1914, Japan challenged Germany with a seven-day ultimatum demanding the withdrawal of its naval forces from Chinese waters and the delivery of Tsingtao, its leased territory in the Chinese province of Shantung. When Germany did not respond to the ultimatum, Japan declared war on 23 August 1914.

After two months of heavy bombardment on the garrison of Tsingtao (where 3,744 men, mostly naval personnel, were surrounded by the sea and on Chinese territory by fifteen-fold superior forces), German Navy Captain Meyer-Waldeck, who was also governor of Tsingtao, capitulated on 7 November 1914. The German East-Asia Squadron could be of no help. Faced with the threat of the whole Japanese fleet, its few ships had withdrawn before the outbreak of the war and in late October stood off the Chilean coast to attack enemy naval units and shipping in the Western Hemisphere. The squadron's last ships were lost in action in November.[14] Four small gunboats (*Cormoran, Iltis, Jaguar,* and *Luchs*) and the Austrian cruiser *Kaiserin Elisabeth* were scuttled at Tsingtao shortly before the capitulation, after expending all their ammunition.

The survivors of the siege, mostly naval and marine personnel, were taken prisoner and for sixty-two months were detained in several POW camps, among them Bando near Tokushima and Matsuyama on the Japanese island of Shikoku. During the long detainment, the German POWs occupied themselves with educational programs, worked on road and bridge construction, and raised cattle in their camps. Through these programs they came into close contact with the local population. The Japanese treated their German prisoners so well that, after their final release in 1920, a number of former POWs either stayed in or returned to Japan to work as scientists, technicians, or businessmen. Parts of the camp of Bando are preserved to this day as a memorial.

Japan also took possession of the German colonies and assets in the Pacific Ocean. Article 119 of the Treaty of Versailles stipulated that the German Empire had to relinquish all of its colonies in trust to the League of Nations, which would, in turn, mandate them to victor nations. Under these premises, Japan placed the German South Sea Territories north of the equator under its administration in 1920. The Japanese, like their German predecessors, administered these archipelagoes mostly by their navy.

These events notwithstanding, right after the end of World War I many Japanese specialists came to Germany and numerous contacts with German veterans and German industry developed. This was due to keen Japanese interest in German war experience and technology and happened on a semi-official level. Although Japan was a cosigner of the Versailles treaty, Japanese officials not only turned a blind eye to violations but actively (though secretly) supported such activities whenever modern technology and know-how could be acquired from the German side.

POLITICAL RELATIONS AND BLOC FORMATION

Most of the former German South Sea colonies had been declared protectorates of the German Empire during the 1880s after trading posts had been established there by German overseas trading companies during the 1870s. The

Marianas, the Carolines, and the Palau Islands had been bought from Spain in 1899 after it had lost its war against the United States.

The parts of the German colonial territories mandated to Japan after 1920 amounted to only 1,034 square miles, or 0.1 percent of the former German colonial possessions. No essential natural resources existed on these archipelagoes. Since the brief war between the two nations had been fought fairly and honorably, little animosity remained between them, except for some unpleasant memories for German enterprises in Japan that had suffered economic setbacks due to the war. The Japanese handled the commercial restrictions imposed by the Versailles treaty with relative laxity. The Most Favored Nation clause, granted all victor nations, remained valid for Japan, however, until 1925.

Initial rapprochement efforts between Germany and Japan were first noticeable in the early 1930s, when their governments and industries began to feel uneasy about possible future supply gaps. With limited resources of essential raw materials on their own territories, especially crude oil, both nations began to search for means to secure access to these critical commodities.[15] Both have-nots, having come late to colonial acquisition, saw themselves in the same boat, rowing against the economic tide with undersized oars. Moreover, Germany, after having paid a suffocating burden of reparations, found itself with acute balance-of-payment problems for buying abroad. Japan had learned the value of German technical proficiency, through its use of disclaimed German patents after the war, and now demonstrated keen interest in obtaining additional German know-how.

Closer political relations began to materialize only in the thirties, heavily influenced by the often diverging aims of the agencies involved, on both sides, in the making of foreign policy. In Japan the army, the navy, the foreign ministry, and the prime minister all had an important say in these matters, and, since the forces were nominally responsible only to the emperor, it was difficult to reach clear decisions whenever there was dissent on foreign policy issues. This situation was worsened by often violent internal struggle within the forces and the foreign ministry. As a result, the strengthening of political ties with Germany was an extremely cumbersome process.

On the German side, the decision process was not burdened with obstacles to such a large extent, since Hitler had quickly secured dictatorial power also in the field of foreign policy making. But there were vested interests in Germany that supported close ties with China, where German industry and the Wehrmacht, too, were engaged with huge weapons sales and military support.

THE ANTI-COMINTERN PACT

Ironically, however, the first official political negotiations between the two governments were taken up in a field in which neither Germany's nor Japan's internal stability was of preeminent concern: international communism.[16] On 25 November 1936, Germany and Japan signed the Anti-Comintern Pact in Berlin. Italy joined the two contracting parties less than a year later, on 6 November 1937. Hitler was satisfied to have created a "world-political triangle," whereas Japan, with its uneasiness about Russian policy in the Far East, felt relieved to see essential parts of the German-USSR Neutrality Treaty of 1926 abrogated.

The real motivation for the Anti-Comintern Pact was the alliance treaties that the USSR had signed with France and Czechoslovakia in 1935 and with Outer Mongolia in 1936. Shortly thereafter, the Soviet Union also signed a nonaggression treaty with China. Although the Anti-Comintern Pact was the first distinct step toward future political German-Japanese cooperation, from the very beginning their political goals did not coincide. Japan wanted a free hand for an attack on China, which it undertook only seven months later. Germany wanted to deter the Soviet Union from interfering with its own schemes in Europe.

In retrospect, the assertion made at the war crimes trials, that national-socialist Germany and imperial Japan had, in a secret alliance, conspired to disrupt the international order and between them erect a world supremacy, seems rather far-fetched.[17]

From the very start of political convergence, both Germany and Japan were intent on making use of the other party just to support their own power politics. With the Anti-Comintern Pact concluded in 1936, both wanted to contain the steadily growing power of the Soviet Union from interfering with their independent schemes to establish their own zones of political predominance. There were not even clearly coordinated German-Japanese policies, nor was there ever any subordination to the interests of the alliance. It is not to be denied that at that time both were pursuing expansionist policies, aspired to hegemony in their respective areas of interest, and were prepared to try to change the international status quo by force. However, there was never any real political *cooperation*. Each partner tried to use the other to support its own political objectives. The German-Japanese alliance was one without backbone from the very beginning, with only temporary periods of limited coincidence of interests.[18]

When in February 1938 von Ribbentrop was nominated German foreign minister, he promoted the idea of a closer political alliance with Germany's Anti-Comintern Pact partners, Japan and Italy. His ideas found an echo in some but not all Japanese political circles. Whereas the Japanese army, engaged in fighting China, seemed to see an advantage in a German alliance, the Japanese navy remained very reluctant. Having abandoned its eighteen-year alliance with the British Royal Navy in 1922, the IJN was clearly aware of Japan's logistic shortcomings. Ribbentrop's plans for an alliance with Japan, therefore, would not be realized until September 1940, because of the parties' constant reciprocal distrust and a lack of mutual regard. During all this time Germany, Italy, and Japan independently pursued their own goals in Europe and Asia, respectively.

WORLD WAR II BEGINS

In March 1938 Germany incorporated Austria and occupied the mainly German-populated Sudeten area of Czechoslovakia in October, after the Munich Agreement. Only five and one-half months later Germany invaded the rest of that country. In April 1939, Berlin revoked the 1935 Fleet Agreement with Great Britain, which had fixed the tonnage ratio for their two navies at 35:100, respectively (submarines, 45:100). On 22 May 1939 Germany concluded the so-called Steel Pact with Italy, in which only eighteen days earlier Japan had declined to participate.[19] Then, without even bothering to inform its Anti-Comintern Pact partner, Japan, until two days before the signing, Berlin on 23 August 1939 arranged a nonaggression pact with the Soviet Union. Eight days later, on 1 September 1939, it attacked Poland, thus starting World War II.

At this point, Japan had already left the League of Nations (in 1933) and had let the 1930 London Fleet Agreement expire (in December 1936).[20] But after Germany had concluded its nonaggression pact with the Soviet Union without notifying her Anti-Comintern Pact partner in advance, Japan suspended all negotiations about a Tripartite Pact on 25 August 1939, viewing the German pact with Russia as a breach of article II of the Secret Supplementary Agreement to the Anti-Comintern Pact.

China had resisted Japan's expansionist attempts to gain influence and access to raw materials in adjacent northern-central China, but on 7 July 1937 full-scale hostilities began between the two countries with a military incident at the Marco Polo Bridge near Peking. In November 1937 the German ambassador in China failed in his mediation attempts between Japan and China. Over recurrent Japanese protests, Germany maintained a military advisory group with the Chiang Kai-shek government and continued military aid to China up to mid-1938.[21] Since China was one of the main targets of Japanese expansion, the German support of China was an obstacle to closer relations between Japan and Germany that was only overcome by Hitler's decision to side with Japan in 1938.

On 3 November 1938, Japan proclaimed a "New Order for East Asia." On 27 November 1938 Japan concluded an Agreement for Cultural Cooperation with Germany and, on 28 July 1939, signed a Payment Agreement, which never took effect. However, despite apparent movement in political agreements, the long-planned pact remained idle. The handling of the Tripartite Pact project during all this long time, since its conception in 1938, was symptomatic of mutual indifference to each partner's political objectives, not to speak of the complete lack of a "grand design."

TOWARD STRENGTHENING OF UNANIMITY

In 1936–37 Hitler had wanted the "world political triangle" to deter the Soviets from interfering with his plans to advance Germany's borders to the southeast and east. Japan wanted the same deterrent for its corresponding plans concerning northeast China. During his preparations to invade Poland, Hitler recognized that Stalin was willing to support his invasion plans, provided he got an adequate slice of Polish territory. Consequently Berlin concluded a nonaggression pact with Moscow without regard for its partner Japan, which by July 1938 had repeatedly clashed militarily with the Soviet Union along the Manchurian border.

After successfully concluding the Polish campaign and having, for the time being, contained the Soviets, Berlin was temporarily interested in not straining relations with Moscow. Japan, on the other hand, fighting hard to accomplish its aims in China, complained repeatedly of Berlin's continuing aid program for Nationalist China. However, Germany was critically short of foreign currency and could ill afford to loose its raw-material supply from China, with whom it still had outstanding contracts worth 282 million marks. The trade and credit agreement concluded with the Soviet Union, together with the nonaggression pact, provided immediate relief from this shortfall by allowing Germany access to the vast resources of the Soviet Union.

Japan again protested against German disloyalty, claiming that the nonaggression pact with Russia violated the secret stipulations of the Anti-Comintern Pact.[22] Germany would later claim that Japan's persistent reluctance to shoulder any obligations arising from an alliance had exhausted Berlin's patience. Made confident by continuing military success, Hitler felt that he could do without Japanese support and let the door slam on further negotiations.

Defeating the Western powers had, for the time being, become Hitler's main objective. The allusion of the commander in chief of the Kriegsmarine, Grand Admiral Raeder, to the desirability of the support of the very powerful Japanese fleet appears not to have impressed Hitler at the time. Basically land-oriented, he never grasped the concepts of naval warfare.[23] Still, there were German efforts to make Japan turn from its traditional anti-Russian attitude toward an anti-British position. It was felt in the German foreign office that the enemy constellation had changed and that, for both Japan and Germany, England had become "enemy number one."[24] However, at the time Japanese officials, especially in the Japanese navy, aware of their critical supply situation, refused to share these beliefs.

In the long run German victories did not fail to impress the Japanese, and they began to fear that they might be deprived of their due share in Asia if Germany won a decisive victory in Europe. As early as 1938 initial direct contacts between Japanese and German army high commands had already been established via the Japanese ambassador, General Ōshima. First ideas and suggestions were exchanged. Neither the Japanese nor the German navy was informed at that time.

In spite of continuing conflicts of interest, when World War II broke out, the small German navy cherished rather unjustified hopes that the big Imperial Japanese Navy could be enticed to lease or sell some of its long-range submarines to Germany for operations in far-off waters and to make available Japanese bases for German use.[25] The Japanese turned down such a request from the Germans on 8 December 1939. Nevertheless, they mentioned that arrangements for an exchange of intelligence and logistic supply for German units could be negotiated.

Hitler mentioned Japan again at a conference with his supreme commanders in July 1940. He talked of Russia as the "East-Asiatic sword of England and America against Japan." For Japan, however, he visualized a role as an East-Asiatic sword, so to speak, for Germany against America. Hitler saw the pact mainly in a deterrent or counter-deterrent function against U.S. intervention. He expected it to neutralize the United States and to isolate England.

In July 1940, after Norway, Denmark, the Netherlands, Belgium, and France had been occupied by Germany, the Japanese foreign office conceived a detailed draft for the "strengthening of unanimity between Japan, Germany, and Italy."[26] The contents were agreed on at a meeting with representatives of war and navy ministries, the army general staff, and the admiralty.

With Germany having occupied countries with colonial possessions wealthy in raw materials in Southeast Asia, there was concern in Japan that Germany could make claims to this wealth, which, Japan felt, belonged to its appropriate zone of hegemony. On the verge of a possible reallotment of interest spheres, Japan faced a dilemma: It wanted to establish its proper realm without interference from Germany but also without shouldering undue obligations to comply with possible demands from its allies.

THE TRIPARTITE PACT

On 1 August 1940 preliminary talks simultaneously got under way at Tokyo and Berlin. Now the Japanese felt that the time was ripe for talks with the other Axis Powers with the target of reaching a fundamental agreement among them to establish a new order in Europe and Asia, respectively.[27] The Japanese proposition for recognition of particular hegemonic claims and mutual assistance was first conveyed to the Germans together with the draft of a secret supplementary protocol that contained proposals for the establishment of Joint Military and Naval Commissions and a Joint Economic Commission.

It seems that the German decision to play the Japanese card again was taken between 7 and 13 August, when it became clear that, even after the collapse of France, England remained resolute. The Japanese army was willing to conclude a military alliance, but the navy, concerned about a possible curtailment of its liberty of action, remained reserved. It adamantly refused to be drawn into an open-ended commitment to fight both the Western Powers and the USSR.[28] The navy gave its unreserved consent only on the condition that, in the event that Japan should be attacked by a power so far not involved in the European or Chinese war, Germany and Italy would come to Japan's assistance with all their means and resources.[29] (See appendix B, para. III.)

After some German amendments to the original Japanese draft, the Tripartite Pact was finally signed on 27 September 1940 in Berlin, supplemented with the secret protocol and two confidential notes. (See appendixes A and B.)

The supplements were not sent to Berlin, and Hitler seems not to have been informed about them. Only Ott and Ribbentrop knew of them and had agreed to them. Based on these supplements, the IJN was ready to endorse the Tripartite Pact because they believed a) that the Germans now were ready to offer the Japanese complete access to modern technology in order to build up Japanese fighting capabilities, b) that the Germans were willing to settle all problems related to the former German island colonies, which were now in Japanese possession, by selling their claims at a low price to Japan, and c) that Germany was willing to act as a mediator between Japan and the Soviet Union. The supplements can be found in appendix B.

Article 4 of the Tripartite Pact provided for the invocation of technical commissions, and on 20 December Japanese Foreign Minister Matsuoka, together with ambassadors Ott and Indelli, signed an agreement to organize the joint committees. The committees were to consist of three "general committees" in each capital and be headed by the foreign ministers. The respective ambassadors made up the other members. Each general committee was to be assisted by subcommittees for military and economic affairs. The attachés of the services were to be automatic members of the military affairs committees, which included other specialist personnel as required.[30]

These committees should have become the natural places for the coordination of all important questions concerning cooperation, but they did not meet before Pearl Harbor and only met afterward for protocol and courtesy. Thus the committees obviously served propaganda purposes only. Hitler and other important German (but also Japanese) executives had no intention of having their freedom of decision inhibited by letting the committees actually function.[31]

In a directive of 5 March 1941, Hitler stated that the "objective" was "to induce Japan to actively act in the Far East" to "tie down strong British forces" and direct the main interest of the United States toward the Pacific. The directive further authorized passing German warfare experience on to the Japanese and offering military-economic and technical knowledge, as well as coordinating the operational planning of both navies.[32]

The main concerns on the Japanese side pertained to the establishment of their "Greater East Asia Co-Prosperity Sphere." These concerns are evident in the preamble of the pact, article 2, and the two supplemental notes (see appendixes A and B). Japan wanted to be assured of German and Italian military support against Great Britain in case the British should militarily interfere with its intended accession to the natural resources in Dutch and French colonial territories. The pact itself did not grant assistance against attack by any power already involved in war with the contracting nations.

In February 1938 Hitler had declared that Germany had no territorial interests in East Asia. Germany's former colonies were regarded as having very limited value for the German Reich, which did not want to get involved in the Pacific. Germany had several times declared itself not to be concerned with the administration of its former Pacific colonies or those of its defeated enemies. But it wanted not to prejudice possible arrangements of a later postwar period. And it wanted Japanese guarantees of unrestricted access to the raw materials of the French and Dutch colonies, which it so urgently needed.

These islands were of great strategic importance, however, for Japan, which since 1937 had fortified them and used them as naval and naval air bases.[33] Under the heading of mutual assistance, Japan had declared its intention to possibly provide Germany and Italy with raw materials from Asia and the South Seas, but for compensation it expected liberal transfer of modern weapons, machinery, and technical know-how. Japan had gotten assurances of military assistance in Asia without having to shoulder a reciprocal commitment in Europe or the Atlantic. (See appendix A.) Again, as in 1939, the Japanese navy sustained complete freedom of action. In September 1940 the alliance only could be contracted because both partners passed over their differences deliberately.

In April 1941 Hitler refused to have the visiting Japanese Foreign Minister Matsuoka informed of the imminent German attack on the Soviet Union.[34] Matsuoka for his part did not tell the Germans that, on his way back, he would sign a neutrality pact with the Soviets at Moscow, which remained valid until the end of the war, contrary to German wishes.

Japan's efforts to get the Anglo-American embargo on scrap iron and petroleum lifted by last-minute negotiations worried its German partner throughout 1941. But although Ambassador Ōshima seems to have acquired Hitler's agreement to enter into war against the United States, the Japanese attack on Pearl Harbor on 8 December, 03:00 Tokyo time, came as a complete surprise for the Germans. Throughout 1941, perhaps the most decisive year of the war, the Axis powers neither marched nor struck in unison.[35]

On 11 December 1941, Germany, Italy, and Japan contracted an Agreement about Joint Warfare excluding individual conclusion of peace for any partner. Finally, on 18 January 1942, a secret Tripartite Military Agreement was concluded between the German and Italian armed forces and the Japanese army and navy (separately). By its terms both navies on 11 September arranged a Communications and Intelligence Agreement. (Both agreements are reprinted in appendix D.)

These agreements, even if in a very restricted way, became a basis for the practical cooperation between the German, Italian, and Japanese navies for coordinating strategies, tactics, and operations on a staff and command level. This convention provided for the setting up of naval commissions in the respective capitals. It also established a boundary line between the European partners and Japan along the 70th degree of east longitude in the Indian Ocean. (See appendix D.)

2

Two Navies Prepare for War

The way the respective naval establishments of Germany and Japan were organized and the way they undertook the planning of their operations differed substantially, virtually ensuring conflict and confusion in important operations as they contemplated war with rather different motives.

THE GERMAN NAVY: ORGANIZATION

In wartime, supreme command of the German armed forces was vested in Adolf Hitler, in his capacity as Führer and Chancellor of the Reich. In the German armed forces the Navy High Command (*Oberkommando der Kriegsmarine,* or OKM), like the high commands of the other two services, was placed under a joint forces staff: the High Command of the Armed Forces, *Oberkommando der Wehrmacht* (OKW). No separate ministries existed for army and navy.[1]

The highest command authority, headed by the *Oberbefehlshaber der Marine* (ObdM, commander in chief, navy) was the OKM in Berlin, with its regular headquarters staff organization. As of January 1942 the ObdM maintained a permanent representative at Hitler's headquarters.

Naval operations were planned and coordinated by the Naval War Staff, *Seekriegsleitung* (Skl.). It was headed by the *Chef des Stabes der Seekriegsleitung* and was composed of two main branches: the operations divisions proper, e.g., naval operations (*Operationsabteilung* [1/Skl]) or U-boat operations (*Unterseebootführungsabteilung* (2/Skl BdU op), and the Navy Command Office (*Marinekommandoamt*, later renamed *Quartiermeisteramt* [Skl/QuA], or Quartermaster Office).

All ships and vessels of the German navy were organized in type commands under Fleet Command (*Flottenkommando*). The submarine type command under Admiral Dönitz as *Befehlshaber der Unterseeboote* (BdU), COMSUB, acquired a special position when in February 1943 Dönitz became ObdM. He retained direct operational command of the German submarine force. This is why, from this date on, the submarine operations division functioned as an integral part of the Naval War Staff.

BdU directed the German submarine forces on two chains of command: operationally, as BdU op and administratively, as BdU org. Administratively the submarine force was subdivided into various theater commands, *Führer der Unterseeboote* (FdU), which were organized in varying numbers of U-boat flotillas, *Unterseebootsflottillen*. These were based in special submarine bases (*U-Stützpunkte*) in German, Italian, and occupied ports. Operationally, BdU op maintained direct operational command over all U-boats on patrol in the Atlantic. The less important theaters in the Mediterranean, the North Polar Sea, the Black Sea, and the Baltic were led by the FdU subcommands.

Special conditions existed in the Pacific and Indian Oceans after 1943. The remoteness of the East Asian theater made radio communications difficult, and so did the delicate situation of the boats having to use Japanese naval bases and to repeatedly cross the swap-line between the German and Japanese operations areas on 70 degrees east longitude. Thus the German naval attaché staff in Tokyo became a link of BdU op in the chain of command as a kind of relay station.

From the beginning of the war, the disposition and administrative and logistic control, as well as naval control of shipping for the Pacific and Indian oceans, was vested in the German naval attaché in Tokyo. He also was in charge of the regional installations of the Naval Supply Service, or *Etappendienst der Kriegsmarine,* in the area. This control was utilized to advise the captains of the German raiders operating in both oceans and to direct the loading and routing of the German and Italian merchant ships employed as blockade-runners between the Far East and Europe.

The German naval attachés, apart from their affiliation with their respective German embassies abroad, until October 1943 were subordinated within the naval organization to the Naval Attaché Group (*Marineattachégruppe* (MAtt) reporting to the chief of staff of the Naval War Staff. After that date, as members of the *Marineattachéabteilung,* they reported directly to the chief of staff of the Navy High Command.

The Tokyo naval attaché, like others in overseas service, had another operative responsibility besides his attaché duties. For the observation of the political, military, and economical developments abroad, the German navy maintained the Naval Special Service (*Marinesonderdienst,* or MSD). Established in peacetime under *Amt Ausland/Abwehr,* the MSD was subordinate to the OKW and was prepared, as to organization, personnel, and communications techniques, to act in wartime as a kind of blockade-running shipping agency. Operationally it was under the Naval War Staff, Quartermaster Office, and as of May 1944 served directly under Navy High Command as *Generalreferat Admiral Quartiermeister* (AdmQuA III).

Its local organizations abroad came under the name of *Etappendienst,* or Supply Service. The naval attaché in Tokyo was, at the same time, head of the Supply Service East Asia (*Etappe Ostasien*). The Supply Service East Asia was responsible for safeguarding German merchant vessels in the Pacific and Indian oceans against seizure by the Allies. It also arranged for their transfer into neutral or Japanese ports, the provision of sea and rail transport, and the acquisition of supplies and war-essential raw materials. *Etappe Ostasien* also oversaw the loading of the cargoes, the routing of blockade-runners, and the supply of naval raiders and auxiliaries at sea or in port. The activities of the Supply Service East Asia were controlled by the attaché's chief of staff.[2]

Because of the amount of radio traffic and the unstable reception conditions, the attaché in Tokyo persistently requested a radio link of his own with the Naval War Staff, independent of the foreign service net, which he was finally granted after November 1942. He felt that the need was urgent because of the high security risk of the intelligence exchange he maintained with the Japanese naval staff. Since the spring of 1942 he had been able to establish his own communication station, with German naval operators, but had been obliged to forward his coded messages to the authorities through Japanese navy transmission stations. It took a long time until he finally was granted permission to transmit directly to German naval authorities.[3]

In a way the naval attaché in Tokyo had to act in the function of a theater commander and direct the tactical deployment of the units in his area under the directive of the Naval War Staff (Skl.). In this function he was designated the Deutscher Admiral Ostasien (German Admiral, East Asia). The Etappe Ostasien organization and personnel were separated from his office as of April 1943. His chief of staff (*Kapitän zur See* Vermehren) stayed in charge.

As for the merchant raiders, the number of blockade-runners to be supplied and routed, and finally the submarine fighting and transport effort in the Indian Ocean, it turned out to be advisable to set up a subordinate command and logistics organization in this area. Admiral Wenneker, the Tokyo attaché and Deutscher Admiral Ostasien, had first suggested installing German naval bases, with their own logistic and communications installations, at Japanese naval bases in November 1942, but the Japanese agreed to their establishment only after long delays.

German naval bases were finally established at Penang and Singapore (*Shonan*) on the Malay Peninsula and at Jakarta (then Batavia) and Surabaya on the island of Java. Singapore and Batavia reported operational on 17 May and 22 May 1943. From March 1944 these bases came under a separate area commander, the Chief of the Southern Area (*Chef im Südraum,* or CiS), *Fregattenkapitän* (Commander) Dommes, responsible via the attaché in Tokyo to the Skl. His tasks were mainly administrative. He had to process Japanese requests for German operations in the area and inform the Japanese submarine command of pending German operations and intentions. He had to assign bases with repair, staging, and recreation facilities for German units and provide German or Japanese escort on fixed safety routes. He had to fit out the units in port with supplies, provisions, and cargoes for their next missions and maintain radio communication with them on approach and departure routes. Finally, he had to report to the Naval War Staff via the Admiral Ostasien at Tokyo.[4]

German U-boats operating in the Indian Ocean were allocated to various U-boat flotillas based in French Atlantic ports until September 1944, when all boats began to be transferred to the new 33rd U-boat Flotilla set up at Flensburg, in northern Germany. In addition to existing bases in the Far East, another German submarine base was installed in Kobe, Japan, also in 1944, mostly for boats in need of replacement batteries.

THE JAPANESE NAVY: ORGANIZATION

Before World War II, the Supreme Commander of the Japanese armed forces was the emperor. The emperor had the authority of supreme command (*Tōsui-ken*) over the army and navy under the imperial constitution (generally called the Meiji Constitution, promulgated on 11 February 1889; it came into effect on 29 November 1890). The general staffs of the army and navy, responsible for executing his supreme command, also were responsible for the defense plan in peacetime. For wartime only, Imperial General Headquarters (IGHQ) was established to conduct operational and strategic matters.

The IGHQ was established first in 1894 for the Sino-Japanese War, then reestablished in 1904 for the Russo-Japanese War, and again in November 1937 for the so-called China Incident. During the Pacific War it was continuously in operation. In IGHQ there was no chief of staff, since, strictly speaking, there were two components: a navy department and an army department, each acting independently. When it was necessary to meet, the army and navy general staffs met as the Imperial General Headquarters (*Daihon'ei*) staff in their own offices. But when they needed to report to the emperor, they went to the palace as IGHQ staff officers.

In November 1937 an "Imperial Headquarters–Cabinet Liaison Conference" was instituted to adjust policy between the government and the supreme command. Attendees were the prime minister, the army, navy, and foreign ministers, and other ministers as required, representing the government and the army and navy chiefs of staff of the IGHQ. If necessary, the vice chiefs of staff of the army and navy could attend. The name of the conference was changed to "Supreme War Council" in 1944, but there was no change in function.

The Imperial Conferences (*Gozen-kaigi*) were essentially meetings in the presence of the emperor to get imperial sanction for policy decisions prepared beforehand by his advisers. Usually the emperor said nothing at these meetings.

The central institutions of the navy were the Navy Ministry (*Kaigunshō*) and the Navy General Staff (*Gunreibu*), whose functions were entirely distinct. The navy minister and his staff were responsible for preparing the force of arms required for the operation plan of the Gunreibu. This meant ship construction, weapons procurement, personnel and training, mobilization of naval forces, and political matters and budget proposals before the Diet (parliament).

The Gunreibu was responsible for fleet movement, operations, and war plans. The Gunreibu had four sections: Operations (1st), Armament and Mobilization (2nd), Intelligence (3rd), and Communication (4th); it controlled the Combined Fleet (*Rengō kantai*), under which in turn came the several regional fleets and flotillas.

Until the end of World War II, the Japanese government usually operated under a bureaucratic cabinet system, and parliamentary power was limited. The cabinet was based not on parliamentary power but on the emperor's decrees. Consequently the cabinet had no power over the command and operations of the armed forces, these being the concern of the IGHQ, whose heads were very powerful as direct advisers to the emperor. The building up, maintenance, and control of the armed forces were the responsibility of the minister of the army and the minister of the navy, who similarly had direct access to the emperor. The Diet could intervene in military affairs only when voting on the annual defense budget.

Submarines were especially important in the cooperation with the Germans. In the war's initial stages, submarines in the Indian Ocean were divided in a dual command structure. Old-type or short-range submarines were under the command of the Southwestern Area Command (Southwest Fleet Commander); the modern, long-range U-cruiser submarines were under command of the Combined Fleet via the commander of the Sixth Fleet. Operational areas were divided according to range, the Bay of Bengal and the vicinity of Ceylon being mainly the operational area of the Southwest Command's submarines. Large fleet-type cruiser submarines were mainly deployed to the western side of the Indian Ocean and the Gulf of Aden.

On 17 April 1942 the Eighth Submarine Group was formed and deployed at Penang for the planned Indian Operation. In April 1943, I-27 and I-29 of the 14th submarine division were also transferred to the 8th Submarine Group. In May the newly constructed I-37 was added, along with I-8 and I-10; repairs were finished and they came under the command of Rear Adm. Ichioka Hisahi. But the impact of American landing operations in the Pacific resulted in the gradual redeployment of these submarines to the homeland. On 20 February 1945 the Eighth Submarine Group was finally disbanded, and until the end of 1944 Japanese submarine operations in the Indian Ocean were reduced to occasional patrols south and east of India.

The Tokyo Communication Group was responsible for submarine communications, conducted on very low frequency (VLF) and high frequency (HF). The Tenth Communication Group at Singapore operated in the Indian Ocean from June 1944. For the submarines in the Indian Ocean, several codes were used for radio communications. The "D" code was used until late June 1942; later the "RO" code was usually used for operations.[5] Between the German and the Japanese navy, the cipher codes "Togo" and "Tirpitz" were designated but, as the navies had no combined operations, never used. In any event, radio communication often proved to be unreliable.

PLANNING AND REALITY

It is hardly surprising that two navies with such dissimilar organizations and chains of command, with such widely disparate national objectives, would plan, in effect, two different wars.

GERMAN PLANNING

After the German navy had been reduced to third-rate status by the stipulations of the Versailles treaty, it was unable to develop any serious contingency plans during the early twenties. The *Reichsmarine* was involved in bitter internal struggle and shaken by the domestic upheavals in Germany that closely resembled civil war. Its leadership even had to face the possibility of its being abolished as a separate branch of service. However, by 1923–24 the situation had become halfway stable again, and navy staff had started considering scenarios with Poland, France, and Denmark as possible enemies against which the Baltic Approaches had to be defended.

When French and Belgian troops occupied parts of western Germany in 1923, the navy started considering how to fight a possible blockade by France and Belgium of its North Sea supply routes. Admiral Zenker, Raeder's predecessor as commander in chief of the German navy, soon assigned this *Zufuhrschutz* ("supply defense") a decisive role in a future war.

The basic dilemma of the German navy, however, was that it was simply too weak to stand any chance at all in a major war. For this reason, considerations of a conflict with the British were excluded a priori. It was only with the changing constellation of the second half of the thirties, when the "Versailles system" crumbled and the ambitious "Z" Plan provided for a new oceanic fleet that would again be able to challenge the British on the oceans, that farther-reaching plans began to form. The "Z" Plan" was intended to be completed by 1949. Hitler gave priority to his continental plans and likewise to the German army and air force and started World War II in 1939—a full ten years too early for the navy.

Accordingly, Raeder's first entry in the war diary of the Skl. was deeply pessimistic. He expected that the most the German navy could do in this war was "to die with grace." Then the successes of operations against Allied shipping with raiders, armed merchant cruisers, and U-boats led to considerably more optimistic views during the early years of the war, and they gained momentum when Japan entered the war on the Axis side. But these successes were not the result of thorough long-term planning and preparation. They were the result of more or less makeshift, improvised reactions to a situation for which the navy—called the Kriegsmarine ("war navy") since 1935—simply did not have adequate forces.

Even their sharpest weapon, the U-boat, became blunt, especially after Allied deciphering allowed a more or less continuous reading of even the most secret radio transmissions on the Axis side. The U-boat offensive collapsed in the first half of 1943. After the bases in France were lost after the Allied landings in 1944, the German navy was reduced to a coastal role, unable to play more than a marginal part until the final defeat of Hitler's Third Reich.

JAPANESE PLANNING

The war planning that actually formed the basis for the Japanese navy itself— not its operations alone—on the eve of World War II began in the early years of the century. In 1907 the *Kokubō Hōshin* ("Guidelines for the Defense of the Empire," sometimes also translated as "National Defense Policy") were given imperial approval. At the same time, the emperor approved other documents: the "Required Forces for National Defense" (*Kokubō Shoyō Heiryoku*) and its attachment, the "Principal Operational Plan of the Imperial Armed Forces." The "guidelines" and the other documents, which were to be the basis for the yearly contingency plans of both services, mentioned Russia as the main hypothetical enemy and the United States, Germany, and France as secondary possible adversaries of imperial Japan.

Since the defense of the empire was premised on attack by a foreign power, the guidelines required Japanese forces strong enough to conduct offensive operations against Russian and U.S. forces in East Asia.[6] The main forces deemed necessary for the navy would consist of eight battle cruisers and eight battleships; thus the planned fleet was called the "eight-eight fleet."

Although the guidelines and related documents were intended to support the planning of both services, in practice there arose considerable rivalry between them. The army considered Russia as the main hypothetical enemy, while the navy viewed the United States in that role. A "magic figure" emerged at the War College around 1907: If the Japanese navy were to have a 50 percent chance of victory in a conflict with America, it had to have 70 percent of the strength of the U.S. Navy. This "70 percent principle" was to have a crucial influence on the Japanese navy's attitude in the Washington and London conferences regarding naval matters in the twenties and thirties.

However, it was only during World War I that the U.S. Navy developed into a really powerful potential enemy, when U.S. fleet plans envisioned a "navy second to none" that would even challenge the traditional leading role of the British Royal Navy. Even before the outbreak of World War I the Board of Grand Admirals (*Gensui fu*) and court circles had realized that it was beyond Japan's financial capability to actually build the eight-eight fleet. The U.S. fleet plans made the Japanese naval position even more precarious, since it seemed now increasingly difficult to actually stick to the 70 percent principle.

Recognizing the financial dilemma, though, was of little consequence until 1921; by then the naval budget had almost doubled compared to 1916. The first revision of the guidelines in 1918 had made no changes in the list of hypothetical main enemies. Only the list of secondary possible adversaries had seen changes: China was now among them, and Germany and France had been crossed off the list because they were not considered a threat in the Far East any more. But the financial facts could not be ignored any longer, and the Navy Ministry (responsible for financial affairs) was able to dominate the Navy General Staff (responsible for war planning and operational matters), and thus the Washington treaties, calling for limitations in the building of capital ships, were concluded. This, however, was only possible against fierce resistance of the Navy General Staff, which can be traced in the second revision of the guidelines of February 1923.[7] The most prominent feature here was that now the United States was clearly identified as the most probable enemy with which "sooner or later a conflict very probably will occur." This stood in stark contrast to the treaty concluded only a short time before in Washington.

From now until World War II the main theme of war planning in the Japanese Navy was to intercept a U.S. fleet thrust into the western Pacific. This was expected as a reaction to a Japanese taking of the Philippines; meanwhile, the U.S. forces would already have been worn down by submarines and night attacks by torpedo-carrying light surface forces. Then the decisive battle would take place—an encounter of the main fleets. After a Japanese victory, favorable peace terms would have to be arrived at, with the Japanese in a position of power at the conference table.

In 1936, after the Washington and London treaties had expired, the guidelines were revised one more time. Here, the operational scenario mentioned above basically remained unchanged, but Great Britain appeared on the list of potential enemies. This was remarkable insofar as the British had been formally allied with Japan from 1902 to 1922.

Japan entered the war with a plan called "Operations in case of a war with the United States, Britain, and the Netherlands during Operations against China" nominally in force. But World War II saw relatively little of the Japanese interwar naval planning, because the Japanese Fleet Commander, Admiral Yamamoto Isoroku, planned the surprise attack against the U.S. Navy at Pearl Harbor and was able to push the plan through against the Navy General Staff.

Sheer luck saved the U.S. carriers at Pearl Harbor. When Japan made another attempt on them at Midway, the deciphering of Japanese radio traffic played an important role in the devastating defeat of the Japanese fleet. Its remaining strength was soon drained in the battle of attrition in the Solomon Islands. Thus the offensive capability of the Japanese fleet was effectively paralyzed by the summer of 1942.

IJN VS. USN: THE MOST PROBABLE ENEMY

The idea of an "attrition plus interception" operation had always formed the core of the Japanese navy's plans for its armaments, weapon systems, fleet formation, education, and training ever since 1907, when it began to consider the U.S. Navy as its potential enemy. The idea became a formal concept around 1917 and was formulated officially in 1923 as the "Doctrine of the Imperial Armed Forces." The operation plans that the navy decided to adopt were to wipe out the American fleet in the Far East at the onset of hostilities and jointly with the army to seize the Philippines and Guam in order to destroy American strongholds in the Western Pacific. After that, the following operations were envisioned:

1. Dispatch submarines to the area where the American fleet was located to monitor its movements and, should it set out, shadow and track its subsequent movements, while in the meantime attacking it repeatedly to diminish its strength.

2. Deploy land-based naval aircraft to the South Sea Mandated Islands to attack the enemy fleet once it comes within range, in cooperation with the carrier-borne planes, to further reduce the enemy's strength.

3. Carry out night attacks, when the enemy fleet has entered the arena of the planned decisive battle, with an advanced body of cruisers and destroyers supported by fast battleships to deal a major blow to it; then after daybreak execute a decisive battle with the entire force centered around battleship units to annihilate the enemy.[8]

However, by the Washington and London naval limitation treaties, the Japanese navy's tonnage ratio was fixed at 3:5, relative to either the British or the U.S. navy in terms of battleships, and at 7:10 for auxiliary ships. So the IJN sought to compensate for inferior strength by several means. One of these was the efficient utilization of torpedoes by submarines, cruisers, and destroyers. Then the successful development of the "long-lance" (Type 93) torpedo, with a range of forty thousand meters, brought about a rapid advance in torpedo tactics around 1935. Around 1937, modifying three light cruisers into heavy torpedo-equipped cruisers, carrying ten 4-barrel torpedo launchers, was incorporated in the annual naval defense plan.[9]

Around the same time the Type 94 carrier bomber (D1A1, "Susie"), a great advance over previous types, was officially introduced. Then came long-range flying boats, land-based bombers, and similar aircraft to become effective adjuncts of carrier-based forces. By 1936, the Type 96 land-based medium bomber (G3M2, "Nell"), which had a range of 6,100 km and was capable of both torpedo attack and bombing, was ready for service.

After Japan officially renounced the Washington Treaty, the IJN gave greater emphasis to land-based naval air, on the basis of the slogan, "Try to make the most of the geographical advantage that only we have."[10] The Third Replenishment Plan of 1937 increased the air arm by fourteen groups to fifty-three groups, and the Fourth Replenishment plan of 1939 added seventy-five more, for a total of 128 groups. Finally, the Fifth Replenishment Plan of 1940 provided another 160 for a grand sum of 288 groups. The latter also included a major expansion of land-based naval air forces and plans for the deployment of large and medium-size attack planes—mainly in Micronesia, close to the expected area of the anticipated decisive battle.[11]

Along with these developments, in 1938 a "Combined Naval Air Wing Rule" was instituted to ensure efficient operation of the land-based naval air groups. In January 1941 the Eleventh Naval Air Fleet was newly organized to form a unified command of the land-based air units. In April of the same year, the

First Air Fleet was set up to coordinate carrier-based aircraft in large numbers.[12] Thus, the major role in the overall interception-attrition operation began to shift from submarines and advanced bodies of cruisers and destroyers to aircraft.

UNDERSEA WARFARE PLANNING

With the development of undersea weapons technology, however, the submarine again became more and more important in the operations of the Imperial Japanese Navy. The Gunreibu assigned submarines critical duties in connection with the interception-attrition operation, making them responsible for reconnoitering the enemy fleet at anchor, pursuing it when under way, and attacking it to whittle down its strength in preparation for the anticipated "decisive battle" of the main fleet.

On the basis of such operational concepts, the Japanese navy endeavored to develop large submarines with sufficient range to cross the Pacific and return without refueling and also with enough speed to shadow the U.S. fleet. In 1924 the IJN had inaugurated the I-51 (*Kaidai* type), a "cruiser submarine," with a size of fifteen hundred tons in standard displacement, which could make twenty knots on the surface and ten knots submerged and had eight torpedo tubes. In 1932, the navy built submarine I-5, which carried aircraft for reconnaissance. The I-5 was the first such vessel, the only one in the world used for real operations.[13]

At the time of the London Conference, Japanese naval planning envisioned an important role for submarines. Specifically, in case of a war with the United States, the navy planned to dispatch six cruiser submarines to the area of the Hawaiian Islands for monitoring and pursuit. Once the enemy's main force set out, some three dozen submarines would proceed to prepare for the decisive battle. Consequently, at the London Conference Japan argued for 78,000 tons of submarines, but had to settle for less. With only eighty-five submarines presumed to be available for operations, plans for their disposition were worked out in 1931 as follows:[14]

Off the West Coast of the United States: 4 mine-laying submarines.
Off Hawaii: 9 cruiser submarines for monitoring the U.S. fleet.
Fleet Submarines: 27 cruiser submarines for pursuing and attacking the U.S. fleet.
Marianas Theater: 9 medium submarines.
South Sea Islands Theater: 9 medium submarines.

Southeast Theater: 9 medium submarines.
Philippines Theater: 9 large submarines.
Home Defense: 9 medium submarines.
Total Submarines: 85

Following this operational concept, the navy had pursued several ambitious projects in submarine warfare. Immediately after World War I, they had invited German submarine designers, technicians, and former German U-boat officers to Japan. With their assistance I-51 was laid down under the naval program of 1919, launched in 1921, and completed in 1924. I-51 was the first fleet-type submarine (abbreviated as Kaidai) in the Japanese navy, with a displacement of 1,500 tons surfaced, speed of twenty knots surfaced and ten knots submerged, and a cruising range of twenty thousand miles. Then the initial four Junsen-type (cruiser type) submarines, I-1 to I-4, were built in 1926 and 1929. These submarines displaced 2,135 tons and ran at 18 knots surfaced, with a cruising range of 24,400 miles.

With the construction of these boats, both Kaidai and Junsen, Japanese submarine construction progressed technically and operationally. In 1937, I-7, a command boat with a displacement of 2,525 tons and a surface speed of twenty-three knots, designed to accommodate a flag officer, was built. Then in 1941, another flag-cruiser submarine, I-9, with a displacement of 2,919 tons, a surface speed of 23.5 knots, and a range of sixteen thousand miles at 16 knots, was completed.[15] Finally, under the Fifth Replenishment Plan of 1940, the navy built the *Oyodo,* a submarine command cruiser, which carried six seaplanes and was designed to command submarines engaged in interception operations.

In 1933 the IJN also began work on the midget submarine program, very secretly. For purposes of secrecy those subs were called *Kō-Hyoteki* ("A-target"). The Navy General Staff believed that this weapon, if properly developed, would give the inferior Japanese fleet an important advantage in the decisive battle.

In 1938 three submarine tenders for midgets, first the *Chiyoda,* followed by the *Nisshin* and *Chitose* (each about 11,000 tons), were completed. The navy planned to use these vessels as seaplane tenders in peacetime, but in war each would carry twelve midget submarines. They would move into the path of the enemy fleet just before the decisive battle and launch the midget submarines from astern at intervals of a thousand meters while steaming at twenty knots.[16] But this was not put into practice. "A-target" subs were used only at Pearl

Harbor, Sydney, and Madagascar. After the defeat at the battle of Leyte Gulf, this weapon was modified to become a suicide weapon named *kaiten*, a human torpedo.

That operations were not carried out as planned in the prewar days was mainly due to the influence of the commander in chief of the Combined Fleet, Admiral Yamamoto Isoroku. Less than a year before the beginning of the war, Admiral Yamamoto submitted a paper, "Comments on Armaments"[17] to Navy Minister Oikawa Koshirō. His premise was that the war plan to secure resources in the western Pacific and strengthen the strategic position by checking the activities of the American fleet would never achieve a convincing victory. He pointed out that the war games of the Navy General Staff were usually suspended when it appeared that Japanese forces would be gradually whittled away. He insisted that the navy had to "deliver a fierce attack on the American fleet at the outset of hostilities to demoralize the U.S. Navy and the people of the U.S.A. beyond remedy." He thought that Japan could not win if it assumed a defensive posture at the start. If it did so, the more powerful U.S. Navy would decide the timing and direction of combat and would come to do battle with its entire strength.

In other words, Yamamoto maintained that the traditional interception-attrition strategy would leave the initiative in the hands of the U.S. Navy. Further, lying in wait for the Americans would dangerously diffuse Japan's forces. Later, Yamamoto argued, "Unless the Imperial Navy takes the initiative and keeps pounding the enemy, how can we fight a prolonged war? We must always deliver fierce blows to the enemy and hit him where it hurts. Otherwise we cannot possibly establish ourselves in a defensible position."[18]

Nowadays many critics point to Yamamoto and his idea of continuous offensive operations as being responsible for the unfavorable developments of the first year or two of the war. They say that, because of Yamamoto, the navy had to fight at Midway without proper preparation and Japan got involved in the campaign on distant Guadalcanal, a campaign that was to sap the nation's strength with no gain. They maintain that the Japanese navy should first have secured a defensible economic sphere and should have refrained from risky offensive operations. This would have been a better preparation for a drawn-out war.

At that time there were many officers, principally in the army and Navy General Staff, who favored the traditional interception-attrition operation. They believed that the coordinated use of carriers and land-based aircraft would make the best use of the empire's geographical extent, particularly its holdings in Micronesia. There was, therefore, a split in the Imperial Navy's strategic thinking. On the one hand, Admiral Yamamoto and the Combined Fleet advocated an aggressive approach. Yamamoto's position was dominant at the start, but damaging vacillation occurred in Japanese strategy later in the war, especially after his death. Then by the end of June 1943, almost the whole of the Combined Fleet had withdrawn to the homeland. This move was forced on the Japanese mainly by an acute shortage of naval air power—a state of affairs resulting from the continuous loss of pilots in the offensives undertaken according to Yamamoto's philosophy of continuously attacking Allied air power in the Solomons and New Guinea.

3

The Axis in Southern Waters

Severing the enemy's supply lines with raiders is one of the traditional roles of small navies fighting stronger opponents. Germany was obliged to move its naval forces south to cut off the supply routes between Great Britain and her Indian and Pacific resources.

GERMAN RAIDERS

In its World War I confrontations with the much larger navies of its enemies, the Imperial German Navy had successfully used its overseas cruiser squadron and merchant ships, converted into auxiliary cruisers, to interdict the transport of supplies. In World War II interdiction of enemy supply was again one of the main goals of German naval strategy. At the very start of the war at sea against the Western allies, the German navy dispatched their three diesel-powered, fast "pocket battleships"—*Deutschland, Admiral Graf Spee,* and *Admiral Scheer*—into the Atlantic to wage a *guerre de course.*[1]

The newly constructed heavy cruisers *Admiral Hipper* (13,900 tons) and battleships *Scharnhorst* and *Gneisenau* (31,800 tons) followed suit. But these vessels were turbine powered. Turbine propulsion gave them a much shorter endurance than that of the so-called pocket battleships and made them less suited to raiding operations. The diesel-powered ships, designed to comply with the tonnage restrictions imposed by the Versailles treaty of 1919, were—

with their speed, endurance, and heavy armament—specially suited for commerce raiding.

Whereas the *Deutschland,* under the command of Kapt.z.S. (Captain) Wenneker (who would later be promoted to rear admiral and serve a second term as Tokyo naval attaché from April 1940 to May 1945) operated only in the North and South Atlantic, the *Admiral Graf Spee* (Kapt.z.S. Langsdorff) and *Admiral Scheer* (Kapt.z.S. Krancke) rounded the Cape of Good Hope in November 1939 and February 1941, respectively, and operated in the Indian Ocean south and north of Madagascar. Off the Seychelles Islands the *Admiral Scheer* sank four merchantmen (19,170 tons). Despite being sighted on 22 February 1941 by an aircraft from the HMS *Glasgow,* she evaded interception by units of the British Eastern Fleet operating off Italian Somalia and returned to Kiel Harbor safely after a five-month mission.

Nevertheless, these thrusts into the Indian Ocean were only an extension of the operations in the South Atlantic. There was no coordination with the Axis partners, nor was there, in early 1941, any operational assistance for the desperate defense of the weak Italian colonial forces, fighting for survival against the British invasion on the Horn of Africa.

AUXILIARY MERCHANT CRUISERS, THE HILFSKREUZERS

Given the small number of capital ships available to the German navy, the diesel-powered pocket battleships could not be spared in sufficient numbers for effective anti-supply operations, despite their desirable speed and range. From the outset of the war, therefore, fast merchantmen were especially earmarked for conversion into *Hilfskreuzer* (auxiliary merchant cruisers, or AMCs).

The AMCs were fast, modern turbine- or diesel-powered vessels of 7,500 to 20,000 tons displacement, with a complement of up to 420 men. They looked like regular cargo ships, with furnishings to change their visual characteristics, and carried a relatively heavy armament of six 5.9-inch guns and two to four 3.7mm and two to four 20mm antiaircraft guns, as well as two to six 21-inch torpedo tubes. All ships had two reconnaissance float-planes; some also had an MTB (motor torpedo boat). They could carry and drop up to four hundred mines. All military equipment was carefully camouflaged but could be rapidly dismasked.

From early 1940 until late 1943 the *Hilfskreuzer* vessels operated under experienced commanding officers in all seven oceans, often very far from home waters, on missions that lasted twelve months and more.[2] Most of the officers and crew were hand-picked former merchant marine personnel, experienced in worldwide service. This established a very special sense of unity and mutual dependence and was an advantage during their long, and at times monotonous, missions.

Nine German auxiliary cruisers were converted and commissioned during the war—*Atlantis* (Rogge), *Pinguin* (Krüder), *Orion* (Weyher), *Widder* (von Ruckteschell), *Komet* (Eyssen), *Thor* (Kähler/Gumprich), *Kormoran* (Detmers), *Michel* (von Ruckteschell/Gumprich), and *Stier* (Gerlach). Seven of . them operated in the Pacific Ocean, and five of them in the Indian Ocean as well. They had to transit all the way from home waters. During the shipping season of 1940 one (AMC *Komet*), on her way out, even used the North Siberian sea route, entering the Pacific through the Bering Straits. Altogether these nine ships sank or captured 138 cargo vessels with 857,533 gross register tons.

A number of Allied ships were also sunk by mines in waters as far away as Australia and New Zealand. On the island of Nauru, a phosphate production plant was heavily damaged by shore bombardment. Twenty-three ships— including two whaling factory ships with 22,200 tons of whale oil and nine of their eleven whaling boats—were captured and sent, with their cargoes, as prizes to ports in occupied France or to designated Asian ports in the Japanese realm.

In the Indian and Pacific Oceans alone, the booty of the German auxiliary cruisers comprised thirty-nine ships totaling nearly 250,000 tons. They successfully fought three British auxiliary cruisers (*Alcantara*, *Carnavon Castle*, and *Voltaire*) and sank one of them, as well as the Australian light cruiser *Sydney*.

THE AUTOMEDON DOCUMENTS

Of special importance during these AMC missions was the capture of the British freighter *Automedon* on 11 November 1940 in the southern Bengal Gulf by AMC *Atlantis* and the seizure of the British passenger freighter *Nankin*, with 185 passengers aboard, on 10 May 1942 in the Indian Ocean by AMC *Thor*.

On *Automedon*, underway from Liverpool (via Durban, Penang, and Singapore) to Hong Kong and Shanghai, all the bridge crew had perished during the assault, without being able to destroy highly sensitive papers.[3] The German prize officer, Lt. Ulrich Mohr, made a meticulous search that yielded top secret British War Cabinet minutes of 8 August 1940. He also found a CoS (chief of staff) report on the defense of Singapore and the Far East; the complete order of battle for the land, air, and sea forces of the area; the new Merchant Navy cipher tables and call sign tables; and maps and information about minefields and swept channels.

Aware of the importance of these papers, the commanding officer of AMC *Atlantis*, Captain Rogge, on 16 November 1940 dispatched the earlier prize *Ole Jacob* to Kobe in order to forward the captured papers to the German naval attaché in Tokyo, Rear Adm. Wenneker. They arrived on 4 December, whereupon Wenneker cabled the essentials via Siberia to the Seekriegsleitung in Berlin, at the same time requesting permission to hand over copies of the captured papers to the Japanese naval staff. He sent the original papers on 6 December by courier via the Trans-Siberian Railway to German naval headquarters.[4] Permission to release copies to the Japanese was granted on 11 December, with the condition that Berlin was to be named as the source.

Because of the British statements contained in the CoS report—that "in the event of Japanese intervention against Britain," as "in the present situation" the British were "unable to send a fleet to the Far East" and, as they were "unable to prevent damage to own interests . . . [they] should retire" and "restore position later on"—the Japanese had serious doubts about the authenticity of the documents. As Germany had been pressing them to intervene on their side in the south, they suspected that they were being manipulated by the Germans.[5]

THE SEIZURE OF THE NANKIN

Another windfall for the Axis was the capture by AMC *Thor* of the British steamer *Nankin* on 10 May 1942 on her way from Fremantle, Australia, to Colombo, Ceylon. Not only was she fully loaded with provisions and equipment for British garrisons in India; she also carried a large amount of freshly printed Chinese currency for Chiang Kai-shek and fifty-six bags of courier mail that the Germans seized.[6] The main assets were "most secret" intelligence summaries, issued by the Combined Operations Intelligence Center in Wellington, sent to the commander in chief, Eastern Fleet at Colombo. From this material it could clearly be inferred that the Allies had cryptanalytic access to the Japanese fleet cipher, "JN25b." The German ship *Regensburg* was dispatched as courier by the German naval attaché in Tokyo, to pick up this extremely valuable material.

The capture of these important papers might have changed history, had they reached the Japanese naval staff without delay. The Japanese were still in the last planning stage for their assault on Midway. If they had immediately learned that the Americans had succeeded in breaking their operational cipher, they certainly would have activated an anticipated code change. As it happened, Capt. Gunther Gumprich of the *Thor*, unaware of the papers' paramount importance, kept the *Nankin* (as German prize renamed *Leuthen*) and the *Regensburg* with him for several days for transloading cargo and transshipping passengers. The *Regensburg*, with her precious Allied documents—compromised on 10 May!—did not reach Japan until 18 July, nor had any prior notification reached the Imperial Navy staff.

The new Japanese fleet cipher, prepared for a code change on 1 April and then 1 May, was activated on 28 June, only weeks after it could have turned the tide of the Japanese disaster at Midway on 3 June 1942.

THE LAST MISSIONS OF THE AMCS

By then most of the German AMCs had been withdrawn from service. The few still operating in Asian waters could use Japanese facilities directly and operate from Japanese bases. Only two, however, put into Japanese ports. *Thor* entered Yokohama for overhaul and logistic supply on 9 October 1942. On 30 November, while berthed alongside supply ship *Uckermark*, she and the *Leuthen*, her former prize, were destroyed with considerable loss of life and material by an explosion on the *Uckermark*.

Michel, after her first mission under Captain von Ruckteschell, put into Kobe for a refit by Etappe Ostasien on 2 March 1943 and left port again for her second mission, now under Capt. Gunther Gumprich, on 21 March. After operating west of Australia and off the Chilean coast, she returned to Japan. Just ninety miles from reaching port again, she was on 17 October torpedoed and sunk by USS *Tarpon*. Part of her crew reached the coast in floats and rubber boats. On this last mission of a German auxiliary cruiser during the war, *Michel* sank three ships totaling 27,623 tons. The surviving crewmembers of these ships were used as personnel reserves and to fill up the supply organization.

BLOCKADE-RUNNERS

German supply ships that replenished German raiders often had to transport the raiders' prisoners ashore. In January 1941, MS *Ermland*, after delivering her goods at Lamotrek Atoll, took on some 330 prisoners and, on orders of the Seekriegsleitung, was directly dispatched to Europe.[7] Admiral Wenneker, aware of the scarcity of many war-essential raw materials in Germany, was dismayed.

He had tried in vain to have the ship carry raw materials, available in the Japanese realm, as well.

Up to this time, raw materials from East Asia, badly needed for the German wartime economy, had been transported all five thousand miles from Vladivostok to the Ural Mountains on the double-tracked Trans-Siberian railway system and on through the European Soviet Union. It was becoming obvious that, as long as it was possible, bulk transport of essential goods would be much more effective by sea than by rail. So, even as Admiral Wenneker was failing with the *Ermland,* preparations were being made to use the German merchant ships available to Etappe Ostasien in transport missions—as blockade-runners—to Europe. In light of the considerable risk of loss on their long trajectories, in spring 1941 routing the merchant ships via the North Siberian Seaway seemed feasible.

Starting in 1941 the blockade-runner service became the main task of the German Supply Service East Asia.[8] This was not an easy job, however. The material shortages suffered by the German economy were also taking their toll on Japan. After the Germans occupied the Netherlands and France, the Japanese feared that Germany might claim these countries' Asian colonies and their natural resources. It was only after Germany abstained from claiming such rights, for the time being, that the Japanese consented to making part of their resources available and allowed German ships to take on cargo directly in local ports.

The situation overall put quite a strain on German means and personnel. Fuel and needed materials had to be bought and stored in considerable quantities. Often special packing or processing procedures were required. The assigned ships had to be steered to suitable loading ports and sent out under operational control to Europe. The German passenger liner *Scharnhorst,* berthed at Kobe, was used as a depot ship for stores and provisions fuel and as an assembly point for personnel. (The *Scharnhorst* was later sold to Japan and its hull used for an aircraft carrier.)

On 20 August 1941, the German Navy High Command (OKM) established priorities for material to be procured, in the following order:[9] crude rubber, tungsten, ferrotungsten, molybdenum, tin, copper, mineral oils, leather and hides, oils and fats. Bills of lading included oil seeds, vegetal and animal oils, food products, quinine, opium, and iodine.[10] The Japanese navy also provided samples of their "long lance" torpedoes and Allied guns captured at Hong Kong and Singapore for German examination. In exchange, out of the French port of Bordeaux, ships transported modern weaponry and aircraft, factory equipment, machinery, propulsion engines, optical instruments, crude glass, mercury, aluminum, scrap iron, and so on. Meanwhile, there was an extensive transfer of know-how, with the release of blueprints and assignment of German experts to Japan.

When the Etappe activities became too demanding for the attaché staff in 1942, Capt. Werner Vermehren of the Marine Special Service (Marinesonderdienst or MSD) was sent to Japan as Admiral Wenneker's deputy to head Etappe Ostasien. Admiral Wenneker had on 7 November 1942 first proposed using facilities in Japanese-occupied territories in Southeast Asia as German supply bases. But it took until early 1943 to achieve Japanese consent and start planning, installing, and manning a German service organization with the necessary equipment and radio links to direct it. Thus German naval supply bases at Penang, Singapore (in Malaya), and Jakarta (on Java) would not be ready for service until 8 June 1943. Another base at Surabaya (Java) was added later.

The original fifteen German vessels available to Etappe had been augmented by two suitable German ships sent from Chile and two raider prizes. From Europe five blockade-runners had arrived during the first half of 1942.[11] Cargoes for all ships had to be acquired and prepared for shipping. The ships had to be repaired and fitted out. Clothing, food, entertainment, and medical care for their crews had to be provided. After December 1942 the ships could be equipped with guns, captured by the Japanese at Hong Kong or Singapore. Safety routes to protect the ships from attacks by their own Axis submarines had to be established.

Of the ships available, from December 1940 until October 1943, thirty-seven loaded blockade-runners departed from Asia for Europe, of which some made the trip several times. Among them were also four Italian blockade-runners. Six of these ships were prematurely recalled, so that thirty-one actually undertook their transit voyages. The Japanese also sent one Japanese ship, the MS *Asaka Maru* (7,399 tons, Nippon Yusen KK, Tokyo) on a two-way voyage with goods to Europe in exchange.

Until the United States entered the war, fifteen blockade-runners were routed around Cape Horn; after that, sixteen went around the Cape of Good Hope. Of these thirty-one vessels, three were sunk by enemy action, eight were scuttled when approached by enemy forces, and two were accidentally sunk by German submarines. One ship, MS *Odenwald*, was captured by USS *Omaha* in fall 1941 in the U.S. neutrality zone before the United States entered the war.

Seventeen blockade-runners would actually complete their voyages and deliver their war-essential cargoes at the port of Bordeaux in occupied France. Of the twenty-two loaded ships sent from Europe to Japan between December 1941 and June 1943, seventeen reached their Asian destination safely. The overall percentage of losses of the blockade-runners amounted to 45.16 percent. It should be noted, however, that between December 1940 and November 1942 it was only 16 percent. Losses mounted steeply thereafter, so that in 1943, of thirteen ships dispatched from Japan, only two reached the German realm.

As the risks grew steadily, especially after the Allied air surveillance gap over the Middle Atlantic was plugged, the Axis tried to concentrate the shipping period in the dark winter months during bad weather. When this approach proved not to be of much avail, the Skl. decided in August 1943 to discontinue fitting out surface ships for this purpose altogether. The last ship to get home with her cargo was MS *Osorno* (6,951 long tons, HAPAG lne, Hamburg), which reached the estuary of Bordeaux on 26 December 1943. During the overall effort about 114,000 tons of commodities reached their destination in Europe, 44,495 tons of which were crude rubber alone; 48,000 tons were lost and 30,500 recalled. (With the rubber brought in by *Osorno*, German requirements could be filled until November 1944.) *Burgenland,* the last ship out, sailed from Yokohama on 29 October 1943 but had to be scuttled when approached by enemy forces at the latitude of Natal on 5 January 1944.[12] About a week later the German Armed Forces High Command (OKW) finally decided to discontinue surface blockade-running.

ITALIAN SUBMARINES WEST OF AFRICA

During the summer of 1940 the Italian navy, in agreement with the German Navy High Command (OKM), had established their own submarine command, BETASOM, in the Atlantic.[13] Starting in September, twenty-seven Italian submarines, after operating in the Atlantic in separate groups, were transferred to a new Italian installation in the Bordeaux base at the Bay of Biscay. Before the Italian positions in Somalia, Italian East Africa, were lost, four Italian submarines (*Archimede, Galileo Ferraris, Guglielmotti,* and *Perla*) transferred to Bordeaux as well, with underway replenishment by the German navy, early in March 1941.[14]

The first Italian submarine to leave this new base on a North Atlantic mission in October 1940 was SS *Malespina*.[15]

It was agreed between the German BdU, Admiral Dönitz, and BETASOM that these Italian boats should operate under overall German operational command, including the assignment of operational areas and decisions on the mode of cooperation. Within the framework of this command authority, BETASOM was to have full responsibility and independence.[16]

The initial relocation of the Italian submarines into the Atlantic did not, however, justify the high-flung expectations of the German submarine command. Whereas during October and November 1940 the average German submarine could sink 1,115 tons per day, the Italian submarines sank only twenty tons per boat per day. It was not that their Italian crews were less dedicated or ready for action than their German comrades, but that they had been trained according to a completely different conventional submarine doctrine. They could not fit into the reconnaissance and radio reporting system. And their big, unwieldy submarines were little suited to mobile, surface night action, against well-escorted convoys, on the main routes across the North Atlantic, in extremely rough weather conditions. It was agreed among both submarine commands to task the Italian submarines in areas with less Allied air cover.

On 15 May 1941 they concurred on Italian operations areas west of Gibraltar, an area in the North Atlantic south of the German dislocations and in the sea area west of Freetown in coordination with the German forces.[17] Two Italian submarines (*Cagni* and *Da Vinci*) even extended their operations into the Indian Ocean. Operating in these remote areas, they could reach a sinking quota of 65.67 tons per boat per diem.

Of the thirty-two boats ultimately transferred, operating out of Bordeaux, independently or together with German submarines, twelve were lost in action. Ten were recalled to the Mediterranean in 1942.

Seven of the boats remaining at Bordeaux were eventually converted into cargo carriers by the removal of their artillery, ammunition storage, torpedo tubes, attack-periscopes, and some battery cells. From late April 1943 they were sent as transports to Southeast Asia under the codename of "Aquila." Two (*Tazzoli* and *Barbarigo*) were lost underway, but three Italian submarines (*Cappellini*, *Guiliani*, and *Torelli*) reached their ports of destination during July and August. One (*Cagni*) was still underway southeast of the Island of Mauritius on 8 September 1943, the day of the Italian capitulation, and put into the South African port of Durban on 19 September.

After the capitulation, those Italian submarines still at Bordeaux (*Finzi* and *Bagnolini*) and the three in Japanese-occupied ports (*Cappellini*, *Guiliani*, and

Torelli) were seized and later commissioned in the German navy with the type denominator "UIT" (UIT-21 to 25). One boat (*Bagnolini*, UIT-22) left Bordeaux under German command on 23 August 1944 but was sunk off the Cape of Good Hope. The remaining *Finzi* was destroyed in August 1944 before the Allied forces reached Bordeaux.

The five Italian submarines that eventually reached the Indian Ocean from Bordeaux carried twenty-eight passengers and 650 tons of cargo. With the three boats arriving in Southeast Asia, sixteen passengers and 355 tons of materiel reached their destination. This corresponds to 55 percent of the total.[18]

THE AXIS SOUTH OF THE TROPIC OF CANCER

Grand Admiral Dönitz, BdU, always saw the interdiction of the enemy's logistic and economic supply as the main operational task for the German submarine arm. Even under the strangulating effect of the Allies' growing ASW efficiency, he was very reluctant to take any of his forces away from the enemies' vital supply routes in the North Atlantic. Nevertheless, when the Allied anti-submarine warfare effort began to drastically diminish the U-boats' success, Admiral Dönitz finally decided to move his submarines to more distant, less threatened sea areas. Their operations areas were gradually moved to the south along the American and African coasts and ultimately also around the Cape of Good Hope into the Indian Ocean. This coincided with the commissioning of the bigger Type IX boats. When the new German Type IXC and IXD subs, with their longer ranges, became operational, Admiral Dönitz could begin to look for more remote operations areas on other essential supply routes.

In the eastern Atlantic he gradually had the bigger submarines, as they became available to him in larger numbers, operate farther to the south, beyond the approaches to the Mediterranean. There, from spring 1941 until fall 1942, they sometimes again operated in company with the Italian Atlantic subs. In October three Italian submarines (*Archimede*, *Bagnolini*, and *Barbarigo*) operated southwest of Freetown and in the Gulf of Guinea as well.

After some missions on the convoy routes between Gibraltar and England, the German submarines were consecutively targeted against convoy traffic off the African West Coast of Sierra Leone in the Gulf of Guinea and the estuary of the Congo River.[19] During 1941 they sank in these sea areas more than a hundred ships totaling 500,000 gross tons. In order to give them enough time in their operations area, underway replenishment by German naval units had to be provided.

In October–November 1942, five German long-range submarines of the types IXC and IXD2 operated as task group *"Eisbär"* ("Polar Bear") around South Africa from the west coast to the Mozambique Channel. They were U-68 (Merten), U-159 (Witte), U-172 (Emermann), U-179 (Sobe), and U-504 (Poske). After underway replenishment from a German Type XIV submarine tanker, together they sank twenty-eight Allied merchant ships, with a gross tonnage of 182,174 tons.[20] Another group of three boats—U-177 (Gysae), U-178 (Ibbeken), and U-181 (Lüth)—sank twenty-five ships totaling 134,780 tons. An Italian submarine, the SS *Cagni* (Roselli-Lorenzini), after exiting the Mediterranean, sank another two ships. This confirmed that shifting the emphasis of the submarine effort to more remote, less guarded sea areas still held good chances for success.

After the "Eisbär" success, another submarine group called *"Seehund"* ("Seal"), consisting of U-160 (Lassen), U-182 (Clausen), U-506 (Würdemann), U-509 (Witte), and U-516 (Wiebe), was dispatched in December 1942 and January 1943 from the *Lorient* submarine base into South African waters. After refueling from a Type XIV submarine tanker in the South Atlantic, they reached their operations area on both sides of the Cape of Good Hope. Here these five boats sank seventeen ships (100,577 tons) and damaged another three (22,353 tons). Four of them, after another replenishment by a Type XB submarine, returned to their French bases, but one was lost on her way back.

4

The Japanese in the Indian Ocean

On 7 December 1941 Japan had entered World War II with its successful surprise attack on the U.S. fleet at Pearl Harbor on Hawaii. Simultaneously amphibious landing operations were started to occupy the Philippines, followed by other landings on the islands of the Indonesian archipelago.

On 26 December 1941, after completion of the landing operation against the Philippines and Malaya, Japan's submarine forces were reorganized into three groups—"Kō" ("A" Group, 6th Squadron), "Otsu" ("B" Group, 5th Squadron), and the Malaya submarine group (5th Squadron)—as the Dutch East Indies Group "B," under command of Rear Adm. Daigo Tadashige, was assigned to the Bay of Bengal for deployment. "B" Group operated in the Indian Ocean from the end of January to the middle of February and then returned to Penang. During this deployment, they sank eleven Allied ships (37,063 tons) and damaged three (17,256 tons). The first victim of Japanese submarine operations in the Indian Ocean was the British SS *Kwangtung* (2,626 tons), which was sunk on 4 January by gunfire off Chilachap. The first Japanese victim was I-60, on 17 January, in the southern approach to Sunda Strait, sunk by the British escort ship *Jupiter*.

On 1 February, for the Dutch East Indies invasion operation, submarines were reformed again into three groups and deployed in the Indian Ocean: "Kō" ("A," Fourth and Sixth Squadrons), "Otsu" ("B", Fifth Squadron), and "Hei"

("C", Second Squadron). Boats that had returned from Hawaii and American West Coast operations were also added to the Indian Ocean operations. These submarines were deployed there from early March to the middle of April and sank nineteen Allied ships (82,886 tons) and damaged three (14,747 tons).

After having occupied Malaya and Java, the Japanese army advanced into Burma and took Rangoon on 8 March 1942. With the initial strategic objectives attained, there arose differences of opinion about the conduct of the war between army and navy. Should Japan continue the offensive operations, or should she take a defensive stance to hold what she had taken? And if she continued offensive operations, should she go westward against Britain or eastward against the United States?

In early February 1942 it was apparent that the navy and the army disagreed sharply. The IJN insisted on following up the advantages gained by conducting more offensive operations against the United States fleet, while the army favored a defensive strategy, fortifying the occupied areas once the Southern Area was conquered. The army was concerned about Japan's overall ability to sustain a protracted war and the specific limitations of war potential and limited military capabilities. Taking both into account, the army considered resolving the Chinese conflict and, if a chance should present itself, advancing to the north into Russia in the wake of a German victory at the eastern front in Europe. Thus the army opposed any further major operations, be it in the Hawaiian, Indian, or Australian theater. The army insisted on a defensive strategy but pointed out that they did not advocate abandoning further expansion altogether. The army's intention was to postpone expansion until the entire "Co-Prosperity Sphere" had become fully self-sufficient and Japan's war potential was sufficiently built up.[1]

The Japanese army had repeatedly been asked by the German Armed Forces High Command (OKW) and Army High Command (Oberkommando des Heeres or OKH) in Berlin, as well as the German Ambassador, Eugen Ott, in Tokyo, to participate in the war against the Soviet Union and was quite fascinated by the Germany victories on the Eastern Front. In July 1941, the Japanese army thus had begun the Kwantung Army Special Mobilization Exercise in Manchuria, aiming to attack the Soviet Union in September if the Soviet Siberian Army moved to the front in Europe. In this exercise fourteen divisions, with 50,000 men and 220,000 horses, including ammunitions and provisions, were prepared for war on the opposite side of the Pacific only four months before Pearl Harbor, but the army could not push through the cabinet a campaign against the Soviets.[2]

In early February 1942, after Japan had completely achieved the strategic objectives of its "First Stage Operation" of the war, the army, spurred by expectations of a German victory and by German requests, again withdrew forces from the Pacific theater to reinforce the Kwantung army in preparation for an attack on the Soviet Union. Thus, in early June 1942, the Kwantung army reached the peak of its strength during the Pacific war, totaling sixteen infantry divisions, two tank divisions (after September), one cavalry division totaling 650,000 men, 675 tanks, and 750 aircraft.[3]

Meanwhile the navy advocated following up on the advantages gained and pursuing more vigorous operations against the United States fleet. The IJN's Combined Fleet (*Rengō kantai*) staff was especially aggressive. They planned to conquer Hawaii and hoped that this would force the American fleet into the much-desired "decisive battle." But when it became apparent that this project could not be carried out because of insufficient air power to destroy the American land-based air assets, they decided on advancing toward the west. They drew up a plan to destroy the British Eastern Fleet, occupy Ceylon, and establish contact with the Axis in the Middle East. Accordingly, the Combined Fleet conducted war games for this operation from 20 to 22 February. But this far-reaching plan was not approved, because of the army's objection. The army opposed such an operation, contending that it would risk Japan's readiness against the Soviet Union in Manchuria and would weaken the war effort in China.[4]

At the outbreak of war, Japanese planners had not considered invading either India or Australia. They sought only to sever their links with Britain by taking Burma and granting it independence, which would stimulate the Indian independence movement, and by disrupting sea communications. The army, fascinated by German victories in the Eastern Front campaign, although worried about Australia's being used as a base from which an Anglo-American counteroffensive might be launched, opposed the Westward Advance campaign and the idea of advancing to Australia. They were unwilling to provide the necessary troops for the disposal of the navy. Thus, the thrust into the Indian Ocean area become a limited one, largely restricted to the occupation of the Nicobar and the Andaman Islands.[5]

On 7 March 1942 a limited offensive, which would not cause a heavy drain on Japan's military capacity and could isolate Australia and effectively prevent her becoming a useful base for the Allies, was agreed upon. And finally, the army and navy agreed on a new plan, named "FS" Operation, that had been worked out during April and May. It provided for the seizure of the Samoan Islands, the Fiji Islands, and New Caledonia, and it anticipated the seizure of Port Moresby.

Japanese leaders clearly understood the weakness of Britain's position in India but could formulate no concrete plan concerning India because Japan did not have the military capability to attempt military measures against it. The planners at IGHQ hoped that by occupying Burma they could disrupt cooperation between India and Britain and activate an anti-British movement in India by propaganda, whereupon the Indian people would rise against British rule. Moreover, Japanese leaders were relying on the success of Germany's and Italy's operations in the Near East and the Suez areas, hoping that the progress of the Axis would propel India toward independence. But those deliberations were destined to assume no concrete form.

Even so, after the unexpected victories of the first-stage operations, the army and navy staffs at IGHQ reached an agreement on 15 January 1942 concerning India, stating that "further strong measures should be taken toward India with the objective of disrupting her communications with Great Britain and the United States, thus urging her to abandon her co-operation with Great Britain and accelerating the anti-British movement." And at a Liaison Conference (between General Headquarters and the government) in February 1942, the political and propaganda aspects of granting independence to Burma and India were adopted in a statement entitled, "Outline of National Policies in View of the Changing Situation."[6]

As the army advanced into Burma, the Japanese navy advanced into the Indian Ocean. In India, the National Congress Party, after a speech of Gandhi's, passed a resolution calling for a withdrawal of British forces from the country. Since the British of course did not comply with this, a passive resistance movement arose all over India. But Japan did not have the military and political power to take advantage of this opening. The chief of staff of the Combined Fleet, Vice Adm. Ugaki Matome, wrote in his diary quite self-accusingly: "Japan is the proposed leader of East Asia. Is Japan ready and able to help the Indians gain independence? If not, we are not worthy even as a neighbor, not to speak of as a leader of Asia."[7]

The Combined Fleet's far-reaching operations plan for a seizure of Ceylon was not approved by the Gunreibu (Navy General Staff) and also met opposition from the army. The army was unwilling to place the necessary troops for an operation against Ceylon at the disposal of the navy. So, instead of a conquest of Ceylon, the Combined Fleet decided on 14 February to have a task force under Admiral Nagumo carry out air raids in the Indian Ocean theater. (Nevertheless, one week later they conducted war games that included a scenario with an assault on Ceylon and making contact with Axis forces in the Middle East aboard the flag ship *Yamato.*) It is noteworthy that this operation was not planned for the sake of a joint strategy. Nagumo's operation merely represented the lame remnant of the original plan for a powerful thrust into the Indian Ocean, which in turn was only a substitute for the original plan to conquer Hawaii, which had proven unfeasible.

Admiral Ugaki wrote in his diary that his young staff officers had concluded that it was better to operate toward the west, since there were no promising possibilities against Hawaii. Despite some differences between their ideas and his, Ugaki approved this plan and called the idea to attack first in the Indian Ocean a mere reversal of the order of the attacks that he originally had had in mind. He now considered the objectives of this proposed operation:[8]

1. Destruction of the enemy fleet.
2. Invasions of strategic points and destruction of enemy bases.
3. Furtherance of the anti-British movement in India.
4. Connection between the Axis powers.

One of the operation's two main goals was to smash the British Eastern Fleet. The Japanese offensive began as passive resistance spread through India. Then, the fall of Singapore rendered 55,000 Indian soldiers captive to Japan. These Indian troops could have been of decisive importance for Japan. They should have been immediately transformed into freedom fighters and incorporated into the Indian National Army under command of the Indian revolutionary organization. But the Japanese did not use Indian prisoners of war at this first stage, because Japan was fascinated with her own victory.

Among Japanese military and political leaders there had arisen an ambition to extend the scope of the Greater East Asia Co-Prosperity Sphere to include India. Therefore, the Japanese army did not want the Indian National Army to take credit for the liberation of India. Japan chose to recognize them as useful auxiliary units that were good only for propaganda purposes. Thus dreams of the Greater East Asia Co-Prosperity Sphere, to be erected by the

Japanese alone, stalled the political and military measures that Japan could have taken to support the Indian uprising.

JAPANESE OFFENSIVE OPERATIONS IN THE WEST

On 15 February, Singapore surrendered. Meanwhile Nagumo's task force of four carriers, two battleships, and three cruisers launched 188 strike aircraft against Port Darwin. Shore-based naval air forces from Celebes also took part in the raid. This attack sank twelve transports, and Darwin was put out of action as a base for several months; thus the last reinforcement link to Java was broken. On 9 March 1942, Adm. Yamamoto Isoroku entrusted the overall command of the Ceylon operation to Vice Adm. Kondō Nobutake, commander in chief of the Southern Force. But actual execution was entrusted to Vice Adm. Nagumo Chūichi, who had attacked Pearl Harbor, and the Malaya Force (Southern Expeditionary Fleet), commanded by Vice Adm. Ozawa Jisaburō.

The Nagumo Mobile Force started preparations for a carrier task force attack on British forces in the western area of the Indian Ocean and sortied from Staring Bay in the south of Celebes on 26 March. This fleet, including five large fleet carriers, had about four hundred aircraft of the First Air Fleet, four fast battleships, two heavy cruisers, one light cruiser, and eight destroyers. In the morning of 5 April, 128 carrier planes took off before dawn and attacked Colombo, where they did heavy damage to land installations. But they sank only one destroyer in dock and the armed merchant cruiser *Hector* and the submarine depot ship *Lucia,* plus a merchant ship, in the harbor, because the British had gotten wind of the attack through signal intelligence.

However, in the afternoon, search planes detected the British cruisers *Dorsetshire* and *Cornwall* off Ceylon, which were seeking to join the British Eastern Fleet under Vice Adm. Sir James Somerville. Japanese dive-bombers sank the two ships with "the best accuracy rate ever achieved by naval aircraft"— nearly 87 percent direct hits.[9] Then on the morning of 9 April, Nagumo's second attack hit the port of Trincomalee, sank a merchant ship, shot down fourteen aircraft, and damaged shore installations. After these air raids, a search plane reported sighting the old British aircraft carrier *Hermes* about noon. In the course of the afternoon, Japanese dive-bombers sank *Hermes,* the destroyer *Vampire,* the corvette *Hollyhock,* a tanker, and a transport ship.

While the operations of the carrier group off Ceylon proceeded, a smaller force under Vice Admiral Ozawa sailed on 26 March 1942 from the Strait of Malacca toward the eastern coast of India and the northern area of the Bay of Bengal. Divided into three groups, this force consisted of a heavy cruiser, a light cruiser and six destroyers, supported by the Fourth Air Squadron (which attacked Allied shipping between Calcutta and Madras). At the same time, six U-cruisers of the Second Submarine Division were also deployed to the Bay of Bengal and in the vicinity of Ceylon. Their task was to reconnoiter the waters near Ceylon and take up positions in the most important passages through the Laccadive and Maldive Islands, providing a degree of protection for the western flank of the Japanese fleet. Altogether, at the cost of seventeen aircraft, Japanese naval and naval air operations in the Indian Ocean produced British losses of one carrier, two heavy cruisers, thirty-one merchant ships totaling 153,603 tons, and seven additional transports. In addition, about forty British aircraft were shot down by Japanese carrier aircraft.[10] British trade and military traffic on both sides of the Indian Ocean were temporarily completely disrupted. Yet because the British Eastern Fleet had escaped destruction, the actual aim of the operation was not attained.

Because of the attack on Colombo, Prime Minister Churchill told President Roosevelt on 7 April that it seemed that the Japanese might be contemplating the invasion of Ceylon and asked whether the Pacific Fleet could take action that would compel the Japanese striking forces to return to the Pacific.[11] On the 17th the President replied that he declined to send American ships into the Indian Ocean, but he offered to temporarily replace some of the home fleet's battleships if they were sent to support the Eastern Fleet. He also stated that measures were at hand in the Pacific which "we hope you will find effective when they can be made known to you shortly."[12] Then Doolittle's air raid was conducted on 18 April. It caused a hasty shift on the Japanese side, which now gave priority to the operation to capture Midway.

Meanwhile, after the outbreak of war, the Japanese navy deployed thirty-one submarines, out of a total of forty-two, to Far Eastern waters. They sank forty-one vessels (188,892 tons) and damaged five more (34,299 tons) before Nagumo's air raids on Ceylon in April.[13] Penang, opened on 20 January 1942, was to be the base for these submarines. On 1 March, a general order concerning submarine operations was issued by IGHQ that can be summarized as follows:[14]

1. Submarines will be dispatched to the Hawaiian area continuously and will also be deployed at the east coast of Australia and New Zealand and the west

coast of the United States and the Panama Canal, to cut the enemy's sea lines of communication between Australia and America.

2. Southern Command is to deploy submarines to the Indian Ocean and at the west coast of Australia to cut sea lines to the Atlantic and the Indian Ocean.

3. Occasionally auxiliary cruisers and submarines will be dispatched to the Panama Canal, southern Africa, and the west coast of America to cut sea lines of communication.

Under this concept of operations, on 10 March, the Eighth Submarine Group (consisting of eleven submarines, among them four I-type submarines capable of carrying sea planes) was organized and deployed to Penang. They formed into three groups. Group *Otsu* (B), consisting of three cruiser submarines, one of them (I-27) carrying a midget submarine, and group *Hei* (C) consisting of three cruiser submarines, two of them (I-22, I-23) also carrying midgets, were assigned to Australian waters.[15] The third group *Kō* (A), deployed at the east coast of Africa, had five new ocean-cruising I-type submarines, three of which (I-16, I-18, I-20) carried a midget submarine on board. Also attached to "Kō" division were the two armed merchant cruisers, *Aikoku Maru* and *Hōkoku Maru*, carrying eight 15 cm guns and two seaplanes.

The operations of the three submarine groups were aimed primarily at the destruction of shipping in the Indian Ocean and in southern Australian waters. Altogether they sank thirty merchantmen with nearly 150,000 gross registered tons (GRT) during this operation, while losing only one submarine (I-28). "Kō" group alone sank twenty-two ships totaling 103,516 tons.[16] Furthermore, on 31 May 1942, it dispatched three *Kō-hyōteki* (midget submarines) into Diego Garcia, where they sank one tanker and damaged the old British battleship *Ramillies*. The armed merchant cruisers mainly operated in the central and western parts of the Indian Ocean, sinking one ship of 6,757 tons and capturing two others, and supported the I-boats.

By these activities the Japanese presence in the Indian Ocean became a serious problem to the British, and the Royal Navy had to reinforce their escorts in the area. To further increase operations in the Indian Ocean, Japanese naval planners intended to deploy the First and Second Submarine Divisions to Penang in June 1942 after these had finished repairs and operations in the northern Pacific. That would have added sixteen more I-type subs for the continuation of the successful operations there, and for July three more cruiser subs of the Thirtieth Submarine unit, plus the boat I-8, were scheduled.[17] But all these deployments were canceled after the Doolittle air raid on Tokyo.

THE INDIAN OCEAN THEATER: TWO VIEWPOINTS

The Japanese navy had opposed the Tripartite Pact, because they saw no value in an alliance with the weak German navy, which could not be of much assistance in a war against Japan's naval enemies in the Pacific and Indian Oceans. But after the Tripartite Pact was concluded, the Japanese navy accepted the support of German merchant cruisers and submarines and requested that German naval power be deployed to the Indian Ocean. The Japanese navy counted on these forces to prevent a British attack from the rear of the main battlefield in the Pacific. So a month before Pearl Harbor, a representative of Japanese Naval Intelligence, Capt. Maeda Tadashi of the Gunreibu Third Section (Europe), as well as the Japanese naval attaché in Berlin, requested details of the number and operational areas of German naval forces. Captain Maeda also proposed recognition signals for cruiser and submarine warfare in the Pacific and Indian Oceans. In the course of these conversations, they stressed that such operations would be very valuable for Japan. On 12 December, Admiral Nagano, Chief of the Gunreibu, expressed the hope that the Germans could shift the focus to the Suez area from the Eastern Front.[18]

Meanwhile the German navy had hopes for Japanese naval power. This became apparent in a document, "Assessment of the General Strategic Situation Following the Entry of Japanese and USA into the War," which was circulated on 18 December 1941 by the Seekriegsleitung within the navy and also handed over to the head of the Japanese inspection commission in Germany, Vice Adm. Nomura Naokuni. It stated, inter alia:[19]

> Closer cooperation between the German and Japanese navies arises from the operational deployment of German cruisers, auxiliary merchant cruisers and U-boats in the Indian Ocean and the activities of the blockade-runners employed for the purpose of importing the rubber and other raw materials urgently required for the European conduct of the war, as well as the eventually planned far-ranging deployment of Japanese cruisers and submarines for the war on shipping. So far as the conduct of war in the Indian Ocean is concerned, the German Naval War Staff [Skl.] would place a particularly high value on deployment of Japanese submarines against the important center of the British conduct of war in the Middle East, that is, in the western Indian Ocean and in the Persian Gulf.

Following this, the German navy repeatedly demanded that a strong fleet be sent to the Indian Ocean from the Japanese side. The chief of the Skl., Vice Adm. Kurt Fricke, talked to Admiral Nomura, now a member of the Tripartite Military Commission in Berlin, explained the African and Middle East situation to him, and emphasized that the operational focus point had to be Egypt. Finally the German requested from Nomura that the deployment of the Japanese fleet for the interruption of British naval communications in the western Indian Ocean should coincide with German and Italian operations in Egypt.[20]

On 8 April, in the course of these discussions, Admiral Nomura decried the lack of progress toward a simultaneous offensive and emphasized the necessity for a simultaneous attack on the British Middle East position, with Germany and Italy coming from the Mediterranean and the Caucasus and Japan from the Indian Ocean. Japan was ready for a thrust into the northern Indian Ocean against British supply traffic to the Red Sea and Arabian Sea, provided that Germany and Italy started a push against the Caucasus and Suez. Otherwise, any drive by the Japanese navy against the Arabian Sea and northern Indian Ocean would be pointless.

The Gunreibu had advised Admiral Nomura on 3 April that the IJN was going to deploy two armed merchant cruisers and several submarines, from the middle of May to the middle of July, to the Arabian Sea and the east coast of Africa. On 4 April they added that, besides those forces, they were planning even more active operations in the Indian Ocean in the near future, as the Combined Fleet was planning the "B" Operation.[21] The subsequent cancellation of these operations aroused considerable mistrust of its Japanese partner in the German navy, especially since the IJN did not reveal the real reasons for this, in particular the precise extent of the Japanese losses at Midway.

The Gunreibu stated that, before any German-Italian move against the Caucasus and Egypt, it would be essential to carry out a drive against enemy sea communications in the western Indian Ocean, in order to prevent the enemy's bringing up more forces. Quite irrespective of any time fixed for German operations, there was an urgent necessity for disrupting enemy supply lines in the Indian Ocean. If Allied sea communications in the Indian Ocean could be broken, this would be of decisive importance for German land operations. Admiral Fricke repeated that a prerequisite for a joint attack on Egypt and the Caucasus was the Japanese navy's cutting of British supply lines, and urged that the Imperial Navy should accordingly adopt a defensive stance in the Pacific against the Americans and take the offensive against the British in the western Indian Ocean. On 7 April, the Gunreibu answered to the German navy that the Japanese navy's main theater was still in the Pacific and its main aim the destruction of the American fleet in the Pacific, but that the Japanese navy would send submarines to the Indian Ocean.

CANCELLATION OF THE ASSAULT
ON CEYLON AND "B" OPERATION

Planning for the action against Ceylon rested fundamentally on the extent of German success in the Northern Africa campaign. There was no plan for the Japanese army in the area of the Indies, and it depended on German success. The Ceylon operation would have been allowed to proceed only if the German army in the Near East had stood on the brink of decisive victories.

In early May 1942 the advantage achieved by the German army in North Africa had placed the British Near Eastern Army in an extremely critical situation, which the Japanese army general staff saw as an opportunity to unite Japanese and German forces by a thrust through the Indian area. Debates over a landing on Ceylon were revived at the end of May and the beginning of June. Meanwhile, however, the Japanese navy had lost four of its best carriers during the first days of June in the fateful Battle of Midway; they now faced a serious shortage of battle-ready ships for a Ceylon operation. Yet the army, spurred by the setback at Midway, now took the position that the Ceylon operation was an absolute necessity. So the Japanese Army General Staff issued Directive No. 1196 of 29 June. In brief, it contained the following points:

> The goal of the operation is the destruction of enemy forces in the area of the Indian Ocean. Ceylon is to be captured first, to provide Japanese forces with bases for further operations.
>
> Participation of one to two army divisions and most of the Combined Fleet will be necessary for the capture of Ceylon.
>
> Commencement of the operation seems feasible when the British are defeated by the progress of German forces in North Africa and the Near East.
>
> In preparation for this operation:
>
> a. The Thirty-Eighth and Forty-Eighth Divisions, located in Java and Northern Sumatra, would be brought together and emphasis placed on training them for amphibious operations in the tropics.

    b. All attainable information on the enemy will be energetically
       collected.

    c. This operation will be called Operation Number Eleven, and is
       issued without any accompanying orders for its execution.

The IJN took a different view of a landing on Ceylon after the Battle of
Midway; it greatly appreciated the need to defeat the British Eastern Fleet in
the Indian Ocean. Adm. Nagano Osami, chief of the Gunreibu, expressed this
position in a memorandum to the throne on 7 July: "The plans drawn up in
agreement with Germany and Italy for interrupting enemy supply and destroy-
ing the enemy fleet in the western part of the Indian Ocean would bring about
a generally most favorable situation."

In July 1942, when the Combined Fleet became aware of German and Italian
plans for the occupation of Alexandria and Malta, it began to study actions
in the Indian Ocean. The Gunreibu agreed, but the Combined Fleet was suf-
fering from a shortage of naval air power and battle-ready ships after the serious losses in the Battle of Midway. Admiral Ugaki, chief of the Combined Fleet,
was cautious about the new Indian Ocean operation, proposed by Germany.
He wrote in his diary that "the proposal of positive operations in the Western
Indian Ocean is a matter of great importance. But I can't approve it until I can
be quite sure of its success after careful study."[22]

Thus only a few surface ships and land planes were ordered to carry out
offensive operations. To this new mission, the Seventh Division (two heavy cruisers), the Sixteenth Division (two light cruisers), and the Third Torpedo division (one light cruiser and eleven large Fubuki-class destroyers), and Second and
Fifteenth Destroyer Divisions (total, seven destroyers) were assigned to the first
Southern Expeditionary Fleet and formed up with it at Mergui, on the west coast
of the Malay peninsula. Preparations were also made for the participation of
twenty naval reconnaissance planes based at Singapore, Sabang, and Rangoon,
as well as sixteen planes that could be catapulted from shipboard.

On 7 July Admiral Nagano reported to the emperor on this operation and
got permission to carry it out. Admiral Nagano explained to the emperor that
the German advance made possible a Japanese advance to the Middle East, to
establish contact and to cooperate with the German advance. The navy was
going to send surface combatants of the Second and Third Fleets to the center of the Indian Ocean, but if the war situation progressed well, it would
deploy these forces to the eastern coast of Africa.[23]

But this operation was canceled because of the American landing on Guadalcanal on 8 August 1943. The result was that the forces allotted for the Indian Ocean had to be transferred to the Solomons, and the plans for offensive operations in the Bay of Bengal had to be abandoned.

Though no formal directive was issued to cancel preparations for an operation against Ceylon and in the Indian Ocean, the defeat of Japanese carrier forces at Midway in June 1942 proved to be decisive stroke in eliminating any possibility of a subsequent Japanese fleet movement into the Indian Ocean to conduct a coordinated offensive against the British.

Looking back at the year of 1942, a discouraged Admiral Ugaki wrote in his diary on 31 December:

> The year 1942 is going to pass tonight. How brilliant was the first-stage operation up to April. And what miserable setbacks since Midway in June! The invasions of Hawaii, Fiji, Samoa, and New Caledonia, liberation of India and destruction of the British Far Eastern Fleet have all scattered like dreams. Meanwhile, not to speak of capturing Port Moresby, but the recovery of Guadalcanal itself turned out to be impossible. Looking back over all these, my mind is filled with deep feelings. Though it's the fortunes of war, it's most regrettable.[24]

But the Indian Ocean was still a good hunting ground for submarines, and the Eighth Submarine Group was still operating there busily. As in the Indian Ocean, the Allied merchant ships were still not escorted, and ASW forces were not well organized. Only two ocean-cruising and three old fleet-type submarines were deployed, but by the end of November 1942 these five submarines had sunk ten cargo ships, without losses of their own. The Indian Ocean was a relatively easy area for a Dönitz-type tonnage war.

After the evacuation of Guadalcanal in early February 1943, the Imperial Navy shifted its attention from the Pacific to the Indian Ocean. The Combined Fleet issued a "No. 3 Stage Operation Order" on 25 March 1943. Based on the Third Stage Operation Order issued from the Gunreibu, it provided for "the dispatch of submarines and surface combatants to the Indian Ocean and west coast of Australia, and the disruption of enemy sea lines of communication. Also a surprise attack on enemy key areas will be conducted and if a chance to do so presents itself, Cocos Island will be seized in cooperation with the army."[25]

The Eighth Submarine Group (mainly First and Fourteenth Submarine Units, commanded by Rear Adm. Ishizaki Noboru) was reformed and the number of submarines increased to six in early June. On 12 September, the Eighth Submarine Group was reorganized under command of the Southwestern Area Commander, and the Thirtieth Submarine Unit (three I-class boats) was added to it (command was changed from Ishizaki to Ichioka Hisahi). By these changes of operational policy, the number of submarines in the Indian Ocean was gradually increased and at the end of 1943 totaled eleven boats. As a result, from 20 March to 18 November 1943, twenty Allied vessels (122,588 tons) were sunk, and from 27 November 1943 to 19 March 1944, nineteen (127,769 tons) were sunk or damaged.[26]

Meanwhile, 1943 was the turning point in the war; the Axis was on the defensive in the East and the West. The Germans abandoned Tripoli in January, the Japanese retreated from Guadalcanal in February. American assault operations began against the Gilbert Islands in late 1943. The Allied counteroffensive commenced a year earlier than Japanese expectations.

In this situation, Naval General Headquarters judged the main Allies' advance to be the Pacific theater, but as Italy surrendered in September and the British attacked Burma, the Japanese High Command (IGHQ) saw the necessity of being prepared for a possible joint Anglo-American attack against Sumatra, the Andamans, or the Nicobar Islands by sea. The Gunreibu therefore issued the Third Stage Operation Order consisting of "Z" and "Y" plans on 15 August 1943. The "Z" plan was the operation order in case of attack from the Pacific; "Y" plan was to counter an Allied advance into the Indian Ocean and provided measures in case of Allied attacks against an area containing the Andaman Islands, Nicobar Islands, Sumatra, Java, and Timor. If this area was threatened, the Combined Fleet would move into the Indian Ocean.[27]

The IGHQ and the government also thoroughly altered Japan's war plans with the revised policy that was approved at the Imperial Conference of 30 September 1943. The new emphasis was on withdrawal from exhausting engagements in remote Pacific areas. Japan would retrench her position, contracting the front to dimensions more appropriate to her resources; this core defense zone was defined as the area containing the Kurile Islands, Ogasawara Islands, the middle and western parts of the South Seas islands, western New Guinea, Sunda, and Burma. This area was named the "Absolute Defense Zone," and its establishment meant, in effect, the abandonment of westward expansion and a withdrawal of forces from the Indian Ocean to the Pacific Ocean.

In response to the American advance in the Pacific, submarines were gradually deployed to the Pacific, and at the end of April 1944 there remained only four in the Indian Ocean. In August, two newly built RO-class boats were added, but in early October two returned for repairs and only two remained in the Indian Ocean. Because of this decrease of submarines, from 21 March to 17 July 1944 only six (42,019 tons) Allied ships could be sunk. The Japanese boat I-166 was torpedoed and sunk in the Strait of Malacca by the British submarine HMS *Telemachus*. This was evidence of the loss of sea control even near her home port of Penang.

Due to the increase of Allied ASW forces and the continuing development of anti-ASW techniques, the Indian Ocean was no longer an easy hunting ground for Japanese submarines. With the American advance toward the Japanese homeland, submarines were fanatically thrown into battle, regardless of losses. Six submarines were lost in the interception operation to protect surface combatants and convoys in the Gilbert Islands counterassault operation. Also, many submarines were ordered to attack landing forces or to transport small amounts of supplies to isolated islands. Submarine crews were opposed to such duty. They strongly argued for using their boats for interception operations against enemy sea lines of communication (SLOC), but they were ignored.

In June 1944, U.S. troops invaded Saipan, and in October MacArthur landed at Leyte Gulf. As a defense measure against the American offensive, boats RO-113 and RO-115 were transferred to the Pacific in late January 1945 and on 20 February, respectively. The Eighth Submarine Group now was dissolved, and Japanese submarine operations in the Indian Ocean came to an end.[28]

On only one subsequent occasion did Japanese naval ships conduct offensive antishipping operations in the Indian Ocean. In March 1944 the cruisers *Tone*, *Chikuma*, and *Aoba* of the Seventh Cruiser Division advanced to the steamer track between Aden and Australia and sank one merchant ship of 6,100 tons. Apart from this operation, only Axis submarines continued their offensive antishipping patrols in all parts of the Indian Ocean and neighboring theaters, and these actions had little effect on relative force levels in these waters.

5

Axis Submarine Operations in the Indian Ocean

After the Japanese opened hostilities against the United States of America on 7 December 1941, Germany declared war against the United States on 11 December in accordance with article 3 of the Tripartite Pact—which called, however, for German participation only in case of Japan's being *attacked* by a power not involved in the European or Sino-Japanese conflicts. The Imperial Japanese Navy then proceeded southwestward. After Japan had occupied Malaya, Singapore, and the Dutch East Indies, the IJN operated against the British Eastern Fleet.

As of April 1942 it operated against Ceylon, Madagascar, and the East African coast with carrier groups and submarines. With these operations it noticeably inhibited Allied logistical supply for the North African theater. When the enemy was able, despite heavy losses, to start a counteroffensive in the Southwest Pacific, the IJN advised Admiral Wenneker, the naval attaché in Tokyo, that it would welcome German submarine operations in the western Indian Ocean, because it had to dislocate its naval forces to counter the new threat.

GERMAN SUBMARINE OPERATIONS

After the first of the German Südraum bases had become operational in June 1943, German submarines operating in the Indian Ocean could make use of these bases as well, provided underway replenishment could be furnished. The big IXD2 and XB types could even reach their destination without refueling. The first German submarine to berth at Penang on 15 July 1943 was U-511 (Schneewind). Under the code name of "Marco Polo," she was en route, with high-ranking passengers, to be delivered as a present to the Imperial Japanese Navy.[1]

In the spring of 1943, submarines began to be loaded with war material for the Japanese ally, in addition to their regular war loads, to supplement surface blockade-running operations. Because transport by surface blockade-runners had become extremely risky and unreliable, it was only logical to load the bigger boats to capacity with urgently needed crucial raw materials to carry home, even though their loading capacity was extremely limited. But Admiral Dönitz could not accede to sending submarines out on solely transport missions. He ordered that these boats should, on their trajectories, combine their transport missions with regular fighting missions.

In March 1943 the Kriegsmarine dispatched five of its new Type IXD2 and two of its IXC boats to operate between 26 April and 10 June off the southeast African coast and around Madagascar.[2] After underway replenishment out of AO (auxiliary oiler) *Charlotte Schliemann* southeast of Madagascar, these submarines sank thirty-six merchant ships totaling 201,653 gross tons. One boat (U-197) was lost, and the rest, except U-178, returned to their French Biscay base at Bordeaux. U-178 (Dommes) entered Penang on 27 August 43 for logistical supply. Meanwhile, in April, U-180 (Musenberg) had exchanged personnel and material with the Japanese submarine I-29 (Izu) southwest of Madagascar and reached her home port safely.

Another submarine task group called *Monsun* (Monsoon) departed from Bordeaux and Kiel during June–July 1943. These eleven IXC boats were to operate in the Indian Ocean.[3] For this operation they had to be replenished in the Middle Atlantic by tanker submarines and again in the Indian Ocean by surface supply ships. After their fighting mission, they were due to return to their European bases, but their commanding officers were free, in the alternative, to enter the German base at Penang. Three "Monsun" boats (U-506, U-509, and U-514) were sunk en route in the Atlantic.

In September and October 1943, five submarines (U-168, U-183, U-188, U-532, and U-533), after replenishment at sea out of tanker submarines and another replenishment from AO *Brake,* operated off the East African coast, in the gulfs of Aden and Oman, in waters of the Chagos Archipelago, and off

Bombay, sinking six freighters totaling 33,843 tons. The "Monsun" group missed some targets because of torpedo failures.

U-533 was lost in the Gulf of Oman. After all four submarine tankers (U-160, U-462, U-487, and U-847) had been lost, another sub (U-516), originally assigned, had to turn back after acting as a substitute tanker. The remaining four boats (U-168, U-183, U-188, and U-532) safely reached Penang with their cargo during October and November.

Reinforcement for task group "Monsun" was sent out in the autumn of 1943. It consisted of three IXC boats (U-172, U-510, U-508). In addition, three more IXD2 boats were sent out (U-848, U-849, U-850), which were to operate independently. After the boats departed from their Norwegian and French ports, five were sunk on their way out in the Atlantic. Only the remaining U-510 (Eick), after underway replenishment by U-219 (Burghagen) in Middle Atlantic and AO *Charlotte Schliemann* southeast of Madagascar, reached her operations area.

In the Gulf of Aden and north of the Nicobar Islands, Eick sank five merchant ships (31,220 tons) and damaged one more. U-510 finally entered Penang on 5 April 1944.

As the record shows, sending German submarines out in task groups centrally controlled from Submarine Command in Europe, on trajectories of more than thirteen thousand miles covering more than 100 degrees of latitude, proved to be very complicated and unproductive. Diesel supplies enabled Type IXC40 boats to just reach their destination with economical speed. The bigger boats had a little more reserves. But even for these, fuel-consuming underway operations were out of the question without underway supply. Returning commanding officers therefore proposed to have these submarines transit directly to their Southeast Asian base and back; between such journeys, they could operate on one or more patrols out of these bases with freshly maintained weapons and equipment, acclimatized complement, and an updated intelligence picture.[4] But Submarine Command did not follow these recommendations.

After the initial reinforcement of "Monsun," from January 1944 until May 1945 twenty-four submarines were dispatched independently to the Indian Ocean theater. Besides three torpedo transports of the VIIF type, most of these were big IXD2 boats with a 265-ton cargo loading capacity. Almost all boats were loaded to capacity with logistic supplies for the Südraum bases or raw materials, modern weapons, and advanced technique for the Japanese ally.

Eleven were lost before they could round the Cape of Good Hope. One had put to sea only shortly before the German capitulation and surrendered with her valuable cargo to the U.S. Navy DD *Sutton* and put into Portsmouth, New Hampshire.

Twelve independents reached the Indian Ocean and there fought targets of opportunity where they could find them, from the African coast off Durban up to the Gulf of Aden, around Madagascar, the Seychelles, and the Maledive and Laccadive Islands. They sank twenty-six ships totaling 164,051 gross tons, with the loss of two German submarines. Of the ten that reached their Südraum bases, one was sunk by the British submarine *Trenchant,* while waiting to be escorted into Penang. Her cargo was salvaged only in 1973.

Even with logistical supply, ammunition, and torpedoes being brought out to the Südraum bases and supply of fuel and provisions being organized locally, Admiral Dönitz stood on principle. He would not let his boats leave these bases for the Indian Ocean on interim fighting missions before finally leaving port for Europe loaded with urgently needed raw materials. They had to seek out and destroy targets en route, even though their full load could only be taken on at the expense of fewer torpedoes carried.

Between January 1944 and March 1945, six submarines (U-168, U-181, U-183, U-195, U-510, and U-532) had to return to their Südraum bases from seven missions with underway action in the Indian Ocean, either because of engine trouble or failure to achieve underway supply. Both tankers (AO *Charlotte Schliemann* and *Brake*) available for this theater had been scuttled when enemy forces, aided by a compromised German code, approached them. So, instead of being supplied by the tankers, U-532 and U-168 had to turn around to pick up the tankers' shipwrecked crews and take them back to port. On return to their bases, all these submarines had to unload and get refitted for another homebound mission. On their aborted missions they sank seven freighters totaling 36,158 tons around the Maledives, Laccadives, and the Chagos Archipelago and damaged two more.

Seven boats, after missions with the other submarines in the Indian Ocean (where they sank another seven ships totaling 42,610 tons), were able to round the Cape of Good Hope. Only two—U-178 (Spahr) and U-188 (Lüdden)—were able to deliver their goods at Bordeaux before the Allied invasion of Normandy. U-1062 (Albrecht) was lost in the Cape Verde area while waiting to be supplied by outbound U-219. Because of the compromised German submarine code, the USN task groups 22.1 and 41.7 waited ready for action at the supply position.

By the time U-510 (Eick), U-843 (Herwartz), and U-861 (Oesten), three of the remaining four, were able to enter German bases in France and Norway, using their cargoes for the German war effort was no longer possible. On an attempt to reach Kiel in the Baltic Sea, U-843 (Herwartz) sank in an air attack in the Kattegat. U-532 (Junker), the last boat, was surprised by the German capitulation and surrendered to the British Royal Navy at Liverpool.

There was final action also in Southeast Asia. On recommendations of Lüdden, commanding officer of U-188, on his return, three boats were tasked for a mission around Australia.[5] Two (U-168 and U-537) were sunk directly after leaving the base of Surabaya by the Dutch SS *Zwaardvisch* and the USS *Flounder*. Only one—U-862 (Timm), not aware of now being alone on this mission—reached her operations area.

On his patrol counterclockwise around Australia and to northern New Zealand, Timm was able to sink two ships totaling 14,356 tons. With a reduced compliment of only eight torpedoes and one misfire, Timm had to be economical with his shots. As the Japanese feared an Allied landing on the Malay Peninsula, he was, when navigating in the Cook Straits, prematurely recalled on 19 January 1945 by the Chef im Südraum (CiS), in order not to leave him without operational control and logistical support. He reentered Jakarta on 15 February 1945. The American Liberty ship *Peter Sylvester*, which he torpedoed seven hundred miles west of Perth on 6 February, was the last merchant ship sunk by a German submarine in the Indian Ocean during World War II.

The last patrol in this theater was run by U-183 under Schneewind. She left Jakarta on 22 April 1945 for operations east of the Philippines, but was sunk in the Java Sea south of Borneo on 23 April by USS *Besugo*.[6]

ITALIAN SUBMARINE OPERATIONS

Of the eight Italian submarines remaining at Bordeaux, after having been modified into transport vessels, seven became operational. They were loaded and in May 1943 set out for Southeast Asia. *Enrico Tazzoli*, code-named "Aquila I," and *Barbarigo*, code-named "Aquila V," were lost shortly after departure. *Ammiraglio Cagni* ("Aquila VII") defected after the Italian capitulation and entered Durban on 20 September 1943.

The four other boats—"Aquila II" (*Reginaldo Guiliani*), "Aquila III" (*Comandante Cappellini*), "Aquila VI" (*Luigi Torelli*), and "Aquila IX" (*Alpino Bagnolini*)—reached their Southeast Asia destination. After the capitulation they were taken over by the German navy in the Südraum bases under the numbers UIT-23, UIT-24, UIT-25, and UIT-22, respectively. UIT-23 was lost on 14 February 1944 in Malacca Straits, torpedoed by the British submarine *Tally-ho,* and UIT-22, after having been taken over in Bordeaux, was lost to Allied air attacks south of the Cape of Good Hope.

RÉSUMÉ OF GERMAN INDIAN OCEAN OPERATIONS

Operational control of the German submarines in Asian waters remained with COMSUB in occupied France. The CiS in Penang tried hard to provide them with all the local information. In the Atlantic the captains were accustomed to depending on reliable intelligence information via radio messages from home. Here, with the Japanese intelligence picture less accurate or not handed over with sufficient details, captains at sea had to rely much more on their own intuition and operational experience. During the rainy summer monsoon season and with the frequent tropical storms, it was exceptionally difficult to find suitable targets.

All told, of the forty-three submarines sent out by the German navy on combined fighting and transport missions into the Indian Ocean, eighteen reached their destination. Thirteen of them set out fully loaded on their return journeys; only seven of them reached European ports. Three subs, including U-180, arrived at Bordeaux before the end of war. One had just reached the submarine base of Trondheim in Norway, and one entered St. Nazaire base only after the invasion. One was sunk in the Kattegat en route to Kiel after reaching Kristiansand, Norway, safely, and the last one had to capitulate at Liverpool on 17 May 1945. Submarine losses thus amounted to 61.5 percent.

It should not be overlooked that a U-boat's cargo capacity was only about 3 percent of that of a surface blockade-runner. Altogether, the boats that returned to Europe were able to land about sixteen hundred tons of urgently needed material—about 20 percent of the cargo capacity of a single surface vessel.

On 19 November 1942 Hitler stated that he wanted transport submarines to be constructed for the German navy. Planning for three large types of more than three thousand metric tons displacement (types XI, XV, and XVI) was initiated but later discontinued. So no specially constructed cargo submarines were used in World War II, as they were in World War I. Of 217,415 tons of raw materials loaded on surface and submarine blockade-runners, 113,805 tons reached Germany and could be utilized for its war industry, a percentage of 52.3 percent. By the end of the war, 47.4 percent of the crude rubber loaded for

Europe had actually arrived there. For other commodities the percentages were 60.3 percent for oils and fats, 33.4 for metals and ores (tin, tungsten, and molybdenum), 9.5 percent for cinchona (quinine) bark, and 70 percent for general cargo.[7]

TECHNICAL AND LOGISTICAL PROBLEMS

German U-boat operations in the Far East suffered from numerous technical and logistical problems. Designed for operation in moderate climates, they carried no air cooling system and had insufficient food refrigeration capacity. Thus fresh food was in very short supply on extended missions. These boats were small by today's standards and had very confined living quarters, with cots being shared in turn by two or three crewmen. For a crew of about sixty, including officers, there were only two heads available and no fixed washbasins for regular petty officers and enlisted men. There were only one or two makeshift sprinkling nozzles installed in the bilges for seawater showering. Consequently the extremely long missions—lasting up to 225 days in tropical waters of up to 36 degrees centigrade—were very trying to the boats' crews. In addition to that physical strain, underway crews had to lend a hand for repair work in machine and shipyard repair shops during their stay in Südraum ports.

The torpedoes used were mostly battery driven. Their engines could be regularly checked and balanced underway, but batteries could not be serviced properly. Their performance was thus very erratic and was the reason for many torpedo misses. Indeed, German submarine batteries and those of the Italian boats, with batteries altered at Bordeaux to enlarge their transport capacity, were ill suited for extensive use in tropical areas. After arriving in their Southeast Asian bases, some of them needed a replacement of cells. As this was possible only in Japan, these boats, before setting out on their journey back to Europe, had to go to Kure to have this shipyard job done there. Three of them (U-196, UIT-24, and UIT-25) could not successfully be refitted and were utilized for shorter transport missions between bases and Japan.

Especially after Japan had entered the war, it was difficult to acquire all the different materials, goods, provisions, and facilities necessary to maintain operations and satisfy the requirements of the ship's crews. The Japanese were running short of some of the same materials themselves, and rationing became more stringent the longer the war lasted. In the occupied territories in the south, raw materials were abundant, but the Japanese were very short of finished goods and expendable supplies. So the German Supply Service purchased needed materials wherever they could get hold of them and tried to keep stocks of the more essential ones like diesel and lubricating oil. In general, German logistical requirements could be managed more conveniently in occupied territories than in the Japanese homeland, where everything had to be handled on a higher level and thus in a more formal way.

Quality standards often failed to meet the requirements of German machinery, and the choice of foodstuffs was limited. Consequently, even with the goodwill of Japanese officials, the German navy and their supply organization had to set up and organize local procurement, store, and upkeep facilities of their own. Much had to be bought from local traders or producers, often at considerable risk for both sides with a war economy in force.

In comparison with the very modest rations of the Japanese submarine force, the much more differentiated German food requirements were very difficult to comply with. For the very long passages between Asia and Europe, all kinds of canned food was required. Rye bread had to be specially baked; meat and sausages were provided by a local German butchery plant; potatoes, vegetables, and fruit were grown in the mountainside recreation areas of the German Südraum bases. A special problem was the production of cans for the preservation of all these foodstuffs. Not only was it difficult to find a plant with sufficient output, but it was also nearly impossible to get tin sheet for manufacturing all the cans required.

For a four-month mission of one submarine, fifteen tons of food in more than twenty major categories were needed. Acquisitions often had to be accomplished on a makeshift basis, with local firms or producers, frequently bypassing Japanese authorities. An exceptional stroke of luck was the capture of the steamship *Nankin* by the raider *Thor* on 10 May 1942 on her way from Fremantle, Australia, to Colombo with supplies for the Burma front. The forty-two thousand cases of canned meat, twenty-eight thousand cases of fruit and vegetables, eight hundred tons of flour, and the Australian butter, fresh meat, and bacon in her six huge cold-storage chambers were a highly welcome supplement to the German supplies.[8] Parts of them even lasted until the end of the war.

The Japanese authorities put many offices, housing, berthing, and recreation facilities for all Südraum bases at the Germans' disposal.[9] Staff office buildings were installed in former German foreign service property, public buildings, or hotels. Air bases were set up at available air strips. Radio receiving and transmitting stations were installed at suitable places with equipment mostly brought over from Europe and manned by German personnel. All these offices and complexes were manned with laid-up or rescued crews of German merchant ships or naval vessels and former staff personnel of German trading firms in Asia. A car pool and storerooms for goods to be transported to Europe were available. Young Germans living in the Japanese realm were also drafted and billeted there after military training. For entertainment special German sailor's clubs with taxi-girls for dancing were set up.

Once in a while sports contests were held between personnel of both navies. Very essential were recreation camps with sports grounds to reinvigorate the exhausted ships' crews between two missions. These were run higher up in mountain areas, where the climate was more agreeable and healthy. Even a small hospital was established and manned with ship's doctors, medics, and a nurse. On Java such a camp was set up on the premises of a former German tea plantation at an altitude of more than a thousand meters. Cattle were raised there and vegetables were grown to help with the provisioning of the submarines.

Escorts for German ships or submarines leaving or entering port were not available in sufficient numbers, nor were they adequately equipped. German naval air stations were set up at Penang and later at Jakarta. They were manned with former AMC aviators and equipped with the remaining Arado 196 seaplanes of the AMCs, later supplemented with Japanese Navy *Reishiki* planes.[10] These planes were utilized for reconnaissance and escort missions above the approaches to the bases.

The quality of shipyard facilities varied widely between bases. Docking space was available at Kobe, Singapore, Surabaya, and, to a certain extent, Tanjung Priok, but not at Penang. It was a rather long time before the Japanese managed to reconstruct the heavily damaged maritime and naval facilities in their occupied territories. The supply lines they tried to establish between these parts and their home country were not effective because of lack of shipping space and surface and air escort. Because of heavy Japanese requirements, the availability of docking space for German units was always problematic. But for hull repairs and change of cargo in their ballast keels, all submarines had to dock regularly between missions. Machine shops were available in all bases. In some, German work crews composed of base personnel or ships' crews had to assist the shipyard workforce.

Work quality matched that of German bases in France. Repairs were executed with great precision, if matching parts could be provided as samples, whereas welding and hull repairs did not match German standards.[11] Ordnance and ammunition, repair-shop supplies, and spare parts, including ships' propellers, had to be provided from Germany. Replacement torpedoes were brought from Europe by special Type VIIF submarines with a load capacity of thirty-nine torpedoes. Run-down submarine batteries were serviced or replaced at Kobe in Japan. The equipment for German medical installations and radio stations also had to be brought out from Germany.

Japanese base facilities were under the jurisdiction of whatever force had occupied the area. In navy installations, the reception and care for German units was warm and hospitable, while in army-run places they were rather impersonal and more correct than friendly. Penang and Surabaya were run by the navy; Singapore (except the naval base of Seletar) and Jakarta were run by the army. In the latter places all German requests had to be forwarded to the authorities in charge by naval flag officers attached to the local army command. With the many well-known frictions between the Japanese navy and army, this was a very inconvenient, slow-working, and ineffective arrangement. In Singapore, where army port facilities at Keppel Harbor had to be used, German personnel were not allowed to enter workshops. (Technical stores and spare parts were in very short supply.)

Circumstances in Penang and Surabaya, which had been occupied by the Japanese navy, were much more convenient. A German torpedo-balancing unit was set up at the Japanese balancing shop at Penang. Results fully matched German standards. Later on a mobile balancing shop was installed on the auxiliary supply ship *Quito*.

When Germany surrendered in May 1945, six German submarines (including two former Italian boats) still in the Japanese realm were taken over by the Japanese navy. They were the U-181 (Freiwald), which became I-501; U-195 (Steinfeldt), I-506; U-219 (Burghagen), I-505; U-862 (Timm), I-502; UIT-24 (Pahls), I-503; and UIT-25 (A. Meier), I-504. They did not become operational again, and after the Japanese capitulation were seized by British, Dutch, and U.S. occupation forces and later scuttled.

6

Practical Cooperation and Exchange of Experience

With the beginning of World War II, the first political accords between Germany and Japan began to develop. With the Tripartite Pact, concluded 27 September 1940, and its secret supplementary protocol (see appendix B), military cooperation between the three powers was stipulated, and the formation of special military commissions in the three capitals was agreed on. The Imperial Japanese Navy stated that it was "firmly convinced, that, in regard to the world-political situation after the conclusion of the Tripartite Pact, it is extremely necessary for Japan and Germany to strive for a closer contact and build up a firmer cooperation between the Japanese and the German navies in order to enhance their mutual strengths."[1]

In Berlin, Vice Adm. Nomura Naokuni, as head of the Japanese naval element of the military commission, was directly attached to the German Naval War Staff (Seekriegsleitung or Skl.). With these commissions, an instrument would have been available for coordinating military planning and strategic concepts among the Axis powers. But they never were put to practical use. Fundamental differences between the nations and their leadership were too predominant. Ethnological backgrounds and historical development and traditions were too far apart, resulting in deep-rooted mutual misunderstanding and distrust. Moreover, totalitarian systems characteristically do not share resources or information with their allies.

Hitler, who had little interest in or understanding of global naval strategy, did not see engaging his allies as a coordinated effort for a common goal, but only as diversionary measures to relieve enemy pressure in his own area. The German leadership was not really aware of the deep rift between the Japanese army and navy or of the fact that, in the Japanese armed forces, there existed no superior coordinating command comparable to the Armed Forces High Command (OKW). The military commissions were seldom convened and could not practically contribute to the military or operational coordination of the Axis powers.

Moreover, there was fundamental strategic disagreement even between the navies. The German navy, small in comparison with the powerful Japanese surface fleet and naval air arm, but possessing a strong war-experienced submarine fleet, regarded Great Britain as the main enemy. They felt that the most effective approach to breaking the British will to fight would be to cut the British Isles off from all outside supply, from abroad as well as from other parts of the Commonwealth. They thought that their Japanese ally should also concentrate his efforts on this task, at least with his submarine forces in the Indian Ocean.

Japan, vividly aware of its own overseas supply problem, wanted primarily to use its powerful striking fleet to deny the Western powers, especially the U.S. Navy, access to the western Pacific. In Tokyo the German naval attaché, Admiral Wenneker, maintained contact with the top echelon of the Imperial Japanese Navy. Widespread residual allegiance to Great Britain among flag-rank personnel, extreme security awareness, and natural distrust of all Europeans complicated his tasks in many respects.[2] Although Admiral Wenneker was able to maintain a good personal accord with a number of high-ranking officers in the Gunreibu, his official contacts, especially in the Navy Ministry (Kaigunshō), remained rather formal. As a personal judgment he stated that, while he could mostly achieve his goals with the Gunreibu, which he saw as "favorably disposed" toward German interests, people in the Kaigunshō seemed to him rather reserved, "slow-thinking," and neutrality-minded to the letter.[3] Hardly ever was he granted permission to inspect modern naval equipment or ships. He complained in his war diary on 13 March 1941, "The reserve of the Japanese concerning their own armament conditions and their material is regrettable. With all inquiries in this direction, again and again I run against closed doors."[4] Admiral Wenneker did not even have concrete advance notice of Japan's opening of hostilities against the United States.[5]

On the medium command level, cooperation with Japanese harbor and naval base personnel, shipyards, industry, and trading firms was different, depending on circumstances. More often than not, detours from official routes had to be invented. But in general there was a willingness to help and comply. Again, security was always a problem. Thus, when German technical specialists had been brought out at considerable effort to share their technical know-how, they regularly were either not employed at all by the Japanese or dismissed after a short time.[6]

In Germany, on the other hand, technical exchange with the Japanese ally was sponsored on all levels by the government. A fairly large number of Japanese technical specialists had been dispatched to Berlin as members of the attaché staff of the Japanese embassy. When Japanese submarines put into the German submarine bases on the Atlantic coast, their crews were given briefings and weapons instructions. It was noticed but widely accepted that while the front row listened to their instructors, other crew members were dismantling equipment and meticulously scrutinizing it. The Japanese crew sent to Europe to man U-1224, the second German submarine to be handed over to the Imperial Japanese Navy, completed the full German submarine training program in the Baltic before departure. Likewise, equipment and blueprints for reconstructing the submarine in Japan were handed over to the crew.

The indirect approach via the "naval attachés" (posted with local army command) eventually eased, but only after the office of the German Chef im Südraum (CiS) had been established, and after the newly designated K.Kapt. Wilhelm Dommes visited with Vice Adm. Fukudome Shigeru, commander, Southwestern Fleet, at the Singapore naval base, Seletar, and with the naval commander at Surabaya.[7] Given the Japanese armed forces' high regard for seniority, it might have been wiser to nominate a German flag officer for the CiS billet.

The Japanese knew that Dommes, even after his promotion to Fregattenkapitän, was not the most senior German staff officer in the Südraum and that his nomination had bypassed his seniors—an unheard-of move in the Japanese navy. Had it been possible to bring out an officer of higher rank and experience to deal with his Japanese counterparts, all of them of flag rank, it would have been easier. But it is questionable that such an officer could have done any better than Dommes did. A German flag officer as CiS would have had more leeway in making decisions. As it was, though, the Skl. maintained more independence from Japanese operational interference by having Dommes defer to COMSUB, which could override it.

With Cdr. Dommes, relations at Penang were excellent from the start, with the local submarine commander, Rear Adm. Ichioka Hisao, with his chief of staff, Commander Iura, and later Rear Adm. Uozumi Jisaku, and with Captain Maruyama, as liaison officer. They went out of their way to give all possible help and support. The same held true at Surabaya with Captain Fuji, commander of the Japanese submarine base, and his staff. At first, arriving German submarine commanders shared little information concerning operations with their Japanese colleagues, but once closer personal contact was established, submarine captains on both sides began to exchange information more freely.[8]

MUTUAL COOPERATION

In the secret military agreement signed on 18 January 1942 (see appendix D), Japan, Germany, and Italy established an operational boundary between Japan and her western allies at 70 degrees east longitude in the Indian Ocean. At a meeting of the Military Commission of the Tripartite Pact on 24 December 1941, the Italian element had proposed common naval action in the Indian Ocean to support the campaign in North Africa. But neither the European nor the Asian partners were prepared to act otherwise than in their own national interests, nor were they willing to coordinate their strategic planning and subjugate their operations to common objectives.

The OKW emphasized the necessity of strategic German-Japanese coordination. But the German leadership, in requesting Japanese support, did not consider Japanese objectives and basic interests. They were even unaware of the circumstances of Japanese decision making and wrongly assumed that the Japanese navy would automatically honor any understanding between the OKW and the Japanese ambassador in Berlin. They seem not to have known about the fundamental strategic disaccord that often surfaced in dealings between Japanese army and navy high commands.

As a relief for the Italian forces fighting in North Africa, Germany had in February 1941 formed the *Afrikakorps*. At that time it had urged Japan to take Germany's side in its struggle against Great Britain because it felt that there was a unique opportunity to challenge the British position in Asia.

After Japan had finally entered into the war ten months later, both sides were ready for a certain adjustment of their independent strategies. But again, each Axis partner wanted the other to initiate operations in its own area as a prerequisite for its own engagement. Whereas Germany wanted the Imperial Japanese Navy to seize Singapore, interdict United Kingdom maritime communications, and sever supply routes for the North Africa campaign in the northern Indian Ocean as indispensable conditions for its own advance in the Middle East and the Caucasus, the Japanese side requested that the Germans seize the Suez Canal and Egypt and conduct major landing operations on the British Isles.[9]

EXCHANGE OF EXPERIENCE

There are always limits to the exchange of information between the militaries of different nations. High-handedness on one side and touchiness on the other may stand in the way of a frank exchange. But more often exchange is impeded by fear of a security breach. Exchange on a high level normally is carried out only after careful consideration on both sides. As noted earlier, German captains continued throughout the war to be hampered by poor intelligence due to mechanical problems and the Japanese tendency to keep information to themselves.

In January 1941 the Skl. wrote a memorandum for a briefing of the German chief of state by the commander in chief of the German navy. This memorandum about Japan's role in the Tripartite Pact emphasizes close collaboration between the German and the Japanese navies. It states the German expectation that neutral Japan should provide any help "short of war" in the fields of supply, exchange of intelligence, and manipulation of public opinion to reduce the British position in the Far East. In order to avoid the three powers' pursuing separate strategies, the memorandum declared it essential that a combined staff or "Supreme War Council" should be assigned "to engage in constant deliberation about . . . joint strategy, as well as arriving at mutual agreements about the conduct of war by the Tripartite Powers in order that all military operations in every theater would form part of a strategic whole."[10]

Such a supreme war council was never constituted, but once Japan had entered the war, at least the General Commission and the naval element of the Joint Military Commission provided by the Tripartite Pact and the Military Agreement would have been suitable instruments. (See appendix A, art. 4; appendix B, para. I; and appendix D, para. III.) In the Military Agreement it was explicitly laid down that military cooperation and operational planning between the partners' high commands should be coordinated, making use of the general and military Commissions. Cooperation in the collection and exchange of information essential for operations was also postulated. But Hitler himself seems to have been disposed against using these instruments for political or strategic coordination that might have unduly committed him. As a means of exchange, however, the navy used them regularly.

There was a frank and open dialogue between the Skl. and Vice Admiral Nomura on strategic and operational questions, intelligence, war experiences, weapons development, logistics, and other matters. The same held true with visiting Japanese military and naval missions. But the Germans often had the impression that although opinions given and material handed over were always warmly received, the information and material handed over by the Japanese side, more often than not, did not match in importance what they received. Often necessary exchange of information on an operational level was overlooked because orders for such an exchange had not been properly promulgated. On both sides security played an important role. In the German navy, however, directives were handed down all the way to squadron level to facilitate inspections of installations, ships, and weapons, advise on new developments, and exchange operational and tactical experiences.

German submarine captains putting into bases in Southeast Asia and Japan at first were disappointed to discover how meager was the information they could derive from their counterparts. Again the coordination decreed by the Military Agreement was lacking, or appropriate orders had not been passed down. Japanese units at sea or in port did not normally enjoy the same volume of situation reports and enemy intelligence that German commanding officers were used to relying on. But the German commanding officers soon found out that, with personal acquaintance and resulting mutual trust, their Japanese partners and submarine squadron staff personnel would do their utmost to oblige. Apart from this, personal exchange was very rare, partly because of the language barrier, at least on the petty-officer and enlisted level. By tradition the Japanese were more reserved and discreet in these matters.

JAPAN'S FAILED HOPES FOR INDIA

As described in chapter 4, Japan hoped that the Axis advance in the Middle East would inspire India to shake off British rule but was not equipped to move against India militarily. The policy was more of a hope than a plan, and nothing came of it. And when Foreign Minister Tōgō Shigenobu urged Ambassador Ott to make a joint declaration of independence of India and the Muslim countries, Germany ignored the Japanese proposal. Berlin's answer was a cautious and passive one.

At the Liaison Conference of February 1942, Japan decided to announce the independence of Burma and India, and on 16 February, at the Diet, Prime Minister Tōjō Hideki declared that "the Japanese Empire stands steadfastly by the Burmese people in their long-standing aspirations to build a nation of their own, India now holds a golden opportunity to rise from her state of barbaric enslavement and march as comrades-in-arms toward Great East Asian co-prosperity in her hands; the Japanese Empire shall spare no effort to assist the peoples of India in their patriotic endeavors to regain their rightful independence."[11]

But such a statement merely addressed political and propaganda aspects of Burma's and India's independence. No positive action ensued when the army and navy staffs at IGHQ reached an agreement on 15 January 1942 concerning India, stating, "Further strong measures should be taken toward India with the objective of disrupting her communications with Great Britain and the United States, thus urging her to abandon her cooperation with Great Britain and accelerating the anti-British movement."[12] The chief of staff of the Combined Fleet deplored Japan's inability to grasp the opportunity presented by Gandhi's call to expel the British, but the fact remained that Japan could not take on India alone.

HITLER AND THE "YELLOW PERIL"

Why did Germany reply so coolly to the Japanese proposal? Because of Hitler's racial prejudice and his overestimation of Japan's chances of victory. Hitler viewed the Japanese with suspicion—as a "Yellow Peril"—because of his racial bias. He did not wish to see the British presence in India replaced with Japanese rule there. So when Singapore fell, Hitler, speaking privately about Japan, observed, "Yes, a relief, an immense relief. But it was also a turning point in history. It means the loss of a whole continent, and one might regret it, for it's the white race which is the loser."[13]

After Japan's sweeping initial victories, "Yellow Peril" suspicion became a factor in Germany again, and the German Home Affairs Ministry had to dispatch the following order to tranquilize those tendencies and to maintain cooperation with Japan.[14]

It has already been pointed out that particularly stupid people are trying either to belittle the success of our Japanese Allies or to question their significance for Germany by speaking of a "Yellow Peril" which menaces even Germany. It must be stated again that any person who repeats statements like these in a thought-less, parrotlike manner is a traitor to his country and does Germany the gravest harm in the midst of a decisive life and death struggle. Since discussion of this theme has been taken up in certain intellectual circles[,] it is necessary to challenge it resolutely wherever this phrase is used and, if necessary, to report the persons who persist in using it.

Influenced by his racial prejudice, Hitler resisted a joint declaration on Indian independence because he saw it as support for establishing a Japanese "Yellow Man" supremacy in India. Milan Hauner, who has written about Axis strategy in India, contends that "Hitler and his lieutenants could not understand the importance that race and the anti-colonial struggle could have in their propaganda campaign. If a joint strategy had been applied to India, the war might have taken a different course, not only in India, but also in the Islamic world."[15] But lacking that joint strategy, the Axis lost an important opportunity for using India against the Allies.

The German army counted on pitting the Japanese Kwantung army against the Soviet army on the Siberian front. Meanwhile Hitler counted on the Japanese navy, intrigued especially by the Japanese navy's stunning success at Pearl Harbor. In early February 1942 he said, "Rangoon, Singapore, and most likely, also Port Darwin will be in Japanese hands within a few weeks. Japan plans to protect this front in the Indian Ocean by capturing the key position of Ceylon."[16] Furthermore, he observed that the Japanese "have recognized the great strategic importance of Madagascar for naval warfare; according to reports submitted they are planning to establish bases on Madagascar in addition to Ceylon, in order to be able to cripple sea traffic in the Indian Ocean and the Arabian Sea. From there they could likewise successfully attack shipping around the Cape."[17]

Aside from these mutual overestimations and fascinations, there arose a confrontation of national interest between Germany and Japan over the potential spoils of war. In addition to this strategic split between the countries, their respective armies and navies did not always work together toward the same objectives.

DIFFERING STRATEGIES: THE USE OF SUBMARINES

Before the war, not only the IJN but also the U.S. Navy planned to use submarines to attack warships. After Pearl Harbor, the U.S. Navy quickly changed their subs' target to the merchant ships, but the Japanese navy did not and thus did not use their submarines to their best advantage.

After the battle of Midway, submarine operations were the only effective operations in the Indian Ocean. The Germans repeatedly asked the Japanese navy to deploy submarines to the Indian Ocean and change their target from heavily protected warships to merchant ships. The Japanese navy, however, continued to view the capital ships as their main objective. The IJN closed its eyes to modern notions of total warfare and remained committed to the traditional idea of the "decisive battle," and it wanted to exploit its superior forces to bring that about. Hence, it failed to recognize the possibilities that lay in the interruption of the enemy's sea supply lines.

Early in the war, Japan used submarines in reconnaissance and shore bombardment missions; later, they were ordered to perform transport duties for isolated islands. After the American landing on Guadalcanal, most submarines were withdrawn for transportation duty and to intercept strongly protected carriers and landing forces; without efficient radar and sonar equipment, however, they had little hope of success. Furthermore, after the Battle of the Marianas, all I-submarines were called home to be equipped with gear for carrying the *kaiten* or "human torpedo." Thus, submarines were sent to intercept the well-defended U.S. fleets in the Philippine Sea, Leyte Gulf, Iwoshima, and Okinawa, and finally fell prey to their superior ASW defense. The use of Japanese submarines in the Pacific war is shown in the following tables.[18]

The German Army and Navy High Commands also had differing strategic objectives. The German Naval High Command (OKM) sought to attack the British in the Middle East, while Hitler, the OKW, and the Army High Command opposed the navy's strategy. Hitler and his generals were absorbed in the Russian War, and the Japanese army, whose most important enemies

Table 6.1. Japanese Submarines and Additional Tasks

Area	Recon (Air)	Recon (Periscope)	Bombardment
East Pacific	7	17	19
South Pacific	33	41	10
North Pacific	6	17	0
Indian Ocean	10	15	1
TOTAL	56	90	30

Table 6.2. Transport Missions

Area	Successful	Unsuccessful	Total	Losses
Southeast	200	14	214	8
Northeast	42	4	46	3
Mid-Pacific	38	7	45	8
Total	280	25	305	19

were China and the Soviet Union, waited anxiously for the German army's victory. These strategic conflicts between the German army and navy resulted in lack of coordination between them in important instances. Since Dönitz favored his "tonnage theory," for example, he did not send submarines to help Rommel's operations.

Along with these internal difficulties, the German and Japanese navies had strategic differences that complicated cooperation. The German navy's main enemy was Great Britain, and its main target was the merchant ship, but the Japanese navy's main enemy was America and its target was the American warship. Because of these differences, the two navies followed separate courses: Hitler's navy primarily fought the Allied merchant fleet in the Atlantic, and Hirohito's navy primarily fought Allied men-of-war in the Pacific.

EVALUATION OF THE INDIAN OCEAN OPERATIONS
From a naval point of view, the Indian Ocean was the only area where the Tripartite Pact navies might have cooperated with similar objectives against the same enemy. Furthermore, the Indian Ocean was the only route possible for exchanges of war materials and military technologies among the Axis powers. But this area was not effectively used, primarily because of mutual egotism, mutual distrust based on traditional racial prejudice, and mutual overestimation and fantasies of victory. The Axis navies had no common political or military objective in the area, and each partner tried to use the other to support its own political and military aims. Strategic differences within the German military and between the German and Japanese armies and navies only made matters worse, and the Indian Ocean operations came to an end without success.

Along with these differences in strategic views, there were also conflicts about the most effective use of submarine forces. Examining the statistics reveals that the Japanese navy deployed 187 submarines during World War II and lost 128 of them. Eighty-eight submarines were lost in limited battle areas against well-protected combatants. Japanese submarines sank only twenty-three combatants, including two carriers, one escort carrier, and one heavy cruiser. They sank sixty-seven merchant ships totaling 357,715 tons and damaged forty-one ships totaling 321,428 tons. In all, 111 Japanese submarines were lost in the Pacific. In the Indian Ocean, the Japanese navy deployed thirty-eight submarines on 105 sorties. They sank 118 merchant ships (600,057 tons), damaged fifteen ships (95,754 tons), and lost only four subs from the beginning of the war to the end. The Japanese effectively ended submarine operations in this area on 20 February 1945, when they disbanded the Eighth Submarine Group.[19]

In autumn of 1942, the German submarine U-504 entered the Indian Ocean, and shortly afterward the German navy committed fifty-seven U-boats (four came out twice, and U-181 three times), excluding the cargo boats, to Indian Ocean operations. Thirty-five were lost in action and another six were interned by Japan. Between October 1942 and the end of the war, however, 151 Allied ships (892,111 tons) were sunk and eleven ships (86,568 tons) were damaged. During World War II, German submarines sank 2,520 ships (12,548,463 tons) and damaged 330 ships (3,186,055 tons). Fifty-one U-boats, excluding the cargo boats—that is, 6 percent of the 863 U-boats that made war patrols—accounted for 7.1 percent of the total Allied tonnage lost to U-boats in the war.[20] This means that the German success ratio was higher in the Indian Ocean than in the Atlantic and the Mediterranean, and that the Japanese success ratio here was almost the same as that of the Germans. Furthermore, although the number of Axis submarines increased in 1943 after the arrival of German U-boats, Allied shipping losses stayed at approximately the same level as in 1942. These figures suggest that Japanese and German submarine operations in the Indian Ocean were successful tactically, but not strategically.

PAYING THE PRICE

The Indian Ocean submarine war was poorly planned and directed, and bitter memories remain among the submariners who participated. In August 1945 Capt. Ariizumi Tatsunosuke, commander of the First Submarine Division, which consisted of big I-400–type submarines capable of carrying three aircraft, shot himself a day before entering Yokosuka. He was a vet-

Table 6.3. Percentage of Ships Attacked That Were Sunk,
Damaged, or Escaped

Year	1942	1943
Sunk	59.5 (54 ships)	65.8 (50 ships)
Damaged	4.5 (4 ships)	10.5 (8 ships)
Escaped	36.0 (33 ships)	23.7 (18 ships)
Total attacked	**91**	**76**

Note: Attacks reported to British naval authorities.
Source: Ministry of Defence, *War with Japan*, 3:121.

eran warrior who had accomplished a sixty-four-day round trip to Europe and had sunk fifteen ships during the war. Why did he commit suicide? Because he faced being tried and sentenced as a war criminal for his massacre of unarmed merchant seamen of the Dutch SS *Tjisalak* and the American SS *Jean Nicolet*.[21]

After the war, almost all Japanese submarine commanders who participated and survived were tried as B-class war criminals for inhuman behavior in the Indian Ocean: machine-gunning survivors as they clung to lifeboats and rafts. Many submariners, not only commanding officers but also petty officers, were convicted and spent seven to twenty years in Sugamo prison. The Yokohama War Criminal Court convicted four captains and five admirals: Vice Adm. Komatsu Teruhisa, commander in chief of the Sixth Fleet (Submarine); Chief of Staff Vice Adm. Mito Hisashi, commander of the Eighth Submarine Group; Vice Adm. Ichioka Hisashi; Rear Adm. Ishizaki Noboru, the chief of the operations department at the Gunreibu and Vice Adm. Nakazawa Tasuku. Of the commanding officers and staffs of submarine flotillas, two commanders, four lieutenants, and one petty officer were also found guilty.[22] The Singapore Military Court convicted the commander of the 16th Cruiser Squadron and the commanding officer of the cruiser *Tone*. Rear Adm. Sakonji Naomasa was executed by hanging, while Capt. Mayuzumi Haruo was sent to Sugamo prison for seven years.[23] At the criminal trial, the accused commanders and commanding officers insisted that they had been following orders from their superiors, while Admiral Nakazawa's defense counsel claimed that the orders had come from the Germans.

The records of the International Military Tribunal for the Far East contain the transcript of a conversation between Hitler and Ōshima that occurred on 3 January 1942. In that conversation, Hitler mentioned the powerful ship-building capability of the United States and insisted that, in order to compete with these capabilities, the Axis forces must kill the crews when sinking Allied merchant ships because their crews required a long training period. He claimed that he had already ordered U-boat commanders to do so. Ōshima agreed and expressed the will to comply.[24] Though Hitler issued the order, the German navy adhered to the Geneva Convention and did not kill shipwrecked personnel or prisoners. The only case on record is that of U-852, whose commander, Kapitänleutnant Eck, ordered survivors of the freighter *Peleus* killed on 13 March 1944. He and his executive officer were sentenced to death by a British war tribunal at Hamburg and executed. At his trial he claimed not to have acted on orders but on his own decision, trying to camouflage the until-then unknown presence of German submarines in that area.

The first massacre carried out by the Japanese occurred on 18 January 1943, after the cruiser *Tone* sank the British SS *Behar* during an Indian Ocean raid operation. *Tone* rescued about eighty survivors, but after returning to port the commanding officer was reprimanded by higher authorities for not executing his orders faithfully. He then had sixty-five of the survivors killed on board. It is said that the order was issued not in writing but orally from the commander of Southwest Fleet.[25]

As for the submarines, in early February 1943 staff officers from the Gunreibu instructed the commander in chief of the submarine fleet on Truk Island to kill merchantman crews. On 20 March 1943, chief of staff of the Sixth Fleet issued the massacre order, saying that, except for those who might be valuable for intelligence gathering, all crews had to be killed. The first war crime committed by a Japanese submariner, however, did not occur until 13 December 1943. Commanders were reluctant to carry out the order because it was considered very dangerous for a sub to surface close enough to kill the crew of a stricken ship; the risk of detection by Allied forces was too high.

Eventually, submariners did obey the order. It was first executed by a most brilliant and experienced officer, Captain Ariizumi, who had graduated from the Naval War College and had knowledge of international law. Why he committed this crime will be understood if one considers the letters he left behind after his suicide. In one, he wrote to his wife, "I am not ashamed of my behavior because my family has been a faithful samurai family since Tokugawa times, for three hundred years. For the navy our three generations have served, and participated in the Sino-Japanese and Russo-Japanese Wars, and I fought bravely in this war. I am a warrior and there is no cowardice in me." In another letter for the navy authorities he wrote, "[I]f the honor of the Imperial Navy is considered stained by my behavior, please purify it by my blood."[26] Submariners, then, followed their orders faithfully and did what they saw as their duty, regardless of the danger of being detected by the enemy. In the end their devotion to the motherland brought them to capital punishment or prison as perpetrators of war crimes.

After the conclusion of the Tokyo Military Court, Ambassador Ōshima confessed that had spoken with Hitler on 3 January 1942 about killing crews of sunken Allied ships and that his defense counsel had advised him to deny that he had ever sent a telegram from Berlin advocating the practice. After his talk with Ōshima, Hitler ordered Dönitz to have the crews of Allied merchant ships killed, but the German navy avoided the execution of his order.[27] On 6 September 1942, a discouraged Hitler grumbled in one of his private talks that "if they were to threaten more drastic reprisals, we will retort by hanging the captains of all ships sunk. . . . The Japanese do this [i.e., kill prisoners of war], while we entertain them with coffee and cognac."[28]

KRUG'S OPINION

Fundamental differences seriously impeded the effective collaboration of Germany and Japan from the very beginning. Conflicts existed in many fields. There were disparate standards and traditions in political, military, and naval reasoning and a wide dissimilarity in doctrines and procedures between the oceangoing Japanese big-ship navy and the much smaller German navy, accustomed to using its potential covertly against superior naval forces.

The extreme geographical distance between the Axis allies, located nearly opposite one another on our globe, complicated the cooperation among them. As a strategic link the Soviet Union could have bridged the vast geographical gap between them, but since the Russo-Japanese War of 1904 the antipathy against Russia had remained strong in Japan. The Anti-Comintern Pact of 1936 had further strengthened these resentments. In spite of this, in November 1940 Germany and Japan agreed to concede to the Soviet Union an advance toward India—without, however, granting it to the USSR as a zone of influence.

In a supplementary note to the Tripartite Pact, Germany had on 27 September 1940 assured Japan of her good offices "to promote a friendly understanding

... between Japan and Soviet Russia." When on 22 June 1941 Germany attacked the Soviet Union without consulting its Japanese ally in advance, Japan regarded this as a breach of the 1936 pact. It claimed that Germany's action was "not in conformance with the spirit of this agreement." The Japanese Foreign Minister Matsuoka, who signed a neutrality pact with the USSR in Moscow just before his return voyage from Berlin in April 1941, did not inform his Allies beforehand, either—committing just as clear a breach of the same agreement.

In retrospect it seems difficult to believable that authoritarian governments of that time felt so little compelled to abide by the substance and wording of international treaties and agreements. Such attitudes further damaged the sense of mutual reliability among partners. The Japanese political framework was by far the more conservative and traditional, whereas the German concept was much more unconventional and radical. On the political and high command levels, both countries tended to use each other as an auxiliary to advance their own national goals and to relieve enemy pressure on their forces, though such actions clearly conflicted with the spirit of military cooperation. This tendency was especially strong and ruthless in Hitler's reasoning.

The rationale of the German armed forces had been handed down from the former German Empire. They were accustomed to trusting in their government's decency and, like other armed forces, were bound by oath. Hitler's very unconventional approaches to political and strategic problems perplexed not only his opponents but his own military leaders as well. His astonishing initial successes were persuasive and made it extremely difficult to articulate reservations about his often rash and intuitive decisions.

Even though Hitler knew of the immense disadvantage of fighting a war on opposite fronts, he decided to attack Russia. He claimed that he took this step to prevent a pending attack from their side; whether this was an actual threat is still occasionally discussed today. When the German advance in Russia came to a halt in December 1941, Hitler assumed direct command of the German army himself, but he could not stem the tide rising against Germany. In a global conflict, which the war became with the entry of Japan, his engagement with the Soviet Union was an eminent drawback.

Japan was impressed by Germany's "lightning war" successes and did not want to miss a unique opportunity, but they still had misgivings about Germany wanting to use a Japanese attack merely to get relief in its own struggle. The Japanese navy, especially, always aware of Japan's precarious shortage of raw materials and natural resources, tried hard for a long time to avoid all obligations. Even after Japan had finally entered the war and occupied most of Southeast Asia, it still felt ill at ease concerning German claims on colonies of the German-occupied European countries. To ease Japan's anxieties, on 22 May 1940 Germany stated explicitly that it was not interested in taking possession of these areas nor of its former South Seas colonies that it had mandated to Japan. Hitler himself repeated this position in his Directive No. 24 on 5 March 1941. (See appendix C.)

Though the Japanese military was bound to a very strict code handed down from the times of the samurai and the German side stood on Prussian military principles of highly loyal service to the state, there were analogies in their ways of thinking that were seemingly affirmed by German army instructors serving in Japan and by Japanese naval officers who had studied in Germany after the Anglo-Japanese naval alliance was canceled in 1921. In this field there was mutual understanding at troop and unit levels. Here both sides generally made all possible efforts to collaborate in all practical ways.

At government, interservice, and upper navy levels, however, each side's lack of adequate understanding of the other's peculiarities seems to have provoked dissension. Mutual arrogance after military successes and general distrust further complicated relations. These difficulties were especially apparent in intelligence and communications exchange. Neither partner was aware of the extent to which enemy code-breaking had compromised their cipher systems, and any suspicion of breaches in code security deepened their mutual distrust. Although the navies reached a communications agreement in December 1942, they rarely used it.

The essential exchange of technical expertise and equipment was also inadequately coordinated. The Japanese were very keen on obtaining all possible information about technical developments and sent people to Germany to get it. In general they wanted to develop innovations on their own, so they speedily discharged foreign specialists from their obligations. They quickly studied new technology, such as jet engines, missiles, and radar equipment, from samples and blueprints and then reproduced it—alarming German industry, which had misgivings about supplying patents without proper reimbursement.

The German side was not so quick to assimilate Japanese technology. An automatic depth-control device for submarines, brought to Europe in a Japanese submarine, was adapted to similar technology in Germany and put to use. The famous Japanese "long lance" torpedoes, brought to Europe from

Japan in blockade runners, were never used for the German navy. Their propulsion engines were never studied seriously at the German torpedo test facilities because they were supposedly too busy testing the Walter hydrogen-peroxide propulsion system. A certain German self-conceit in the technical fields may also have played a role in the lack of interest in Japanese technology.

In the end, the blind forces of institutions and political machines doomed the uneasy alliance of Germany and Japan, despite the many personal interactions and innumerable personal sacrifices it generated.

PART 2

Forming the Axis Challenge to Anglo-American Naval Power

7

Building Navies, 1919–1933

German-Japanese relations from the first half of the thirties until the defeat of Hitler's Germany would be quite a tempting subject for any historian, because little interest has been paid the subject thus far and, moreover, primary sources have gradually become available to researchers over the postwar years. The records of the German naval attachés, Wenneker and Lietzmann, were remanded to German archives in the second half of the seventies. These do, however, have gaps from 1942 on, and no records dating from the spring of 1943 have survived.

On the Japanese side, nearly all reports of the attachés in Berlin seem to have been destroyed. However, new releases of documents on the German and Japanese attachés' radio traffic, deciphered and translated during and after World War II, became available during the eighties and nineties.[1] Thus it has become possible to shed new light on the naval dimension of an alliance that was the twentieth century's most powerful attempt at violently changing the existing world order and, in the process, especially challenging the Anglo-Saxon sea powers.

German-Japanese naval relations were by no means an "invention" of the thirties but date back to the time right after the end of World War I.[2] As early as 1919, several Japanese commissions visited Germany in search of technology and expertise that they could use for the planned "eight-eight fleet," for which large amounts of steel also were contracted in Germany. The most important visit from the naval point of view was probably the one in the fall of 1919 from Rear Adm. Katō Kanji, who was to become one of the most influential flag officers in the Japanese navy.[3] He was on a year-long information-gathering journey through the United States and Europe. After his return to Japan he reported enthusiastically on the quality of German aircraft, submarines, and all kinds of technology usable for naval purposes.[4] A run on German technology set in that lasted until 1924, and it was estimated that several thousand Japanese took up residence in Germany solely to obtain know-how for the Japanese services.

The Japanese also established contact with the German Navy High Command (then called the *Marineleitung*), hired numerous naval experts, and built submarines according to German plans and with the assistance of German technicians and the Reichsmarine. Moreover, although Japan was a cosigner of the Versailles treaty, she encouraged German firms and even the Marineleitung to conduct joint developments in fields that the treaty specifically forbade to the Germans.[5] The explanation for Japan's helpful attitude was that the British and Americans, her former sources of naval "high tech," had become very reluctant to give military or naval support to Japan, now considered a rival and no longer an ally.

Although the Japanese "run" slowed somewhat after the conclusion of the Washington treaties in 1922, the special relationship persisted into the early thirties. For instance, in 1932 Admiral Raeder, commander in chief of the Reichsmarine, describing "our outlook" regarding foreign navies, cites "good relations with Japan, especially considering the very considerable orders that have been placed with German industry for a long time by the office of the Japanese naval attaché."[6]

For the Reichsmarine the Japanese contacts were quite welcome but had to be kept strictly secret to avoid any irritation on the part of the Anglo-Saxon sea powers. The main goal of the Reichsmarine was to shed the "Versailles shackles," which required maintaining good relations with Great Britain and the United States. Only those two nations could, if they chose, effectively support German wishes for equal rights (*Gleichberechtigung*) at sea. Therefore, the German naval delegate at the Geneva Disarmament Conference was instructed to support Anglo-Saxon positions as much as possible. Such instructions by no means signified that the idea of a future war against the British or the Americans had been rejected by German naval leaders; they merely affirmed that discord had to be avoided, temporarily, for political reasons.[7]

A decisive point for the future relations of the German and Japanese navies was reached in 1930, when at a conference in London the regulations of the Washington Treaty, which had only applied to capital ships, was extended to cruisers. This was met with ardent resistance from Katō Kanji, now vice admiral and chief of the Japanese Navy General Staff (Gunreibu). Katō Kanji had been a member of the Japanese delegation at the Washington Treaty negotiations and had had a bitter struggle with Katō Tomosaburō, the naval chief delegate at Washington, against whom he had advocated the "sacred 70 percent" principle. Thus Katō Tomosaburō represented the Treaty Faction (*jōyakuha*) against Katō Kanji, who became the leader of the Fleet Faction (*kantaiha*).

But Tomosaburō not only prevailed over Kanji at that time but also initiated internal reforms clearly aimed at subordinating the Gunreibu to the minister of the navy; he even considered subordinating the navy to the civilian cabinet.[8] He seems to have realized that the independence of the armed services from the cabinet was a major problem for a properly functioning administration. Indeed, the independence of the armed forces from civilian control had been inherited from the Prussian constitution, which had been chosen as the blueprint for the Meiji Constitution, specifically with the aim of preventing the cabinet and parliament from having control of them.[9]

Right after the Washington Treaty was concluded, Katō Tomosaburō became concurrently minister of the navy and prime minister, while Katō Kanji became vice chief of the Gunreibu. However, the treaty faction leader died in August 1923, leaving nobody who could effectively counter the rising influence of Kanji and his followers. As the 1930 London Conference approached, he was determined not to allow a violation of the "sacred 70 percent" principle again. When he discovered that Navy Minister Takarabe and his deputy, Yamanashi, were about to let this happen, he tried to prevent it by reporting his opinion to the throne (his privilege, in his capacity as chief of the Gunreibu and according to article 11 of the constitution). Although his opponents could not stop him from doing so, they made sure that his message reached the throne too late. They maneuvered through court circles and ensured that it would arrive after the delegation in London had been instructed, with imperial consent, to adopt the navy minister's line.

Kanji, now unable to prevent the conclusion of the treaty, in an unprecedented move had his deputy Suetsugu go public with a press conference. Here he claimed that to ignore the Gunreibu's opinion constituted a violation of the emperor's prerogative of command (*Tōsuiken*). This led to an uproar in the public, in the press, in parliament, and in the navy in favor of Kanji's position. Although he had to retire after this incident, it had become practically impossible to push through a policy adhering to the Washington and London treaties within the navy, since the majority of naval officers, especially the middle and junior echelons, supported the Fleet Faction. This in turn implied closer ties with Germany. Katō Kanji had repeatedly shown his pro-German tendencies.[10] When the Japanese navy decided in 1934 to let the treaties expire in 1936, the possibility of a new armament race—maybe even an armed conflict—with the Anglo-Saxon powers sometime after 1936 came in sight.

It was therefore no coincidence that, from 1934 on, the German navy was seen as an important source of technology in the expected armament race and even as a potential ally or at least diversionary factor in an armed conflict with the Anglo-Saxon navies. But, for the time being, the Reichsmarine was still a third-rate naval force, at best. So the Japanese navy, Versailles treaty notwithstanding, decided to give the Germans some development aid in a field that could give the German fleet considerably more punch in the future: construction and operation of aircraft carriers.

Thus the origins of a constellation, with the British and U.S. navies on the one side and the German and Japanese navies on the other, can be traced to 1933, the year in which German naval attachés were reinstalled abroad. This event is a logical starting point for a closer look at the relation of the two navies up to and during World War II.

8

Rapprochement, 1934–1936

The mid-thirties were for the Reichsmarine, which was rechristened the "Kriegsmarine" in March 1935, a time of significant changes. The navy was successful in gaining the necessary means for rearmament,[1] the way to which was paved by Germany's withdrawal from the League of Nations and the Geneva Arms Limitation Conference. Already—with a plan for restructuring the German fleet drawn up in November 1932 that foresaw (among other things) an aircraft carrier, sixteen submarines, and the buildup of a naval air wing—the building plans aimed far beyond the limitations set by the Treaty of Versailles.[2] Then the alternative rearmament plan of 1934 left behind it the majority of tonnage and caliber limitations.[3] The rebuilding of the fleet should have been, according to this plan, completed by 1949 or, according to the plan of 1936, completed by 1945–46.

Germany's break with the Treaty of Versailles, already executed on the planning level, became noticeable to the outside by the proclamation of the German *Wehrhoheit* in March 1935. (The German term signifies a nation's right to determine the size and composition of its military.) The break was recognized, practically speaking, by England with the German-British Fleet Treaty in June of the same year.[4] The latter treaty did not mean an actual abandonment of further-reaching armament plans but was, rather, the contractual securing of gains that could be realized by the Kriegsmarine in subsequent years, given its personal and technical capacities.[5]

The modern ship material that the Kriegsmarine possessed at the end of 1936 consisted of three *Panzerschiffe* (armored ships), six light cruisers, and thirty-five new submarines in service. Under construction were four battleships, four heavy cruisers, two aircraft carriers, nineteen destroyers, and one submarine.

The operational plans of the navy tended from 1934 onward to be stronger in the direction of the protection of Germany's shipping in the North Sea and the destruction of enemy shipping in the Atlantic and the Mediterranean. France was considered the main enemy, whereas England was temporarily discounted because of poor prospects for success against the Royal Navy. Meaningful diversionary strategies (such as gaining Italy as an ally) were increasingly recognized. Naval aviation was considered to be indispensable for oceanic warfare and was incorporated into the planning.[6] Just as in the mid-twenties, the navy assumed for itself an indispensable, even war-deciding role in a future armed conflict.[7] The waging of war in the Atlantic was to be directed by the Naval War Staff (Seekriegsleitung, or Skl.) which was subordinate to the Marineleitung (from 1935 on, *Oberkommando der Marine*, or OKM). The waging of war in home waters was under the jurisdiction of the fleet commander.[8]

Given Germany's interests in the Atlantic and Mediterranean, it was largely Hitler's and Foreign Minister von Ribbentrop's strong interest in good relations with Japan that furthered the German Navy's contact with the Imperial Japanese Navy (IJN).

For the IJN the abandonment of the Washington Treaty system was the most influential factor in the field of foreign policy in the mid-thirties. It led to a significant intensification of armament efforts leading, in turn, not only to competition with the Japanese army for resources but also to a conflict about military objectives. Aviation, beset with problems due to extremely fast development in technology, figured prominently in these efforts.[9] The changed situation was acknowledged by the Japanese military with the third revision of the "Guidelines for the Defense of the Empire," for which imperial consent was obtained in June 1936.[10] The most important change was that England was now considered a potential enemy for the first time.

The overall foreign policy background to the IJN's post–Washington Treaty actions included the Somalia crisis of September 1935; the passive stance of the Western powers toward the German *Rheinlandbesetzung* (literally, "occupation of the Rhineland"); the beginning of the Spanish Civil War; and the formation of the Berlin-Rome Axis in October 1936, followed by the signing of the Anti-Comintern Treaty the following month. These events seemed, at least outwardly, to indicate a growing cooperation of the revisionist "have-nots," Germany, Italy, and Japan.

THE IJN: RAPPROCHEMENT
AND TECHNICAL COOPERATION

In early 1934 the IJN undertook initiatives aimed at an intensification of its relationship with the Reichsmarine, in the wake of which developed, within the next two years, a connection between them that represented the high point of their relationship in the whole time frame between 1919 and 1945.

That Japanese interest in products of the German armaments industry had not lessened was apparent when a representative of the Krupp firm in January 1934 confidentially asked the Foreign Ministry if an order by the Japanese navy for "ship steel," actually meaning armor plating, was unobjectionable from a foreign policy standpoint.[11]

In February 1934 the Japanese indirectly reached for a rapprochement by promoting contact between the Japanese Naval Society and the German Fleet Society.[12] In March, however, a more definite signal was the announcement, from the Japanese naval attaché, Endō, of the first official visit of the Japanese navy to Germany since the end of the World War I. The commander in chief of the training squadron of the IJN, Vice Adm. Matsuhita Hajime, intended to head for the French harbor of Marseilles at the beginning of May.[13] From there he wanted to go to Paris, on 7 and 8 May, and then to Berlin and afterwards London. The official character of the visit was emphasized by the squadron commander's request for visits with the *Reichspresident, Reichschancellor,* minister of air, minister of defense, and the head of the Marineleitung.[14]

Not only were these wishes fulfilled, but, in addition, the foreign minister received the Japanese admiral as well. Besides these receptions, there also took place a dinner with the Japanese ambassador and the head of the Marineleitung. Moreover, Matsuhita laid down a wreath at the Ehrenmal Unter den Linden, toured the Tempelhof airport and the Potsdam palaces, and participated in a joint reception of the German-Japanese Society and the Japanese Club in Germany. The program almost resembled one for a head of state.[15]

In his speech at the banquet of the Japanese ambassador, Nagai, for Matsushita, Defense Minister von Blomberg emphasized the "exceedingly cordial reception that the German training cruisers had always received during their recurring visits in Japan," thanked them for it, and expressed the hope that Japanese ships would soon also visit German harbors. He continued, citing the "upstanding feeling of friendship" that the "whole German people" had shown toward the Japanese, which had, especially in recent times, been enhanced by the Japanese people's understanding of the "national renewal of Germany." He compared the samurai spirit of the Japanese armed forces, with its emphasis on knightly bravery and unconditional sacrifice, with the spirit of the German officer corps, claiming that this was why representatives of both services had always understood each other so well.[16]

Similar in nature was the speech of the former head of the Marine-leitung, Admiral (Ret.) Behncke, at the reception of the German-Japanese Society and the Japanese League in Germany.[17] Behncke, at that time the chairman of the German-Japanese Society, also referred to the strikingly friendly reception given German ships in Japan and made known his wish for a speedy Japanese warship visit in Germany. He then went on to say that, since the Reich had been led by von Hindenburg and Hitler, the German people had become a people of a national unity similar to Japan's and similarly focused on a national struggle. Like the Japanese in East Asia, the Germans would struggle in Europe for a "peace of honor," "equal rights," and the "right to live." Nothing but distance would divide the two and, beyond all political day-to-day questions, their inner attitude and national character (*völkische Wesensart*) were identified by the admiral as important common traits.[18]

One can surely assume that the retired admiral, who had been "raised" in the Imperial German Navy, went beyond politeness here and conveyed a position that was shared by his comrades, based on their upbringing and selection as imperial naval officers. These sentiments were also shared by Raeder, who was present during Behncke's speech and also spoke, although his speech has not, unfortunately, been preserved. As a retiree, though, Behncke had greater freedom and could speak unburdened by political or tactical considerations.

Behncke's speech reveals, moreover, that another Japanese naval delegation was abiding in Germany for study purposes independently of Matsushita's visit. That IJN delegation was also present at the reception and also expressly greeted by Behncke.[19]

The answering speech given by Matsushita is not in the record, but a summary, taken from newspaper clippings collected by the Foreign Ministry, has survived.[20] He declared that, although both peoples were thousands of kilometers apart and were culturally different, they nevertheless shared the same courage and proficiency. This was the reason why, based on their sense of justice and their fanatical love for their fatherland, both occupied a special place among the peoples of the world. In his opinion it was no coincidence that both, just at the same time, had a plethora of international difficulties to contend with and longed for a peace that should, however, be a "just" peace. It would be "in the interest of the welfare of mankind . . . especially between both of our countries to set a goal for ever-closer cooperation."

Matsushita continued that the Japanese people and the Japanese navy had a special understanding and the highest appreciation for Germany. The "numerous officers sent each year to foreign countries" by the Japanese navy were . . . received in such a very friendly way [in Germany] that they felt here just like back home and could return to Japan enriched by impressions and information."[21]

Mashsushita was given a farewell by Lt. Cdr. Bürkner of the Marineleitung, as well as Behncke and Hack from the German-Japanese Society, on 9 May at the Bahnhof Zoo station, as he left for London. (No German or Japanese records of the London visit are extant.)

Matsushita expressed himself very positively at his departure from Berlin and let it be known that he judged his reception there to have been far more favorable than the one in Paris.[22] The visit also attracted attention from foreign observers, specifically, Captain Rowan, the assistant U.S. military attaché. In reporting the visit, he also took the opportunity to convey his general observations about the current German-Japanese relationship.[23] According to him, the visit of Matsushita had elicited exceptional attention and interest, not only in official circles of the German Reich but also in business and industrial circles.

Rowan considered the speeches of Behncke and Matsushita at the reception of the German-Japanese Society to be particularly noteworthy. On the whole he received an impression of unusually close and friendly relations, raising conjecture about a possible secret alliance. The Japanese side played the more active part but was met willingly by the Germans, especially under the NSDAP (Nazi) administration. The beginning of the friendship stemmed, he thought, from the time before 1933; it was, however, hindered earlier through the friendship of the German government with China and Russia.

THE JAPANESE IN GERMANY

Rowan, the American assistant military attaché, noted that the markedly closer ties between Germany and Japan in this period were revealed by, among other things, the changing array of foreign students at German universities. Whereas in the past the Americans, followed by the Chinese, had been the most numerous, the numbers of Japanese students had nearly caught up.

Japan had also bought large quantities of armaments from Germany during the recent outbreak of hostilities in China, even though the same goods could have been acquired in the United States at far less cost because of the shorter transportation route. The acquisitions were admitted neither by the German nor the Japanese side, but the assistant attaché considered the proof as conclusive.

The American also knew interesting things to report about the spy networks and contacts of the Japanese in Germany and wrote that the Japanese military attaché had explained to him that approximately 150 agents were working for him and that other departments of the Japanese embassy carried the same amount. A large number of them were probably Japanese students, who collected intelligence as repayment for financial support through the Japanese government. Among them were, however, also some whose qualifications raised Rowan's doubts as to whether getting a university education was really their main purpose. Thus one of the students at the Berlin University had been a professor of chemistry at the University of Tokyo.

Lieutenant Colonel Thomas, at the *Heereswaffenamt* (Weapons Section, Department of the Army), had imparted to Rowan that the Japanese attaché visited the place three to four times as frequently as the other attachés; moreover, a few months before, a German officer had been deployed as an observer to the Japanese army in Manchuria. The American suspected that there were further cases, unbeknownst to him, of special privileges for Germany. It was, however, his opinion that "as usual Japan has received more than she has given in exchange."

According to Rowan, the reason for the especially good relationship of the two countries at that time could be found in the fact that they were currently in similar positions in the world. In political terms both had placed themselves contrary to the majority of the world opinion and had deemed it necessary to leave the League of Nations for the pursuit of their goals. Their position was also similar in economic terms. Both required more territory and markets. This was, certainly, in the foreground (contrary to the policies of the state administration, which aimed for self-sufficiency) but was, however, necessary for the immediate future if autonomy was to be achieved. Beyond that, the American suspected that there had to be even more concrete reasons, such as, for example, the threat from a common enemy, which he suspected was the Soviet Union.

As totally beyond doubt he saw, though, that the now evolved cordiality had no personal basis. It was unthinkable that "the Japs" would develop any kind of truly brotherly feelings toward Western peoples, and some Germans did not hesitate to speak openly with Americans about their own attitudes. The assistant attaché summed up the German view: "We are encouraging close and friendly relations with Japan because it is to our advantage to do so, but we must never forget that we are white people and they are not."[24]

THE GERMANS IN JAPAN

Further clear signals of the IJN's interest in closer contacts with the German navy were observable at the end of 1934. One was a reception given for two former German naval officers, who went to Japan nearly simultaneously for aviation matters.[25]

Early in November Senior Lieutenant (Ret.) Breithaupt arrived in Manchuria to negotiate with the authorities there about the purchase of airships from Germany.[26] Paul Wenneker, the German naval attaché and senior among the *Wehrmachtsattachés* at the Tokyo embassy, reported that representatives of the Japanese armed forces had always been present at the negotiations, and, after Breithaupt had arrived in Tokyo on 20 November, it had become altogether clear that the IJN had been the main interested party. So Breithaupt had been given an active-duty admiral in support and the IJN had prepared various events for him.

When Breithaupt requested meteorological data for evaluative proposes, he received these at once. A flight was arranged to show him the intended areas of zeppelin operations. The Japanese navy was mainly interested in the use of zeppelins for reconnaissance of the sea areas east of Japan. Wenneker was sure that the negotiations would lead to the purchase of airships (which, however, did not occur) and expressly warned:

> It has become known to me that the transaction might be in danger for the sole reason that it is not wanted by certain authorities on the German side (impairment of the American transaction or similar things). To this I would like to remark that after the negotiations have progressed well, a cancellation by the German side can only result in great consternation on the Japanese side. This is under certain circumstances able to seriously endanger the presently existing good political relationships as well as the navy-to-navy relationship.[27]

In the Marineleitung provisional plans were immediately made for counterdemands to the Japanese in the case of a sale.[28]

The second visitor was Lieutenant Commander (Ret.) Coeler, who now stood in the service of the Air Ministry (*Reichsluftfahrtsministerium*, or RLM) and was the director of the air traffic school in Warnemünde.[29] He had left Germany on 21 September 1934 and arrived in Japan from the United States on 25 November; he stayed for two months in order to be instructed in the organization of naval aviation. The high point of his stay in Japan was an inspection tour of the Japanese aircraft carrier *Akagi*, which he took with Wenneker at the end of January 1935.[30]

This concession on the part of the Japanese was without precedent and a temporary high point of a development that had started in the spring of 1934. Wenneker had repeatedly petitioned for the inspection of ships of the Japanese navy in the meantime. The IJN finally relented; on 10 January 1935 the German attaché had the opportunity to tour the battle cruiser *Kongo*, the cruiser *Tama*, and the submarine I-2.[31] The attachés of the other states were also shown these craft in the first half of January 1935. The inspection tours, however, took place singly; the reason given Wenneker was that individual tours enabled them to adjust the level of accommodation. He was to be shown the highest.

The actual inspection tour, which took place in the naval station of Yokosuka, was preceded by a talks with the station commander, Adm. Suetsugu Nobumasa, who wore, Wenneker noted, a seldom-seen parade uniform for the occasion.[32] He stressed the IJN's interest in the "energetic buildup" of the German navy and showed personal interest in the building plans and experience with the new German Panzerschiffe, in particular regarding the devices for fire control and range finding. Suetsugu also spoke about the approaching fleet conference for the extension of the treaties of Washington (1922) and

London (1930). He made it clear that Japan could never do without full parity with the Anglo-Saxon sea powers and would also never agree to abolish the submarine, which Wenneker called Suetsugu's "favorite weapon."

When Wenneker remarked that Japan would then have to count England as a possible opponent, Suetsugu replied that, though he thought this improbable, Japan would accept such a case without hesitation. Especially during his assertions about the parity principle did Wenneker observe in Suetsugu—whom he described as an "extraordinarily strong personality"—an "inner passion, obviously only checked with difficulty." Wenneker described this confidant of Katō Kanji as a "leader who enjoys the confidence of the whole navy" and as an "idol of the young officers."

The whole discourse took place in Japanese, because even though Suetsugu, as former attaché in Washington, had a good mastery of the English language, as a "self-confident conservative Japanese" he used only his own native tongue.

The German specialist of the Navy General Staff, Lieutenant Commander Maeda, who escorted Wenneker, had no German and only little English language ability. The German attaché was therefore forced to rely on his own Japanese skills. The speech barrier was quite obviously a major impairment of the visit, although Wenneker remarked that the Japanese officers on board the inspected ships and boats certainly did not refuse to use foreign languages and made a serious effort at being understood. But time and again they had been lacking knowledge of even simple technical terminology. Wenneker therefore suggested, "due to the expected expansion of the relationship between the two navies" (aircraft carrier questions, etc.), to emulate other nations and send language officers, who would later be reserved for the attaché post.[33]

Wenneker was clearly somewhat disappointed by the degree of accommodation shown him, which he judged as "average at best" and to which he remarked: "By the great accommodation that was shown the Japanese attaché and *the numerous commissions* in Germany, one was allowed to expect and one had to expect more" (emphasis in original).[34] On the other hand, he mentioned that he had been treated considerably better than all the other attachés, who had merely been led across the deck.

Wenneker also pointed out a certain reservation on the part of the Japanese when showing the vessels, which was explained by the fact that these stood in a "technical and especially weapons technical sense on *an unimaginably backward level for our conceptions*" (emphasis in original).[35] Particularly the artillery seemed backward to Wenneker, who was himself a trained artilleryman.[36] This impression was confirmed by him in conversations with other attachés.[37]

THE CARRIER INSPECTION

Wenneker thus had decisive leverage, not just to get answers to questions concerning naval aviation that the Marineleitung had already transmitted to him some time earlier, but also to push through the inspection of an aircraft carrier, seemingly already requested by him at the end of 1934.[38]

A tactical advantage proved to be the fact that these negotiations took place shortly before 20 January 1935, the scheduled date for Coeler's departure (which in fact was postponed to 30 January). Wenneker could urge that Coeler should logically take part in the inspection of a carrier and that a quick decision was therefore necessary, and he received additional support for his request through Endō, the former attaché in Germany.[39]

Wenneker rated the fact that the inspection was finally made possible for him as extraordinary, because it was without precedent for a foreigner; even the Japanese were allowed to get near the ship only under stringent conditions.[40] In keeping with the stringent Japanese security measures, which stated that no civilian was allowed to set foot on board the ship, Wenneker could not take a translator on board with him. However, he received the opportunity for a discussion before and after the inspection tour with the help of a translator.

The courtesy shown during the inspection he judged to be conspicuously high. The Japanese had shown themselves to be unreservedly open and had unconditionally answered all questions, except for one (concerning landing intervals).[41] They endeavored to point out and explain the different installations. The visitors were also informed about the experience gained with the installations, as well as about their differences from other carriers, and reported that they had won valuable experience and insight.

Wenneker characterized the tour of the carrier as "incredibly impressive" and pointed out how important it was to the IJN to keep the inspection tour secret. The Germans were even expressly asked to disclose nothing about the fact that they had inspected a carrier. The Japanese were afraid of diplomatic difficulties if it were to become known. For reasons of secrecy Wenneker and Coeler were asked to appear in civilian clothes, and the journey was not made with Wenneker's official vehicle but with a car of the Kaigunshō (Navy Ministry).

The reciprocal German effort, the inspection of the fire-control unit of the *Admiral Scheer*, was viewed by Wenneker as not detrimental, since he considered the Japanese to be unable to duplicate the complicated devices, even if they could study them in a detailed manner.[42]

This was exactly what the Japanese did when, apparently early in February 1935, they let themselves be instructed about the installations of the German ship as reciprocation.[43] Despite the very far-reaching accommodations of the Japanese, the Marineleitung had not agreed to meet the Japanese guests without reservations.[44] The orders issued on 30 January to the ship concerning the visit were contradictory. For example, they gave orders, on the one hand, regarding a few especially protected devices, to "organize the tour in such a way that the device does not come in appearance to the Japanese," to show them "only upon demand" and then give only general explanations.[45]

On the other hand, the ship's leadership was instructed to "be in keeping as much as possible with the wishes and questions of the Japanese and *to achieve the impression of a great and open-hearted cooperation*" (emphasis in original).[46] This situation led to uncertainty on the part of the German artillery officer who led the tour, with the result that the Japanese were extensively informed.[47]

A few days later the Marineleitung was informed by the RLM that the Japanese naval attaché had offered to allow a German naval construction engineer a comprehensive study of Japanese aircraft carriers and in return had asked for the plans of the latest dive-bomber of the RLM.[48] When the Marineleitung gathered the opinions of the bureaus about this, the Construction Bureau astoundingly spoke out against it. The head of the *Kommandoamt*, though, Rear Admiral Guse, put great value in acquiring insight into the practical air traffic on a carrier and named as candidate for dispatch Senior Lieutenant Czech.[49] He also made sure that, despite the negative vote of the Construction Bureau, a back door stayed open for the dispatching of an engineer.[50]

At about the same time a high-ranking member of the technical section of the Japanese Naval Aviation Department, Captain Wada, wrote to Wenneker and asked him for support in negotiations of the firm Aichi Tokei Denki with Heinkel. Aichi mainly worked for the Japanese navy and wished to acquire two airplanes, including instruction in construction for two or three of their engineers.[51] How important Heinkel was for Aichi and also indirectly for the IJN was revealed in the statement of a leading member of the Aichi firm that Heinkel was the only foreign firm with which they cooperated. In addition, he pointed out that Coeler had visited Aichi offices during his trip and had been treated very accommodatingly there, as Wenneker confirmed.

In the middle of March, then, there were the first signs of a further intensification of contacts in the area of aircraft carrier construction. Wenneker reported that the Japanese navy was considering an exchange of engineers with the German navy, whereby the Japanese thought to send aircraft carrier specialists to Germany.[52] At the same time the Japanese signaled a desire for information about torpedo explosives and construction details of the Panzerschiffe. The Marineleitung, however, did not react to these signals.[53]

Two weeks later Wenneker could add that the Japanese were inclined, after the completion of the first German carrier, to give the German navy assistance with the especially difficult initial training in carrier flight operations. For this, German pilots could either train in Japan, or Japanese could be dispatched to Germany as instructors.[54]

In the same month Wenneker had a conversation with the commodore of the naval flying squadron on the *Akagi*. He gave Wenneker further detailed information about the Japanese carriers and informed him that the Japanese attaché, Yokoi, had reported extraordinary approval of the German cooperation during the inspection tour of the *Admiral Scheer*. The Kaigunshō therefore felt "morally obligated" to answer further inquiries about carriers without reciprocation. The officer offered that he wished to be the first Japanese to take off and land on a German carrier. The Kaigunshō would approve of his dispatch to Germany upon German request.[55]

A good month later Wenneker received further hints in a similar direction. This time, the head of the Gunreibu's German Section, Lieutenant Commander Maeda, consulted him for information he needed for a lecture on the topic "potential strength of the German navy and its reconstruction." With this lecture Maeda wanted to draw attention to the benefits of a closer cooperation with Germany. He characterized this as an easy task, since there were hardly any officers in the IJN whose sympathies did not lie with Germany and its navy. He imagined a cooperation to be mainly an exchange of experience.

Wenneker immediately remarked that such an exchange had to give both sides the same benefits. He made known his wish to take part in exercises at some point with Japanese ships at sea and pointed out that this had been arranged for the former Japanese attaché, Endō, on board the German cruiser *Königsberg*. Maeda replied that he had suggested that Wenneker take part in the air operations on a carrier at sea and that approval was soon to be expected, perhaps even without reciprocation. At the same time he named the areas in which the Japanese were interested in receiving information from the Kriegsmarine. In this case it dealt with participation in heavy-caliber shooting, questions about fire control and distance measurement, construction details of the underwater hull of the Panzerschiffe, and the composition of the explosive charges of the German torpedo warheads.[56]

Wenneker's commentary in his report clearly shows that the Japanese played the more active part in the question of cooperation: "In case an exchange is found to be at all useful, I ask that requests be submitted from our side."[57]

NEGOTIATIONS

Although a request by the Japanese can be deduced from these procedures, there were no formal proposals for cooperation. Such a proposal was not made until the beginning of July 1935 when Wenneker reported that the Japanese had officially proposed an exchange of experience through the attachés or the dispatch of specialists. The area of exchange was not only to be concentrated on aircraft carrier questions; the Japanese side also offered instruction about submarine development. As a counterweight, more airplane designs and information about submarine propulsion, fire-control devices, and torpedo explosives was requested.[58]

The German navy—now termed the Kriegsmarine—accepted this offer. There followed, however, tough negotiations over the exact content of services, which dragged on until the end of September and were only ended when Wenneker threatened to send the German commission home; the Germans were already on their way to the United States, from where they were to board a ship to Japan.[59] During those negotiations both sides tried to "improve" their positions. The Japanese sought expanded information about fire-control devices by trying to define them as being already a part of the original, previously agreed-upon "service package" of the Kriegsmarine. Wenneker tried to extend the instructions to tactical matters as well.[60]

It was agreed that the Japanese navy would arrange an inspection tour of the *Akagi* for the German commission, especially of the installations important for air operations and of the carrier planes, as well as making available the plans for these areas. In addition, day and night takeoffs of all carrier-borne airplane types were to be demonstrated, in which the German pilots were expressly allowed to participate. Answers to questions concerning the construction of the carrier, the ship's routine, and air operations were also to be given.

The Kriegsmarine would reciprocate with descriptions of fire-control systems and their construction and usage; inspections and the handing over of plans, as well as permission for the purchase of trial pieces, were planned.[61] Beyond this the intention was to supply the Japanese with samples of torpedo explosives and information about composition and properties, to give manufacturing methods along with the required materials, and to arrange an inspection tour of the factories. The same thing was to happen for the most modern ship armor (of over 30cm thickness).[62] For this the IJN put special emphasis on a "reasonable price." Over the dive-bomber they negotiated separately with the technical bureau of the Luftwaffe and the Heinkel firm.[63]

The commission, consisting of Major Roth of the Air Ministry (RLM), Lieutenant Commander Czech, and *Marinebaurat* (naval construction engineer) Ohlerich, started their journey under strict secrecy on 9 September, arrived in Japan on 2 October, and left on 17 November 1935.[64] Although the leadership of the commission rested with Roth, and therefore with the Air Ministry, they were not, while in Japan, under the command of Colonel Ott, the military attaché. Ott also represented the interests of the newly founded Luftwaffe, but under the command of Captain Wenneker. The reason for this was that the IJN was the host, and there was no independent air force in Japan. Right after their arrival the commission was received by the navy minister, Admiral Ōsumi, and his deputy Hasegawa, as well as the head of the Naval Aviation Department, Shiozawa, and the head of the Construction Bureau, Nakamura. The commission was also invited to dinners given by the above named, as well as by Rear Admiral Takasu, head of the Third Group of the Gunreibu, and the commander of the Second Aircraft Carrier Squadron, Rear Admiral Katagiri.

They were constantly attended by the newly designated naval attaché for Berlin, Commander Kojima, as well as Lt. Cdr. Maeda Minoru of the German Section and the technical specialists, Lieutenant Commanders (engineers, fire-control) Ōhashi, Sawai, and Inagawa.

During the Germans' stay, the Japanese went even beyond what had been agreed upon, in that they offered not only the previously agreed-upon inspection tours and demonstrations but also showed the airfield of the naval station Yokosuka, the naval shipyard there, and the Nakajima and Kawanishi aircraft works. Beyond this the Japanese military attaché in Germany, General Ōshima, had arranged an inspection tour of the facilities of the Japanese Army Air Force. The commission could not, however, make use of this offer because of time constraints.[65]

Since the commission, given the difficult negotiations about the actual content of the exchange, had not expected overly intensive cooperation from the Japanese side, they were now pleasantly surprised. Their leader reported enthusiastically:

> The originally unplanned-for reception by the navy minister himself, the thorough preparation of the ... extensive program, the most willing consent to special wishes and questions of the commission, the more than willing, cooperative, and downright comradely attitude of the escort and the specialist officers, and the continually encountered pose of honesty and friendliness ... of the inspected stations deserve to be mentioned favourably.[66]

The commission explained this behavior, which they viewed as unusual with respect to a foreign military commission, from four viewpoints:

1. the high standing that Wenneker had been able to achieve with the Japanese navy,
2. the similarity of the foreign political situation in which both countries found themselves,
3. the trust exhibited by the Japanese that the transmitted information would actually be held secret by the German side, and
4. "through the high esteem for the re-awakened and re-strengthened German Nation, for the serious view of life and the hero worship of the Germans, but also at least in part for the quality of German technology and the German inventor's spirit."

The assessment of the cooperation with the Japanese ended with the observation that " the commission ... encountered difficulties nowhere and ... the relationship to the Japanese, both officially and privately, surpassed every expected boundary."[67]

Wenneker shared the positive judgment of the commission and did not conceal that

> the cooperation of the Japanese authorities was quite beyond all expectations, so great, that it often astonished me, someone who I believe can claim to be somewhat familiar with the conditions in this country. I believe I can state that never has a foreign commission been so openly and willingly attended to and in addition been so personally and heartily received by the Japanese navy as this

commission. Not only that everything that was wished for was explained and shown with great openness, the Japanese also produced new proposals, new documents and materials, which had not even been requested for from our side.[68]

Especially impressive were the practical demonstrations on the carrier. Here the Japanese had managed "with great deployment of airplanes to give the commission a brilliant, extremely realistic picture of the operations on a carrier," which of all the demonstrated efforts none of the participants would soon forget. Both officers had also been allowed to experience take-offs and landings as passengers aboard aircraft while on the carrier and "if they had demanded to fly themselves, then this wish, too, would have been fulfilled."

As a reason for the extraordinary friendliness Wenneker named the fact that the IJN had high hopes of trading with the German partner, considering their otherwise isolated position, and wanted to give a good impression from the very first. In the Anglo-Saxon countries the Japanese were hardly allowed any insights anymore. Somebody had also explained to Wenneker that "the fable that Japan can only take and not give should be abolished."

Despite all his enthusiasm, however, he also added a few sobering thoughts. It was unclear to him what else the Japanese would have to offer in any further exchange, now that they had probably totally exhausted themselves. He presumed that, in the meantime, in the area of submarines, "where the Japanese are by all accounts achieving considerable things," there could still be interesting things for the German side.[69] In addition he could not estimate whether or not the proffered information would actually compensate for the German contributions.[70] Nonetheless, he ascertained that the Japanese had done their utmost and that "in any case a plethora of very valuable experience was gathered." Even before the completion of the evaluation, there could be no doubt that the journey was going to be viewed as a success.

MAEDA'S APPRECIATION

An interesting illumination of the attitude of the Japanese officers toward the German visitors could be seen in the farewell of the ever-present escort of the commission, Lieutenant Commander Maeda.[71] Maeda described his words as his own personal convictions, at the same time explaining, though, that he was convinced that he was articulating a "common basic idea of the greater part of the Japanese navy and the Japanese people in general." His observations could at least be taken as representative of the "state of mind" of many of the younger officers at this time.

First he termed it as the most profound wish of the Japanese navy that the service rendered may be of true value to the Kriegsmarine in their rebuilding effort and attributed the "not at all coincidental" achievement of the Japanese-German cooperation to the similar fate of both nations, the same mentality of both peoples, and especially to the efforts of Wenneker, who enjoyed the trust of the Japanese.

Maeda attributed the relationship between countries to be, nearly without exception, dictated by "personal interest" (a fact that sadly also held true for Germany and Japan). His remark was surely an allusion to the difficult negotiations continuing until shortly before the arrival of the commission in Japan, in which both were "wrestling for expansion" as strenuously upward-fighting countries "that strove for a higher ideal."

Despite "deep friendship" they, too, could not avoid making decisions based on their own interests when problems arose. Also the recently accomplished technical exchange was, to be frank, "ultimately a profit-trading, in which each side tried to get as much useful information for the development of one's own navy and to give as little as possible oneself."

Such profit-trading could not be allowed, however, to be "the final goal of our mutual efforts." In his opinion states, too, had to strive for higher ideals. To make his point he introduced three thousand years of Japanese history.[72] The imperial state–founding ordinance of ancient times had as its foundation the Japanese ideal state, whose goal was the creation of a world "in which the whole mankind of Earth is able to equally enjoy peace and good fortune." And he continued that this was also the reason that "our striving for world acknowledgment . . . is considerably different from selfishness or nationalistic strivings." The keys to understanding this were the imperial rescripts. Maeda's oratory rose to a level of passionate, even fiery rhetoric, when he elucidated the highly idealistic, even religious context, in which he placed the cooperation with Germany:

> The imperial rescripts are truth itself. For us Japanese the imperial rescripts have a higher value than the Bible. There is no doubt that you, too, are able to thoroughly understand the eternal vitality and the ideal of Japan through the imperial rescripts. I can only urgently recommend the study of the imperial rescripts to all foreigners who want to understand Japan.

The Japanese people are prepared . . . to sacrifice themselves for the real-ization of the holy duty of Japan, since they strongly believe that its ideal, to realize true peace and true prosperity for mankind on Earth, free from tem-poral and spatial conditions, has eternal truth. Japan is furthermore prepared to walk the path to the realization of the holy work, hand in hand together with other capable countries with the same ideal. . . . And now we have found Germany, the re-aspiring German empire.

Japan was endeavoring to build a better world, he said, and Maeda's speech peaked with the request: "You, Germany, be a friendly and good coworker of Japan! That is my deepest wish from my innermost depths."

Near the end of the speech Maeda eventually pointed out the cultural dif-ferences between East and West that complicated a true understanding of the "Japanese heart." He also alluded to the fact that in Germany there were very few who actually understood this—perhaps just one, the former Ambassador Solf. Such an understanding, though, was greatly wished for in Japan. On the other hand, he averred, the Japanese navy was wrestling for a corresponding understanding of the German side:

"We, who hold in the highest regard the Kriegsmarine of the German Reich, which is with an iron will and by a thorough plan re-emerging, are with all strength endeavoring to understand the true Germany, the true German spirit."

In the same spirit Maeda concluded with an idealistic appeal:

"The actual work is just now beginning. Do we not want, together hand in hand, to build as the main driving powers a new world, which greatly differs from that of other peoples, that would build merely on selfishness?"

And at the end he asked the Germans "to take the true heart of Japan home" with them.

Despite the seeming exuberance of these statements, Maeda should hold true as representing the mentality of the greater part of the Japanese officer corps, especially of the younger members. Just a short time later, in February 1936, it came to the "revolt of the young officers," motivated by idealistic rea-sons that were closely related to those stated in Maeda's utterances. That the viewpoints violently represented in this unsuccessful putsch were not re-stricted to the captains and lieutenants of the army, who were leading the revolt, revealed itself in the restrained sympathy that was also found in the higher echelons of the army and even the navy, even though some of their most senior officers became targets of assassination attempts.[73]

WENNEKER'S APPRAISAL

While the Japanese generously offered their services, previously agreed upon, exhibiting great cooperation in the trade of technical information, the Kriegsmarine showed itself hesitant, since the negotiations were still in progress.[74]

In response to Raeder's thank-you telegram, conveyed by Wenneker to Navy Minister Ōsumi, for the friendly treatment of the commission, the latter showed himself to be extraordinarily pleased and expressed his hope that the trade could be continued in the near future. Of all the nations, he had the greatest trust in Germany and tensions between both countries were unthinkable. He hoped, however, "that also the German reciprocal services, over which the negotiations would soon be concluded, could find full appreciation in his Ministry."[75] In other words, the negotiations were still going on and the result was still unclear.

Even in April 1936, five months after the departure of the German commission, the negotiations had not yet been concluded. In the meantime the Japanese side had applied for inspections in Germany, that had seemingly been granted.[76] Wenneker immediately submitted an extensive wish list for his own inspections, and pointed to the great number of Japanese officers in Germany.[77] He expected consideration of his wishes equal to that which the Japanese were expecting of Germany.[78] He informed them that the repetition of this had achieved "understanding" with his intermediaries, and they had promised "betterment."

At the next meeting the Japanese had, however, made him aware of a clear annoyance about the delaying of the exchange deal. Despite more than half a year of negotiations, the manufacturing of armor had still not been demonstrated to the Japanese in Germany. Neither had any agreement been arrived at concerning their wish to fix prices only after the presentation of the corresponding plans. Concerning this Wenneker emphasized that these considerations were still being separately negotiated "on the side" in Berlin and should have no influence upon the inspection tours that had been applied for. He requested of his superiors in Berlin that he be allowed to "treat the Japanese accordingly ruthlessly" if they did not accord him more cooperation.[79]

In the return letter to Wenneker's inspection applications,[80] the chief secretary of the Japanese navy minister thanked the German attaché again for the
good treatment that the Reichsmarine had always shown the Japanese officers
during their inspection tours. The fact that both navies "enjoyed a special,
friendly relationship" brought with it the result that "the majority of Japanese
officers that were posted abroad to study and to inspect chose Germany for
their abode. Captain Tayui specifically requested that notice be taken of the
Japanese navy's endeavors to burden the German navy as little as possible. In
addition the Japanese side planned "with consideration in regard to the special relationship between Germany and the Japanese navy . . . to give exceedingly special treatment" to Wenneker's applications. Except for a few smaller
parts in regard to the inspection of the cruiser, Wenneker's applications were
granted. Tayui, however, requested absolute secrecy, especially about the ship
inspections, toward the other attachés stationed in Japan.

Wenneker, who had asked for clearance of his inspection applications by
the end of May 1936, reported in June about his observances.[81] While in the
preliminary report from 18 June he characterized the cooperation of the
Artillery School and the naval air installations as good, on the ships as satisfactory, and on the docks and arsenals as adequate, his report after completion of the inspections at the end of June was naturally more comprehensive.
Here he emphasized that it took several "strong hints" that the considerable
cooperation accorded the Japanese officers in Germany up till then would
be strongly restricted if the German attaché did not receive an "at least
halfway equal treatment."[82]

Wenneker's report revealed the discord that still existed in the relationship
of both navies. Admittedly, the Japanese had overcome tradition, because up
until now it had been "an iron rule never to let a foreigner have access to modern material . . . The other attachés had up till now never seen modern material."[83] So to him, to his own surprise, once again, more than he had petitioned
for was offered.[84]

Nevertheless, he also reported that the granting of the permits had created
"a big headache." The main resistance had come from the Gunreibu. Only since
the Kaigunshō, the Navy Ministry, had once again regained its position of
power, as a result of the actions taken after the revolt of the young officers in
February, had it become possible to bring about the inspection tours.

Another problem had been to win the support of the commanders of the
ships that were to be toured, and Wenneker assumed that to the crew he was

not represented as an attaché but as a company representative, since he was requested to appear in civilian clothes. His escort from the Navy Ministry had as his main concern to make sure that the guest was actually shown what had been agreed upon. "It has been my experience that the front disregards the instructions from above and sees it as a matter of honor to reduce the already rather sparse program."[85]

Once again the language barrier was a considerable obstacle, since the Japanese could barely speak English or German, and Wenneker was forced to rely on his own "naturally insufficient" knowledge of Japanese.[86]

The cooperation during his visits he had already characterized as good to adequate, adding, however: "That means by our standards. By Japanese standards it must be seen as considerably more than the norm." The visits had allowed an interesting insight into the activity and methods of the Japanese navy, but the technological yields were small.[87] About the brand-new cruisers of the *Mogami* class, he reported that they were not seaworthy because of severe construction errors, and it was debated whether their refurbishing would even be worth the effort.

Especially remarkable were the thoughts on military policy that the attaché encountered during his inspections. Surprised, he discovered "that compared to not even half a year ago, when the Japanese navy had, as usual, . . . imperturbably considered America as the only future enemy, a change in this view has recently set in, even at the front . . . Not just exclusively America, but in the first place also England was seen as the future enemy."[88]

Wenneker had gathered knowledge of this changed view from his conversations with the commanders on his inspection trips in May and June, as well as through talks with the senior officers of the Navy General Staff and with the chief of staff of the Combined Fleet, Rear Adm. Nomura Naokuni.[89] The origin of this change of attitude he suspected to be in the Navy Ministry and outlined it: A war with America would be "pure madness," because Japan was economically dependent upon it. Problems between both of them existed at most because of China and perhaps because of the Philippines. Both questions, however, were not acute, and a solution would probably not be hard to find.

In the case of Great Britain the case was totally different: "Every future, and in the long run unavoidable, expansion of Japan" had to necessarily come up against British positions and with that the resistance of Great Britain. Of course it was totally out of the question that England, in any way and in any position, would give up the field voluntarily." On the contrary it felt the

Japanese threat and tried with all its might to neutralize it. It began "to start an encirclement of Japan, in similar form, to which Germany had experienced before the World War."[90] The British were interested in a war between Japan and the Soviet Union and acted in this manner.

A special danger emanated from the Japanese army, which would have liked to destroy the Soviet Union "better today than tomorrow." The navy, however, viewed such a war as a "national disaster." The goal of Japanese politics had to be "to prevent these policies of England, no matter what the cost."[91]

9

Cooperation with Caution

Information about the position of the Japanese navy in view of the pending second London Fleet Conference was obtained by Wenneker from conversations and from his cooperation with the German press representatives in Japan. For example, Admiral Suetsugu, the base commander of Yokosuka, granted an interview to Fürst Urach, the correspondent of the *Völkischer Beobachter,* who was sent to Tokyo to determine the Japanese position on the pending conference.[1] The representatives of the German press coordinated their articles about the conference with Wenneker before they were sent to Germany, so that he could monitor their reporting. In the interview with Suetsugu he had given Urach a few questions to ask, not all of which the Japanese admiral, however—much to Wenneker's regret—would answer.[2]

The conversation, which took place on the same day that the Japanese government obtained the consent of the Tennō for the cancellation of the Washington treaties, was revealing. The admiral did not respond to the question regarding the oil supply of the fleet and simply did not react to the question of what the IJN planned to do if the conference failed. The Japanese would, however, demand parity; of that he left no doubt.[3]

Certain points, apparent from reports in previous years, surfaced again in the interview. Suetsugu indirectly labeled the navy as being the more important of the two branches of the armed service.[4] Thus the IJN recruited their enlisted personnel mainly from the peasant population; the city population was not considered good enough. Suetsugu was also of the opinion that it was practically impossible for foreigners to understand Japan. The phraseology of the Japanese language often did not lend itself to translation, and the Japanese national consciousness was "totally different from that which could be encountered in Europe and America." In addition, it had developed over centuries in a "specific Japanese way." That is why "Europe and America cannot understand us."[5] This meant nothing other than that Germany did not form an exception in this matter.

Racist overtones were also noticeable in Suetsugu's comments. He observed that the Japanese were a "very pure race" because of their island location and from this had synthesized a rationale for a belief in "superiority" and a "privileged position."[6]

Asked for his opinion about German submarine warfare during World War I, he explained that it had failed because of a lack of will on the part of the German government. Submarine warfare could only be successful through full concentration on either the enemy merchant or military fleet. (The spirit of the German fleet, he averred, had been magnificent.) Finally, he especially emphasized that he viewed the submarine as the strongest and most useful attack weapon in modern maritime warfare.[7] Technological advances in the area of antisubmarine warfare he called an incentive to "overcome all difficulties through the harnessing of moral powers."[8]

Suetsugu's opinions about the outcome of the upcoming fleet conference were concisely presented the following month in his conversation with a Japanese journalist, whose translation Wenneker sent to Berlin.[9] The Japanese admiral viewed it as a certainty that the United States would not accept the Japanese demands. In that case there would be no treaty at all and that would be a good thing.[10] At the same time he stated that Japan could not initiate an "overwhelming" construction program.

THE LETTERS OF ADMIRAL YAMAMOTO

In the meantime the preliminary discussions on the fleet conference that was supposed to extend the treaties reached in Washington in 1922 and London in 1930 were concluded in London. Here the Japanese naval delegate, Vice Adm. Yamamoto Isoroku, had represented the Japanese standpoint on common tonnage limits, and this proposal had not been accepted by his British and American colleagues, so that the talks had ended without result. Yamamoto's letters shed light on the course that the Japanese navy now planned to sail and on the role that Germany played as a historic example.

In correspondence that he wrote during the conference, he observed that the time had come for the Japanese Empire, in view of its increasing power since the Washington treaties, to dedicate itself "with all circumspection" to "the creation of its own good fortune." The example set by Germany—"had it only waited just five or ten years" it would now have stood in Europe without rivals—told one that the next task was to "build our strength quietly and with circumspection." Even though the current conference would probably not be successful, he was under the impression that "the day was not far on which we will cause Great Britain and the United States to bow before us." For the navy "the most important task is to achieve rapid progress in the area of aviation."[11]

On his way back from London, Yamamoto visited Berlin, where he met with Ribbentrop and Raeder. Though there are no documents about the content of the talks, the visit fits into the picture of the increasingly friendly attitude of the IJN toward the German side, even if the actual idea in this case came from Ribbentrop.[12]

The proposed (by Ribbentrop) meeting of Yamamoto with Hitler was prevented by the Japanese ambassadors in London and Berlin and very probably was also not accepted by Yamamoto. It had depended on the assignment of the "middleman," Dr. Hack. Ribbentrop had ordered Hack "in a very careful way to inquire if there was enthusiasm in Japan for a German-Japanese-Polish alliance against Russia." The Japanese diplomats viewed the help of a representative of the "rival" navy as an unwelcome intrusion in their sphere of influence; to a Japanese naval officer, though, an offer of alliance against Russia looked like the passionately fought politics of their rival, the army.[13]

WENNEKER'S OBSERVATIONS

Wenneker reported a little later from Tokyo that the Imperial Japanese Navy had succeeded, through its propaganda activity and its firm stance in refusing the proportion regulation, to regain considerable prestige in the eyes of the public. Thus the domestic political effects of the London preliminary discussions earned for the IJN what it had once lost by the Shanghai incident of 1932 (provoked by the actions of their army in Manchuria).

Through the announcement of the German rearmament in early 1935, the hope of a stronger commitment in Europe with respect to England was enhanced. At that time there were still reservations about England, but

Wenneker made it clear that, despite all the veiled statements, the goal of the Japanese fleet construction was the creation of a hegemony in the Far East. The way to accomplish that was confirmed through the happenings in Manchuria and recently through the proclamation of German rearmament.[14] About the attitude of the Japanese navy with regard to German rearmament, Wenneker added that it was greeted there with "nearly unbridled joy." Numerous officers had personally conveyed their best wishes to him.[15]

THE GERMAN-BRITISH FLEET TREATY

Expectations in Japanese naval circles that were tied to a German fleet buildup were revealed in Wenneker's report about the German-British Fleet Treaty. The Japanese had already been confidentially informed before the beginning of the negotiations by contacts within the German navy[16] and described the German demands as moderate and legitimate.[17] The German fleet buildup found a positive echo in the Japanese press and an even better reception in the navy.[18] One reason Wenneker gave for this was that "the World War did not lessen but rather strengthened sympathy and admiration, . . . understanding of the unjustness of the Versailles treaty and understanding for the German position," which was similar in its difficulties to that of the Japanese. The essential point was, however, the IJN's hope that the strength of the Kriegsmarine would grow to such an extent in the near future that it could bind large parts of the Royal Navy and thereby limit its deployment in the Far East.[19] The Japanese hoped that the German side, like the Yamamoto delegation in London, would present itself as unyielding.

When it was revealed that the Germans were prepared to meet British wishes at least halfway and to limit themselves to 35 percent of the British tonnage, the Japanese side was disappointed. They repeatedly warned Wenneker that the treaty "means almost as much as an alliance, at least, however, a cooperation in close contact for the future."[20] The Kaigunshō, since April, and even during the German-British negotiations in London, had repeatedly signaled that it was inclined to support a German participation in the upcoming fleet conference. It had hoped for the support of the Germans for the Japanese position. Now, however, the IJN let it be known that by such participation "the solid front of powers that recognize the proportion principle would just be enlarged." This was not what Japan wanted. Wenneker reported that there was no doubt in his mind that the change in the attitude of the IJN was based on their annoyance with the conclusions of the German-British Fleet Treaty.[21]

An indication that the relationship between the Kriegsmarine and the Royal Navy had temporarily actually gotten closer was the fact that the English naval attaché, Captain Vivian, allowed Wenneker to view an exhaustive report to the Admiralty about the capabilities of the Japanese navy during the London negotiations. The timely meeting could hardly have been a coincidence. Wenneker was able to photograph the report and send it under strict secrecy to Berlin. Vivian had explained that the report represented the fruits of the labor of the British attachés since the World War I.[22] Wenneker remarked that the report essentially showed "how little even the English, who had worked together with the Japanese navy for decades, basically knew of the Japanese."

Vivian did not exhibit a particularly flattering impression of the IJN.[23] In most points Wenneker agreed with him. He excepted, however, the capabilities of the officers from Vivian's harsh criticism. His expressed confidence in his judgment on this point, based on his much closer association with the IJN, showed what kind of privileged position he actually enjoyed.[24]

THE KEELUNG INCIDENT

Both Wenneker's special position, as well as the mistrust of the Japanese toward the relationship of Germany with Great Britain, became clear especially during the Keelung Incident.[25] In the middle of November the naval attachés in Tokyo had invited a few senior Japanese officers for tea, among them the minister of the navy, his deputy, and the deputy head of the Gunreibu. The British attaché and his assistant had canceled their participation a few days before because of reports of mistreatment of British crewmen by Japanese police at Keelung, in Taiwan. Thereupon the chief secretary of the navy minister, Captain Tayui, asked Wenneker to see him and made it known that the Japanese considered this an affront. He asked Wenneker to remind the English attaché in an appropriate manner "of his duties" as co-host. Tayui acknowledged that this was actually the concern of the Soviet attaché, who was the doyen of the attaché corps but was considered to be totally "uneducated."

Subsequently Tayui presented the Keelung incident again in a way that was very unfavorable to the Royal Navy and ended his remarks with the statement that he was doing this so that Wenneker would be informed about how things stood with the English navy, with which the Kriegsmarine was connected through the Fleet Treaty and "otherwise also maintained a relationship." Tayui did not pursue the subject, but Wenneker assumed, from other conversations, that he was alluding to recent statements in the press about mutual promises of friendship between the German and British navies.[26]

Wenneker gave little credence to the depiction of the Keelung incident by Tayui and the Japanese police and commented: "Naturally a rapprochement (of the German and English navies) does not fall into line with the Japanese naval policy . . . [the IJN] in the future had hoped for a binding of the British fleet through the Germans."[27]

When the Japanese delegation under the leadership of Admiral Nagano and Ambassador Nagai departed for the London Fleet Conference in the middle of November 1935, the Japanese position had not changed from the one held in the preliminary conference. Wenneker quoted Nagano as saying that there was "no shaking" of the Japanese demand to revoke the proportion principle, and he did not believe that the conference would produce a result under these conditions. At the same time the Anglo-Saxon naval attachés had clearly signaled Wenneker that their governments would never accept the Japanese demands. The German rearmament was commented on in the Japanese press in such a way that it complicated the conference. The general tone, however, was positive.[28]

THE JAPANESE BUILDING PLANS

Earlier the Marineleitung (the German Navy High Command) had received a petition from the Japanese for talks with Ribbentrop and Raeder. It was unusual that this petition made its way via the Japanese military attaché in Berlin, General Ōshima, to the head of the Abwehr, Admiral Canaris, and from there had been passed on to the Marineleitung. Army and navy usually acted strictly separately. They asked for a secret "working dinner" and let it be known that the visit should primarily document "how well one understood the good intentions of Ambassador Ribbentrop during the visit of Admiral Yamamoto."[29] So the visit did not concern the Kriegsmarine (which in any case was quite knowledgeable about the Japanese position at the conference from Wenneker's reports) as much as it concerned Ribbentrop, whose expectations had not been completely met by Yamamoto's sojourn in Germany.[30]

The failure of the Fleet Conference in January 1936 was no surprise for the Kriegsmarine. Interest now focused on what the Japanese planned to do after the treaty expired at the end of 1936. Wenneker indicated that the failure of the conference was registered quietly and with sighs of relief in the Japanese public, but with joy and enthusiasm in the IJN. Senior naval officers had exclaimed that the world would probably silently accept "a new orientation of Japanese policy in East Asia based upon fleet equality," just as it had learned to live with "the withdrawal of Japan from the League of Nations, the Manchuria Incident, the cancellation of the Washington Treaty, and the new advance in China."[31] Although a "hardening of America's attitude" was expected, this was not, however, ascribed any special meaning, since one presumed that the American construction program could not catch up, even in several years' time.

While the commerce and foreign ministries accepted a worsening of the relationship with England only reluctantly, the "English danger" was less important for the navy.[32] Rather it saw a gain in its prestige, the achieved complete freedom in construction, the possibility of the expansion of bases in the Pacific, and, with that, increased chances of achieving long-term goals, namely, an expansion in the direction of the "southernly lying resources" as the decisive, essential gains.

In pursuit of their goals Wenneker expected the Japanese to increase construction activity, especially for cruisers and submarines with a large range. Both types were especially important for economic warfare, which Wenneker falsely assumed would "give the war at sea in the Pacific . . . its characteristic features."[33] He also reported on Japanese plans to build capital ships of fifty to sixty thousand tons. The question of whether or not Japan's industry was even capable of such an extensive construction program, he answered in the affirmative.[34] New extensive naval armament had to strain the resources of the country, however, and Wenneker predicted a heightened rivalry between the navy and the army. In any case "tensions between the army and the navy had a well-founded tradition in Japan." He was sure that the increase of fleet tonnage depended on "foreign political strategy questions," in which the navy's influence was seen as a further result of the outcome of the conference.[35]

Parts of Wenneker's reports about the expected new Japanese construction program seemed to have leaked to the public, because at the beginning of February a Japanese press agency reported from London that Japan was planning a "secret navy" with "mighty ships." The agency drew upon reports of a correspondent of the *Daily Press* who in turn drew upon reports of a "naval attaché at the embassy of a certain European country that had not taken part in the conference." Wenneker was thereupon humorously notified by the liaison officer of the Kaigunshō that only he could be meant by this. The officer soothingly added, however, that they did not believe Wenneker capable of such things and, moreover, believed the message had been dreamed up in London.[36] However, from then on the Japanese cloaked themselves in secrecy about their construction plans, even toward Wenneker.

That meanwhile the Japanese navy actually intended to build ships with a tonnage of fifty thousand tons or more was soon verified. This was confirmed by Wenneker not just indirectly from conversations that he had with Japanese officers and other naval attachés in Tokyo, but also from information that he received from German corporate representatives in Japan. In this way he came to know that the IJN had ordered the largest forge press available in Germany at the beginning of 1936. The negotiations for further specialty tools for work on very large projects was still continuing. The businessman who passed on this information remarked that the Japanese obviously wanted to build especially large ships. He was also asked if he knew anything about the size of ships other powers intended to build.[37]

Even though Wenneker had a privileged position in comparison to the other naval attachés, the Japanese kept their building plans carefully concealed even from him. Only the consultations over the 1937–38 budget gave rise to new clues: it was approximately ninety million yen higher than previously, and the IJN had set up a five-year plan requiring a one-billion-yen minimum.[38]

JAPANESE NAVY VS. ARMY

Because of this favored treatment, in comparison to other attachés, Wenneker was viewed by American and British attachés as a potential source of knowledge about Japanese plans. Especially his British colleague, Captain Rawlings, explained to him quite directly that it was his mission to "ferret out the Japanese secret no matter what the cost." He used every chance he had to make contact with Wenneker and consequently made certain concessions, as his predecessor had done during the negotiations for the German-British Fleet Treaty in the summer of 1935. The concessions consisted of "lending" the plans for the Japanese naval stations Kure and Yokosuka, so that Wenneker could photograph them.[39] Rawlings, however, did not receive any information in return.

To Berlin Wenneker reported in October 1936 that for some time now the Japanese had viewed Great Britain and not the United States as the main enemy. He also confirmed the navy's aversion to a military engagement in China. Numerous naval officers had explained to him that they rejected the continental politics of the army after their own bad experiences in the Shanghai incident of 1932 and in view of the high potential costs. His confidants had, moreover, indirectly pointed out the totally differing goals of the navy: "Our goals lie in a totally different direction, and they are pointed to the areas that are of true benefit to Japan."[40]

In yet another aspect did the Japanese navy differ from the army. Mainly during the pre-fleet negotiations, Navy Minister Ōsumi had stated that the strong inner tensions present in the army that had figured in assassination attempts within this service did not appear in the navy with the same severity. He had accomplished this by transferring most of the high-ranking members of the Treaty Faction to the reserves.[41] The few that were left were removed from active service by his successor, Nagano.[42] At the end of 1936 the highest posts in the IJN were held by men who had either personally made sure of the end of the treaty limitations at the London negotiating tables or, as members of the emperor's family, had kept themselves apart from "political" issues, yet still stood close to the Fleet Faction.[43]

THE FEBRUARY 26 INCIDENT

Its greater inner unity made it possible for the IJN to use the coup of the younger officers from February 1936 to its advantage. As opposed to earlier incidents of this nature no naval officers were involved.

Led by company and platoon leaders, troops of the 1st and Guard Divisions occupied central installations in Tokyo on the morning of 26 February 1936. Among the leading personalities targeted for assassination in the coup were three admirals, Prime Minister Okada Keisuke, the Lord Privy Seal and former prime minister Saito Makoto, and the Lord Chamberlain of the Tennō, Suzuki Kantarō.[44]

In Wenneker's report about the events in February, his perceptions of the internal and foreign political situation and the intentions of the Japanese navy are revealed as in a looking-glass, which is why we shall look at it here in detail.[45]

Wenneker reported that the reaction of the navy to the coup was that it had immediately and unmistakably stood against it. Heavy naval forces were deployed at Tokyo and Osaka, the Kaigunshō was immediately protected by several hundred marines, and landing forces with armored cars and artillery in Tokyo, and 250 airplanes on the naval airfield in Yokosuka were placed in combat readiness. Ruthless suppression of the revolt and the release of the corpse of the supposedly murdered Admiral Okada (whose brother-in-law was in fact the murdered man) were immediately demanded from the army.[46] The naval negotiators made it clear that naval troops would otherwise use force of arms.[47] Wenneker was of the opinion that the navy, if need be, would not have hesitated to take "even more drastic steps," after a senior naval officer had explained to him that the navy "was aware of its great responsibility" and was prepared "to justify the trust that was placed in it," and with all determination, "to take appropriate actions." For this one would "not have recoiled from acts of violence" and was prepared "for the most extreme case."[48]

Two aspects were the main reasons for the immediate and decisive reaction of the navy: on the one hand, high-ranking former flag officers had been targets for assassination; on the other hand—and this was the deciding factor—the navy would have had to place itself under the army if the coup had been successful. Since the Manchurian Incident the army had continually expanded its influence on foreign and internal political issues, and after a successful coup "the navy would have been politically, but also from a budget standpoint, reduced to second place."

The officers who associated with Wenneker explained that the IJN was completely in agreement over the handling of the revolt, since a terrorization or takeover of power would also have meant a takeover of the navy. Never would they have allowed such a thing.[49]

However, Wenneker knew that despite the apparent outer clarity, "the inner attitude of the officer corps" was "considerably more complicated." He referred to the participation of younger naval officers in earlier attempted assassinations and pointed out that their motives had earned sympathy, even among the naval leadership. As examples of sympathetic flag officers he named Katō Kanji,[50] Suetsugu, Nomura Naokuni, Kobayashi, and Mazaki. Nomura had even literally explained in a conversation with Wenneker shortly after the revolt:

> The army officer who comes into closest contact with the peasant class, the backbone of the nation, has noticed more and more clearly the dangers that arise out of its destruction for the benefit of industrial development and capital. From the leading posts of the army decisive action was not to be expected because of their connections with capital. Parts of the younger officer corps took matters into their own hands. There was simply no other way left. . . . We

should be thankful to the officers for their sacrifices. No harm was done to the nation due to their actions, as serious as these are to be taken; quite the opposite, the prelude to the necessary reforms is started.[51]

The remarkable thing about Nomura's observations is that he paid practically no attention to the assassination attempts upon certain people and even upon members of his own branch of the service. As a result, Wenneker considered his views too extreme and assumed that they were shared "to the same extent" by only a few senior naval officers. He held a statement of the adjutant of the navy minister to be representative of the majority view, when he declared that the path the younger officers had taken was "totally wrong." But the navy "knew how to appreciate" their motives. Moreover, the adjutant continued, the navy drew its "best forces" from the peasant class, whose "destruction" would have "catastrophic consequences."[52]

In any case, the gain in prestige was clear. The IJN now expected a higher potential influence for itself, as the adjutant explained. The continental policies of the army had, until then, been carried out exclusively, to the detriment of the navy. Without the navy the other greater powers would have intervened long ago.[53]

Wenneker judged this more cautiously and saw the that the navy had achieved "at least a temporary gain" in influence. After all, it now found itself in an advantageous position. The new Navy Minister Nagano energetically exploited this, bringing about personnel and organizational changes in the navy and raising a number of internal and foreign policy demands.

The internal measures consisted, first, of discharging the last proponents of the treaty and also a few notably radical flag officers, who all too clearly seemed to sympathize with those who had led the putsch.[54] Second, besides expanding the training department, Nagano investigated the organization of the Naval Aviation Department and restored the predominance of the Navy Ministry over the Navy General Staff.[55] That additional funds were demanded for the coming year (fifty million yen, specially earmarked for the replacement of the big ships and naval aviation) was almost self-evident.

Beyond that, a fact-finding committee under Deputy Navy Minister Hasegawa was created to concern itself especially with a reform program, besides certain naval organizational duties. The reforms included such central points as the elimination of fragmentation in the formulation of foreign policy, the "strengthening of the national spirit," the "purification of political life," the reorganization of the tax system, control of the national resources, and much more.[56] With this the navy's claims to far-reaching influence in important political areas were substantiated.

Wenneker interpreted these developments as very comprehensive and as by far overstepping the realms of the navy. However, he took this as an indication that the navy was willing to respond to "only [mainstream opinion]" and was not truly prepared to seriously cooperate on reforms. The most important indication of this, he thought, was that a demand for agrarian reform was completely missing—despite the fact that this was, "the most important program point of any reform in Japan." Thus it would be revealed that the navy, even though it recruited over 90 percent of its enlisted personnel from rural areas, had stronger ties to industry and industry's capital resources. The navy was dependent on industry and therefore interested in its strength. Since the "best forces" volunteered for the navy, it did not have recruitment problems and was therefore not as close to the plight of the rural population as the army.

Much more important to the IJN than domestic political reform, obviously, was a commitment of foreign policy orientation toward its favored goal of a "southern advance." About this time the navy's slogan for this policy appeared increasingly in the press: "Defense in the North and expansion in the South." Only an expansion in this direction under the protection of the fleet could solve both of Japan's most pressing problems: lack of resources and overpopulation.[57]

With these kinds of publications it was always pointed out that this expansion was to take place peaceably. Wenneker, however, pointed out in all clarity: "It is, however, self-evident that this assertion . . . does *not* correspond to the true attitude of the navy. What the navy would like is the exploitation of the areas in question with Japan as master of these areas and not under the sovereignty of a foreign power. Such a *forceful* expansion is to be expected with certainty as soon as England is seriously bound by a conflict in Europe in which it is itself actively engaged" [emphasis in original].[58]

This raised the notion of a diversionary, strategic confining of the Royal Navy by the Kriegsmarine, to which Wenneker, considering the decision of the IJN for a forceful thrust to the South, even attributed decisive meaning.

In September Wenneker took inventory of the navy's demands and remarked that the points debated by Hasegawa's fact-finding reform committee were still only on paper.[59] Obviously it was not really interested in such matters. Meanwhile the navy had achieved considerable success in the much more important area of ship construction policies. Japanese shipyards were currently producing to the limit of their capacities. The outlook was good for the naval budget of the coming year, the first not under a treaty, to consist of 770 million yen. That was 85 million more than the current budget and even 35 million more than the increase that the navy had demanded in March!

Wenneker went on to report that the IJN's earlier announced intensification of the southern thrust policies had not materialized. The main reason for this, according to Wenneker, was the lack of expansion of "the war engagements in Europe [that were] with certainty expected."[60] The navy did manage, however, to considerably lessen the continental policies of the army. Notable also was the friendly farewell that had been extended to the U.S. naval attaché, Captain Rogers. The British Captain Vivian, who had taken his leave three months earlier, had not been treated in such a friendly way, and Wenneker saw in this the efforts of the Japanese to create a positive relationship with the U.S. Navy.

The IJN had cleverly understood how to use the revolt of the young army officers to its own advantage, even though the motivation of these officers was not foreign to many naval personnel. Even high-ranking naval officers sympathized with them. Navy Minister Nagano had immediately taken a hard stance, almost to the limit of a civil war, to the coup and so had gained the advantage over the army in being able to present the IJN, after the collapse of the revolt, as loyal to the state and showing unity within the ranks. To the outside the IJN raised claims to far-reaching influence on important areas of policy. Internally Nagano reduced conflict by retiring the proponents of those sympathizing with the radical wing, as well as the conservative treaty faction, and reestablished the predominance of the Navy Ministry (Kaigunshō) versus the Navy General Staff (Gunreibu). While the IJN soon quietly dispensed with the practice of claiming to influence general political questions, it stayed hard on truly important aspects: cementing its foreign political goal to give preference to southern expansion (versus the continental plans of the army) and increasing its budget.

Wenneker emphasized in his reports the internal political aspect of the navy's greater closeness to economic circles and to industry, compared to the army, and the foreign policy aspect of an increasingly deepening antagonism of the Japanese navy versus Great Britain. He maintained that this could most probably peak in a forceful thrust to the south, resulting in a confrontation of the Japanese navy with the Royal Navy if and when the British were confined by a diversionary strategy in Europe. This had to be of direct interest to the Kriegsmarine.

10

Drawing Closer

Above and beyond the contacts already mentioned, there had been other visits, mainly initiated by the Japanese navy, and they increased in 1936.

The first visitor was, however, a German, Senior Lieutenant (Ret.) Hashagen, whose visit to Japan in the summer of 1934 was arranged by Wenneker and who stayed there for several months.[1] He had been a very successful submarine commander in World War I and informed the Japanese navy about German experiences with submarine warfare. The Japanese regarded his comments highly and in gratitude invited Hashagen to a dinner given by Deputy Navy Minister Hasegawa, during which the Japanese presented Hashagen with a Japanese sword.[2]

In the middle of May 1935 an eighteen-man mission under Captain Matsunaga arrived in Germany from London. The Japanese were on an extended study tour through America and Europe and stayed in Germany until the end of the month. They visited naval installations in Wilhelmshaven, Kiel, and the Naval School in Mürwik and then continued to Paris.[3]

Shortly after the departure of that mission, Wenneker reported that he had heard through the press that a Japanese engineering officer had received a command to Germany.[4] Notably, the officer had not been announced. Only when Wenneker inquired did the Navy Ministry give him the less than precise information that the Japanese officer (Lieutenant Commander Okuda) was going to Germany for language studies and "studies of general military affairs." The fact that a specialist was being sent did not, however, speak for the validity of this information.

At the beginning of 1936 there appeared in Tokyo an unofficial, but in Japanese government circles well-known, visitor: the businessman Dr. Hack. Besides his negotiations regarding a German-Japanese film, during his visit he also led negotiations for the delivery of aircraft and aircraft parts with both of the Japanese service branches. Hack did not plan visits with just the heads of the army and navy; he also met with members of the Foreign Ministry, the imperial court (including an audience with the Tennō), and leading industrialists of the country.[5]

The Japanese handling of the deployment of two submarine specialists, who left Japan in the middle of January 1935 for Germany, was different from the case of Lieutenant Commander Okuda. This time they were announced by name to Wenneker, and he was informed that they were to travel Europe after Germany for "the sake of studies." The length of their stay was not specified.[6]

The notification of deployments to Germany remained the exception, however. As happened in the summer of 1936 almost monthly, Wenneker nearly always had to receive the information from Japanese billeting posts.[7]

Only Capt. Wada Misao, who together with a coworker left Japan in September for a three-month stay in Germany, visited Wenneker beforehand and explained the purpose of the trip to him. Wada's mission during the three-month stay in Germany was to study at different firms the possibilities of lowering the costs of aircraft production.[8] Wada had labored hard to ensure the visit of the German aircraft carrier commission, and Wenneker recommended that his wishes be fulfilled, within the realm of possibility, according to the demands of reciprocation.

In February 1936 Commander Kojima, the current secretary of the navy minister, was appointed the new naval attaché in Berlin as replacement for the departing Yokoi.[9] Apparently the Kriegsmarine had not been very happy with Yokoi, because Wenneker mentioned that Kojima was "undoubtedly, considerably superior." But even with Kojima Wenneker, at least, did not seem truly content. Although he spoke English and German well, the working relationship with him "had not always been easy." Even though he obviously endeavored to show great cooperation, he was often overly afraid, even with minor matters, to reveal anything considered secret. He was especially guarded on military political areas, and Wenneker reported candidly: "Here I actually never managed to hold a halfway open conversation with him."[10] Wenneker remarked very appreciatively about the former attaché Endō, with whom he remained in contact and who, just like Wenneker himself, had preferred the appointment of the only other officer prepared for Germany, Commander Takada.[11]

After the training cruiser trips of 1934–35 had suffered from budget constraints and Japan had not been visited in those years by German warships, the Marineleitung decided to allow one of the two cruisers that were to sail into foreign waters between the autumn of 1935 and the summer of 1936 to head for Japanese harbors.[12] The *Karlsruhe* was selected to visit Nagasaki and Yokohama from 27 February to 12 March.[13] Because of the coup on 26 February, the visit could not take place as planned.

Anticipating the arrival of the ship, Wenneker had gone to Nagasaki, where he registered "the greatest cooperation" on the part of all those Japanese involved with the preparations for the visit.[14] Originally Wenneker had wanted to go on board the *Karlsruhe* together with the German ambassador and the consul general in Kobe, for the voyage to Yokohoma. This, however, did not occur, since news of the coup arrived from Tokyo. Wenneker and the ambassador immediately returned there via train. From his private residence the attaché phoned the Navy Ministry, which instructed him to redirect the cruiser to Kobe.

Wenneker understood this but thought it a pity, because the German colony in Tokyo had made such extensive preparations and had looked forward to the arrival of the ship with high hopes. Especially in view of the Japanese public and of the "leading representatives of headquarters, whose views of the new Germany were not quite right," he judged that contact with the crew of the cruiser would have been "extraordinarily fruitful." To this end a great banquet had been planned, with representatives of the naval and foreign ministries, as well as a reception at the embassy with invitations for the entire diplomatic corps and a parade of the crew through the main streets of Tokyo to the emperor's palace. These and further arrangements made in conjunction with the IJN had to be canceled because of the repercussions of the coup. The navy minister nevertheless insisted on honoring the captain and the executive officer of the *Karlsruhe* by awarding them medals.[15]

A meeting held during the visit of the ship's leadership in Tokyo with representatives of the IJN had to take place in the naval officers' casino, which lay outside of the government district, since the government district was still vigilantly guarded even a month after the collapse of the coup. Wenneker reported that the reception by the representatives of the IJN in Kobe and Osaka, which was also visited by a detachment from the ship, was especially hearty, supposedly to make up for the change in the original plans. The visit of the ship had left a "strong impression" on all posts, and he recommended that at least twelve days be reserved just for Tokyo during the next visit.

In the summer Wenneker reported that, on the occasion of the coronation of the English King Edward VI, two Japanese ships under Nomura Naokumi were to be deployed to Europe and that they would also visit Germany.[16] With this the very first visit of Japanese warships in Germany was proclaimed.

The personnel traffic mentioned showed that the main areas of interest of the Japanese navy continued to lie in the technical areas and especially with submarines and airplanes. The deployment of specialists to Germany for the purpose of study still went unreported to the Kriegsmarine to some degree, indicating that they were still trying to acquire armaments technology of interest to them by avoiding the Kriegsmarine.

The planning for the visit of the *Karlsruhe* shows that the heartiness of the reception was intensifying, compared to earlier visits of German warships to Japan. The parade planned to proceed through the main streets of Tokyo to the Imperial Palace was an especially demonstrative element. With the announcement of the first visit of a Japanese warship, it became evident that there existed the desire on the part of the Japanese to strengthen the relationship.

TRADING INTELLIGENCE

An initial trade of intelligence between the navies began in 1935 when the German naval attaché in Moscow was given access to intelligence on Soviet submarines in the Far East by his Japanese counterpart. Since the sketches made available were not particularly good, Wenneker was asked by the Marineleitung to determine if they had better material in Tokyo, against which the Kriegsmarine could check its own documents.[17] When he inquired at the Kaigunshō about this matter, the Japanese proposed to exchange their current state of knowledge and also exchange all future intelligence about the Soviet navy.[18] A decision regarding this Japanese suggestion has not been retained in the files. There are, however, clues that this happened in September 1936 at the latest.[19]

About the negotiations that led to the conclusion of the Anti-Comintern Treaty in November, neither navy was informed in detail, nor did either have any notable interest in it.[20] Wenneker himself had only heard of it eight days before the signing and reported that he was not congratulated about it, nor was it even mentioned to him by any of the Japanese naval officers. If he mentioned the topic, he was met with skepticism. He thought that this was only natural, because the IJN had not taken part in the negotiations, which had been led by its great rivals, the army and the Foreign Ministry. The IJN had assented to the treaty only after getting a guarantee from the army that a state of war with the Soviet Union was not being considered. A senior naval officer made this remark to Wenneker about a war with the Soviet Union: "A war with Russia would be the ruin of Japan, no matter how the war ended." Wenneker suspected that the IJN had also agreed, because they hoped for a clouding of German-English relations.[21]

THE LIMITS OF COOPERATION

Looking back on the period from 1934 to 1936, it is clear that the actual foreign policy goal of the Japanese navy was the creation of a hegemony in East Asia. Especially the areas of Southeast Asia that were rich in raw materials were to be included, as was clearly recognized by Wenneker in March 1936. He immediately reported to Berlin that this goal, in case of a doubtful outcome, would also be pursued with force. The tool for this was, however, a fleet that had to be superior to the Anglo-Saxon naval forces in this region. Consequently, the intermediate goal was the abolishment of treaty restrictions. In the long run they would require an increase of high-quality armaments technology in order to take on any potential enemies with the fleet, which was to be newly strengthened when the treaty ended.

Japanese industry had not fully caught up with the technological lead of the Western industrialized nations, and Germany, whose technology had been urgently recommended to the Japanese navy by Katō Kanji shortly after World War I, took on a highly important role as the only possible supplier after the IJN's decision to break out of the Washington Treaty system.[22] This decision was forced through internally, as Wenneker observed when the main proponents of the Treaty Faction were discharged at the end of 1934 and its last survivors in March 1936.

In view of the expected confrontation with the Anglo-Saxon sea powers and the ready acceptance of possible hostilities with England at the latest around the turn of the year 1934–35, the IJN must have judged very positively that the proclamation of German military sovereignty, which included a massive rearmament of the Kriegsmarine, made possible the confinement of the Royal Navy to Europe. Accordingly, however, there was very noticeable disappointment about the seeming agreement of the Kriegsmarine and the Royal Navy through the German-British Fleet Treaty only a quarter of a year later. However, the treaty's effect on Japan was negligible because the Kriegsmarine still had scant strength. Moreover, the treaty did not alter the decisive, important role of the Germans as a source of armaments technology, especially in the areas of aviation, submarines, fire-control systems, diesel engines, and specialty tools for ship construction.

The most important aspect for the IJN was to defend its foreign policy program against an internal political opponent that considerably outweighed the danger posed by the Western navies: the Japanese army. The IJN saw itself as the more important branch of service, since only it could keep an enemy from the shores of the Island Empire and create the prerequisites for the autarchy of the nation through a thrust to the south.[23] This meant securing the necessary means for its fleet construction program against the demands of the competitor and preventing the fixation of the official policy on the continental goals of the army, as well as preventing its constant dominance in national policy. As Wenneker's reporting revealed, the IJN was, in light of the February coup of the young officers, even prepared to use force for this purpose, even though the goals of the revolutionaries also found sympathy in the navy. The chance to better one's own inner political position versus the competition was used without hesitation.

The situation of the Kriegsmarine was, in comparison to the IJN, more advantageous in foreign policy terms, because it had achieved the intermediate goal,[24] striven for since the end of World War I, of a revision of the Versailles treaty and done this without incurring the threat of a confrontation with one of the great sea powers in the near future. Domestically, the Kriegsmarine had no hope of even approximating the influence of the army and the foreign office (*Auswärtiges Amt*). It did profit, however, by the interest of Hitler and Ribbentrop in the creation of a good position relative to England and to Japan, through which it gained a limited autonomy. Through the fleet treaty with England and the rapprochement of the Japanese navy, it came out of its isolation, lamented in 1932 by Raeder.

The IJN did not possess, however, the importance for the Kriegsmarine in the mid-thirties that the Kriegsmarine, Japan's presumed key to modern armament technology, held for the Japanese. The Japanese navy was the third strongest in the world, but the question of an alliance had not (yet) posed itself to the Kriegsmarine, which anyway was too weak and therefore uninteresting as an ally at this point in time.

Beyond that, however, there were similarities in opinions about both the national and foreign political orders in the officers' corps of both, though difficult to judge in concrete ramifications.[25] There were only limited concrete points of interaction that were of interest to the Kriegsmarine. The most important point was Japanese experience in the field of aircraft carriers, classified as most important by the Germans from 1934 onwards, and of which the German side had absolutely no experience of its own. The situation described above showed that exactly this was recognized by the Japanese and used by them as an introduction for technical trade, the initiative for which, having come from the IJN, is explained by its isolation.

This isolation also explains why the Japanese, to the astonishment of their German partners, fulfilled more than just the accepted conditions during the visit of the German aircraft carrier commission.[26] It is interesting to note that the Japanese took on the role of the stronger partner who gave developmental aid. After decades of learning from foreigners, they had now achieved a level of development in the field of aircraft carriers, then as now a high-tech field, that was superior to that of various Western industrialized nations.

The fact that they were able to teach one of their earlier teachers was proof of their advanced level and had to have, especially in view of the rule of proportion as set by the Washington and London fleet treaties—which were viewed as discriminatory—a special psychological meaning for the Japanese naval officers.[27]

A comprehensive, trusting relationship was, however, not created, as there was quite an extensive Japanese network of spies in Germany and only limited willingness on the part of the Japanese to report on the officers who were deployed to Germany for "study purposes." The areas of specialty of those experts (aviation and submarine engineers) demonstrated the main points of the newly created cooperation, just as persistent Japanese silence in other areas (tactics, armament plans after the expiration of the treaties) marked their boundaries.[28] Here also, Wenneker's reception, preferential in relation to other foreign attachés, found its limits. Nor did both sides' attempts to "adjust" the negotiated terms, shortly before the arrival of the German commission, necessarily point to a pre-existing, trusting relationship.

Also interesting is the Germans' reluctance to accept, in February 1935, the IJN's offer to permit German specialists to inspect a Japanese aircraft carrier, which came by way of the German Air Ministry (RLM). In order to accept, the Kriegsmarine required an additional, direct invitation in the summer. This rather hesitant attitude, especially as displayed by the head of the Construction Bureau, seems quite astonishing.[29]

On the German side the limits of cooperation were marked by veiled orders for the completion of the reciprocal services (inspection of the *Scheer*) and the half-hearted way in which the Japanese were instructed in confidential details, like the production of armoring. At the same time the delays also showed a fragmentation of the decision-making processes, which on the German side were divided between the OKM, the RLM, and industry.[30] A similar fragmentation was noticeable on the Japanese side between the Navy Ministry, the Naval General Staff, and the Fleet, which led to complications for Wenneker's inspections, for which he had to bring considerable pressure to bear.

Finally, there appear in the above-mentioned reports also isolated, racially colored elements that could never quite be excluded during contacts, as in the specifically mentioned "white" consciousness, which the U.S. attaché in Berlin reported as coming from some of his German conversational partners, or in the comments of Suetsugu or Maeda when there was occasional talk of the practical inability of foreigners, including the Germans, to understand Japan. In view of the friendly-to-very-friendly contacts among naval personnel of both sides since the 1920s, such viewpoints seemed, however, to basically make no difference.

In the spring of 1937 the relationship between the two navies was rather ambiguous. Considerable effort in protocol for demonstrations of friendship stood opposed to noticeable reservation as soon as either side was asked to cooperate on concrete questions. German officers and cadets were offered a tour of the Japanese battleship *Yamashiro* during the visit of the training cruiser *Emden* at the beginning of the year. Wenneker complained, however, that only a sporting event aboard was shown and the visitors were only led across the deck; any possibility of an inspection of military or technically interesting aspects was avoided.

Wenneker responded firmly to this event. For a visit planned for the end of May of the Japanese cruiser *Ashigara* in Kiel, he urgently recommended that the expected Japanese requests of access to German ships and docks be limited to the same measure of cooperation that the Japanese had shown, that is, only allowing superficial impressions. He also pointed out that the "surprisingly numerous staff" of the *Ashigara* probably stood in "some kind of relation" to the Japanese inspection wishes.[31]

The actual purpose of the voyage of the cruiser, as Wenneker heard it, was to represent the Japanese Empire at the coronation ceremonies for the English King.[32] Wenneker, shortly before leaving the ship, invited Rear Adm. Kobayashi Sonosuke, who was to board the *Ashigara* for the journey, and his staff, as well as the CO and executive officer, to a tea house. In the ensuing conversation the admiral maintained that the main purpose of the voyage lay in the visit to Germany. In England it would simply be the "execution of formalities" and besides, the relationship to the Royal Navy was "anything but heartwarming" because of the still unresolved Keelung incident.

Wenneker further reported that Kobayashi had told him that he wanted to go to Berlin with his staff and hoped to be received there by Hitler. He based his hopes on the fact that "up until now all German cruiser commanders that visited Tokyo were introduced to the Emperor." Furthermore, Admiral Matsushita, during his visit to Berlin in 1934, had been received by the Reichspresident. Wenneker surmised that they intended to show Berlin to the whole crew, for which they expected considerable reduction of transportation costs and free tickets.[33]

A novelty was the presence aboard the *Ashigara* of five civilians and Maeda, who had been promoted to the rank of commander in the meantime.[34] The civilians consisted of three media representatives, one artist, and Professor Fujisawa Chikako.[35]

Wenneker's characterization of Maeda and Fujisawa clearly showed his sober appraisal of their strongly nationalistic viewpoints. He characterized Maeda as "that sort of officer" who had never been in foreign lands and who, therefore, had totally wrong impressions of them, held Japan in comparison to "all other nations, even if not in civilizational context, but in spirit and morality as incredibly superior," and, believing in a godly mission of Japan, stood for a spreading of the Japanese spirit over the whole globe.

In this Maeda was strongly influenced by Fujisawa. He had been temporarily employed at the training department of the Navy Ministry and counted as a consultant in the interpretation of "issues related to the interpretation of the state." He spoke German flawlessly and had recently published a few articles that had also appeared in Germany. Wenneker described these as stamped "by an arrogance unparalleled and for which one can only spare a smile."[36]

In spite of all the friendliness that was expressed before and during the visit of the *Ashigara*, Wenneker did not receive any insights into the intentions of the Japanese navy. The new construction plans, in particular, were kept strictly secret. To direct questions of foreign attachés concerning them, the same answer was always given, namely, that the construction program had not yet been decided upon. It was also pointed out to Wenneker that the dockyard in Kure had recently been shown to the U.S. attaché, at which time he had been able to see for himself that nothing was being constructed there. When, however, Wenneker asked the American for his impressions, he answered that they had carefully kept him from the really interesting places during the inspection, and he therefore had not been able to glean any impressions of the actual construction activities going on there.[37]

The official proclamations were opposed by other statements. For example, the IJN, in answer to a question asked in parliament as to whether or not the new British and American fleet building programs represented a threat, replied that they did not, and therefore the new building program already planned did not have to be modified. Wenneker judged the first part of this statement to be unbelievable and concluded from his conversations with his Japanese contacts that the Anglo-Saxon armament was viewed with great discomfort. The fact that the IJN had accepted a budgetary increase of only 63 million yen over the previous year was simply explained by the fact that it estimated the outlook for higher appropriations as unfavorable, since the army had managed for the first time in a long while to push through demands that lay significantly higher than those of the navy.

Another reason he saw was that the navy had repeatedly declared that the abolition of the treaty limitations on fleet armament would not result in an armament race.[38] Wenneker did not believe this, however, and pointed out that the Japanese navy had just refused a British proposal for a treaty on the limitation of the caliber of battleship artillery to 14 inches. Such a qualitative limitation was described as unsuitable if tonnage limitations were not included at the same time. The German attaché contended that it was safe to assume that the Japanese navy already had ships under construction with a displacement of over thirty-five thousand tons, which they wanted to arm with significantly heavier artillery than the British proposal would have allowed. To diverge from their current construction policy was something the Japanese were under no circumstances prepared to do.[39]

Even from Nomura Naokuni, usually friendly to the Germans, now rear admiral and head of the Intelligence Department (Third Group) of the Navy General Staff, Wenneker could not get any details about the new construction program. Nomura did tell him that the program had already been decided upon before 1 December 1935, but it was kept top secret and was known only to those directly involved. Wenneker might believe him or not, but even if he, Nomura, wanted to, he could not divulge any information. Details would only be published after the new constructions were in service.[40]

In the summer of 1937 Wenneker reported more details about the displacement and caliber of the Japanese battleships[41] under construction, which became more precise at the beginning of 1938. But even Wenneker's successor, Captain Lietzmann (who served between September 1937 and February 1940), reported tersely: "The Japanese themselves keep strictly silent about their new constructions."[42]

Despite this reticence on factual issues, Wenneker was still given preferential treatment, which was evident at the annual dinner held by the navy minister for the foreign naval attaché corps in Japan. The Soviet attaché was not assigned the seat of honor next to Navy Minister Yonai, even though as longest serving and therefore doyen, he had a claim to this according to protocol. Instead Wenneker was assigned this seat, whereupon the Soviet attaché left in protest when the minister arrived.[43]

Preferential treatment did not hinder Wenneker, however, from suggesting sharp countermeasures after an incident involving the German steamer *Potsdam* in the harbor of Yokohama. When the ship had passed the naval station of Yokosuka while approaching Yokohama in April 1937, it had been overflown by a Japanese naval plane, from which a *Potsdam* passenger was seen taking pictures of the old torpedo boat *Yukaze*. Acting on reports provided by the navy, police detained the steamer for several hours in Yokohama. The passengers had to surrender their films and received them back only after they had been made useless. Wenneker commented: "Since such incidents occur very often in Japan, it would be time to check if it were not appropriate to treat Japanese steamers in Germany in a similar manner."[44]

Wenneker's and Lietzmann's reports in the years 1937 and 1938 about the attitude of the IJN toward the Anglo-Saxon sea powers must have been very informative for the Kriegsmarine. The "Z" Plan to build an oceanic fleet to go against Great Britain would finally be accomplished. The reports of the German attachés clearly showed distinct anti-British tendencies in the Japanese navy, with at the same time a milder attitude with regard to the United States.

JAPAN "FLIRTING WITH AMERICA"

Wenneker reported that among the Japanese since 1936 the large Pacific maneuvers of the U.S. Navy had not been portrayed as a threat or used as justification for their own armament. This "flirting with America" even went so far that the great new fleet armament of the United States was described by Japanese newspapers as "not in any way being pointed against Japan." They described this rather as an expression of the "traditional strivings" to own a fleet that was "second to none."[45]

From Adm. Nomura Naokuni, Wenneker learned in April 1937 that the Japanese-American relationship was currently "better than ever before." However, the British side made strenuous efforts to heighten earlier tensions in the relationship with the U.S. Navy, with the goal of locking the Japanese fleet into the Pacific, through the Americans, in case of a conflict in Europe.[46] Also, the resolution of the Keelung incident did not improve the IJN's relationship with the Royal Navy.[47]

While stressing that the relationship with the United States was good, the Japanese did not fail to consider meeting a maritime threat from America with armaments measures. This was evident indirectly from Wenneker's reports, such as when he reported answers given by Navy Minister Yonai in parliament upon inquiries about a possible air threat against Japan by the United States.

On that occasion Yonai had observed that Japan would obviously feel threatened if the United States deployed strong air units to the western Pacific and explained: "If our program is completed with the budgetary year 1939–40, there will be no danger, just as there is no cause currently to view the situation as critical."[48] The Japanese armament program, then, did indeed orient itself toward a potential American threat.[49] Yonai was, however, obviously working hard for appeasement and indeed also looking to the relationship with Great Britain, because when Wenneker asked him directly in April 1937 about the attitude of the Japanese navy toward the strong British armament effort, the minister replied with the hint that England was not feared. The Japanese navy would retain its standpoint of "being non-threatening and conducting no invasion," and in conclusion he emphasized the closeness of his standpoint to that of Foreign Minister Sato by quoting him: "If we do not want to, there will be no war."[50]

MORE ARMY-NAVY CONFLICT

Wenneker submitted a report in May 1937 that focuses on the army-navy struggle occasioned by the replacement of Hirota's cabinet by Hayashi's.[51] At the same time, though unintentionally, Wenneker illuminated internal differences of opinion within the IJN. During formation of the Hayashi cabinet, the navy had rejected the war hawk Suetsugu Nobumasa as navy minister and instead entrusted Yonai with this position.[52] Not only did he seem to be the right man to put the mighty rival in his place, but he was also chosen in order to limit tensions within the navy. (Wenneker described the proposal to name Suetsugu as navy minister as a "request without doubt inspired by the army.")

Yonai understood well enough, on the occasion of parliamentary inquiries about the tensions within the armed forces, to present this as purely an army problem, by which the role division of both branches of service during the "2-26 incident" of the previous year benefited him: "The problem of discipline seems to be more a part of the army, not the navy, and insofar as it concerns the navy, there is nothing to be said about it."[53] In addition, the economic weakness of Japan, which heightened the rivalry between both services, and the domestic situation, which hindered foreign policy decisions, were unmistakably judged here by Wenneker:

> There can exist no doubt at all about the fact that Japan's inner strength is totally inadequate in the long run to withstand an armaments race with any theoretical opponents on sea or land, meaning at least England and Russia. One branch of the armed forces must necessarily come up short, and it is the navy's standpoint, that if it is affected, the existence of the Island Empire will be endangered, which would not be the case by a reduction of the army.[54]

From the "only superior authority," the Tennō, a resolution of the conflict could not be expected, since he was completely in the hands of his advisers, who came from the army and the navy, and even if he were to reach a decision, it would be "very doubtful that it would even be recognized."[55] So decisions about the foreign policy issues of the services were dependent upon their domestic position, and in this Wenneker saw the only reason for the domestic activities of the IJN. In this it allied itself more with the forces that aimed for the continuation of the status quo and compromise, such as the last of the

Genrō, Saionji Kimmochi, and circles of the Imperial Court and "big business," than with those propounding strong political changes.

Strong forces that did not shy away from a more direct confrontation with the British were nonetheless present in the Japanese navy, as confirmed by Wenneker through a British colleague whom he quoted as saying: "God preserve the Japanese army for us. It has so far spared us from a Japanese southern expansion and will continue to do this. A relinquishing of the diversionary continental policies and a transfer to the navy of large sums spent on Manchuria and the army would have had catastrophic consequences."[56]

Thus the deciding factor in holding off "catastrophic consequences" for the British in the Far East was not frugality in the IJN's expansion policies but funds limitations due to competition with the army.

Still, it was hinted at in Yonai's comments in April that he was determined not to let matters progress to a warlike involvement with Great Britain at the moment. It was a course on which he could, at least temporarily, also set the middle ranks of the Navy Ministry, because in November 1937 Lietzmann, newly replacing Wenneker, reported that the intention of the navy to push England out of Asia, often openly spoken about, at least currently was being followed "only step by step and with great care." This impression he had obtained from conversations with those in the mid-level echelons of the Navy Ministry.

In view of the war between China and Japan, which had started in the interim, Lietzmann still, however, estimated the danger of a Japanese-British incident in South Chinese waters as high, basing his estimate on a recent conversation that the German professor Haushofer had had with Navy Minister Yonai. Haushofer verified his impression that Yonai wanted to avoid an impending conflict with the British if at all possible, and Yonai pointed out that South China was an area in which Great Britain had special interest.[57]

Subdhas Chandra Bose aboard I-29. *Maru* Magazine

I-30 berths at Lorient. *Schöpke, Propaganda Kompanie*

Sudhas Chandra Bose addressing gathering. *Schöpke, Propaganda Kompanie*

I-8 enters Brest submarine pen. *Info Zentrum Flotte*

Commander Uchino addresses a reception for I-8. *Info Zentrum Flotte*

I-8 sports demonstration at a French castle. *Info Zentrum Flotte*

Commander Uchino inspects German installations. *Info Zentrum Flotte*

Four German submarines at Penang base pier. *Schöpke, Propaganda Kompanie*

Commander, Submarine Squadron 8, and Chef im Südraum at welcoming ceremony. *Schöpke, Propganda Kompanie*

Korvettenkapitän Erhardt, Base Commander, Penang. *Schöpke, Propaganda Kompanie*

Kapitänleutnant Schneewind and Commander Ariizumi at a party. *Schöpke, Propganda Kompanie*

The CO of U-183 samples German submarine food with Japanese officer. *Schöpke, Propaganda Kompanie*

The explosion of the supply ship *Uckermark,* at Yokohama. *Krag*

German naval aviators with pilots from CVL *Ryuho. Hoppe*

U-511 arrives at Penang. *Maru* Magazine

11

Bargains and Treaties, 1938–1939

After his return to Germany, at the beginning of December 1937, Professor Haushofer wrote an exhaustive report about his trip, a copy of which he sent to Raeder for his own personal instruction.[1] In this report he pointed out the efforts of the Japanese naval leadership to avoid confrontations with British and American naval forces in South Chinese waters.[2] Nonetheless, a long-lasting condition of irritation had probably set in. For the China conflict itself, Haushofer prognosticated that this would bind Japanese strength for years to come, and maybe even overwhelm it. Despite any and all massive attempts, he averred, it would be impossible to break Chinese resistance. In this case modern military technology and the rough treatment of the population would change nothing.[3] Nevertheless the professor viewed a lasting China conflict as being in the interests of Germany, because it would cause "such a strong withdrawal of Russian, English, American, and even French (Indochina) attention to the Far East that German politics in Europe could gain very welcome relief."[4]

Despite caution on the part of the Japanese naval leadership, incidents with British and U.S. naval forces arose very soon within the framework of the fighting in China. Late in 1937, on the Yangtze River, Japanese army artillery units fired on the British river gunboat *Ladybird*, and Japanese naval aircraft, in another incident, attacked the American gunboat *Panay*, the British boats *Cricket* and *Scarab*, and some civilian craft of Standard Oil. The *Ladybird* and the *Panay* suffered fatalities, and the latter was sunk.[5]

Characteristic of the differing attitudes toward the British and the Americans were ensuing comments and reactions, about which Lietzmann continuously reported.

While the *Panay* incident had been extremely discomfiting to the navy, and the navy was trying very publicly to calm the Americans in order to avoid a break with them, the Japanese had repeatedly revealed in talks that, with reference to the British protests, they thought one could safely treat England as quite negligible.[6]

From a department head of the Gunreibu, Lietzmann heard that "in general the American seemed to be a sensible and quiet, deliberating man with whom one could talk." The British, on the other hand, had forfeited even the last bit of remaining sympathy "with their constant nagging, petty protests, and involvement in things that did not concern them." Especially in the younger officer corps, the anti-British feelings had reached a boiling point that "made occasional excesses within the framework of the current engagements understandable." Not only could such frictions hardly be counteracted, but this attitude had indeed to be promoted, "in order to be as well prepared as possible" for confrontation "that would come sooner or later."[7] A warlike conflict with the British was already viewed as unavoidable.

Nearly a year later Lietzmann found these impressions further verified.[8] The "department head" in the Navy General Staff, whom he had quoted before, he identified as his "old friend" Nomura Naokuni, the head of the Gunreibu's Third Group (intelligence service). Nomura enjoyed special esteem in the IJN in general, and his viewpoints represented, according to Lietzmann, not the personal opinion of a single person, but rather the official opinions of substantial naval posts.

Despite this hostile attitude, no activities of the Japanese navy in the actual British sphere of interest (South China) had so far occurred. A confidant of Admiral Nomura attributed this cautious behavior to the fact that the *Panay* incident had already alarmed the United States, which should not be additionally disquieted. Lietzmann himself saw "economic consideration to the American friend, whose financial help one hoped for in the future development of China," as the main motivation for the momentary caution of the navy in the pursuit of its "southernly directed maritime goals."[9]

During various festivities on the occasion of the first anniversary of the Anti-Comintern Pact, Lietzmann also had a chance to speak with various active and retired Japanese flag officers. He reported that they themselves had all explained that the Japanese navy now understood "Tirpitz's exclamation about perfidious Albion." This was because they were currently having the same experiences with the British as the German navy had had around the turn of the century. After a decade of friendship with England, this was painful, but "fate had to run its course and just this destiny had made a confrontation with England sooner or later unavoidable."[10] The British were viewed by the Japanese as the actual perpetrators in the occupation of the Paracel Islands, a group of small islands and reefs in the South China Sea southeast of Hainan, by France.[11]

During a dinner at the end of July 1937, Lietzmann had the opportunity of a conversation with Rear Admiral Inagaki,[12] the deputy of Yamamoto Isoroku. Inagaki spoke about the probably long duration of the war in China and commented bitterly about the English, without whom this war would, in his opinion, have long since been ended. Germany as well as Japan, he continued, had "even if for different reasons, the same interest in the defeat of England." For this goal Germany surely had to re-arm for a few years; Japan was currently not in a position to do this, since it was tied up in China. But in the end "China was . . . in the eyes of the Japanese navy only a means to an end, only a resting point on the way to a final settlement with *England*."[13]

Despite differences of opinion between the navy and the army, which the admiral had judged as being only "superficial," "Japan would at the proper time employ its imperial national forces in order to decisively defeat England in the Far East." Until then one had to "fight it indirectly, which meant damaging it in a non-violent way, politically delaying it or binding it in other ways." According to Lietzmann's report, Inagaki's observations culminated with the pledge of armed support in case of war: "In case of a European conflict the German navy could, in case we wanted to know about it, be certain that the Japanese navy would stand by the German navy and, seizing the opportunity, would move against England."[14]

Lietzmann came to the conclusion that the friends of the British in the younger, middle-aged, and senior officers' corps of the Japanese navy had obviously turned into a minority essentially without significant influence. The main attack point of the Japanese navy was currently British sea power in the Far East, as in Australia and New Zealand. The British were characterized by the Japanese navy as an "enemy," the United States, on the other hand, as "friend." Lietzmann, though, reported doubts here, about whether or not "a possible or probable cooperation between the United States and England had been considered thoroughly enough" by the Japanese officers. The possible point in time of unleashing an attack against England had not been estimated precisely, since that would be determined to a considerable degree by the domestic constellations in Japan. But Lietzmann was sure that it would happen if England were tied up elsewhere, and Japan felt itself capable of doing it. From the Japanese viewpoint a possibly unique chance had to be taken advantage of before the British completed arming themselves, in about four years.[15]

On the eve of the Sudeten crisis, it became apparent to the Kriegsmarine that in a conflict with the British it could quite probably count on the Royal Navy's having to face a considerable diversionary-strategic burden from a probable Japanese intervention in the Far East.[16] This was a perspective that had to be greeted joyfully by the Kriegsmarine, especially in view of its relatively weak condition until the "Z" Plan was realized.

A worsening of the relationship between the British and Japanese navies, clearly emphasized in Lietzmann's reports, provided the occasion for Ambassador Ott, after he had personally reported to the Reich's foreign minister, to order the attaché to conduct a study of this topic. The result was his report, "Considering a State of War between Japan and England or Japan and the Anglo-Saxon Powers," which Lietzmann presented at the end of August and which circulated during the Sudeten crisis among the naval leadership.[17]

Even though it actually was an internal embassy report, Ambassador Ott had passed the study on through Lietzmann "for the personal information of the commander in chief of the Kriegsmarine," asking, however, that beyond that no use was to be made of it. Lietzmann had based his work, for the most part, on a publication of the Skl.'s Third Department (naval intelligence) for internal naval use, entitled "Study of Foreign Navies," and even partly plagiarized it; however, his study is no doubt a spotlight on how the maritime situation in the Far East appeared to the German naval leadership.[18]

In his observations Lietzmann first considered the possible timing of the conflict and focused his attention especially on the main domestic competitor of the navy, namely, the Japanese army. From there, also, voices could be heard that described a conflict with England as a "national end goal," but only "in the long run" and on the "China-Russia path," and only after victorious wars against those two countries. Lietzmann credited the army with a realistic perception of the chances of keeping America and Britain divided.[19] Since Japan was currently weakened by the China War, a confrontation with Russia would be unthinkable before another four or five years had passed. From this one could conclude that a war with England was to be expected considerably later, "certainly not before ten years from now."

An earlier attack, with the single goal of forestalling the arming of the British at sea (expected to be completed around 1941), was ruled out by Lietzmann, then made conditional on England's being tied up elsewhere.[20] Such a drain on England was also considered a decisive factor in the case of "development according to plan," meaning after "a solving of the Russian business" and subsequent creation of economic and military preconditions for the battle against a modern, greater power—a war of aggression against England. In contrast, a war against a Great Britain unburdened by another conflict would be a "risk for Japan, the taking of which can probably not be calculated," since time, in Lietzmann's opinion, was working for Japan.[21]

The expected war between Japan and Great Britain was characterized by Lietzmann as a "sea war, combined with air operations" in which, on key points, "the strongest efforts" of the army would also be necessary. Since the goal of the war from the Japanese point of view was the achievement of maritime supremacy in the western Pacific and at the same time the final expulsion of the Royal Navy from this area, the army was faced with the task of conquering the British bases, of which Singapore was the most important.[22] Even if Great Britain were already engaged elsewhere, Japan would have to use its "entire national war-waging capability."

However, such remarks raised the weak point of just this capability, namely, the comparatively weak economic position of Japan in wartime. Lietzmann elaborated that Japan would have to undergo the "greatest efforts" in economic and financial areas, in order to be able to meet a future confrontation with the Anglo-Saxons. Just to recover from its weakened state since the war in China would take at least three years. Of special importance, however, were Lietzmann's comments to the effect that Japan was dependent for up to 70 percent of its imports of raw materials from the Anglo-Saxon countries and the Dutch East Indies (e.g., oil for the navy) and that, in the case of a war with England, it could at least expect an embargo by the United States.[23] In view of this, Lietzmann concluded:

It will therefore all depend on whether or not Japan takes a firm stance on creating a source of raw materials in Manchuria and Northern China, that will lessen its dependency upon imports and arm itself through stockpiling for all kinds of future decisive confrontations.

The fact that Japan now possesses a rather weak capacity for successful warfare against a modern great power is concluded from this without further ado.[24]

In conclusion Lietzmann judged the battle strength of the fleets of Japan, Great Britain, and the United States and analyzed in detail the bases of these countries in the Pacific and their relevance in a possible conflict. In view of its "spirit" and "discipline" he judged the Japanese fleet as excellent. It was prepared for "ruthless action." The "spirit" of the Royal Navy he described as good, but he had ascertained that discipline there left a lot to be desired in recent years.[25] The U.S. Navy he equated with the Royal Navy in this respect.

The training of the Japanese he judged as not broad enough and therefore "for example, not fully able to match that of the German fleet." War experience, also, had been absent for a long time. Aside from the lack of war experience, training and tradition made the British "in any case a first-class opponent." What the training of the Americans was worth had first to be proven in a war situation. As far as the will to fight was concerned, Lietzmann judged the Japanese as "surely not being inferior to the tough English" but superior, on the other hand, to the Americans.

He seemed to see no significant differences between the three navies in the technical area, recognizing, at most, light advantages with the Anglo-Saxons. While armament and the armoring of ships by the Japanese corresponded to "modern viewpoints" and their naval aviators had "proven their efficiency and their heroism," the English were in the first two areas a "first-class opponent" and the U.S. Navy corresponded to all modern demands in every way.[26] As for the operative and technical abilities of the potential opponents, Lietzmann did not see himself in a position to pass judgment.

Considering the geo-strategic backdrop of Japan and the Anglo-Saxon powers in terms of bases in the Pacific area, Lietzmann came to the conclusion that Japan, on the basis of its dense network of bases in the western Pacific and its potential, in contrast to its opponents', for concentrating its entire fleet, possessed "a truly strong bulwark against enemy attacks." Not the least because of airfields and fortifications built on former German colonial possessions of the South Sea Islands (in violation of the treaty terms), Japan also possessed an "excellent base for its own offensive purposes."

As for the Anglo-Saxons, the attaché saw the fortress of Singapore as by far the most important base, its extension having just been completed a few months prior. The British planned, after completion of their maritime armament, to deploy a fleet there with five modern battleships as its nucleus. The scheduled fleet deployment indicated that a main focus of British foreign policy actually lay in the Far East. Singapore was the key position, covering India "against surprises from the East," dominating the passages from the Indian Ocean to the Pacific, and, lastly, controlling the oil fields on Borneo and Sumatra, the real key areas. From the oil fields of Sumatra came the majority of oil for the Japanese fleet.[27]

The very high status that Lietzmann attributed to Singapore was revealed by the fact that he introduced his thoughts on the matter with the words:

> The strong interest that England is forced to show for the European situation should not be allowed to cloud the fact *that the main emphasis of British foreign policy does not, or just not for the time being, lie in Europe, but in the securing of its sea power connections and its far Eastern possessions"* (emphasis in original).[28]

Within this framework Lietzmann also pointed out that worry about Japan was observable in Australia and New Zealand, especially since the expiration of the Washington treaties.

No other Anglo-Saxon base could be compared to the importance of Singapore: Hong Kong was unfortified and could not be held indefinitely against a threat posed by the nearby Japanese bases.[29] The U.S. bases at Manila and Guam were also unfortified. Pearl Harbor and the bases on the Pacific coast of the American continent were not of much importance because they were too far away.[30] Lietzmann saw the U.S. Navy as a serious threat to the Japanese side only if the Americans used Singapore to support the English in a conflict with the Japanese.[31]

In conclusion, the naval attaché expressed his opinions about the "fated" (his word) war between Japan and Great Britain, namely, that the conquest of Singapore was of decisive importance for the Japanese (pointing out that a Japanese attack was to be expected in case of a strategic binding of England at a different place) and that Japan still needed quite a long time in order to be prepared, especially in economic areas, for this conflict.[32]

THE CHINA PROBLEM

In the meantime a problem had arisen out of the war between Japan and China that also strained the maritime relationship of Japan and Germany. It is well known that Chiang Kai-shek was supported by German military advisers and received military material in large quantities from foreign countries, among them, in leading position, Germany. Even though this was first and foremost an army problem, and the Japanese Navy Ministry indicated its tolerance in view of Germany's need for hard currency, eased in considerable measure through the sale of war materials to China, in the long run the shipments did lead to noticeable annoyance in Japanese naval circles.[33]

Lietzmann reported in October 1937 that the shipment of war materials on ships belonging to German shipping lines was constantly pointed out in Japanese radio shows and newspaper articles.[34] He himself recently had been questioned repeatedly about the current German shipments by the Navy Ministry, although in a friendly way, and had replied that orders predating the conflict between China and Japan were still outstanding, the filling of which according to "existing customs was self-evident." Further shipments had, however, been stopped "for a fairly long time." Furthermore Lietzmann referred to the fact that foreign transports on German ships, according to international trading regulations, could not be inspected and asked for concrete information about shipments on German ships.[35]

From Captain Kondō, the first adjutant of the navy minister, the German heard that the British embassy had recently given information to the Japanese Foreign Ministry about French and German weapons shipments to China via Hong Kong.[36] Even though the Kriegsmarine was not directly concerned in this matter, Lietzmann, considering that he had been asked remarkably often about the situation, took this opportunity to call its attention to the discord among the political interests (focused on China) on the German side. He urgently advised a definite settlement as to which side should be given priority. Although "Japan is treated by us in press and public announcements as a friend, the practical help . . . is given to China in terms of war shipments and military advisers." Lietzmann warned against playing both sides against the middle and advised a clear backing of the Japanese and prohibiting German shipping lines from transporting war shipments to China.[37]

The Japanese quickly accepted Lietzmann's plea for concrete instructions about German shipments to China. They started right at the beginning of November 1937 to hand over detailed lists.[38] Since the Kriegsmarine had requests from the Chinese for construction of submarines and the training of their crews and ten cadets, Raeder now saw the necessity of a fundamental settlement on how to deal with Chinese armaments orders and requests for help. He solved this with Defense Minister Blomberg on 12 November.

Raeder informed the Japanese naval attaché Kojima that China had ordered submarines in Germany long before the outbreak of the war with Japan. Those would be built but not handed over for the duration of war. Blomberg gave his approval for the German shipyards and factories producing submarines, S-boats, minelayers, torpedoes, and mines for China to be ordered to declare these goods as being produced for the German navy. The training of officers, officer candidates, and submarine crews, as requested by the Chinese, was to be fulfilled, but with the exercise of "greatest discretion." Finally, the whole package of Chinese requests was to be checked again in the spring of 1938.[39]

Interesting here is a comparison of the various examples of this document, of which thirteen were produced. While the first seven routing numbers were destined for Blomberg and other non-naval personnel in the RKM (War Ministry), the last six served internal naval use. Besides the "external" example destined for Blomberg, two other "internal" ones have been preserved.[40] Exclusively on the last two copies, a footnote of Raeder's is found that clearly marks the orders to the German shipyards to designate ships for China as ships for Germany, purposely fooling the befriended Japanese:

> This order is supposed to hide from the Japanese, if possible, the building and construction of this war material for China, according to my previous statement, and prevent unnecessary unrest through newly disclosed information. Therefore, knowledge of the destination of the constructions and manufactured goods to China is to be limited by all the bureaus involved to absolutely necessary personnel.[41]

These dictates were used by Raeder not only to fool the Japanese but, at the same time, also to prevent those Chinese residing in Germany from detailed inspections of the respective companies; with this notice for the need of secrecy, they were denied lengthy stays at the companies.[42]

Lietzmann, who in the meantime had once again reported that the Japanese had received hints from the British naval attaché about the continuing German and Italian armaments shipments to China via Hong Kong, was now informed about the sense of the consultation between Raeder and Blomberg.[43] The footnote was kept from him. He was able, however, to detect from the information given that the Japanese were being misinformed. The message mentioned that the submarine question—whether Germany was building submarines for

China—had come up during Raeder's verbal explanation to Kojima but that all further Chinese construction orders and training requests were being kept quiet. At least it was acknowledged, in the spirit of Lietzmann's previous recommendations, that the political ties to Japan should fundamentally have priority over the economic ties to China.[44]

Despite their disgruntlement, the Japanese wanted to avoid any straining of the relationship. Efforts by the Japanese navy to avoid a break with the Kriegsmarine, despite the China shipments, were revealed in comments that Kojima had made in a conversation with Raeder. Kojima had pointed out the considerable difficulties created for the Japanese army attaché by the German advisers in China, as well as by the German aid shipments for Chinese land troops. In the same breath, however, he remarked that the Japanese navy minister had noted that such cases were not evident in the affairs of the navy and that the wishes of the Japanese navy were always treated with great preference by the German navy commander in chief.[45]

The polite but substantial accusations of the Japanese about the Chinese shipments were funneled through the OKM to the Wehrmachtsamt (from 1938 onwards and hereinafter named OKW, for Oberkommando der Wehrmacht, Armed Forces High Command) for testing and commentary, where the comment was made that the Japanese lists "were mistaken nearly throughout,"[46] and later even that they were correct "in no single case."[47] The last claim originated with Canaris, who had the first Japanese lists checked.

In order to be able to judge Canaris's statement correctly, it is worth examining it more closely. He limited his investigation to (a) only "true" war material, (b) the question of whether these were German shipments, and (c) the thirteen steamers mentioned in the Japanese lists. Thus the investigation was indeed limited so as to give priority to the obviously desired solution: The listed ships had either not transported the questionable freight, or it was of foreign extraction. In this way consideration of the question as to whether or not, or to what extent, the German shipment occurred was carefully avoided, and Canaris could in "good" conscience discontinue the checking of Japanese lists and even argue with the Japanese claims.[48]

To verify that the illusion so created did not correspond to the facts, one can find numerous clues in the records. The continuing German shipments, mainly via the "loophole" Hong Kong, were mentioned in a study by the Kriegsmarine on the question of why Japan was hesitating to declare war on China.[49] They were also found in appeals from Ambassador Dirksen to stop these shipments.[50] And they appear in other reports of the German embassy.[51]

The extent of the IJN's disaffection as a result of the Germany-China shipments, based on their quite detailed knowledge about the particulars of those shipments and the resulting game of hide-and-seek of the shipping lines, emerged in a report of Lietzmann's from the spring of 1938. It concerned the events surrounding the German steamer *Crefeld* in Yokohama. This report showed how carefully one has to judge Canaris's later claims of the falsity of the Japanese accusations.[52]

The *Crefeld*, a freighter and passenger liner of the Norddeutsche Lloyd firm, had suffered severe damage before its arrival in Yokohama on 8 April 1938, putting into question the ship's maneuvering ability. It was supposed to serve the Germans and Austrians in Kobe on 10 April for the vote on Austria and the Reichstag election and after that take on a large shipment of soybeans in Korea. In the latter it dealt with a temporary bargain, valid until the beginning of May, that was especially favorable to the German Empire and promised good "hard currency" profits. There was, therefore, from the perspective of the German government, great interest in a fast docking for repair of the ship.

Because of the China conflict, the Japanese navy had received power of disposal over all shipyards and docks in Japan. Lietzmann now approached the Navy Ministry and referred to the urgency of the repairs. However, he received the answer that the ship could dock in two months at the earliest. When he expressed dissatisfaction with this, he was told by naval officers of the Gunreibu that the waiting period might possibly be shortened by one month but that this would involve great difficulties and higher costs.

Lietzmann now visited the Navy Ministry for several days in a row and finally achieved permission for the *Crefeld* to dock on 18 April.[53] As a condition, though, the Japanese insisted on claiming the ship as having been chartered for Japanese naval purposes for the time being. Lietzmann described the attitude of the Japanese navy as "conspicuously unfriendly" and reported that they had tried to make it clear to him a day later that it had been a special favor in this instance, since the prepared dock had originally been reserved for the Italian cruiser *Montecuccoli*, which now had to wait. Lietzmann remarked to this: "The falseness, I want to say childishness of this information was revealed on the same day through a press release, wherein the cruiser . . . within the framework of a long-prepared program . . . was mentioned as going into dock at Yokohama according to plan."[54]

The essence of the problem would, however, soon become clear when the Navy Ministry pointed out to Lietzmann that the German ship had considerable amounts of American ammunition for China on board. The ministry soon weakened that statement, saying that the ship did not currently have ammunition on board but was, however, known to be a supplier of war materials for China.

The German attaché then heard from the captain of the steamer that he actually had had, on the previous voyage, bombs, loaded in Philadelphia, that had been transferred in Hamburg to a different ship going to Hong Kong. In order to double-check if the German steamer itself had perhaps gone to Hong Kong with the bombs, a Japanese police commission had come aboard the *Crefeld*. The first officer had been able to prove, with the help of the ship's diary, that this had not been the case. Neither did the bill of lading point to any explosive material as cargo. By letter, Captain Oelrich of the *Crefeld* informed the attaché:

> Since the bill of lading of the previous voyage contained no clues to the cargo in question, it was all right to show it to the commission. Judging by the comments made, the Japanese seemed to have very detailed information about the ammunition, etc. shipped in the States, since they knew exactly which ships had been part of the transportation of these bombs.
>
> I am informing you of this in case somebody also visits you in this matter at the embassy. I have had all relevant papers removed from the records here.[55]

Lietzmann pointed out in his report that this incident was corroborated by reports of South China Germans, who claimed that the German war materials shipments were "going on with unlessened momentum." The shipments had to be seen as the reason for the growing resentment of the Japanese navy, also notably reserved in other official areas, that stood in strong opposition to the cooperation "that we give from our side to Japanese naval commissions and similar things in Germany."[56]

Fundamentally, Japanese naval officers expected Germany to take a hard line against private economic interests, which they considered her able to do because she was, like Japan, a totalitarian state. There were attempts by Lietzmann's Japanese conversation partners to appear conciliatory, mixed with threats of a break with the German side. The strain was evident in the attaché's statement that high-ranking naval officers had recently let him know, more than once, that "after liquidation of the China conflict, one could hardly demand that the Japanese people favor nations that had in this hard fight supported the Chinese economically with especial stubbornness."[57]

There was a certain consensus that German merchants used the opportunity to "sell outdated things for good money in China," but Germany was a "state of authority," in which, in view of the friendship with Japan, it should not be possible for private businessmen "for their own selfish interests to support an enemy of Japan [i.e., China] that was obviously cooperating with the Soviet Union."[58]

The Germany-to-China shipments presented themselves in a negative light in yet another area. When the German Luftwaffe captain Schubert came to Japan, in order to study the experiences of the Japanese air forces in the China war, Lietzmann had tried to ease his way with the Japanese naval aviators, but he had to report that the result had been "quite poor." The Japanese made it clear that "an instruction in tactical areas was out of the question as long as certain powers give active help to the Chinese through military advisers."[59]

The touchy Japanese reactions were based on the fact that the Island Empire had maneuvered itself into a very difficult position through serious military and political mistakes in the war with China, about which Lietzmann reported to Raeder directly in May.[60] Only after the actual withdrawal of the German advisers and after instituting effective German measures to prevent the China shipments in the summer of 1938 did the accusations of the Japanese navy cease.[61]

INTELLIGENCE SHARING AND THE USSR

Despite the irritations caused by the Germany-to-China shipments, the Japanese navy repeatedly tried to create a closer relationship to the Kriegsmarine. Starting with proposals in the area of intelligence sharing, the attempts at rapprochement continued with proposals for an expansion of the already existing agreements. The Kriegsmarine showed little interest but could not afford to refuse, for political reasons.[62]

The rapprochement was initiated by the Japanese through the delivery in 1937 of an extensive secret report about the Soviet Amur fleet, in line with existing agreements in the framework of the Anti-Comintern Pact.[63] Without having given any vital information out of their hands, the Japanese had nonetheless offered something remarkable to the Kriegsmarine, because, as Wenneker reported, the material shed interesting light on the excellent Japanese intelligence service. He found it astounding how far the inquiries went. He also emphasized that the material had been offered to him without reciprocation.

That this action was supposed to prompt a closer intelligence cooperation was affirmed when, a few days later, Kojima spoke to the Kriegsmarine in Berlin. He proposed a trade of intelligence that went beyond the Soviet navy to encompass the British and any other foreign navies of interest to the Kriegsmarine. Furthermore, a treaty about the exchange of experience and technical aid and support was supposed to be worked out between the two navies.[64] Here the Japanese naval attaché acted parallel to his army comrade Ōshima, who signed certain agreements with Canaris and Ribbentrop on 11 May 1937 that only dealt, however, with cooperation against the Soviet Union.[65]

The German Naval War Staff did not endorse the proposal.[66] Even before the decision-making process was complete on the German side, Kojima made another approach on the same matter at the beginning of July and made new proposals that were considerably limited in comparison to the original ones. The agreement to be finalized was now to contain a sharing of intelligence limited to the USSR, as well as an exchange of technical experience and of tactical and strategic views.[67] Although Kojima handed over a written formulation authorized by the Japanese Navy Ministry, he expressly explained that a verbal agreement was "appropriate and sufficient."[68]

Even though no urgency was considered necessary from the German side,[69] in view of the very general formulations of the Japanese proposal and only a verbal form of agreement in the Marinekommandoamt, there was now no reason not to agree.[70]

Only the head of the Naval Weapons Bureau, Witzell, commented negatively. He warned of the Kommandoamt's prevailing view that the Kriegsmarine had it within its power to regulate the extent of the tradeoff and to avoid opening topics that were, for it, uncomfortable. He viewed it as imperative not to delay resolution of these issues, lest a relationship opposite to what was sought be established, and stated:

> There must, before a formal agreement, be clarity, if we . . . also want to reveal truly important things. If the friendship with Japan is, for political reasons, considered so valuable that we are also prepared to make considerable sacrifices for it, a decision must be reached in favor of the sharing of experience. We must understand that in all technical areas we will be the party giving the most.[71]

Finally Raeder verbally informed the Japanese attaché at the end of August that the OKM was basically prepared for an "occasional trade of experiences in technical areas, as well as about tactical and strategic viewpoints." During this there could also "be traded tactical [things for] technical things," for which the details should be agreed upon case by case, "according to the principle of cooperation, more for more."[72]

As a result of this very loose agreement, an exchange of rather limited extent came into being and was subjected to an interim check in March 1938 by the German side.[73] The German Naval Intelligence Service judged that the material received did not contain "anything truly new" but was nonetheless "of interest" and concluded that a revival of this intelligence trade would lie in the common interest.[74] Despite certain initiatives that Commander Maeda had suggested to Lietzmann at the beginning of 1938, exchanging information about navies other than the USSR's was for the time being not considered. This was also the position of the Japanese Navy Ministry, which the Japanese naval attaché confirmed in Berlin at the beginning of November 1938.[75]

In the area of technical information and other trades, not much had happened. At least the Japanese had handed over at the end of January 1938 a highly classified organization of their united fleet. In the judgment of the German Naval Intelligence people, it brought little new information but was nonetheless seen as proof that the Japanese wanted to get the exchange going.[76] As a reciprocal service the Kriegsmarine sent the Japanese a highly classified piece of information about the probable completion dates of new German warship constructions.[77]

In July 1938 Kojima told the Kriegsmarine that the Japanese military attaché, Ōshima, had informed him that a written agreement about the intelligence exchange between the OKW and the Japanese army concerning the Soviet Union was supposed to be signed by himself and General Keitel from the OKW, which also foresaw annual consultations.[78] Keitel had also said that he was prepared to sign an agreement together with Kojima, which meant that he also wanted to include the Japanese navy in the OKW agreement. Kojima asked the OKM if there was interest in an expansion of the existing agreements, let it be known that he was gladly prepared to do this, and wanted to know if the agreement would be concluded with the OKW or directly with the OKM.[79]

Raeder now declared himself "fundamentally" in agreement with the conclusion of a written treaty and yearly consultations and instituted the guidelines to create the exchange as extensively and as closely as possible. It should be closed between OKW and the Japanese navy; the bureau in charge on the German side would be the Skl. Third Department (intelligence).[80] In terms of the content and realization, the work was, however, supposed to be left to the Japanese, since the suggestion had originated with them, and the OKM awaited corresponding proposals from the Japanese naval attaché.

The OKM especially valued the already initiated exchange of information about the Soviet Union but wanted to limit it to that country, as long as other requests from the Japanese side had not been precisely stated, officially and by clearly naming the respective countries and questions. The attitude of the OKM to this was "fundamentally" positive, but they stated that it had to hold back its decision until they were informed of the details of the Japanese intentions and wishes. Lest the already woven threads of exchange, though heretofore limited in extent, should unravel, the principle of reciprocity of intelligence should be handled generously, and the mutual deployment of officers for this purpose was considered especially promising.[81]

As a consequence of these promptings, a qualitative rise in exchanges seems in fact to have come about.[82] A written agreement, however, does not seem to have been completed until October 1938.[83] However, important areas, such as radio surveillance, still seemed to have been exempted.[84]

The Japanese navy was not yet satisfied with what had been achieved. Endō, Kojima's successor, among others, conveyed requests to the OKM in Berlin to extend the agreement to information about the United States, Great Britain, and France. The same thing was also proposed by the Gunreibu to Commander Menzel, who had been sent to Japan in the spring of 1939, whereupon Lietzmann signed an addendum to the agreement at the end of April.[85] Once again the initiative had originated with the Japanese side, this time from the Gunreibu, which had even pushed for haste in the matter.[86]

In conspicuous contrast, Menzel had been ordered not to mention further questions of exchange or a consolidation of strategic and technical cooperation. It was merely explained to him that, in the case of an outbreak of war, an immediate communications link between the German and Japanese forces would be of the greatest use; otherwise, however, the continuation of this matter had to be a concern of later agreements between both sides.[87] Menzel noticed that the Japanese, time and again, in comradely discussions, had shown interest in what kind of notion the Kriegsmarine had of a future naval war scenario against the British. About their own problems, especially in terms of the continuation of the war in China, the Japanese had been very reticent. They had, however, let it be known that they expected at least another two years of war.[88]

As becomes clear in Menzel's report, the Gunreibu and not the Kaigunshō was the driving force behind the intensification of cooperation in the spring of 1939. The Kriegsmarine had already been able to see signs of activity on the part of the Gunreibu in the beginning of 1938, when Lietzmann reported on suggestions by Commander Maeda that aimed for closer relations between both navies.[89] Maeda, who had been, until recently, the official responsible for Germany in the European Department at the Third Group (intelligence) of the Gunreibu had just taken up his new position as first adjutant of the commander in chief of the Combined Fleet, and Lietzmann judged his proposal to be "without doubt inspired by higher posts."[90]

THE SOUTH SEAS MANDATES

Maeda mentioned two potential problems in the German-Japanese relationship and the further arrangement of the intelligence exchange between both navies. The first of the potential problems was the South Seas mandated area, which had formerly been German colonies. On this Maeda commented that the Japanese navy was prepared to seize the initiative and to take a positive position in this question in case Germany wanted to speak freely and openly about it. His solution seemed, however, to be somewhat fantastic: He proposed "that Japan, without consideration of the Versailles treaty and the League of Nations, simply return the South Seas mandated area to Germany and then buy it back from Germany."[91]

The second problem dealt with the German "economic and other interests in Manchuria, North and Middle China." Here a free and open dialogue was also necessary. And finally Maeda mentioned the desire of the Japanese navy to extend the intelligence exchange also to other greater powers. This proposal obviously aimed to clear away any remaining problems and further deepen the existing cooperation. As far as China was concerned, the proposal was, however, outdated. With the naming of Ribbentrop, who was friendly to the Japanese, as foreign minister in the beginning of February 1938, German interests in relation to China were largely abandoned.

As for Maeda's mentioning the former German colonies in the South Seas, his proposal showed signs of lacking coordination with important authorities within, as well as outside of, the IJN. The service branches in Japan had considerable leeway in formulating autonomous foreign policy based on their constitutional "immediate response." For the aforementioned South Sea areas, however, an autonomous proposal of the navy was really without merit. Their control of the South Sea Islands was unchallenged, and measures like those proposed by Maeda—in addition to causing an international uproar—could not even take effect without the consent of the *Gaimushō* (Foreign Ministry). Beyond that, since buying back the islands would have needed an international treaty, it also would have required the consent of the Secret State Council (*Sumitsuin*). It seems, in view of the careful position of Navy Minister Yonai versus the Anglo-Saxon powers, highly questionable whether such plans even had a basis within the IJN—that is, a basis broad enough to guarantee them a chance of success. The "higher posts" named by Lietzmann were therefore limited to the Gunreibu.[92] The process, however, clearly showed the strongly diverging streams of thought within the Japanese navy.

12

Japan's Response to the Outbreak of War

From the summer of 1938 onward the Kriegsmarine became certain that they had to prepare for war against Great Britain, a war that might occur as soon as autumn because of Hitler's plans for a military operation against Czechoslovakia.

The leadership of the Kriegsmarine must have known Hitler's intentions regarding the Sudetenland by 12 July 1938, at the latest. The files show when Schneewind, head of the Kommandoamt, informed the Fleet Command:

> From the instruction of the Bureau Chief A on 12 July 1938, comments of the Führer aboard *Grille* and Field Marshall Göring aboard *Hermann Schoemann* on 22 July, the following can be concluded: 1) It is planned, to bring the Sudeten German question at all costs to a satisfactory solution, if possible by way of a peaceful agreement, if not, through the use of force. (Führer) 2) As for the point in time in question, the end of September through October 1938 is to be assumed. (Bureau Chief A)[1]

In August, then, the Kriegsmarine saw the necessity of initiating "military-technical consultations in case of war" with the Japanese, as they had already begun doing with Italy since the end of July.[2] The Kriegsmarine wanted, "in keeping with the fundamental attitude that at first a cooperative military action in a conflict is not striven for," to discuss the possibility of each partner's maintaining neutrality while supporting the other in a maritime war. This would mean intelligence cooperation, toleration of the partner's supply ships in the other's own neutral zone of sovereignty, and propaganda support. Hitler consented to these terms on 29 August,[3] whereupon Lietzmann was so instructed[4] and the attaché department brought the request on 15 September to Kojima.[5] He informed them on 29 September that the Japanese Navy Ministry was basically prepared to fulfill the German wishes; details and questions were to be resolved on a case-by-case basis.[6] However, the OKM saw no need for further consolidation after the situation had eased as a result of the Munich Conference.[7]

Within the framework of the Skl.'s operative thoughts, Japan appeared as a counterbalance to the United States and as an important factor in the support of Germany's economic warfare.[8] Germany occupied the Sudetenland in October 1938. By early 1939 the sea areas under Japanese control were among the very few worldwide in which the supply of German naval forces would be possible for an extended period of time.[9] During the Sudeten crisis Lietzmann had, as a leader of the *Grossetappe* Japan-China, completed the appropriate measures for dealing with a period of tension from 16 September onward.[10]

Meanwhile the Gunreibu had begun to inform Lietzmann about movements of France's and Great Britain's Eastern forces. This occurred without knowledge of the Navy Ministry (Kaigunshō), which is why Lietzmann requested in his report to the OKM that no mention be made of it to the Japanese attaché in Berlin, Kojima.[11] Concurrently, Lietzmann had requested of the Kaigunshō that German merchant ships receive protection, especially in Shanghai. After a two-day examination, they replied that the Japanese navy was prepared to prevent any hostilities against German ships in sea areas that Japanese naval forces could reach, in the waters under the new Chinese government and also in Shanghai.[12]

This was in no way a clear pledge to help. On the contrary, the Japanese comments were marked by great care. The promise of support by means of war with the British, made the previous year by Admiral Inagaki, was not to be taken for granted.

During the treaty negotiations that Ōshima had conducted with Ribbentrop since the summer of 1938, no initiative had originated with the IJN that proposed a closer cooperation in the area of intelligence exchange. The Japanese naval leadership—specifically, Navy Minister Yonai Mitsumasa, his deputy

Yamamoto Isoroku, and Inouye Shigeyoshi, head of the Bureau of Maritime Affairs[13]—had no interest in an alliance, and it was especially important to the Japanese to avoid all clauses that would involve the Island Empire in a war with the Western powers in Europe. The "southern thrust" plan of the navy was, in their opinion, best served if pressure could be applied in China, Indochina, and Great Britain and France, threatened in Europe by Hitler. They did not want to burden the IJN with the higher risks of an alliance "domino effect" in East Asia, which Navy Minister Yonai and his followers feared.[14] An intervention of the United States on the side of Japan's opponents was judged by Yonai to be the automatic result of an alliance with Germany and Italy.[15]

Furthermore, the southern expansion could be pushed ahead at comparatively low risk without ties to the Axis powers, considering that in February 1939 the island of Hainan, as well as the Spratley Islands, were occupied and placed under the control of the Japanese navy. Yonai ran into resistance to his delaying tactics within his own ranks and especially in the army, but he was still able to use the extraordinarily ponderous decision-making process to his benefit. The cabinet of Hiranuma was split on this question and the navy minister was able, together with Foreign Minister Arita and Finance Minister Ishiwata, to ward off all utterances from the German side, from the army, and from Ambassador Ōshima, until the negotiations came to a halt because of the German-Soviet Nonaggression Pact.

During all this Yonai entirely understood how to control the internal tensions within the navy, by mediating between his allies Yamamoto and Inoue— who pushed for a tough stand in the denial of the requests made by Ribbentrop, Ōshima, and the army— and his department heads who supported an alliance; he also never quite severed his ties to the army. The fact that the Tennō and conservative court circles supported Yonai's position was, in the end, of decisive importance.[16]

THE GERMAN-SOVIET NONAGGRESSION PACT (23 AUGUST 1939)

The surprising conclusion of the German-Soviet Nonaggression Pact caused a shock in the Japanese public, the Foreign Ministry (Gaimushō), and the army, but not in the IJN. Lietzmann, who assumed on the eve of the outbreak of war in Europe that the "pre-conditions for Japanese help to German shipping and other German concerns do not lie as favorably as in September of 1938," remarked, however, that the IJN had remained quiet, in contrast to the

Gaimushō, the army, and the public.[17] When he explained the pact on the same day in the Kaigunshō, he immediately received a friendly reception from his Japanese conversation partner, Captain Ichimiya, the first adjutant of the minister of the navy. Although the Japanese did not express an opinion of the German-Soviet Nonagression Pact in this conversation, he made a point of their cooperation and interest, present and future, and Lietzmann gathered "the impression of factual judgment and quiet waiting."[18]

Generally there were only a few signs of disgruntlement in the Japanese navy due to the pact. Adm. Ōsumi Mineo, former navy minister and now member of the Supreme War Council, declined to continue his voyage to Germany, where Hitler had invited him together with General Terauchi to attend the Nazi party congress.[19] Lietzmann thereupon received the order from Berlin to lobby at the Kaigunshō for Ōsumi to come to Berlin. His efforts, however, did not meet with success.[20]

Ōsumi's behavior actually had nothing to do with the German-Soviet Nonaggression Pact. Instead it addressed the reaction of the IJN to the outbreak of war. Yonai's successor Yoshida Zengo had avoided a too-clear pro-German demonstration at the outbreak of war. When the cabinet of Abe fell at the beginning of the following year, the groups that had sympathized with Yonai even showed themselves tactically superior to their enemies: The fall of Abe's cabinet and the attraction between the most important power factions were used by the conservative forces of the imperial court to make Yonai premier of the next cabinet in January 1940.[21]

THE TRIPARTITE PACT

Shortly after the outbreak of war the Seekriegsleitung had considered the consequences and the extent of possible support from Italy, the Soviet Union, and Japan. It had noted that, after less than two weeks of war, Italy had made its first promises (if clearly below the Skl.'s expectations) and a start had been made in getting support from the Soviet side. However, by the middle of September 1939 an answer from Japan to the proposition was still outstanding.[22]

At least the Soviet-Japanese treaty about the settlement of the border conflict in Manchuria was viewed with great satisfaction. The Skl. saw in this a precondition for the march of the Red Army into Eastern Poland, executed immediately afterward, and hoped from this to reap very positive consequences for its position versus the Western powers.[23] Just a week later the head of the Skl. ordered the checking of the possibilities of maintenance, refuge, and supply of German Panzerschiffe in Soviet and Japanese harbors.[24] The Skl. saw itself at the beginning of October 1939 in a position to advise the Panzerschiffe that they could, if necessary, dock in Vladivostock and Murmansk for several days, while similar concessions from Japan were hoped for but not yet granted.[25]

From the standpoint of the Skl., what did come out of Japan was certainly not positive. The Gaimushō disallowed the departure of German merchant ships without prior official announcement of their intention to do so, and, to the horror of the Skl., Tokyo Radio reported the dates of departure, so that the German ships ran the risk of falling prey to British and French naval forces.[26] The best Raeder could report to Hitler on 10 November 1939 was that the Kaigunshō had explained that Japan did not want get involved in the European war but would support the Kriegsmarine according to the agreements reached in 1938 and asked for the transmission of concrete requests.

Raeder suggested asking the Japanese for docking permission at Japanese bases for German auxiliary cruisers and submarines, as well as for the conveyance of a few submarines for the battle against the British sea lanes in East Asia. Hitler agreed,[27] and the requests were transmitted to Endō.[28] The Japanese refused, maintaining that the IJN was not prepared to break its neutrality by conveying submarines but, again, would stand by its 1938 agreement to provide other assistance.[29] The Skl. therefore would not permit the deployment of the *Graf Spee* to a Soviet or Japanese harbor in East Asia, since it saw the negotiations as "not yet so far grown" and viewed such a deployment "as being the same as a relinquishment" of the Panzerschiffe.[30]

In the meantime the obvious German victory in the war against Poland (attacked on 1 September 1939) led to nervousness in Japan. The Gaimushō now saw a German attack on the Netherlands in the near future as a certainty and asked itself what would happen to the rich Dutch colonies in such an event. The declaration of a protectorate, or some other measure unwelcome to the IJN, coming from especially the United States, could not then be ruled out.

Naval analysts recommended reducing the Island Empire's economic dependence on the United States and the commencement of war preparations.[31] From the middle of November onward, naval forces were prepared for eventual operations against the Dutch East Indies.[32] At the end of November

Navy Minister Yoshida agreed to guidelines that incorporated the exploitation of the war in Europe in order to complete the "southern expansion."[33]

THE TRADE WAR AND BRITAIN

Meanwhile the main attention of the Skl. was focused on the trade war. Because of the special emphasis that the Kriegsmarine accorded it, Raeder had decided at the end of November 1939 that the first wave of German auxiliary cruisers should deploy in the winter of 1939–40, and the second wave should be ready for deployment in the summer of 1940.[34]

In connection with the trade war, Japanese reactions to initial British attempts to control neutral shipping were of special interest to the Skl., just as was the extent of trade that the Japanese engaged in with the opponents of the Reich. The sharp Japanese protest against the British confiscation of certain Japanese goods bound for Germany, as well as attempts at appeasement by the British in offering especially high compensation, were astutely noted by the Skl.[35]

The trade in Japanese goods with Great Britain was judged by the Skl. as "very opaque." The Japanese were "very sensitive" on the question, making the gaining of clear knowledge more difficult. It seemed probable that the Japanese trade with Great Britain would continue unabated.[36] The Japanese threat, to answer the illegal confiscation of Japanese goods through confiscating the same amount of British goods in Far Eastern waters, must have been welcome news for the Skl.; this time, unlike in World War I, it seemed possible to inhibit, at least, the classic British method of blockade.[37] Thus a friendship with the third largest sea power seemed highly beneficial, even without a formal alliance.

That impression seemed to be confirmed at the beginning of January 1940, when the Skl. received news that also seemed to point in that direction. It was rumored that Tokyo and London were talking about an agreement about shipping German goods to Japan.[38] These hopes were dampened in the same month, however, when on 21 January, not far from the Japanese Naval Station at Yokosuka, a British cruiser stopped the *Asama Maru* and violently abducted twenty-one Germans.[39]

This incident could not have been a complete surprise to the Kriegsmarine. On 5 September Lietzmann, having asked whether or not there were doubts about transporting German draftees on board Japanese ships, had received the answer from the first adjutant of the navy minister: "According to section 82 of maritime war law, warships of warring nations were permitted to inspect neutral ships and take prisoner any encountered draftees of an enemy power.

One could from the Japanese side therefore give no guarantee for the safe passage of German draftees on a Japanese steamer."[40]

The incident led to sharp anti-British reactions in the Japanese public and to protests by the Japanese government.[41] Interesting, however, was the Skl.'s estimation of this reaction: "The strong condemning attitude of Japan is no doubt not based on a special friendly attitude of the Japanese people or the government toward Germans, but rather on the mentality of the Japanese in exhibiting natural resistance against a foreign show of power in an East Asian area in which Japan claims pre-eminence and is prepared to exercise it. The incidents, therefore, hit the Japanese in the most sensitive spot of their nationalism."[42]

The Skl. noted hints of Japanese "retaliation" for the incident,[43] but viewed as "surrender" the directions of the Japanese government to the shipping lines not to transport any more German draftees[44] and its finally negotiated compromise with the British.[45] Moreover, the Skl. critically detected doubts about the German government in their evasive answers and registered a strong disparity between sharp words and dull actions on the part of the Japanese government.[46]

At the end of March 1940 the Skl. assumed that the Japanese were worried about an intervention of the United States in the European conflict, which could have grave consequences in East Asia. The Skl. now expected a Japanese rapprochement to Great Britain and already had concluded that the difficulties, presumably caused by the Japanese, in transporting important raw materials to Germany from East Asia via Siberia could be based on this development.[47] The Gunreibu had in the meantime, through studies of its own, come to the conclusion that a German attack on the Netherlands was improbable, since Germany could only hold open its access to world markets by maintaining friendly relations with neutrals, and judged the chance of a German blockade against Great Britain as favorable.[48]

The prospect of gaining both the Soviet Union and Japan as "friendly" neutrals allowed the Skl. to also hope for the homecoming of numerous German merchant ships that had stayed in neutral harbors as a result of the outbreak of war. It was thought to bring the ships lying off the Dutch East Indies and western America first to Japan and from there, via the sea routes north of Siberia, back into German waters. For those ships whose chances of being brought back seemed hopeless, a sale to neutrals was considered, under the condition that these ships would not be used for trade with Germany's opponents or leased to them.[49] The Skl. had high hopes for the use of the "northeastern sea route" for trade with East Asia, as well as for the transit of auxiliary cruisers into the Pacific, Indian, and South Atlantic Oceans.[50]

The right of disposal of the merchant ships lay not with the Skl., insofar as the ships were not needed for logistical support, but with the Transport Ministry (*Reichsverkehrsministerium,* or RVM). The RVM told the Kriegsmarine with great regret at the beginning of April that it did not plan to bring the ships back from Japan in 1940, since no cargo was going to be available for the ships.[51] In July the auxiliary merchant cruiser *Komet* left for the Pacific via the North Siberian seaway (with Soviet help), where it arrived in September,[52] but the Skl. had to abandon all further hopes of a northeast passage as relations with the Soviet Union deteriorated in June 1940.[53]

The Operations Department of the Skl. evaluated the effects of the trade war with pocket battleships and auxiliary cruisers in January 1940 and deemed its achievements as very favorable. Accordingly, because enemy naval forces were otherwise engaged (the diversionary effect), it planned to deploy in the spring and summer of 1940 five auxiliary cruisers with the main emphasis in the Indian Ocean.[54] For this reason it wanted priority given to the completion of the auxiliary cruisers. During the preparations for the occupation of Denmark and Norway (code named "Weserübung"), the Skl. ran up against opposition from Raeder, who judged the outlook for the auxiliary cruisers more skeptically and ordered that the preparation of the cruiser *Leipzig* be given priority.[55] Thus only two instead of five of the planned second wave of auxiliary cruisers, together with the armored cruiser *Lützow* (the former *Deutschland*),[56] could be made ready to sail into the Atlantic before the German attack on Denmark and Norway on 9 April 1940.[57] And even that plan could not be fulfilled; the ships were deployed in May. For the deployment of new auxiliary cruisers the Skl. viewed the Indian and Pacific Oceans for the time being as secondary areas of operation.

In the meantime Wenneker was surprised to be notified by the Gunreibu that it would welcome an appearance of German naval forces in East Asia.[58] The IJN was not only prepared to tolerate the operations of German submarines from Soviet harbors, but would also support the Kriegsmarine with appropriate harbors in the South Seas.[59]

THE INVASION OF THE NETHERLANDS

The beginning of the "Weserübung" caused conceptual rethinking in Japan. This involved the German invasion of the Netherlands, now expected with great certainty, and its effects upon the Dutch East Indies.[60] Once again preparations for a deployment of Japanese naval forces into the area were completed in order to preempt the Anglo-Saxons.[61] In such a case, however, it was necessary to take into consideration an armed conflict with the United States. Studies of the Gunreibu in May 1940 revealed the Achilles heel of Japan in such a scenario. A war had to be decided within a year, because of the lack of resources, and could at most be conducted for two years. In addition the navy minister pointed out that the sea routes between Japan and the Dutch colonies would be unprotected.[62]

During the French campaign, which began on 10 May, the Skl. perceived heightened Japanese concern about an Allied involvement in the Dutch East Indies, especially after just this had occurred in the Dutch Caribbean possessions. This concern even led to an announcement of troop landings, in case "third powers" should engage in such activities in the Dutch East Indies.[63]

The German successes during the French campaign inspired the Japanese navy to encourage more active use of Japan's friendship by the Germans, that is, engaging Japanese support for operations in the Indian and Pacific Oceans. Thereupon the head of the Skl. ordered the preparation of the Kriegsmarine for Pacific operations; a utilization of Japanese help was also planned for the operations of the auxiliary cruisers.[64] Safe anchorages prepared by the Japanese in the Marshall or Caroline Islands were to be stocked with supplies from Japan and first to be used to supply the auxiliary cruiser "Ship 36." The auxiliary cruiser was supposed to operate between June and September in the areas around Australia and New Zealand and, after being supplied on the way back, also in the Indian Ocean.[65]

At the end of July, the Skl. noted with satisfaction, from the numerous orders of the British Admiralty to the merchant ships in the Atlantic and Indian Oceans, the "very respectable results, of the only partially known successes of our auxiliary cruisers."[66] In the beginning of December 1940 nearly all German auxiliary cruisers were deployed in the Indian or Pacific Oceans or were planned for such deployment.[67] In the Skl. was so impressed by the victories achieved that they demanded the incorporation of the auxiliary cruisers into the *Sonderstufe* and characterized them as one of their best weapons.[68]

The preparation of supply dumps by the Japanese navy was of critical importance for this activity. However, the limits of Japanese willingness to help were immediately revealed, if international interest—for example, by the docking in Japanese harbors of ships captured by German auxiliary cruisers—

threatened to be stirred up.[69] Neither was direct material help given to German warships by the Japanese; on the contrary, supplies for the auxiliary cruisers had to be transported via the Trans-Siberian Railroad into the Far East and brought with German merchant ships from Japanese harbors to the supply dumps.[70] Then, from the spring of 1941 on, the Japanese declared themselves ready to support the operations with Japanese supply ships.[71]

The bombardment of Nauru Island by two German auxiliary cruisers at the end of December 1940 caused considerable irritation to the IJN. Wenneker reported that their shipments of phosphorus were impaired by this event, cooperation was threatened, and possibly the danger of a limitation of support might develop, which was why such actions in the vicinity of the mandated areas should in future be refrained from. The Skl. supported his position on the matter.[72] All in all the Skl. was, though, extraordinarily pleased with the successes of the ships and the unrest they caused in Allied shipping.[73]

In the spring of 1941 there were hints that the shipping traffic between Australia and New Zealand and the British Isles was being increasingly rerouted from the Indian Ocean through the Panama Canal.[74] For further auxiliary cruiser operations in the waters around India, the Kriegsmarine asked for and received support in intelligence gathering. The Japanese navy asked the Japanese consulates and shipping-line representatives to gather information within the entire area.[75]

INDOCHINA

The armistice in France brought up the question of the fate of Indochina, in which the Japanese navy had to be especially interested, since it dealt with an important part of their "southern thrust." An immediate, forceful intrusion was judged by the Japanese as bearing the risk of the armed involvement of the United States, a risk that the IJN in June and July 1940 was not yet prepared to take.[76] This, obviously, did not hinder the political exploitation of the victorious German western campaign and the preparations for an incursion into the French colony.[77] However, during the summer the way was paved in the IJN for a more extensive cooperation with the Germans that was decided upon in September and which was aimed clearly against the United States.

At the end of June, warning voices still prevailed: cooperative investigations by the Kaigunshō and the Gunreibu came to the conclusion that a further southern expansion (including a movement against Indochina) would mean war with the United States, Great Britain, and the Dutch East Indies. Japan would only be able to wage such a war for one year and would be put under pressure to conquer the oil fields in the Dutch East Indies within four months.[78] In early August, however, the operations department of the Gunreibu proposed to commence the move into Indochina.[79] The IJN also around this time took advantage of a chance to enlarge its share of the defense budget and was perfectly ready to take a stronger anti-U.S. stance in exchange for this gain.[80]

Sweeping changes, though, were on the horizon. At the beginning of September Navy Minister Yoshida Zengo and his deputy Sumiyama Tokutarō, both relics of the Yonai faction, were replaced by the team of Oikawa Koshirō and Toyoda Teijirō, who were strongly sympathetic to the more radical middle echelons of the IJN.[81] It also seems that they harbored a fear, also shared by Foreign Minister Matsuoka, that the animosity between the United States and Germany could be only temporary "sibling rivalry" of "whites," after the resolving of which Japan would be confronting a united "white" front unless precautions against this were not created through treaty obligations.[82] This opinion was now shared by the navy.

When the Foreign Ministry subsequently explained alliance proposals to the German diplomats Ott and Stahmer in Japan, the new Japanese Naval High Command created within a few days a consensus for the proposed agreement.[83] This was, though, not a total change in the current Japanese naval policy, because the agreement to the proposal had been granted by the IJN only under conditions: Japan must be able to decide independently about a war with the United States; Germany must guarantee the Japanese possession of the previously German South Sea colonies as final, and efforts for a settlement with the Soviet Union should take place.[84] In addition, the IJN considered the Tripartite Pact, concluded on 27 September 1940 in Berlin, as an instrument of deterrence against the United States. Before the signing, the IJN was still alarmed at the prospect of the U.S. Navy using the British fleet port of Singapore.[85]

But also within the time frame of the treaty's conclusion, which, upon closer inspection, did not specify any binding alliance obligations for Japan, Wenneker repeatedly recognized small "blemishes," pointing to self-interest and especially concerning Navy Minister Oikawa, that did not call for great elation. The signing had to be postponed because, according to Wenneker, "the Japanese themselves still tried at the last minute to gain small advantages (especially in the weapons area) for themselves."[86] When after the conclusion of the treaty the German and Italian naval attachés visited the navy minister and chief of the Gunreibu in order to convey the official congratulations of their navies, Wenneker noted a "quite cool" reception by the minister but got a warmer reception from the Gunreibu. He remarked that at the reception for higher government representatives, given by Premier Konoe on the occasion of the signing, only the navy minister was absent—something that also occurred at the reception of the German ambassador the next day.[87] In view of the composition of the technical commission, specified in paragraph 4 of the treaty, it was announced to Wenneker on 3 October that Vice Adm. Nomura Naokumi would be the leader of the commission being sent to Berlin.[88]

At the Skl. the sharp reaction that the pact had received in the United States had meanwhile been noted.[89] Characteristically, while the German navy was thinking of incorporating Vichy France into the "Berlin-Rome-Tokyo Front,"[90] the Japanese navy wanted the relationship with the Soviet Union cleared up ("to protect one's back") before any confrontation with the United States.[91]

13

Intelligence Exchange

The events of the year before the Japanese entry into the war, including the attitude of the IJN and the occurrences of the year 1942, have been exhaustively covered elsewhere.[1] The present discussion can be limited to aspects that have had only limited mention or none at all, namely, cooperation in the field of intelligence exchange.

THE AUTOMEDON INCIDENT

An extraordinary occurrence in this sector was the capture of the British steamer *Automedon* by the German auxiliary cruiser "Ship 16," the *Atlantis*, on 11 November 1940 in the Indian Ocean, between the Nicobars and Ceylon.[2] During this operation a lot of valuable material fell into the hands of the Germans, among which was the mail for the British Far East Command. In this there were also cabinet papers from 15 August 1940 that dealt with the situation in the Far East and the possible reactions to a Japanese attack on Singapore, as seen by the British.[3]

This material was brought to Kobe by the captured Norwegian tanker *Ole Jacob,* where the ship, to the dismay of the Japanese, entered harbor on 4 December with the German war ensign hoisted. Wenneker received the documents on the following day, sent them to Berlin by safe hand, radioed a summary of their contents, and telegraphically asked for permission to hand over the documents to the Japanese.[4] They were delivered to the Japanese on 12 December.[5]

In various literature the supposition is often encountered that Japanese planning was strongly influenced by this captured material.[6] In actuality, however, the German side seems to have been the one more strongly influenced. Wenneker's compilation of the captured War Cabinet papers arrived in Berlin at a time at which the Skl. especially desired an additional strategic diversion of the Anglo-Saxons. It viewed the situation in the Mediterranean with great worry in the autumn of 1940. It had even considered possible an Italian collapse and Italy's breaking away from the Axis. The expulsion of the Royal Navy from the Mediterranean, seen by the Skl. as decisive for the war, was no longer deemed possible; instead it expected increasing difficulties for its own warfare. The tonnage war with Great Britain was, in view of increased aid from the United States and insufficient production of new German submarines, judged to be favorable for the British in the long run and, at least in the war journals (*Kriegstagebuch*, or KTB), the Skl. wanted more emphasis on the war against Great Britain and postponement of "Barbarossa."[7]

When Raeder reported to Hitler on 27 December to this effect, he received only slightly veiled disapproval for his lobbying to encourage the Japanese to strike against Singapore, as well as for his demand for giving priority to the naval war against Great Britain before "Barbarossa."[8] He obviously was not willing to be satisfied with this response, because when the couriers arrived on 30 December with the original documents from the *Automedon*, he decided on the same day that Wenneker was to be ordered to influence the Japanese in this matter, just as he had presented the idea to Hitler on 27 December.[9] Wenneker's receipt of such an order before March 1941, however, cannot be proven. The war journals of neither the Skl. nor of Wenneker show any such notation.[10]

Even though no clues were found that Japan was ready to enter the war in the near future, the Skl. considered it necessary to set up studies for this in January 1941.[11] The only apparent reason for this was the hope that the Japanese could be riled up by the British weakness in the Far East, as revealed in the *Automedon* documents.[12] That the British would be weakened by the loss of Singapore was not as important as the improvement in the Axis advantage, in terms of tonnage, if Japan entered the war.[13] Thus global diversionary strategic aspects led the German side to hope for a reversal of the tendencies in the trade war apparent since the autumn of 1940.[14]

In addition, for Raeder there had to be, with the arrival of the *Automedon* papers in Berlin, an unexpected occasion for far-reaching hope. After the hesitancy of the Japanese in the first parts of war, the chance now seemed to have arrived for presenting to the Japanese, with the help of these documents, just such a "never-recurring possibility" and "fateful opportunity" that Lietzmann had already described during the Sudeten crisis.[15] They could help the hawks within the Japanese navy, who had pushed for an armed conflict against the British, to a breakthrough.

Concrete plans for a combined effort in case of a Japanese entry into the war were not realized, however. And nobody in the Skl. was sure at the end of February 1941 that the delivery of the *Automedon* material to the Japanese navy had actually led to an increased preparedness for war.[16] For this, however, the Foreign Ministry took the initiative. Ribbentrop ordered Ambassador Ott at the end of February to pressure the leadership of the Japanese for an attack against Singapore.[17] The ambassador accomplished this mission by asking the *Wehrmachtsattachés* of the embassy for support and leading conversations with the heads of the Japanese IGHQ and the Gunreibu.[18] By the beginning of the month he had completed a study, in cooperation with the Wehrmacht attachés, about a possible involvement of Japan in the war.[19]

Wenneker also placed that study before the OKM; in it he incorporated the knowledge gained from the War Cabinet papers captured from the *Automedon*.[20] The attaché had come to the conclusion that Japan was militarily strong enough to successfully accomplish offensive operations against the British possessions on the East and Southeast Asian mainland, Northern Borneo, and perhaps also against the Dutch East Indies and the Philippines. An involvement of the Americans was not to be anticipated, in his opinion, except in the case of simultaneous attack on the Philippines.[21]

Very meager from the point of view of Raeder and Ribbentrop were the results of the discussion that Ambassador Ott and the Wehrmacht attachés of the German embassy conducted with the Japanese to encourage them to move against Singapore. Admiral Kondō explained that the IJN was making all preparations for an attack upon Singapore but that this would only be initiated "when the time has come and no other path remains open." Such an attack could also bring about war with the United States, especially endangering the Japanese merchant marine with American submarines and cruisers, and, finally, "the cause for an active attack in any direction was not yet given," as long as the possibility of obtaining raw materials from the United

States remained. Wenneker gained the impression "that the will to attack in comparison to the last half year had suffered some deterioration in Japan," and saw the main reasons in the recent Italian setbacks.

A further clue to the Japanese reluctance was the statement of a Japanese publicist that he had been asked by the Kaigunshō to limit his previously lively propaganda for an attack on Singapore.[22] Wenneker, on the other hand, was of the opinion vis à vis his Japanese counterparts that Japan now had a chance to realize its goals, the kind that "will not appear in fifty or a hundred years."[23] Such lobbying, however, remained without visible success. Quite obviously the British War Cabinet papers had not significantly affected the careful position of the IJN. The favorable outlook for a strike against Singapore neither changed the dependency on raw materials from the United States, nor did it change the threat from the U.S. Navy, the main enemy of the Japanese navy in the Pacific.[24] These vital factors underlying the attitudes of the IJN were obviously not clearly recognized in the German naval leadership.

The Skl. thus saw itself in the spring of 1940 doubly disappointed in its hopes on the one hand by Hitler, who was not prepared to follow Raeder,[25] who had been significantly influenced by the captured War Cabinet papers, and on the other hand by the Japanese navy, whose doubts could not be eliminated despite the singular chance "in fifty or a hundred years."[26]

INTELLIGENCE GATHERING

Even though the IJN was not interested in an actual coordination of operational plans with the German side, it did have a manifest interest in cooperation in the area of intelligence gathering. This was especially true for intelligence about its main enemy in the Pacific, the U.S. Navy. The deciphered radio traffic of the Japanese naval attaché reveals a cooperation that has been, until now, totally unknown or not recognized as such.[27]

In May 1940 the head of the Japanese Naval Intelligence Service informed the Japanese naval attaché in Washington that an agreement had been reached with the Germans and a meeting between Japanese and German agents was to take place in the Japanese Club in New York. For this a representative of the German intelligence service (*Abwehr*), who was given the code name "Steamer," was to hand over documents for the Japanese navy. For security reasons, no direct contact was to be made with him.[28]

The meeting was delayed, however, because at the end of August the Japanese naval attaché in Berlin was informed that the first contact should now take place in the Miyako restaurant in New York. Obviously, further agreements had been made in the meantime, because now it was said to first get in touch with the contact man for the area of the East Coast and make arrangements later for the area of the West Coast. In addition, the Gaimushō had offered the Germans use of the Japanese diplomatic pouch for the transport of information.[29] The attachés in Berlin and Washington were informed a few days later that the code word for the meeting was supposed to be the code name for the German "Steamer."[30]

Since the German intelligence agent Mand, who was planned for the meeting, was on tour, the meeting could not take place at the specified date.[31] It finally happened on 25 October. Mand handed over a letter, after the arrival of which in Tokyo further dates were to be arranged, and asked to arrange a direct meeting with "Steamer." The delivery of the letter was especially supposed to determine the amount of time it took for the documents to get to Tokyo and inform Berlin of their arrival.[32] This took a considerable amount of time, and the continuation of the operation was delayed until March 1941.

THE "K" OPERATION

Nevertheless, the Japanese were very much interested in cooperation with the intelligence service and sent an officer to Berlin in March 1941 to personally inform the Japanese naval attaché, Yokoi, about the situation in the United States and instruct him about the Japanese naval leadership's interest in this endeavor.[33] In the same month there seem to have been hints of a cooperation with German spy networks in South America and the *Marinesonderdienst* (Naval Special Services), which was run there by the naval attaché in Buenos Aires, Captain Niebuhr.[34]

In order to finally and satisfactorily organize the coordination, a high-ranking representative of the Intelligence Service was sent to Tokyo in the middle of May via Siberia.[35] After a conversation with him, a new meeting was agreed upon in the United States on 22 May and the joint effort was baptized the "K" Operation.[36]

In an unrelated gesture, the Intelligence Service also offered the IJN the transmission of aeronautical knowledge through couriers assigned to the "K" Operation.[37] On the same day the Germans requested that the Intelligence Service be allowed to use the Japanese attaché radio net for the transmission of intelligence to Berlin.[38] Evidently this request was granted, because a few

German-language communications were transmitted over the Japanese connection until the middle of July 1941.[39]

The agreed-upon "K" Operation meeting was highly successful for both sides, and documents were handed over to the Japanese,[40] who considered them so important that they could only be transported aboard a Japanese ship.[41] When they arrived in Tokyo in the middle of August, the Abwehr was immediately notified.[42]

Obviously relieved that the "K" Operation had finally begun, after lengthy negotiations involving an Intelligence Service representative, the Japanese naval attaché in Washington had instructions to keep the closest possible contact with the Germans and to undertake all efforts to ensure its success.[43] Near the middle of July 1941, however, numerous Germans were arrested in the United States, among them, apparently, "Steamer," so the "K" Operation had to be suspended temporarily.[44] This cannot have been the case for too long, however, because at the end of September the Japanese attaché reported that the coastal posts of the U.S. Atlantic Fleet had been changing their call signs on a monthly basis since May. Since the code in use could not be read anymore, he warned, the "K" work had now become very difficult.[45] From that one may conclude that the operation was resumed before it once again ran into difficulties.

BARBAROSSA

Another notable discovery in the decoded naval attaché messages is the point at which the IJN received notice of "Barbarossa." Hitler had forbidden notifying the Japanese of the planned attack on the USSR, and the literature until recently has set 3 June, when Hitler instructed Ōshima, as the date on which the Japanese learned of the plan.[46] Yokoi's radio traffic proves, however, that the Japanese had been notified a month and a half before that.[47]

Even so, a week after the start of "Barbarossa," the Japanese attaché was still without instructions from Tokyo as to the official Japanese attitude to this event. Yokoi complained bitterly about this fact in a long radio message and warned of a loss of face toward the Germans. He asserted that, at the outbreak of war between Germany and the USSR, Foreign Minister Matsuoka had been under the wrong impression, that Japanese participation in this venture was not desired. At any rate, he observed, in Germany the action most desired of the Japanese would be the capture of Singapore. And in light of the Japanese negotiations with the United States, Germans had the impression that there was really little or no inclination in Japan to start the "southern thrust."

Consequently, the German side, as "replacement" for Singapore, had asked for Japanese participation in the war against the Soviet Union.

Yokoi pushed for a decision[48] and contrasted the Japanese reluctance with a German example: Within minutes and with a few telephone calls, Ribbentrop had brought about the decision to recognize, together with Italy, the Nanking government in China.[49] Yokoi concluded, "Germany considers it extremely strange that our attitude should still be undetermined today, when we had advance notice in the middle of April."[50] Yokoi had been kept in the dark by Tokyo for over two months.

Yokoi's situation typified the consequences of a decision-making process as cumbersome as that of the Japanese. For the Japanese representatives in foreign countries, it meant the danger of working abroad for long periods without instructions, even about important developments; the Germans inferred insincerity from the resulting inaction in Yokoi's case.

Despite urgent requests, Yokoi had to wait for another month before he received instructions about the IJN's attitude toward the relevant questions from the head of the Naval Affairs Bureau, Rear Adm. Oka Takazumi.[51] The admiral mentioned a "common fate" of both nations, but the important passages contained criticism of the German partner, underlined the need to keep one's options open, and whined about having to carry the main burden in a war with the Anglo-Saxon sea powers without any help from the Germans.

First, Oka pointed out the internal differences between Japan and Germany, with which the Germans were obviously not familiar enough.[52] Instead of an extensive coordination of their policies, both partners should, rather, concentrate on their own matters within their own spheres of influence.[53] For Japan the conclusion of the war with China had priority. A further extension of the fronts (obviously a reference to Germany's wish that Japan participate in the war against the Soviet Union or attack Singapore) was therefore "only limitedly" possible and even then only after the resolution of the China conflict. German doubts as to the resoluteness of the Japanese were unfounded, but Japan had to decide the time and place of its measures itself, just as Germany also did.[54] Each country was supposed to make its own plans; cooperation was to follow only rough outlines.[55] Only if both nations should get into a situation in which direct reciprocal help should become necessary would the question of cooperation have to be viewed differently.[56]

Anyway, the admiral insisted, German distrust of the Japanese-American negotiations was without substance. Its only goal was to prevent a worsening in the relationship of both countries. Moreover, the German attack on the Soviet Union was the actual problem. Not only had it occurred without consideration of Japan's still unfinished preparations, but it had also worsened Japan's position in the China conflict, and had, beyond that, given encouragement to U.S. war plans.[57] Even in case of a complete victory of the German army the actual problem of the Japanese navy, the rivalry with the Anglo-Saxon navies, remained unsolved. Here the danger was that Japan would be left alone with the risk.[58]

This remarkable document proves that the IJN disapproved of the idea of coalition warfare with the German side. The reasons for their resistance marked the primary constant that decided the policies of the Japanese navy, namely, the knowledge of their own economic weakness and vulnerability in a war with the Anglo-Saxons.[59] Thus the IJN urgently required, not just to settle the strength-draining China war, but also to limit further warlike involvements of any kind (such as movement, according to German wishes, against the Soviet Union, or an attack on Singapore). From this standpoint the Southern Thrust had to enjoy priority, as it promised to eliminate Japan's scarcity of raw materials (especially oil). Of course, it was to be pursued with care, in order not to precipitate an early war with the Anglo-Saxons.

The German side played a subordinate role in these plans, because their actual strength, their very powerful land forces, could not reach the sources of British and American might through their own power, and the Kriegsmarine was, because of its limited strength, hopelessly outclassed by the Anglo-Saxon navies and was, therefore, despite a limited diversionary effect, practically a negligible factor for the Japanese navy. This basic constellation of economic weakness, overextension of forces, and factual inability of the Kriegsmarine to support the Japanese partner militarily did not change after the Japanese entry into the war and remained unchanged throughout the course of it.

That Yokoi's warnings of irritation on the part of the Germans were justified was revealed when Nomura Naokumi tried to explain the Japanese position in a conversation with Groos at the beginning of August.[60] Groos himself commented in his report that Nomura's explanations showed "how hard it was for the Japanese to accept the changing of the situation that occurred through the German-Russian war and make the appropriate decisions."[61] The mistrust that had established itself in the German naval leadership in the meantime is quite drastically visible in the severely bitter and ironic marginal remarks that the head of Skl., Fricke, placed on Groos's report.[62]

While the Japanese navy had been notified at least two months in advance of "Barbarossa," the Kriegsmarine received no definite information from the Japanese side before the attack upon Pearl Harbor. Wenneker reported at the beginning of November that he had heard from a "senior naval officer" that the negotiations with the United States were looking hopeless, the Japanese government was "as good as certain of war with America," and the start of the military "southern thrust" was still to be expected in 1941.[63] The Skl. rated this, however, as "in view of the source, a report not to be judged without skepticism."[64]

Even when the exact time of the Pearl Harbor attack was known, the Gunreibu kept its own representatives in Germany in the dark.[65] Groos wrote in his memoirs that Nomura Naokuni had explained to him at the beginning of November 1941 that Japan would open the war with a sudden attack on the U.S. Navy and confidentially whispered to him on 4 December, "We are attacking."[66] But even if Groos's memories do not deceive him here, this cannot be considered clear information about intentions, location, and time of the Japanese attack.[67]

After the attack on Pearl Harbor, the responsibility for gathering intelligence about the United States for the Japanese navy was transferred from the attaché in Washington to the one in Berlin. He immediately called for an intensification of cooperation in the area of signals intelligence. During a conversation in January, Fricke had given him details about the *B-Dienst*'s breaking into the British codes and the solutions for U.S. codes. In terms of the latter, Fricke complained about a lack of raw data, and to his superiors in Tokyo Yokoi suggested giving the Germans access to such material via Wenneker for their own decoding work.[68]

Throughout the war with the United States, the Japanese labored to reconstruct the information network they had lost there. Agents were trained in Europe, equipped with false identities and papers and sent to Portugal and Spain, from where they were to infiltrate the United States via South and Central America, disguised as business travelers. Among them was a German named Mann, who was possibly a former naval officer.[69] During the attempted infiltration, the Japanese again cooperated with the OKW, but this fact was kept strictly secret from Mann.[70] The lack of contact people in the United States seems to have complicated the operation.[71] The cooperation with the OKW did not stop the Japanese attaché from conducting espionage, by means of well-placed contacts, against Germany and Italy.[72]

14

Intentions and Evasions

In the area of military cooperation, true coordination never developed between the navies of Germany and Japan, either in 1942 or later. The military commission of the Tripartite Pact remained a hollow facade, and the navies did not exchange their operational intentions.[1]

The wording and content of the "military agreement between Germany, Italy, and Japan" of January 1942, which was supposed to secure the operative cooperation in the war alliance, was characterized by the absence of any tangible obligation: The only concrete decision was the limitation of the operational zones through 70 degrees east longitude.[2] Beyond that, there was merely talk of "contact" and "cooperation." Clues as to how this could be realized were utterly lacking. In this the document, which deals almost exclusively with maritime warfare, proves that the IJN's interest in merely loose cooperation had remained the same as Japan entered the war.

But it was not just the Japanese navy that showed disinterest in close cooperation; the important German posts were also unenthusiastic. At the end of December 1941 the Chief of Staff of the Skl. (Fricke) ordered that the attachés should cooperate as usual. Talks with Nomura were to take place, but for immediate questions a Japanese liaison officer was deployed, "who from time to time makes a presentation to the 1.Skl." These were clearly not arrangements for a close cooperation. Meanwhile a memo of the Operations Department of the Skl. expressed hopes for the far-reaching success of a coordinated movement with the Japanese in the near future. In the middle of February 1942 Lieutenant Rost concluded, from a longer situational analysis:

> The current weakened position of England in the Middle East gives us the great historical opportunity to achieve a position with a few divisions in a reasonable amount of time, that in cooperation with Japan will lead to the collapse of the entire British key position at the three-continent junction point and holds war-deciding consequences. The deployment of a few divisions will greatly compensate their lack on the Eastern front through the strategic consequences achieved, not to mention the economic advantages that become clear with the acquisition of the oil in Iraq and the future connection to the raw materials in Asia. If Germany and Japan join hands at the Indian Ocean, the final victory should not be far off.[3]

This quite worthwhile—from a purely operational viewpoint—recommendation for a shift of the main emphasis of the German war effort to the Middle East and to coordination with the Japanese was calculated without considering the decisive players in the game. It represented an attempt by the Kriegsmarine to influence the deployment of forces over which it did not have command. Neither the OKH, nor the OKW, nor Hitler was prepared to redeploy the "few divisions" necessary for the capture of Suez from the Eastern front. Instead the Kriegsmarine was consoled with an offensive into the Caucasus.[4] On this there was again some hope placed in the Skl. In a memorandum Lieutenant Commander Assmann emphasized the results that interruption of the supply lines from the Indian Ocean to southern Russia would have for the support of this offensive and concluded: "For this only the Japanese are capable, judging by the current situation."[5] Not realizing the true situation, Assmann counted on support from the Japanese and was merely concerned about the disinterest of the OKW that had developed in the meantime and wrote:

> The decisions of the Japanese are strongly retarded by a complete lack of official instruction about German intentions. It is to be noted that a generous strategic and operative cooperation does not exist with the Japanese High Command. The initiative for this cooperation must actually come from the *Wehrmachtführungsstab*. The OKW, however, seems not to place any value in cooperative strategic and operative planning with the Japanese.[6]

Assmann pleaded for speedy instruction and, aside from that, thought the Skl. the only post having the necessary strategic perspective for coordination with the Japanese.[7] In contrast to the continental perspective of the OKW and the OKH, the global viewpoint in the Skl. could hardly be made clearer.

The fact, however, that neither the OKW nor the Japanese navy was interested in the closer cooperation mentioned by Assmann and Rost was revealed a few days later. The Japanese had let it be known that they wanted to allow a few submarines and auxiliary cruisers to operate in the Indian Ocean. However, the appearance of a significantly stronger naval force, mainly a carrier battle group, which had operated during early April 1942 in the Eastern Indian Ocean with considerable success against the British Eastern Fleet, was not mentioned to the German side.

The final foundering of the hopes of the Skl. for cooperation was made clear at the beginning of August when the head of the OKW Operations Staff, Jodl, began a situation report for the Japanese with the explanation that the main goal of the year concerning the Caucasus, "namely, to cut off the Soviets from the main part of their oil supply," had been achieved.[8] There was no mention that creating a connection with the Japanese ally in the Near Middle East was an objective, even a secondary one, of the offensive in the area of Army Group South. Instead the protocol remarked concisely: "If the Soviet Union is defeated, the war is decided." In this Japan could "help considerably" by the use of naval forces in the western Indian Ocean.[9]

Not only had the Caucasus Offensive not contributed anything to the Skl.'s goal of a connection with Japan together with an interruption of the Allied sea lanes in the Indian Ocean, but the role of the IJN was seen there as that of a helper in the Germans' war against the Soviet Union. That had to be an unacceptable situation for the Japanese, because there was no actual state of war with Stalin's empire; on the contrary, since the middle of the 1930s it had been a constant part of Japanese naval policy to avoid such a conflict. Accordingly, Japanese support had been promptly withdrawn.

In addition, Japan's situation had fundamentally changed with the decisive loss at Midway, and only three days after Jodl's discourse the first battle in the Solomons began, by which the Japanese fleet lost any maneuvering room for a coordinated offensive movement with the Axis partner. Nomura tried very hard in his reply to Jodl's observations to explain the reluctance of the IJN to deploy in the Indian Ocean and emphasized the necessity for mutual trust. Japan would do everything that was possible.[10] With this he had hit the mark exactly. Trust was not present, and precisely the information from the alliance partner, about what could now still be viewed as possible, was lacking.

The Japanese veiled their true situation after their defeat at Midway in June and during the battle of attrition in the Solomons that began in August.[11] In these battles Japanese sea power was weakened to such an extent that it led to a loss of the ability to conduct strategic offensives at sea. Wenneker clearly understood this situation by the end of 1942, and in December in a situation report he drew a brutally clear picture of it. The heavy setbacks at Midway and the Solomons were for the Kriegsmarine, too, "of grave consequence" because they curtailed the Japanese operations in the Indian Ocean that the Germans constantly demanded. Further large-scale operations were not even considered, because of the heavy losses. Additionally, Wenneker pointed out the very serious situation for the Japanese in the Solomons, the feeble outlook for their reconquest, the weakness of Japanese production, and the catastrophic lack of shipping space.[12]

This last comment earned the attaché a reprimand from the OKW, which considered such reporting to be "psychologically dangerous," claimed that it did not withstand a "sober military analysis," and demanded a "healthy optimism."[13] The Skl. did not share the OKW's weakening grasp of reality, but that did not change matters; Wenneker had seen that a strategic cooperation between the German and Japanese navies had become basically impossible.[14]

THE END GAME

The IJN's posture with respect to cooperation with the Kriegsmarine, as outlined in the instructions for Yokoi at the end of July 1941, for all practical purposes stayed the same until the German capitulation. The German Navy, for the most part, reflected a nearly identical opinion.[15] After the war, a study conducted by the U.S. Navy examining the relationship of both navies, through the use of all available sources,[16] came to this conclusion.

Operational preconditions for a successful cooperation sprang from the need to maintain open sea lanes between the respective spheres of control in Europe and East Asia. The cooperative effort of the navies during World War II can be divided into three main areas: first, the exchange of material, especially important raw materials for the respective industries; second, the exchange of information, in other words, relevant scientific and technical knowledge for armaments and military intelligence experts; third, the direct support of the other partner through the deployment of forces in his area of operation.

One can differentiate among three fairly distinct time periods. The first period lasted from the Japanese entry into the war until about the end of the year 1942 and the beginning of 1943. Within this phase fell the high-flying plans of the Seekriegsleitung and successful operations of the German blockade-runners in operation between East Asia and Europe. The Japanese naval forces were, after great initial successes, seriously weakened by the defeats at Midway and the battle of attrition in the Solomons.

The second phase lasted until the Allied landing in France. It was marked by German attempts to strengthen Japanese fighting power through technical support. In this phase the turning point of submarine warfare came in May 1943, resulting in its extension into the Indian Ocean. Because of Allied successes against German blockade-runners, an increased shifting of transport duties to submarines on the side of the Axis was begun, and the building of U-boats solely for transport was considered but later discontinued.

The third phase, which lasted from the Allied invasion in France until the German capitulation, was marked by an increasing Japanese initiative to persuade the Kriegsmarine to deploy as many submarines as possible to East Asia. This reached its peak as the German surrender approached, in the suggestion to transfer all remaining large boats to Japan and continue the war from there.[17]

THE NEED FOR RAW MATERIALS

The German side had a special need for raw materials (mainly rubber and special ores for precious metal production), whereas the Japanese needed finished products (mainly "high-tech" machines and specialty steel) as well as raw materials such as mercury, which were scarce in the Japanese sphere of influence. After the possibilities of transport via the Trans-Siberian Railway were basically lost, as a result of the German attack upon the Soviet Union, the only promising possibility that remained was the sea route. It was not the first-rate naval power, Japan, but the second-rate naval power, Germany, which carried the main burden of the efforts to maintain the sea routes.

During the first phase the trade in freight ran relatively smoothly. Even so, problems arose that revealed mistrust and unrealistic estimates of the actual possibilities. Thus there were complaints from the Germans in September 1942 about the Japanese reluctance to conclude a treaty for rubber shipments. This led to delays in the deployment dates of German blockade-runners. There were other complaints, about prohibiting German representatives from observing the reloading of blockade-runners in Singapore, about the nonfulfillment of promises for oil deliveries to German ships, and about Japanese attempts to replace contracted cargo with cargo of lesser quality.[18]

Then there were the Japanese orders for over a million tons of steel and exorbitant amounts of aluminum. The cargo capacity for such quantities was not available, nor could the Luftwaffe realistically be expected to reduce its aircraft production for the benefit of shipments to Japan.[19] At the same time the Japanese requested that the Kriegsmarine provide them with more merchant ships to relieve their constant lack of shipping tonnage. The Kriegsmarine had already sold four merchant ships to the Japanese navy and chartered seven others to them.[20] Further accommodation would have endangered the completion of blockade and supply duties.[21]

With increasing Allied successes against the blockade-runners, transport duties increasingly moved to the submarines, a circumstance that imposed limitations in the quantity of transported goods that were more drastic for the German side than for the Japanese.[22] The important things for them, such as construction blueprints and technical specialists, could just as well be transported by submarine. Bulk transportation, which was important for the Germans, was drastically limited.

TECHNOLOGY EXCHANGE

Concerning armaments technology, the Japanese navy received from their German ally, in the second phase of the cooperation, prototypes of torpedoes, mines, guns, radar, and radar-warning devices. It was characteristic of the reserve practiced by the Germans that modern weapons, such as the target-searching acoustic torpedo of the Kriegsmarine (T-5, Zaunkünig), were long denied the Japanese. German submarines that entered the base at Penang within the Japanese sphere of influence were still ordered in April 1944 to destroy all torpedoes of that type that were on hand before sailing into the harbor.[23] Shortly thereafter those orders were changed; these torpedoes could be stored in Penang, but their existence had to be kept secret from the Japanese.[24] When base personnel replied that this would be impossible in the combined German-Japanese torpedo storage facility, Dönitz decided that the Japanese could see the torpedo, but he prohibited all technical explanations.[25]

Only after corresponding representations from Admiral Abe, who had meanwhile become Nomura's successor as the Japanese naval representative in the military commission of the Tripartite Pact in Berlin, did Dönitz promise him, around the middle of the year, complete information about this modern weapon. At the end of September two of them were handed over to the Japanese in Penang.[26]

Characteristic of the entire proceeding was the reluctance with which Dönitz acted. His behavior even repudiated the policy, agreed to in 1941 by his predecessor Raeder, to disclose all operational developments. Apparently he only agreed to it when he noticed that the torpedo could not be kept secret from the Japanese and that further silence on the matter would have aroused irritation on their part.

THE GIFT OF SUBMARINES

A special gesture of support was the presentation of two submarines to the Tennō during the summer of 1943, over strong objection from the navy.[27] The first of the two submarines (U-511) was sailed to the Far East by a German crew and was handed over on 16 September 1943. Vice Adm. Nomura Naokuni returned to Japan on board the boat, and the Japanese attaché commented favorably on the gift.[28] In addition, German engineers were sent to Japan to support the mass production of Japanese submarines according to German designs. In August 1943 a Japanese crew, sent to Europe with the Japanese boat I-8, was trained by the Kriegsmarine and sailed for Japan with the second donated submarine, the newly constructed U-1224, at the end of March 1944. The boat, however, fell prey to the Allied antisubmarine forces in the Atlantic.[29]

The gift of both submarines along with the technical know-how and the training of the crew actually constituted a serious attempt to train the Japanese navy in submarine warfare according to German tactics. The initiative to donate the boats, however, came from Hitler, not the navy. Nevertheless, the Kriegsmarine tried to make a deal for raw materials shipments as a counterservice as late as June 1944.[30]

Possibly in connection with the donation of the submarines and characteristically only after the intervention of Hitler and Dönitz, an inspection of the Japanese battleship *Yamato* was finally made possible in July 1943. The Japanese stipulated strict secrecy, however, in regard to the Italians. They were also not prepared to reveal to Wenneker the actual construction data of the ship, instead giving him merely "nominal specifications."[31]

TELECOMMUNICATIONS AND
INTELLIGENCE EXCHANGE

Dissatisfaction was also apparent in the area of radio contacts and signals exchange. Although a telecommunications agreement was reached, the negotiations were complicated and protracted; it was not in fact fully utilized. The German side was displeased with the practical performance and had a low opinion of Japanese capabilities.[32]

In the area of radio reconnaissance there were indeed partly thought-out plans for far-reaching cooperation, including the mutual placement of personnel in each partner's evaluation organization. These attempts, however, seem not to have been realized in a practical sense. Allied studies on the topic came to the conclusion: "Cooperation was never direct and at best the assistance rendered each to the other was negligible."[33]

Although both sides traded military and political information, the quality was very inconsistent and limited by political and prestige considerations. Thus, German proclamations about progress in the area of advanced submarines were excessively optimistic, while the Japanese masked their true situation in the Pacific.[34] The Japanese in Berlin did not receive any reports from the Japanese attachés in Moscow, for the Germans an especially interesting field, and the Japanese navy was always fearfully anxious not to let any precise details of the Allied resupply shipments to Vladivostok leak to the Germans.[35] Even knowledge from POW interrogations was, for the most part, withheld from the Germans. After the war U.S. analysts came to the conclusion that the area of intelligence sharing was, on the whole, lopsided to the disadvantage of the Germans.[36]

OPERATIONS: THE "MONSUN" SUBS

In operations, too, the cooperation of the navies was only superficial. When in August 1942 German submarines put to sea for operations off the South African Atlantic coast (Operation "Eisbär") the Skl. assumed that this deployment would be matched by corresponding operations of Japanese boats in coastal waters of the Indian Ocean.[37] Near the end of September, however, Dönitz ordered the German boats to operate on the Indian Ocean coast of South Africa, up to the area of Madagascar. The Japanese had not given their permission for this operation.[38] Obviously, Dönitz's orders were a reaction to the fact that this sea area in the Indian Ocean was totally free of Japanese boats.

The negotiations over operational areas for submarines and auxiliary cruisers proceeded until November 1942—very unfavorably, in that no agreement was possible and misunderstandings became more frequent.[39] By the middle of the month the Japanese finally notified the Skl. that the developments in the Solomons compelled them to concentrate their forces there, and only four auxiliary cruisers and five submarines would be available for the Indian Ocean.[40] The boats were to be deployed in the northwest Indian Ocean where since September there had been a few boats in action.[41]

The Skl. came to realize the seriousness of the Japanese situation in the Solomons and the fact that Japanese naval forces could not be expected to intervene in the Indian Ocean anymore, when it was secretly informed that Yokoi judged Nomura's presentation of the situation in the Solomons to be too optimistic. Nomura had fed unfounded German expectations of a Japanese intervention in the Indian Ocean, and Yokoi now held him responsible for the disappointment so created.[42]

In the first days of December the Japanese then offered the Kriegsmarine bases on the Indian Ocean, since "it would be favorable to the situation as a whole, if the maritime forces of the Axis could be deployed in stronger measures to the Indian Ocean."[43] This offer was also, simultaneously, presented to the Italians. An appraisal of the Japanese as "unreliable, " as well as hopes of their strengthened return into the Indian Ocean, were reflected in the language of the Skl.'s comment on the proposal: "Given the already proven mentality of the Japanese, it is to be feared that this willingness to grant bases is also only for a short duration and that numerous difficulties will arise once the Japanese fleet can again more actively operate in the Indian Ocean. Nonetheless, this offer remains tempting."[44] Here the unhappy experience of the negotiations of the preceding months over the demarcation of operational area seems to have left its mark. But the offer was enticing for the Kriegsmarine because in the Indian Ocean, as opposed to the Atlantic, the Allied antisubmarine warfare was a lot weaker, and the German side had a chance to lead the battle, deemed all-important, against Allied shipping space in sea areas that promised good success. Besides, the Japanese were deemed too weak and untrained for merchant warfare with submarines.[45]

The first of the German "Monsun" U-boats arrived in Penang at the end of October 1943. Preceding this were tedious negotiations over details such as the quality of the diesel oil that the Japanese were to provide in Penang.[46] Initially the Japanese did not want to concede to the Kriegsmarine its own radio station and demanded that Japanese communication installations be used.[47] The Germans, however, prevailed in this matter.

In the meantime, in March, the first session of the main commission of the Military Commission of the Tripartite Pact took place. It consisted of the reading of short, previously traded speeches, and Wenneker noted in his war diary that "the entire meeting was in actuality nothing other than a circus. . . . The reports of the Japanese military representatives were very shallow."[48] Cooperation was evidently treated as a mere formality.

Abe, however, saw in August 1943 that the time had come to intensify such formalities to a true cooperation, and he suggested the following measures to his superiors: "By this I mean that we must go beyond the hastily erected framework of previous agreements relating to operations and the conduct of the war; in other words, we must advance a step beyond the sphere of indirect collaboration in our operations."[49] Partly as a symbol of goodwill, two Japanese submarines were sent to Europe with transport missions.[50] But no actual coordination of operations ever developed. Symptomatic of this was the fact that the German "Monsun" boats bound to operate in the Arabian Gulf during September–October 1943 had no information about the three Japanese boats that were operating in the Indian Ocean at that time.

New discrepancies subsequently briefly appeared in September over the respective areas of operation.[51] Characteristic of the "next to one another" instead of the "with one another" attitude was the German proposal that both sides should order a general ban of attack on submarines to avoid damaging each other's boats.[52] This showed that the Germans again expected lengthy and difficult negotiations and in the meantime at least wanted to create a safety minimum. The Japanese, however, now responded with alacrity to German wishes.[53]

In view of such examples, American analysts after the war correctly judged the "Monsun" operation as a German attempt at a geographic diversion of their submarine warfare, but not as a joint operation with the Japanese. The deployment of German submarines in waters nominally claimed by the Japanese navy as their own areas of operation merely called forth the semblance of a joint operation.[54]

Three factors severely affected the deployment of the German boats from Far Eastern bases: the scarcity of supplies from the German sphere of influence, the difficulties that the Japanese ally encountered in providing the promised fuel for the boats, and the growing threat to the U-boats from Allied submarines in the waters around the bases. When the Allies cut off the blockade-runner traffic,[55] the boats going to East Asia had to carry a large part of their supplies themselves, worsening living conditions for the crews aboard.[56] Then, as the Allied offensive brought disastrous consequences to

Japanese shipping, Japanese ability to transport the promised amount of fuel to German bases also decreased. Near the end of 1944, the situation had become so serious that Wenneker had to supply fuel for the boats lying in Surabaya through the German tanker *Quito,* and the submarines could not be deployed until its arrival.[57] Because of the Allied submarine threat, Batavia was selected as the new main base after the end of October, and the last German submarine left Penang the same month.[58]

In the meantime the Japanese naval leadership had instructed Abe to push the Skl. for stronger deployments of German submarines, especially the newly announced Electro boats. Dönitz had refused; Allied troops were advancing to the German borders and active shipping traffic was increasing off the European coast.[59] Two months later, faced with the American attack upon the Philippines, the Japanese repeated their request, using Dönitz's own argument, namely, that the best sea area for a submarine war was where the best chances of success were, wherever they may be. In the area around the Philippines, while merchant shipping density was high, the submarine defense was weak in comparison to that in the Atlantic. German wishes concerning command leadership and supply would be "fully considered" by the Japanese side.[60] All that was achieved, however, was Dönitz's agreement for the deployment of a single boat (U-183), already stationed in the Far East, in the area of the Philippines. It was sunk en route, south of Borneo, by a U.S. warship in April before it had even reached its operational area.[61]

CONTACTS AT THE WORKING LEVEL

Too late to have any significant or practical consequences as to the outcome of the war, in August 1944 Dönitz, pursuant to a decision by Hitler, now issued an order to answer all Japanese questions concerning weapons and equipment. This was to include combat-tested as well as experimental developments. The Navy High Command (OKM) still, however, claimed the power of a case-by-case decision.[62]

That German technicians in Japan did not receive corresponding treatment was evident in December, when Wenneker reported on the experience of the engineers who had come with the two submarines given to Japan in the summer of 1943 to help with their mass production.[63] Instead they were employed entirely in making improvements or new developments of Japanese equipment. Wenneker even doubted that the Japanese had ever intended to use them for building submarines, the function for which they had been requested. With the exception of the welding expert, the engineers lamented that their developments were not tested in practice. Apparently, too, the salary agreements were not kept.

The German naval attaché thought that the specialists were valuable to the Japanese but doubted that they represented a marked contribution to the strengthening of the Japanese defense potential. The practical realization of a close partnership remained unsatisfactory here because of the mistrust of the Japanese partner.

But there were also significant inhibiting factors on the German side. Besides Dönitz's hesitant attitude, which was still noticeable, even after Hitler's decision for a full-disclosure policy on technical matters with respect to the Japanese, there was the decision-making process itself, badly fragmented on important questions about German war planning. A homogeneous leadership or organization was missing, so that, in constantly shifting constellations, the OKW, the high commands of the service branches, and other offices all exerted influence. One result was that the Japanese were sometimes unable to identify the authoritative spokesman in any given situation or the intentions of the German side.

Moreover, German army officers in the OKW and OKH saw little relevance in the Japanese navy where their own plans were concerned, so the IJN was not included in their discussions and instruction. The Kriegsmarine was only marginally represented in the OKW and therefore had comparatively little influence. Of course the Japanese naval officers in Berlin knew this and tried to intensify contacts with other offices that they believed to possess more influence.

In May 1944 Kojima considered these issues, along with the cautiousness of his own superiors in Tokyo, as the actual hindrance to a true, close cooperation between the two navies. They were a stronger hindrance than the now frequent bombing attacks of the Allies on the capital city.[64] Kojima's eloquent complaints and his proposals that the Japanese naval command should offer the Germans true cooperation died away without result. Instead, Abe and Kojima themselves were no longer receiving instructions on a regular basis, and they were still complaining about that in March 1945.[65]

The difficulties that the IJN encountered in their effort to better their contacts to the power centers in Germany did not, however, stop them from establishing and maintaining numerous contacts on the working level. The American decoding of the attaché communiqués allows unusual insights here.

Apparently, in the second half of the war spy activity of the Japanese navy flourished within the German sphere of influence. Meanwhile, as this source illuminates, it was making contact with groups besides the Kriegsmarine—primarily, the Luftwaffe.

As examples, two incidents deserve mention. In November 1944 the Japanese naval attaché in Sweden informed the chief of the Naval Intelligence Service in Tokyo and Abe that a captain of the Luftwaffe, who was deployed as technical assistant to the German Luftwaffenattaché in Sweden, had had a fierce dispute with his superior, as a result had declared himself a "free German," and had gone into exile in Sweden.[66] Thereupon, Abe and Kojima reported to their fellows in Sweden that said captain, who had been stationed in Washington at the time of the Japanese entry into the war, was an excellent judge of the U.S. air forces, whose analysis had always been fully accurate. He looked back upon a long record of service in America and had always "worked closely with the administration of the Imperial Japanese Army and the Imperial Navy." Even after his return to Germany he had continued to achieve "positive contributions." His deployment to Sweden had been regrettable and "a heavy blow for Japan." Since he was now "highly suitable" for investigatory purposes, the attaché in Sweden should test the possibility to continue using him to "Japan's advantage." Abe wanted to check this out as well but cautioned to use great discretion so as to avoid any "unpleasantness" with the Luftwaffe.[67]

The head of the Naval Intelligence Service in Tokyo agreed to this at the beginning of December, warning, however, that U.S. services could lurk behind the matter, since the German was married to an American who was currently in Switzerland.[68] The attaché contacted the German via telephone, also judged the danger to be considerable that he was in contact with U.S. services, and viewed his further use as a great risk in respect to the relationship with the Luftwaffe.[69]

At that time the IJN's relationship with the Luftwaffe was relatively good. The Japanese naval personnel in Berlin had not only received detailed information about German jet aircraft, radar, remote-controlled glide-bombs, and even tests results with antiaircraft rockets and experience with other new weapons, from the Luftwaffe, but had also reciprocated with services important to the Luftwaffe.

Field Marshall Milch had in the middle of October 1943 sent Major General Zellschopf to Abe under strict secrecy and inquired if the Japanese navy was capable of getting five tons of tungsten per month for the Luftwaffe. The

Germans had developed a new large-caliber fighter aircraft cannon with which it was possible to effectively combat the Allied four-engine bombers at a distance of one kilometer. Now the Luftwaffe's problem was getting large enough quantities of raw materials for the production of ammunition for this new weapon. Therefore Milch had decided, through circumventing the chain of command, to initiate contact with Abe directly. Even within the Luftwaffe he kept this move top secret.

Abe judged that a helping hand in this matter on the part of the Japanese might possibly be war-deciding. Despite the materiel superiority of the Allies, he saw a possibility here to enable the Luftwaffe to shoot down the heavy Allied bombers faster than their crews could be trained. Therefore, he rapidly endorsed Milch's proposal and at the same time asked that this information also be kept from the Japanese army.[70]

In the middle of March 1944 some thirty tons of tungsten actually arrived in Lorient aboard the Japanese submarine I-29 and were delivered to the Luftwaffe free of charge.[71] A day after the Japanese boat had entered harbor, Milch's messenger once again visited Abe, once again asked for total secrecy, and as a thank-you for their help gave the Japanese the latest models of remote-controlled glide-bombs, rocket-propelled projectiles, and aircraft cannons, including five hundred rounds of ammunition.[72] This was an example of unbureaucratic and effective cooperation that stood in stark contrast to the tedious negotiations that took place on similar issues between the navies where rights and price issues often played a great role.

That this transaction did not have the effect that Abe hoped for was due, among other things, to the fact that the Allies constantly read his and Kojima's radio traffic. Thus they received early notice of the newest German developments, situation analysis of leading institutions and people, and often also operationally usable information, such as reports about the coastal defenses in France, which the Japanese had inspected shortly before the invasion and about which they had radioed detailed reports back to Tokyo.[73] In other cases, meeting places for Japanese submarines on their way to western France were broadcast. In at least one instance this spelled a death sentence for the subject submarine.[74]

THE FINAL PERSONNEL EXCHANGES: U-234

Near the end of the war, the Kriegsmarine seemed to back down from the opinion that there was little to learn from the Japanese partner. This announced itself in the autumn of 1944 in certain statements of the Skl. to Wenneker.[75]

Despite the sobering report about the experience of the German engineers in Japan,[76] Dönitz developed plans at the beginning of December 1944 to send officers of the Kriegsmarine to the Japanese ally, where they would be deployed on board for training purposes.[77] The Japanese eventually agreed to this wish, reserving the right, however, to decide in which units of the fleet the Germans would be deployed.[78] These plans would not be realized. Two of the officers earmarked for the program embarked on the last submarine sailing to Japan, but Germany surrendered while the boat was still in the North Atlantic and the commander handed it over to the U.S. Navy.

Freight and passengers on this boat, U-234, were extraordinary. Not only were there 560 kilograms of uranium oxide for the Japanese army on board[79]—leading, after the war, to speculation about atomic weapons research in Japan[80]—but also the embarked passengers were all highly trained specialists. Their selection showed the main concerns of both sides.[81] Both Japanese commanders (engineers) Shoji and Tomonaga, the first a jet-turbine and the second a submarine specialist, committed suicide when they recognized that the boat was going to surrender to the Allies.[82]

Three other U-234 passengers were members of the Luftwaffe: The highest ranking was General Kessler, who was being sent to Tokyo as the new Luftwaffenattaché and was described by the Americans as being well informed about guided weapons and fire control devices.[83] Kessler had formerly been a naval officer, had held the position of *Fliegerführer Atlantik* and was a friend of Canaris's. An antiaircraft expert and a radio communications expert were accompanying him in support.[84] The Luftwaffen group was rounded out by two civilian members of the Messerschmidt company, who were specialists in rocket engines and their mass production.[85]

German navy personnel aboard the U-234 as passengers consisted of two groups: two officers, the first that Dönitz sent for training purposes to the Japanese navy,[86] and three officers who were supposed to be posted to Wenneker's staff for support. Two of the latter group were technicians,[87] the third a navy judge.[88] Wenneker needed these people because he was lacking technical specialists in Tokyo, and he needed judicial support because, among several hundred naval personnel under his command, there had been incidents of considerable service violations, such as grand theft and spying, which the attaché could not prosecute. Previously the delinquents had been transported back to the German sphere of influence via blockade-runner, but from 1944 on that was no longer possible.[89]

Two weeks before U-234 sailed into an American harbor, Wenneker in Tokyo had already given the code word "Lübeck" via radio to all submarines remaining in East Asia and informed the Kriegsmarine personnel a few hours later, two days before the surrender in Europe, that weapons had been laid down.[90] Thereupon the Japanese navy took over the boats and the crews were interned.

Plans had been in place since the autumn of 1944 about the Japanese naval personnel in Berlin in case of Germany's defeat. In the event, escape into the Soviet sphere of influence was considered.[91] But this possibility seems not to have been used by a single Japanese. Instead, the Japanese naval personnel who had not been captured by the U.S. Army in Bavaria (together with the majority of the embassy personnel) went to Switzerland or, with the help of the Kriegsmarine, to Sweden. Before this, in the middle of April, Abe had tried to get an appointment with Hitler, to suggest to him that the remaining naval forces of the Kriegsmarine could continue fighting from East Asia. Dönitz had, however, issued a polite refusal on 20 April.[92]

The official "paper traffic" of the German naval personnel remaining in Japan with the Japanese navy continued for a time even after the surrender. Even after the capitulation of Japan, they were still transacting business, such as the negotiations with the Kaigunshō and its representatives over the outstanding charter fees.[93] Only near the end of 1945 did this activity seem to stop, since around then the remnants of the erstwhile command authorities of the Japanese armed forces, which had temporarily continued to exist as a "first and second demobilization bureau" for the facilitation of the demobilization process, were disbanded. The repatriation of the Germans out of Japan did not begin until 1947.[94]

PART 3

Logistical Exchange between the Partners

15

Exchange of Personnel

During World War II the exchange of personnel was always seen as a basis for mutual understanding between Germany and Japan. However, the geographical distance between the two countries alone posed numerous difficulties in transportation of personnel. With the outbreak of war in September 1939, sea travel for German nationals was limited by the Allied sea blockade imposed against German merchant ships. Travelers had to make their journeys via friendly and neutral countries or aboard neutral merchant vessels. Only limited restrictions were imposed on Japanese nationals traveling at sea until Japan officially entered the war in December 1941.

From 16 January to 20 February 1941, members of the Japanese Navy Commission traveled aboard the AMC *Asaka Maru* from Yokosuka via the Panama Canal to Lisbon for onward transfer by air to Germany.[1] United States officials initially insisted on searching the *Asaka Maru* during her transfer through the Panama Canal, relenting only after lengthy negotiations.

In March 1941 President Roosevelt gave orders to search every foreign warship passing the Panama Canal. Likewise the British Embassy in Tokyo informed the Japanese government that Britain would not tolerate a repetition of the *Asaka Maru* trip. This threat was probably triggered by the fact that the British knew that the ship carried civilian and military cargo on the return trip. Consequently the Japanese navy routed the *Asaka Maru* around the Cape of

Good Hope on the way home.[2] Apart from this episode, Japanese merchant vessels generally avoided the European combat zones declared by the belligerent parties after mid-1940.

A safe and more secret alternative for traveling was opened by the German-Soviet Nonaggression Pact of August 1939, enabling the use of the Trans-Siberian railway. Although no exact figures are available, the Trans-Siberian railway route was extensively used for the exchange of civilian, diplomatic, and military personnel, especially blockade-runner crews, technicians, and embassy personnel, during the period from September 1939 to June 1941. This important transportation link was abruptly closed to the Germans when they attacked the Soviet Union on 22 June 1941. Japanese diplomatic and military personnel continued to use the Trans-Siberian route until March 1943 under the auspices of the nonaggression treaty signed with the Soviet Union in April 1941.[3]

Efforts to build up an air communication link between the Axis partners by using long-range aircraft were unsuccessful. Apart from a pioneering Italian nonstop flight across Soviet territory to Tokyo in July 1942, all plans for rapid air transport ended in failure. Although the Luftwaffe had approached its Japanese counterpart to make arrangements for nonstop flights between German bases in the occupied part of the USSR or Northern Norway and Tokyo, using modified Fw 200 or Ju 290 aircraft, the Japanese would agree only if the aircraft were routed around the Soviet Union. The Japanese objection to crossing Soviet territory arose from their intention to avoid diplomatic implications or confrontation with the Soviet Union that might give Stalin an excuse to revoke their mutual neutrality.

Nevertheless, the Japanese also saw the advantage of a quick air link between the two hemispheres to transport military and civilian experts. Especially after the series of military setbacks in early 1943, Japan took a growing interest in studying the latest German military technology to oppose the superior American war potential. In October 1943 the Japanese naval attaché, Vice Admiral Abe, sent a memorandum on the importance of an air link between Asia and Europe to the commander in chief of the Luftwaffe, Reichsmarschall Göring, and asked him to take every possible step for its realization.[4]

But on 1 August 1943, nearly three months before, the Japanese army had attempted to start nonstop flights with long-range aircraft from Singapore, using the southern route via India and Arabia to Europe. However, the first aircraft dispatched on this route was lost, presumably intercepted over the

Indian Ocean by a British fighter from Ceylon.[5] Thereafter the Japanese army and navy seem to have abandoned their attempt for an air link to Europe.

In April 1945 the German air force finally put forward a plan to send high-ranking Luftwaffe personnel by aircraft to Japan, this time using the great circle route from Norway across the Northern Hemisphere via the Bering Strait to Japan. The plan was to use a Ju 290 aircraft converted for extra fuel storage to cover the 7,700 kilometers between the German Bardufoss airfield in Northern Norway and Paramushiru airfield in Japan in a nonstop flight, with a four-man crew and the two passengers. However, the quickly deteriorating military situation soon made any such ideas useless.[6] Given the existing geographical, political, and military situation, transport by way of enemy-controlled waters became the only way to transfer German personnel to and from Japan.

The start of the German blockade-running program at sea between Japan and Europe in April 1941 to import vital raw materials offered an efficient but increasingly hazardous way for transportation of personnel. Blockade-running ships usually offered a limited number of places for passengers or military personnel in addition to their nominal crews. Since the start of the war, numerous native Germans resident in Japan or other Far Eastern countries had applied to the German embassy at Tokyo for homeward transportation to serve in the German armed forces. In addition, merchant seamen whose vessels had been interned or lost in North or South America, together with several former crewmembers of the pocket battleship *Admiral Graf Spee*, having escaped from internment in Argentina, had reached Japan for onward transport.

Between April 1941 and May 1942 at least 136 passengers had sailed on blockade-running ships from Japan to Europe. While several of them were killed in the accidental sinking of the motor ship *Spreewald* off the Bay of Biscay by a German U-boat at the end of January 1942, the majority reached Bordeaux safely. In the same time period, at least fifteen German officers and communication specialists arrived in Japan. Two army officers, Lieutenant Colonel Niemöller and Captain Merkel, carried out a special mission ordered by Hitler himself to deliver unspecified, highly secret weapons samples to the Japanese army. In order to reduce the risk of loss, the two couriers traveled on different ships, each carrying a full set of the special cargo.[7]

However, from 1943 on, the chances for a successful passage between Europe and the Japanese-controlled hemisphere diminished rapidly. The danger was made clear to the German navy in its attempt to return the crews of the auxiliary merchant cruiser HSK 10 (*Thor*) and the supply ship *Uckermark* from Japan to Europe. Both ships had been lost on 30 November 1942 in an accidental explosion during a dockyard layover at Yokohama. When no replacement ships could be provided by the Imperial Japanese Navy, the Seekriegsleitung decided to return the majority of the crews aboard several homebound blockade-running ships. Out of some 640 men designated to return, however, only eighty-seven finally arrived safely at France aboard the MS *Pietro Orseolo* in early April 1943.

Almost the same number were lost under way in early March 1943 when the MS *Doggerbank* was accidentally sunk by a German U-boat in the mid-Atlantic. Others were lost in the sinking of the MS *Regensburg* or became POWs when the MS *Irene* was intercepted by Allied forces. But the majority remained in the Far East after their ships had been ordered to return to Japan on 27 February 1943, following several blockade-runner losses in the Atlantic. About 250 returned to Japan aboard the German motor ships *Rio Grande, Burgenland,* and *Weserland.*[8]

The Germans suffered a similar disaster during the winter season 1943–44, when four out of five ships were intercepted by Allied forces. Among the ships sunk were the motor ships *Burgenland* and *Weserland* carrying, respectively, thirty-six and thirty-seven pro-German Italians formerly serving with the Italian naval base at Singapore or on ex-Italian "Aquila" transport submarines. While two Italians were killed in the sinking of the *Weserland,* the remaining Italian passengers of both ships became prisoners of war.

The total number of passengers leaving the Far East for Europe was more than nine hundred, but less than half of them arrived safely in French ports. Allied action killed 136 under way or when their ships were sunk, while the rest either became prisoners of war or remained in the Far East after their ships had turned back upon orders of the Naval War Staff.

The low level of German interest in its Japanese partner shows in the small number of travelers heading toward the Far East. Only in 1942 were a few officers and technicians dispatched to Japan aboard surface blockade-runners. The majority of them were assigned to the staff of the naval attaché's office in Japan.

TRAVEL BY U-BOAT

When the attempt to break the Allied blockade ring with surface ships was finally abandoned on 18 January 1944, Japanese resistance to German plans for

Table 15.1. Passenger Transport by Surface Blockade-Runner
between the Far East and Europe, 1942–1945

Japan to Europe				
Passengers	1941	1942	1943	1944
Arrived	18	201	178	—
Lost	—	18	117	1
POW	1	10	52*	73
Turned back	—	—	256*	—
Total	**19**	**229**	**603***	**74**

Europe to Japan				
Passengers	1941	1942	1943	1944
Arrived	—	19	—	—
Lost	—	1	—	—
POW	—	1	—	—
Turned back	—	—	—	—
Total	—	**21**	—	—

*Approximation.

air transportation left the U-boat as the only remaining alternative for the exchange of personnel between the two countries. However, cargo or combat U-boats could by no means replace surface transport. The cramped conditions inside U-boats limited the number of passengers that could be taken aboard. As a consequence, from 1943 on, transportation of personnel between the two Axis partners was in a constant state of bottleneck. Only very important, key personnel were selected for transportation on U-boats. Naturally, none of the U-boat commanders expressed pleasure about extra passengers being assigned to his boat.

Civilian passengers, often unacquainted with the spartan living conditions aboard U-boats and without specific U-boat training and duty stations, sometimes suffered badly during the long periods at sea. German technicians who traveled on board Japanese cargo-transport submarines to the Far East later commented bitterly on the Japanese mentality and Japanese food.

The German passengers traveling on I-8 to Japan reported that "life with the Japanese aboard was difficult owing to the difference in mentality, requiring utmost considerateness. The Japanese showed lack of understanding for the use of German canned food except fruits. The majority of it was thrown overboard. Fat was cut away from flitches of bacon and sausages were served cold, etc. The Japanese crew showed free and easy homosexual behavior tolerated by the ship officers."

A German officer embarked on I-29 on its trip to Europe as adviser and pilot for the final leg through the Bay of Biscay remarked that food rations aboard, consisting of rice with sauces and vegetables four times a day, were almost unacceptable to the German palate.[9] In addition, the steadily growing success of Allied ASW operations after May 1943 made such trips increasingly risky.

Among the first passengers carried on a U-boat to Japan was the leader of the Indian National Party, Subhas Chandras Bose, and his aide. Bose was to organize the resistance of the Indian nation against the British colonial government. Leaving Germany on 9 February 1943 aboard U-180, both were transferred on 27 April 1943 to the Japanese I-29 in the Indian Ocean south of Madagascar. They finally arrived at Sabang on 7 May 1943 and from there flew to Japan. Contrary to previous opinion, the transfer of Bose and his aide was not the primary task of this U-boat meeting. The exchange of military equipment and plans was the primary task, whereas Bose's trip to the Far East served mainly for propaganda.[10] In exchange for Bose, U-180 took on two Japanese naval officers bound for Europe.[11]

THE "AQUILA" SUBS

In May 1943 the German U-511 sailed from Lorient in France to Japan with high-ranking military and civilian personnel, including the former chief officer of the Japanese navy liaison staff in Germany, Vice Admiral Nomura; the German ambassador resident in Nanking, Woermann; and the designated leader of the NSDAP organization in Japan, Spahn.[12] U-511 also carried the first group of three engineers, out of a total of eleven, sent on a technical mission to Japan. Their aim was to increase Japan's submarine construction program and generally improve its warship construction efficiency by mass production methods, using the German Type IXC U-boats as a model.

The first three engineers were Heberlein, Schmidt, and Müller from the Deschimag AG Weser shipyard at Bremen, the leading German building yard for the Type IXC U-boats. Heberlein was a specialist for auxiliary engines; Schmidt was a welding technician, and Müller belonged to the construction office for the Type IXC boats.[13]

Two more groups of three German civilian engineers each arrived in the Far East during 1943 aboard the Italian transport submarine *Luigi Torelli* ("Aquila VI") and the Japanese I-8, while two more were lost in May 1943 with the Italian transport submarine *Enrico Tazzoli.*

The ill-fated Italian "Aquila" transport boats that left France for the Far East during May and June 1943 mostly carried Italian or German military and civilian experts sent to build up the U-boat supply and maintenance bases in the Far East, as agreed with the Japanese navy earlier that year.[14] On 4 August 1943, the Japanese U-cruiser I-8 arrived at Lorient with a duplicate Japanese U-boat crew designated to take over the newly completed German U-1224.[15] On its return trip it carried the long-time Japanese naval attaché in Germany, Rear Admiral Yokoi, back to Japan.

SENDING EXPERTS AND TRAINEES

From the experience of the 1942–43 blockade-running season, the Japanese ambassador in Germany, Ōshima, concluded in his reports in the fall of 1943 that the chances for future imports of large German industrial products and samples of military technology by surface ships would soon become impossible. Since submarine transport was unsuitable for heavy cargo, he proposed to concentrate on the exchange of patent rights.[16]

Accordingly, on 10 September 1943, a considerable number of Japanese civilian and military technical experts were appointed to various posts in Germany. They were to study military developments and learn the technology of weapons and machinery acquired from Germany. Some were assigned to undergo training in various technical establishments or in companies engaged in military and technical production. All were assigned to the Japanese military attaché's office in Berlin on a temporary basis.[17]

Transport for the Berlin-bound technical experts was arranged aboard the large Japanese U-cruisers I-34, I-29, and I-52, also employed as cargo transports between Japan and German bases on the French Atlantic coast. However, I-34 was lost on a transfer passage to Penang before the majority of the passengers assigned for the trip had come aboard. I-29 reached Europe in March

1944, carrying a total of fourteen passengers, including the newly assigned Japanese naval attaché to Germany, Vice Admiral Kojima.[18]

Thereafter, disaster befell Japanese submarines engaged on liaison operations between the Axis partners, one after another, because the Allies could predict their movements with great accuracy, thanks to Ultra and Magic message decryption. Between May and July 1944, the Allies sank the I-52, intended as a replacement for I-34 and carrying sixteen passengers outbound to Europe, as well as two homebound boats, RO-501 (ex U-1224), carrying four passengers, and I-29.[19] Except for the sixteen Japanese and four German passengers who disembarked from the I-29 at Singapore before its subsequent loss, the passengers, all Japanese nationals, were killed in the sinkings. The four German passengers were originally scheduled to travel on the German UIT-21, but its operation was canceled after a series of engine breakdowns.[20]

After this series of setbacks, the Japanese navy decided to stop any further submarine operations to Europe for transport liaison. To the Naval War Staff. this important turn in German-Japanese naval cooperation was explained by rising submarine losses resulting from the lack of up-to-date detection sets and technically outdated ship design.[21]

Nevertheless, both the Japanese navy and army still had a great interest in bringing to Japan a number of key specialists working in Europe. Accordingly, the IJN had taken steps to attract German experts in jet aircraft development and mass production to Japan for temporary liaison with Japanese aircraft production companies. While travel expenses and salaries for these experts were to be met by the Japanese government, transportation for them had to be requested from the Kriegsmarine.

Because its policy was to use its outbound U-boats in a dual-purpose role as combat transports, with offensive operations in the Indian Ocean while en route to the Far Eastern bases, the German navy was generally reluctant to offer them for transport of personnel. With the exception of U-180 and U-511 in 1943, none of the operational boats sent to Far Eastern waters until the end of 1944 carried supernumerary passengers. Nor did any of the homebound German U-boats carry any civilian or military passengers.

In April 1944 the Japanese army had asked the German naval attaché in Tokyo about the possibility of transporting a number of army engineers to Europe on homebound German U-boats. The Naval War Staff. quickly rejected this appeal, pointing out that its own officers and specialists had higher priority.[22] Only after repeated requests from the Japanese naval attaché was it finally agreed in August 1944 to carry Japanese personnel aboard future U-boats leaving for the Far East.

On 14 August 1944, the naval attaché requested approval from Tokyo for his plan to negotiate with the German navy for transportation of Japanese personnel aboard outbound German U-boats. He also asked for the order of priority in the return to Japan of twenty-six Japanese or German specialists previously detailed for transport to Japan. The answer clearly showed a significant ranking in the order of priority. Transport of German aircraft technicians and production specialists from the Messerschmidt, Junkers, and BMW companies was given top priority, to be followed by Japanese specialists trained in U-boat construction and the latest developments in the field of homing torpedoes.[23] German approval for transporting up to three passengers on outbound U-boats was reported by the Japanese attaché on 31 August 1944. At the same time, several of the large Type IXD2 U-boats designated for operations in Far Eastern waters were partly converted to accommodate a larger number of passengers by removing the auxiliary diesel generators.

In late 1944 the German navy started to play a more active role in the naval cooperation with Japan. The reluctant or sometimes dilatory attitude of the Japanese navy in all aspects of technical collaboration or the exchange of its own operational experiences with the German navy prompted the commander in chief of the Kriegsmarine, Grand Admiral Dönitz, to dispatch a team of ship construction and electronic experts to Japan.[24] Formal announcement to the IJN about the intention to sail three officers for this purpose by the first available U-boat was made on 23 November 1944.

The officers assigned were Capt. Gerhard Falk, a line officer as well as certified engineer and shipbuilding specialist with long experience in negotiations with the Japanese, who had been responsible for the Japanese naval inspection commission to Germany in 1941; Dr. Heinz Schlicke, a certified engineer with a triple Ph.D., who was the leading German specialist in research and testing of radar, infrared, and direction finding; and the civilian interpreter, Dr. Müller, temporarily promoted to the rank of ensign, who had distinguished himself especially in the training of the Japanese crew of RO-501 (ex U-1224).[25]

Accompanied by the experienced interpreter, these officers were to form a new technical section at the office of the resident naval attaché in Tokyo. Once they were put at the disposal of the IJN as aides, their principal task was to collect important technical and operational experiences. In contrast to his previous restrictive attitude toward Japan, Dönitz now developed even more far-reaching plans for the intensification of the naval collaboration between the two Axis partners.

Previous Allied operations had shown the great value of an independent fleet air arm to support all kinds of operations at sea. The German navy completely lacked fleet air arm formations after a long controversy with the Luftwaffe and its despotic commander in chief, Reichsmarschall Göring. The German naval strategy after 1941 was almost exclusively confined to the concept of the U-boat tonnage war and defensive operations in the immediate coastal areas off German-controlled territory.

On 13 December 1944 Dönitz requested, through the Japanese naval attaché in Berlin, that eight line officers and two engineering officers be assigned to the Japanese fleet for a considerable period of time to collect experiences in oceanic naval warfare. Because practical application was considered more important than theoretical training, full use of these officers in all tasks of the IJN forces was requested. On 13 January 1945 the IJN agreed in principle to the German proposal but wished that such matters as exact assignments for the training be left to its discretion until the arrival of the officers.

Among the officers assigned were Lt. Cdr. Robert Kopp, a communication specialist, formerly radio officer aboard the training battleship *Schlesien;* Lt. Sven Plass, ordnance specialist; Lt. Jobst Hahndorff, fire control specialist formerly commanding a torpedo boat in the Mediterranean, with previous experience on the pocket battleships *Admiral Graf Spee* and *Admiral Scheer;* Lt. Richard Bulla, naval aviator with three years' flying experience and subsequent destroyer commander; Lt. Heinrich Peter-Pirkham, tactician and experienced torpedo boat commander; Lt. Hans Reimer German, navigator with a long service record aboard the heavy cruiser *Prinz Eugen* and the training battleship *Schleswig-Holstein;* Lt.(jg) Heinrich Hellendorn, antiaircraft specialist; Lt. Cdr. (E) Kurt Ziegler, diesel motor specialist with extensive experience on heavy cruisers and pocket-battleships; and Lt. Cdr. (E) Karl Nuber, high-pressure steam specialist with lengthy experience as torpedo boat flotilla engineer in the Mediterranean.[26]

Meanwhile, the commander in chief of the Luftwaffe had named General Kessler, a prominent and long-time advocate for a German fleet air arm, the new air attaché in Tokyo on 15 December 1944. Transportation of General Kessler and his staff of fourteen officers to Japan by U-boat was requested from the German navy.

Apart from General Kessler, the following staff teams were assigned to his party: General Affairs Group, formed by Colonel Wild as chief of staff, Captain Schumann as aide and antiaircraft expert, and Dr. Hähnisch as civilian interpreter; the Operations Group, consisting of Colonel Sandrart, aerial defense expert and former head of the Bremen air defenses, Lieutenant Colonel Stepp, specialist for day and night fighter operations, Major Sauer, ground attack planes and ground co-operation expert, Major Lauerschmalz, aerial mine specialist, and Major Mayer, aerial torpedo expert; Technical Group, formed by Major Parke, a radar specialist, Captain Menzel, radar and radio-controlled weapons, Major Holweck, rocket equipment, Captain Kröpe, navigation and meteorology, and the civilian adviser Dr. Mahlfeld; Intelligence Group, consisting solely of Major Schubert.[27]

These German assignments to Japan, together with Japanese requests for passenger travel, called for transportation for about forty persons in the early months of 1945 to meet all immediate requirements. Owing to losses and damage inflicted by Allied air attacks on North Sea and Baltic naval bases, the German U-boat sailing scheme to the Far East was repeatedly delayed. A new arrangement in December 1944 included the departure of four Type IXD2 U-cruisers (U-873 through U-876) and the Type XB transport U-234 from Germany between 10 January and 15 March 1945. Besides their nominal cargo loads, all of these U-boats were also earmarked for passenger transport.[28] In addition, the Type IXD2 U-cruiser U-864, under repair in Norway after a false start in December 1944, was included in the passenger transport scheme. This boat, now carrying two Japanese technicians and four Germans as supernumerary passengers, was lost with all hands to submarine attack, shortly after its departure in February 1945.

The rapidly deteriorating German position in Europe, which left little hope of reversing the military situation, soon forced the German navy again to reconsider plans. The number of officers intended for training with the IJN was cut down to only five, and the U-boat sailing scheme was similarly reduced. The five assigned officers were Lt. Sven Plass, Lieutenant Hahndorff, Lieutenant Bulla, Lieutenant (jg) Hellendorn and the newly appointed Lt. Cdr. (E) Hermann Schimanski. Previously Schimanski had been chief engineer officer aboard the light cruiser *Emden* since July 1943. Unknown to the Naval War Staff, Plass and Hahndorff had already been lost with U-864. On 8 March 1945 the German naval attaché was told to count on only two more transports (U-234 and U-876) until further notice.[29]

Table 15.2. Passenger Transport by Submarine between
the Far East and Europe 1942–1945

Japan to Europe				
Passengers	1942	1943	1944	1945
Arrived	—	58	16	—
Lost	—	1	14	—
POW	—	—	—	—
Total	—	59	30	—

Europe to Japan				
Passengers	1942	1943	1944	1945
Arrived	1	44	19	—
Lost	—	10	4	8
POW	—	—	—	10
Total	1	54	23	18

Ultimately only U-234, with a total of twelve passengers on board—including two Japanese naval officers—was able to leave for the Far East in April 1945. When U-234 finally surrendered to U.S. naval forces on 17 May 1945, the two Japanese officers, unwilling to surrender, committed suicide aboard the sub and were buried at sea shortly before an American boarding party arrived.[30]

From 1942 to 1945, a total of eighty-nine passengers were embarked on Japanese submarines or German U-boats for transport from the Far East to Europe. Of this number seventy-four arrived at German U-boat bases in France, while the rest were killed when their boats were sunk underway. In the opposite direction, a total of ninety-six passengers sailed for the Far East. Sixty-four arrived at their destination, but twenty-two were lost underway and ten others were on board U-234 when it surrendered to the Americans near the end of the war.

16

Transport of Materials

Apart from the German navy's strategic military intentions toward and expectations of Japan right from the start of the war, a parallel economic interest in Japan and the Far Eastern region developed with the beginning of 1941. This interest focused on the importation of vital raw materials from the Far East that were essential for the German war industry. Germany's increasing need for raw materials from Japan's part of the world compelled its active cooperation with the Japanese navy.

The Japanese perspective was rather similar, but its economic interest concentrated on a comprehensive technology transfer to improve the often inferior technological standards of its military forces and its industry. Importing advanced high-tech production tools, as well as military or civilian industrial products, together with the training of personnel and the transfer of blue prints or patent rights, rated highest among Japanese intentions toward Germany.

Before the outbreak of the war Germany had accumulated stocks of key raw materials as strategic reserves. As the German army advanced through Europe, additional stocks became available in the occupied territories. A stiff rationing system for raw materials from outside the German-controlled sphere prevailed from the beginning of the war, and substitutes like synthetic rubber (buna) or reductions in the overall consumption helped to reduce the dependence on these strategically important materials. However, certain key raw materials like natural rubber, tin, quinine, and opium were not available in the German realm.

With the implementation of the Allied blockade system against German overseas shipping right after the start of World War II, imports of raw materials and other goods from overseas countries dried up very soon. By early 1941, Germany's available stocks of strategic raw materials, especially natural rubber, had dropped drastically. Meanwhile the persistence of the British defense, as well as German preparations for the Russian campaign, increased the urgency of Germany's need to find new ways to import more materials to maintain war production.

Attempts by the German Ministry of Transport to import raw materials, especially rubber, with blockade-runners from South America were soon halted by anti-German political pressure and several losses to Allied sea patrols in the mid-Atlantic. Thus the German interest turned entirely to the Far East and Japan, where a large number of German diesel-powered ships suitable for blockade-running operations had been waiting since the start of the war. At the start of 1941 eleven such ships belonging to the Naval Supply Service organization (*Marineetappe*) in Japan were registered as *V-Schiffe* and available for operations: *Anneliese Essberger, Elsa Essberger, Elbe, Odenwald, Regensburg, Spreewald, Burgenland, Kulmerland, Münsterland, Havelland,* and *Ramses.* Four coal-burning steamers, unsuitable for supply or blockade-running operations, had been sold to Japan in 1940, and the chartering of four others was being negotiated with the Japanese government. Between 27 June 1941 and 2 July 1941, four motor ships—*Quito, Rhakotis, Bogota,* and *Osorno*—arrived in Japan after having escaped from Chilean ports in May 1941.[1] In mid-1942 the German blockade-runners in the Far East were further augmented by the two raider prizes *Rossbach* (formerly the Norwegian tanker *Madrono*) and *Hohenfriedberg* (formerly the Norwegian tanker *Herborg*).

In November 1940 the German Ministry of Transport had made a half-hearted attempt to get three German merchant vessels back to Europe from Japan. The chief of staff of the German armed forces, Field Marshal Keitel, asked the Special Staff for Economic Warfare (*Handelskrieg und wirtschaftliche Kampfmasshahmen* or HWK) on 23 January 1941 to propose a plan for transporting vital materials, primarily natural rubber, by ship from Asia to Europe in case the Trans-Siberian Railway link from Vladivostok to the western border of the Soviet Union could not be used any longer. Ultimately, on 11 March

1941 the HWK was ordered to arrange for the immediate homeward transport of ten thousand tons of natural rubber already acquired by German companies in East Asia. To accomplish the transport the German navy was asked to take all necessary steps to sail the appropriate number of ships from Japanese and Manchurian ports.[2]

The procurement of all sorts of suitable cargo, especially rubber, metals or metal ore, and edible oils, was the responsibility of the German Delegation for Economic Negotiations at the German embassy in Japan and a procurement agency for raw materials, *Rohstoffgesellschaft* (ROGES), led by State Councillor Wohlthat. He was assisted by the management of various German trading companies, notably Illies & Co., Melchers & Co., and Niggemann & Co., which had various branch offices in the Far East. Operations at sea for all blockade-runners, including the establishment of safety routes to protect the ships from attacks by Axis submarines, were planned and controlled by the operational staff of the Kriegsmarine.

The shore organization of blockade-running operations, initially under control of the German Ministry of Transport, was later transferred to the Naval Special Service Division (Marinesonderdienst, or MSD) of the OKW department Ausland IV, in agreement with the HWK and the Naval War Staff Registration, repair, fitting out, and cargo loading of all ships in the Far East was in the hands of the naval attaché in Tokyo, acting as commanding officer of the Marineetappe in Japan. The German passenger liner *Scharnhorst,* laid up at Kobe, was used as a depot ship for stores, provisions, and fuel and as assembly point for personnel. Blockade-runner service became the main task of the Marineetappe from 1941 onward.[3] In 1942 Captain Vermehren of the MSD was sent to Japan and became Admiral Wenneker's deputy to the German Naval Supply Service in Japan.

The French port of Bordeaux on the Bay of Biscay became the main naval base in Europe for blockade-running operations to and from the German-controlled hemisphere. Loading and unloading of all blockade-running ships entering or leaving Bordeaux, together with the organization of overhauling, fitting out, and staffing, were the responsibility of the Bordeaux branch of the MSD in cooperation with the Naval Office Bordeaux and the western branch office of the Fleet Train Unit.[4]

In February 1941 the German naval attaché in Tokyo received preliminary orders to prepare German ships available in his area for blockade-running operations. At the beginning only three diesel-powered vessels were detailed for sailing to Europe. Limitations in docking and repair capacities offered by the Japanese navy caused frequent delays to the German plan. Although dockyard preference was accorded to vessels used for secret supply operations to German auxiliary cruisers operating in the Pacific, other German ships might have to wait weeks for dockyard space. Furthermore, all services offered by the Japanese to maintain and equip the ships had to be paid in yen or foreign currencies, placing a heavy strain on German financial resources in Japan.

To conceal its role in the operation, the Japanese navy also insisted that loading was to take place only at the remote port of Dairen, in Japanese-controlled Manchukuo. On 20 April 1941 the German motor ship *Elbe* finally left Dairen for Europe as the first Axis blockade-runner sailing during the 1941–42 blockade-running season. Prior to this the *Ermland* had successfully reached Bordeaux on 3 April 1941 after having sailed in ballast from Kobe on 28 December 1940 to a secret rendezvous with a German auxiliary merchant cruiser at Lamotrek Atoll to take over about 330 Allied prisoners of war for onward transfer to Europe.[5] Between 5 May and 2 July 1941 the Ausland IV Department at the OKW ordered the German naval attaché to sail four more ships loaded with rubber to Europe. Finally, on 21 July the order was given to sail all suitable ships available for blockade-running operations. Individual departures from Japan were to be so arranged that the ships would arrive at Bordeaux at intervals of about twenty days.[6]

Germany did not have enough oil in Japan to float all diesel-powered vessels available in the Far East for supply runs to Europe. Secret imports of small German oil stocks from Latin America, using Japanese vessels and additional purchases on the open market with the help of Japanese cover companies, could not improve the situation. Toward the end of 1941, existing German stocks of fuel and diesel oil in Japan had been almost depleted. By then, too, the IJN was reluctant to offer oil from its own stocks in the face of the imminent outbreak of war in the Pacific.

The navy's attempt to send a loaded oil tanker to Japan two weeks after Pearl Harbor, to ensure the provisioning of future blockade-runners, failed when the ship succumbed to Allied attack. The German tanker *Benno* left St. Nazaire in France on 22 December 1941 with 9,600 tons of diesel and fuel oil for the Etappe Japan. The ship was bombed by British aircraft off Cape Ortegal in the Bay of Biscay and later was sunk by aerial torpedo while anchoring off Carino, well inside Spanish territorial waters.[7] However, the situation eased considerably after the Japanese occupied the Southeast Asian oil fields in early 1942. Thereafter all

German vessels in the Far East were supplied with Japanese fuel oil, but usually only after wearying negotiations with the relevant Japanese authorities.

In September 1941 the Italian Naval High Command had ordered four Italian ships berthed in Japan into blockade-running operations. At first the Japanese navy denied the necessary fuel supply. After consultations with the German navy, responsibility for fitting out and fueling the Italian ships was formally assumed by the Marineetappe. In exchange the Italians offered to carry some German cargo on these ships. All Italian blockade-runners sailed under their own flags, with Italian crews, but were under German control during operations.[8]

Between April 1941 and the end of February 1942, fifteen ships, including three Italian vessels, had left Far Eastern ports for Europe. All these ships were routed across the Pacific and around Cape Horn. Eleven ships arrived safely at the French port of Bordeaux, but three were lost in the Atlantic to various reasons, and one was ordered to return to Japan as a cautionary measure. The German Naval Operational Staff recalled it because of the British crackdown against German fleet supply ships operating in the Atlantic in the summer of 1941. Total German imports during the blockade-runner season 1941–42 amounted to 74,960 tons, including 32,000 tons of rubber. The three ships that failed to reach Europe went down with 19,200 tons—20.3 percent of the total shipped cargo.[9]

The Naval War Staff nevertheless understood that the Japanese government would support the German effort to import vital raw materials only as long as materials and equipment ordered by the Japanese in Europe were transported to Japan free of charge on outbound German blockade-runners.[10] Shipping transport to Japan started on 17 March 1941 with the Japanese AMC *Asaka Maru*, which had delivered the Japanese military commission to Germany at Lisbon and later moved to Bilbao in Spain to load valuable cargo sent to that port from Germany. The procurement of Japanese cargo was organized by the various relevant sections at the Japanese embassy and the attaché offices. As no other Japanese merchant ships were present in European waters in 1941, the German navy offered a number of its forthcoming blockade-runners outbound to Japan for transport. But sailings were repeatedly delayed by reports of successful British operations against the German supply tanker net in the Atlantic. Finally, though, the German motor ship *Rio Grande* left Bordeaux on 21 September 1941 on the first blockade-runner trip to Japan.

During the shipping season 1941–42 a total of five blockade-runners left Bordeaux and all arrived safely at Japan, delivering 32,540 tons of cargo. Exports to Japan mainly consisted of industrial products like locomotives,

Table 16.1. Tons of Matériel Transported from the Far East to Europe during Blockade-Running Season, 1941–1942

Cargo	Shipped	Arrived	Lost	Turned Back
Rubber	46,234	32,027	10,483	3,724
Rubber tires	1,039	650	293	96
Edible & industrial oils, oil seeds	NA*	30,096	NA	NA
Lard	NA	2,571	NA	NA
Glycerin	608	608	—	—
Mineral oils	NA	700	NA	NA
High-grade metal ores	NA	2,747	NA	NA
Chemicals & asphalt	NA	678	NA	NA
Hemp	NA	780	NA	NA
Tea & coffee	NA	583	NA	NA
Egg products & yolk	NA	379	NA	NA
Miscellaneous	NA	635	NA	NA
Italian load	2,498	2,498	—	—
Total	**104,233**	**74,952**	**19,200**	**7,575**

*NA = not available

turbines, boilers, and agricultural machines; various technical equipment, including complete hydroelectric power stations, scientific instruments, and photographic equipment; chemical and pharmaceutical products; and unprocessed raw materials. In addition, the ships carried supplies and spares for the German ships and offices in the Far East. Some were also used under way as auxiliary supply ships to supply German armed merchant cruisers operating in the South Atlantic, Indian Ocean, and Pacific.

To replace possible losses and older, less suitable ships, in late 1941 the German navy ordered the completion of fourteen fast, long-range diesel-powered vessels, already under construction at various European yards, to continue the blockade-running program.[11]

The success of the previous operations, together with the growing need for certain key raw materials in the German armament and nutrition industries, prompted higher projections from the German ministries of economics and food production for the 1942–43 season. The initial import demand amounted to 440,000 tons, including 270,000 tons of edible oil and fat to replace expected crop failures as a result of the severe winter season in 1941–42.

German war material support for Japan correspondingly increased greatly after the beginning of the Pacific war. The Special Staff for Economic Warfare drew up an ambitious sailing scheme to meet minimum requirements. A total of twenty-two freighter voyages, carrying 140,000 tons of dry cargo from Far Eastern ports to Bordeaux, were planned between August 1942 and April 1943, whereas twenty-six trips were envisaged from Europe to the Far East in the same period. In addition, nine fleet supply tank ships, intended for replenishment operations to supply armed merchant cruisers on their outbound trip, were designated to carry up to 110,000 tons of edible oil to Europe. At Bordeaux and other French ports, extensive preparations took place during the second half of 1942 to ensure the handling and onward transfer of the expected cargo quantities. As in 1941, the IJN declined to permit Japanese merchant ships to participate in blockade-running operations to Europe, referring to its heavy commitments on the Pacific theater.

Sailing times were concentrated in the winter months, when adverse weather conditions and the long hours of darkness in the Northern Atlantic would, they hoped, help Axis ships elude Allied attack. The Japanese control of the Sunda Strait shortened the length of cruises, enabling ships to make the trip to Japan around the Cape of Good Hope with a replenishment stop at Batavia.[12]

GERMAN SUPPLY BASES IN SOUTHEAST ASIA

A proposal made by Admiral Wenneker, on 7 November 1942, to reduce days in port by using only selected South East Asian ports for cargo loading, was frustrated by the Japanese insistence on calling at numerous ports in the South East Asian area and the Japanese homeland. This practice offered the IJN the advantage of using available German ships for transporting Japanese cargo within Southeast Asia and to the Japanese homeland. The Japanese navy left no doubt that it considered this kind of transport aid a precondition for the supply of raw materials required by Germany.[13]

More successful was Wenneker's effort to establish forward German supply bases in Japanese occupied territories in Southeast Asia. Following an agreement with the Japanese navy in early January 1943, the first German naval supply bases at Jakarta and Singapore reported ready for service on 17 and 22 May 1943. The submarine base at Penang followed shortly thereafter, with a further base at Surabaya added in 1944.

After the summer of 1942, increased Allied air and sea patrols, supported by a steady flow of information from signal intelligence, sharply worsened the prospects of the blockade-runners. Especially dangerous was the passage through the Bay of Biscay, where the German navy and air force were unable to provide adequate cover against Allied forces; two ships were lost to enemy action there in the first half of December 1942. In response, on 16 December, the Marinegruppenkommando West postponed departures from France until the German forces could provide more protection through the Bay of Biscay.[14] By then only seven blockade-runners and two fleet supply ships outbound to Japan had successfully crossed the Bay of Biscay, while three inbound ships arrived in France.

Thus the voyages to the Far East planned for the 1942–43 blockade-runner season were reduced by half. Pending the reinforcement of Luftwaffe and naval units in Western France, Marinegruppenkommando West waited until the end of March 1943 to make a final attempt to sail a group of blockade-runners through the Bay of Biscay. Despite intense Allied naval and air force operations, two of them finally arrived at Japan, while a third was intercepted in the mid-Atlantic. In the end, only eight Axis blockade-runners, bringing 24,447 tons of war material and industrial products, arrived in Japanese or Far Eastern ports during the 1942–43 season. Only two out of nine fleet supply tankers designated for the import of edible oil successfully completed their outbound trip. Three outbound freight motor ships with additional 9,382 tons of cargo and one tanker in ballast were intercepted and lost. Several other ships were either damaged in port or withheld in France.

The cancellation of voyages and losses on the outbound route to Japan greatly reduced the number of ships in the Far East available for homebound voyages. Thus only thirteen freighters left from Far Eastern ports between August 1942 and February 1943. Of these only four arrived at Bordeaux, carrying 29,600 tons of cargo. When six ships were sunk and two more damaged by Allied interception or friendly fire, 50,950 tons of cargo, including 27,750 tons of precious rubber, were lost en route. On 27 February 1943 three more ships were ordered to stay in the Far East or the Indian Ocean to prevent their interception in the heavily patrolled Atlantic waters.

Table 16.2. Tons of Matériel Transported from Far East to Europe during Blockade-Running Season 1942–1943

Cargo	Shipped	Arrived	Lost	Turned Back
Rubber	45,320	7,550	27,750	10,020
Tin	7,430	1,290	3,440	2,700
Tin ore	1,870	270	1,300	300
Tungsten ore	1,010	180	430	400
Molybdenum ore	170	120	—	50
Misc. metals	50	50	—	—
Wood oil	1,000	490	—	510
Glycerin	120	—	—	120
Wax	40	40	—	—
Resin, shellac, copal	1,480	440	270	770
Quinine	850	50	400	400
Chemical & pharmaceutical	370	140	80	150
Leather, skins	260	260	—	—
Textile raw materials	300	100	90	110
Mica	40	15	10	15
Edible oil & lard	36,210	13,820	15,680	6,710
Oil seeds	2,750	2,750	—	—
Egg products, yolk	570	500	70	—
Tea	2,700	1,120	630	950
Canned fish	1,710	100	700	910
Spices	250	230	—	20
Miscellaneous	200	85	100	15
Total	**104,700**	**29,600**	**50,950**	**24,150**

The attempt to import edible oil, using tankers, was a total failure. One tanker had already been lost at Yokohama by an accidental explosion, and neither of the two tankers that left the Far East arrived in France. Two more never left port; delayed by extensive repairs, they were not ready to start back before the end of February and thus would not have had the benefit of the dark winter season in European waters.

Despite the disappointing results of the 1942–43 blockade-running season, continuing the transportation link with Japan was considered essential to maintaining the German-Japanese alliance. During the summer of 1943, the German navy worked out a schedule for the upcoming blockage-running season that was intended to deliver the necessary minimum import of key raw materials. The losses from its Asia-bound vessels had left Germany with only six suitable ships in the Far East to deliver raw materials to Europe in the 1943– season—38,000 tons of cargo capacity.

According to the arrangement with the Special Staff for Economic Warfare, that load capacity was envisaged for the transport of 14,000 tons of rubber, 3,000 tons of tungsten ore concentrate, 9,640 tons of tin, 360 tons of cobalt, 4,000 tons of industrial oils, 650 tons of medical chemicals, 300 tons of tanning substance, 500 tons of raw silk, and 4,000 tons of foodstuffs, including lard, edible oils, and vitamins, together with 1,550 tons of miscellaneous materials. For the same period the dispatch of seven motor vessels carrying a maximum of 50,800 tons of cargo was planned in the opposite direction, toward Japan.

In addition to the seven outbound cargo ships, the fleet supply ship *Ostfriesland* was designated for the import of edible oil after intended supply operations for the German armed merchant cruiser HSK 28 (*Michel*) on the outbound route. Subsequent Allied action against ships in French ports and the withdrawal of *Ostfriesland* after the loss of *Michel* on 17 October 1943 reduced the number of available ships to four until the end of 1943.[15]

However, the German naval staff's estimate of the chances of success of this operation in August 1943 is indicated by its ordering that the fitting out of more surface ships for blockade-running be abandoned altogether. When sailings from the Far East started on 27 October 1943, the Allies started intensive barrier operations in the Atlantic, greatly supported by signal intelligence. Eventually only the *Osorno*, carrying 6,890 tons of cargo (including 3,944 tons of rubber, 1,826 tons of tin, and 180 tons of wolfram [tungsten] ore), skillfully evaded the determined efforts of her pursuers and arrived at Bordeaux at the end of December 1943.[16] Its rubber load alone filled German minimum requirements until November 1944.

The next four ships to leave for Bordeaux, carrying 26,205 tons of cargo, were lost to Allied action. When their loss became evident to the German navy, Hitler himself on 18 January 1944 gave the order to abandon any further attempt to use surface blockade-runners for transport to and from the Far East. Accordingly the sailing orders for all blockade-runners, including four ships fully loaded and ready to depart at Bordeaux, were canceled. By June 1944 the remaining ships, *Dresden, Tannenfels, Osorno, Fusiyama,* and *Elsa Essberger,* had been unloaded by the MSD and handed over to the Kriegsmarine for further use.[17]

All told, from April 1941 until October 43, thirty-six loaded blockade-runners departed from Asia to Europe, of which some made the trip several times. Six of these ships were prematurely recalled or returned after damage, leaving thirty actually heading for Europe. Of these vessels, eleven were sunk by enemy action or were scuttled when approached by enemy forces; two were accidentally sunk by German submarines, and one was seized by American naval forces before the United States entered the war. Sixteen blockade-runners actually completed their voyages and delivered their important cargo at the port of Bordeaux in occupied France.

Of the twenty-three ships sent from Europe to Japan between September 1941 and April 1943, including eighteen loaded blockade-runners and five fleet supply ships intended for homeward transport of edible oil, sixteen reached their Asian destination safely. Five were sunk by enemy action or were scuttled when approached by enemy forces, and two were prematurely recalled or returned after damage.

Losses of the German blockade-running ships on the Far East route amounted to 45.8 percent overall. However, ship losses between April 1941 and October 1942 were only 12.1 percent, whereas in 1943 losses rose to 85.7 percent, when, out of fourteen ships dispatched from Japan, only two reached the German realm.

By December 1942 the German naval staff had concluded that the future use of surface blockade-runners probably could not be maintained at the previous level, whereas the need to import vital raw materials would continue as a decisive factor in the outcome of the war. This led to a revival of the World War I idea of cargo U-boats.[18]

At that time U-boats were considered relatively immune to Allied action, permitting a year-round sailing schedule. Given Hitler's order from 18 January

Table 16.3. Axis Blockade-Running Operations, Far East to Europe, 1941–1944

Nationality/ Type	Ship	Gross Registered Tons	Sailed	Departure Port	Cargo (Tons)	Arrived/Lost	Arrival Port/ How Lost
*G M/V	Elbe	9,179	20.04.41	Dairen	7,134	06.06.41	Sunk by aircraft from HMS Eagle, 23°30'N, 36°09'W
G M/V	Regensburg	8,068	05.05.41	Dairen	7,500	27.06.41	Bordeaux
G M/V	Ramses	7,983	12.05.41	Dairen	7,575	30.07.41	Yokohama. Ordered to return 26.06.41.
G M/V	Anneliese Essberger	5,173	20.06.41	Dairen	5,090	10.09.41	Bordeaux
G M/V	Odenwald	5,098	21.08.41	Yokohama	6,054	06.11.41	Seized by USS Omaha, 01°N, 28°W
G M/V	Burgenland	7,320	21.09.41	Kobe	7,039	09.12.41	Bordeaux
G M/V	Elsa Essberger	6,104	14.10.41	Sasebo	6,857	10.03.42	Bordeaux. At El Ferrol, Spain, 11.01.42–09.03.42.
G M/V	Spreewald	5,083	21.10.41	Dairen	6,000	31.01.42	Sunk accidentally by U-333, 45°N, 25°W
I M/V	Cortellazzo	5,292	15.11.41	Dairen	5,238	28.01.42	Bordeaux
I M/V	Pietro Orseolo	6,344	02.12.41	Kobe	7,034	22.02.42	Bordeaux
G M/V	Osorno	6,951	23.12.41	Kobe	6,796	19.03.42	Bordeaux
G M/V	Rio Grande	6,062	31.01.42	Kobe	7,558	10.04.42	Bordeaux
I M/V	Fusijama	6,244	07.02.42	Kobe	6,621	26.04.42	Bordeaux
G M/V	Münsterland	6,408	18.02.42	Kobe	8,192	17.05.42	Bordeaux
G M/V	Portland	7,132	26.02.42	Yokohama	6,814	10.05.42	Bordeaux

Nationality/Type	Ship	Gross Registered Tons	Sailed	Departure Port	Cargo (Tons)	Arrived/Lost	Arrival Port/How Lost
G M/V	*Tannenfels*	7,840	08.08.42	Yokohama	8,406	02.11.42	Bordeaux
G M/V	*Kulmerland*	7,363	26.08.42	Dairen	8,072	07.11.43	Bordeaux
G M/V	*Dresden*	5,567	08.09.42	Saigon	6,091	03.11.42	Bordeaux
G M/V	*Regensburg*	8,068	09.10.42	Singapore	9,000	20.10.42	Batavia. Torpedoed by USS *Searaven*, 12.10.42.
G M/V	*Rhakotis*	6,753	05.11.42	Batavia	6,601	01.01.43	Sunk by HMS *Scylla*, 41°01'N, 10°50'W
G M/V	*Ramses*	7,983	22.11.42	Batavia	9,436	28.11.42	Sunk by HMAS *Adelaide*, 23°28'S, 99°20'E
G M/T	*Hohenfriedberg*	7,892	22.12.42	Batavia	11,606	26.02.43	Sunk by HMS *Sussex*, 41°45'N, 20°58'W
G M/V	*Doggerbank*	5,154	15.01.43	Batavia	6,650	03.03.43	Sunk accidentally by U-43, 29°09'N, 34°46'W
G M/T	*Rossbach*	5,894	18.01.43	Batavia	6,965	08.04.43	Batavia. Ordered to return 27.02.43.
G M/V	*Karin*	7,322	04.02.43	Singapore	7,814	10.03.43	Sunk by USS *Eberle*, 07°S, 21°W
G M/V	*Regensburg*	8,068	06.02.43	Batavia	9,097	30.03.43	Sunk by HMS *Glasgow*, 64°N, 27°W
G M/V	*Weserland*	6,528	06.02.43	Batavia	7,618	23.03.43	Batavia. Ordered to return 27.02.43.

Ship	Nationality/Type	Gross Registered Tons	Sailed	Departure Port	Cargo (Tons)	Arrived/Lost	Arrival Port/How Lost
Burgenland	G M/V	7,320	08.02.43	Kobe	8,735	02.04.43	Kobe. Ordered to return while at Batavia 27.02.43.
Pietro Orseolo	I M/V	6,344	16.02.43	Batavia	8,301	02.04.43	Bordeaux
Irene	G M/V	4,793	18.02.43	Batavia	7,200	10.04.43	Sunk by HMS *Adventure*, 43°18'N, 14°30'W
Rio Grande	G M/V	6,062	25.02.43	Batavia	7,456	05.03.43	Batavia. Ordered to return 27.02.43.
Osorno	G M/V	6,951	27.10.43	Batavia	6,890	25.12.43	Grounded off Le Verdon. To Paulliac 13.01.44.
Rio Grande	G M/V	6,062	29.10.43	Batavia	Unknown	04.01.44	Sunk by USS *Omaha* and USS *Jouett*, 06°40'S, 25°39'W
Alsterufer	G M/V	2,729	10.11.43	Batavia	Unknown	27.12.43	Sunk by aircraft RAF Sdn 311, 46°27'N, 17°40'W
Weserland	G M/V	6,528	22.11.43	Batavia	Unknown	02.01.44	Sunk by USS *Somers*, 14°55'S, 21°39'W
Burgenland	G M/V	7,320	25.11.43	Batavia	Unknown	05.01.44	Sunk by USS *Omaha* and USS *Jouett*, 07°29'S, 25°37'W

Table 16.4. Axis Blockade-Running Operations, Europe to Far East, 1941–1944

Nationality/ Type	Ship	Gross Registered Tons	Sailed	Departure Port	Cargo (Tons)	Arrived/Lost	Arrival Port/ How Lost
G M/V	*Rio Grande*	6,062	21.09.41	Bordeaux	7,220	06.12.41	Osaka
G M/V	*Portland*	7,132	22.10.41	Bordeaux	6,880	01.01.42	Osaka
G M/T[a]	*Benno*	8,306	22.12.41	St. Nazaire	oil	24.12.41	Sunk by RAF torpedo bomber, Carino, Spain, 43°44'N, 07°52'W
G M/V	*Regensburg*	8,068	12.02.42	Bordeaux	5,820	07.07.42	Yokohama
G M/T[a]	*Charlotte Schliemann*	7,747	23.02.42	Las Palmas	oil	20.10.42	Yokohama
G M/V	*Tannenfels*	7,840	08.03.42	Bordeaux	7,250	12.05.42	Yokohama
G M/V	*Dresden*	5,567	16.04.42	Bordeaux	5,370	23.06.42	Yokohama
G M/V[c]	*Uckermark*	10,698	09.09.42	Bordeaux	oil	24.11.42	Yokohama. Lost in port by accidental explosion, 30.11.42.
G M/V	*Weserland*	6,528	09.09.42	Bordeaux	2,960	01.12.42	Yokohama
G M/T[a]	*Brake*	9,925	27.09.42	Bordeaux	oil	23.12.42	Yokohama
I M/V	*Pietro Orseolo*	6,344	01.10.42	Bordeaux	2,960	02.12.42	Yokohama
G M/V	*Rio Grande*	6,062	01.10.42	Bordeaux	2,974	31.12.42	Yokohama
G M/V	*Burgenland*	7,320	04.10.42	Bordeaux	2,899	12.01.43	Kobe
G M/V	*Irene*	4,793	11.10.42	Bordeaux	2,886	20.12.42	Kobe
G M/V	*Anneliese Essberger*	5,173	05.11.42	Bordeaux	2,340	21.11.42	Sunk by USS *Milwaukee*, 01°N, 23°W
G M/V	*Karin*	7,322	06.11.42	Bordeaux	2,738	22.12.42	Batavia

Nationality/Type	Ship	Gross Registered Tons	Sailed	Departure Port	Cargo (Tons)	Arrived/Lost	Arrival Port/How Lost
G M/V	*Elsa Essberger*	6,103	—	—	2,297	—	Voyage canceled after RAF bomb damage, St. Nazaire, 07.11.42
G M/T[b]	*Spichern*	9,323	08.11.42	St. Nazaire	oil	13.01.43	Bordeaux. At El Ferrol, Spain, 11.11.42–09.01.43.
I M/V	*Cortellazzo*	5,292	28.11.42	Bordeaux	2,209	01.12.42	Sunk by HMS *Redoubt* and HMAS *Quickmatch*, 44°N, 20°W
G M/T[a]	*Germania*	9,851	11.12.42	Bordeaux	none	15.12.42	Sunk by HMS *Egret* and HMS *Tanatside*, 45°N, 16°W
G M/V	*Osorno*	6,951	28.03.43	Bordeaux	5,758	04.06.43	Yokohama
G M/V	*Portland*	7,132	28.03.43	Bordeaux	4,833	13.04.43	Sunk by FFS *Georges Leygues*, 05°N, 22°W
G M/V	*Alsterufer*	6,062	29.03.43	St. Nazaire	1,272	19.06.43	Yokohama
I M/V	*Himalaya*	6,240	08.04.43	La Pallice	5,241	11.04.43	La Pallice after RAF bomb damage 09.04.43
I M/V	*Fusijama*	6,244	—	—	—	—	Voyage canceled 01.43
G M/V	*Münsterland*	6,408	—	—	—	—	Voyage canceled 01.43
G M/T[a]	*Sudetenland*	11,309	—	—	—	—	Voyage canceled 02.43
G M/T[a]	*Monsun*	8,038	—	—	—	—	Voyage canceled 02.43

Nationality/Type	Ship	Gross Registered Tons	Sailed	Departure Port	Cargo (Tons)	Arrived/Lost	Arrival Port/How Lost
G M/T[b]	*Passat*	8,998	—	—	—	—	Voyage canceled after bomb damage at St. Nazaire 02.09.42
G M/T[a]	*Taifun*	6,405	—	—	—	—	Voyage canceled 01.43
G M/V	*Kulmerland*	7,363	—	—	—	—	Voyage canceled 01.43
G M/V	*Tannenfels*	7,840	—	—	—	—	Voyage canceled 01.43
G M/T[a]	*Schlettstadt*	8,055	—	—	—	—	Voyage canceled 01.43
G M/V	*Kulmerland*	7,363	—	—	—	—	Voyage canceled after bomb damage, Nantes, 23.09.43
G M/T[b]	*Ostfriesland*	6,135	—	—	—	—	Voyage canceled 10.43 after loss of raider 28 (*Michel*)
G M/V	*Dresden*	5,567	—	—	—	11.43	Voyage canceled after mine hit, Gironde roads, 02.11.43
I M/V	*Pietro Orseolo*	6,344	—	—	—	21.12.43	Sunk after a/c torpedo hit, Concarneau roads, 18.12.43
I M/V	*Fusijama*	6,244	—	—	—	—	Voyage canceled 18.12.43
G M/V	*Elsa Essberger*	6,104	—	—	—	—	Voyage canceled 18.01.44
G M/V	*Tannenfels*	7,840	—	—	—	—	Voyage canceled 18.01.44
I M/V	*Himalaya*	6,240	—	—	—	—	Voyage canceled 18.01.44

[a] auxiliary fleet tanker
[b] auxiliary fleet supply ship
[c] fleet supply ship

1943 to build special transport U-boats, later known as Type XX, it was clear that such U-boats would not become operational before the summer of 1944. Moreover, the theoretical annual transport capacity of twenty cargo U-boats was calculated as 20,000 tons, at best, in each direction. The estimated *minimum* import figure of essential goods was 150,000 tons for the blockade running season 1943–44. It should not be overlooked that one U-boat could carry a cargo of only about 2 to 3 percent of that of a surface blockade-runner. Thus the HWK continued to consider the employment of transport U-boats only as a complementary effort to the use of surface blockade-running ships.[19]

TRANSPORT TO THE EAST

In 1942 the Japanese navy had sent the large U-cruiser, I-30, to France to pick up the latest German radar and sonar devices, requested from the German navy, for a safe return to Japan. The incident was offered as propaganda, a goodwill visit to strengthen German-Japanese naval cooperation. The majority of the cargo load was lost on 13 October 1942 when I-30 sank off Singapore after hitting a mine during its final transfer passage to Japan.[20]

In contrast, a similar operation took place in April 1943, when the German U-180 met the Japanese I-29 at sea in the Indian Ocean southwest of Madagascar to transfer highly secret weapon samples and construction plans for the Japanese army, upon personal orders from Hitler. When the Japanese naval attaché in Berlin had expressed his dissatisfaction with the apparent lack of benefit for the Japanese navy in this operation, the German navy agreed to ship a certain amount of cargo for the IJN as well, in addition to two Japanese naval officers as passengers. In return the IJN handed over to U-180 three of its latest Type 93 submarine torpedoes, together with various other materials and construction plans requested by the German navy in the course of the I-30 visit. However, neither the Japanese submarine I-8 in its next trip to France in the summer of 1943, nor any of the aforementioned Japanese boats, would carry any substantial load of raw materials, despite German requests.[21]

The setback in surface blockade-running operations in early 1943 prompted the use of Italian combat submarines, converted into cargo U-boats, as an emergency step during the intermediate period. Of the nine Italian boats originally designated for cargo transport, two were lost before their scheduled conversion. Removal of the remaining seven's artillery, ammunition storage, torpedo tubes, and some battery cells was completed between March and July 1943. Five of these transport boats, cover-named "Aquila," left France for the

Far East, carrying 650 tons of cargo for the Japanese in addition to supply materials for the buildup of the German-Italian submarine bases at Penang, Singapore, and Jakarta. Only three actually arrived there, delivering 355 tons of cargo. None of them ever returned to Europe.[22]

Parallel to the use of the "Aquila" boats, the Naval war Staff asked the Japanese navy in July 1943 to send one or two of its U-cruisers as transports for rubber and other urgently needed materials. Only after repeated requests did the Japanese navy agree on 24 August 1943 to sail two boats for this purpose in September and October 1943.[23] This was the IJN's first active participation in the blockade-running program between the two Axis partners. Its probable motivation was an intention to keep personnel traveling to and from Europe and bringing back the latest military secrets from Germany.

Actually three Japanese boats were designated for transport missions to Europe after the first boat, I-34, was lost to submarine attack en route in Japanese controlled waters. Thereafter only I-29 made it to France, bringing some 170 tons of raw materials together with two tons of gold to cover Japanese expenses in Europe. The third boat, I-52, carrying a similar cargo and intended as a replacement for I-34, was lost en route to France. Its loss on 24 July 1944 marked the end of the Japanese effort in blockade-running operations.

By the end of May 1944 the conventional design of the German Type XX cargo U-boats then under construction had proven to be no longer equal to modern ASW weapons and tactics. The Type XX construction program was abandoned in June 1944. Instead, the idea was to convert some of the new, advanced Type XXI "Electro" U-boats for cargo transport. Plans were drawn up to reduce the number of torpedo tubes in some of these boats in favor of cargo stowing space. However, none of the Type XXI U-boats completed or under construction was ever converted in this way until the end of the war. Equally unsuccessful were attempts to use submersible cargo containers to be towed by combat U-boats, because towing cargo shortened a U-boat's cruising range, making it insufficient for the trip to the Far East.

The intended completion and use of six large cargo U-boats, captured under construction in Italy following the Italian capitulation, was frustrated by the military situation in the Mediterranean.[24] For the time being, then, German combat U-boats had to be utilized for cargo transport to and from Europe. Combat U-boats sailing from Europe for operations in the Indian Ocean also carried equipment and all necessary spares for the German bases in the Far East.

The use of combat U-boats for transport generally faced a number of problems. Storage room in normal combat U-boats was—and is—usually insignificant, with only about one cubic meter space available for each ton of cargo capacity. Freight goods are often bulky and on average require at least three to four cubic meters per ton. The maximum dimensions of dry cargo are limited by the small openings in the U-boat pressure hull.

Against these realities, the shippers had to account for the nature of wartime matériel. Most of the goods being shipped to and from Japan consisted of space-consuming military or industrial equipment or lightweight raw materials like rubber. A significant part of the cargo load had to be stowed inside the U-boat as ballast, to reach submerging weight, while keeping the normal fighting capability unaffected. In November 1943, U-boats in the Far Eastern bases were ordered to remove their keel ballast (each about eighty to a hundred tons) in order to use the available space for suitable cargo on the homebound trip.

From early 1944 on, U-boats sailing to the Far East generally carried bottled mercury, lead, special steel or aluminum bars, and unmachined optical glass as keel load. Cargo within the pressure hull was principally limited to drawings of important war equipment and models of modern weapons. Several of the long-range Type XB, IXD1, and IXD2 boats were partly converted during 1944 to increase their dry stowage room, by reducing the diesel propulsion unit or replacing the mine-laying equipment in the mine shafts by pressure-proof steel containers.[25]

On 19 February 1944 the Type IXC/40 boat U-843 left its French base at Lorient as the first German combat U-boat assigned to the Indian Ocean, loaded with extra cargo for the Japanese army and navy. The schedule worked out in early 1944 for a round trip of the combat cargo transporters included a four-to-five-month antishipping operational patrol in the Indian Ocean on the outbound trip, two to three months' yard overhaul in the Far Eastern bases at Penang and Singapore, and a four-to-five-month return patrol to a French U-boat base, with intermediate antishipping operations in the Indian Ocean.[26] While the German U-boat command still considered the Indian Ocean a promising operational area in its desperate continuation of the U-boat campaign, the antishipping operations on the outbound trip were still seen as the primary objective. Advances in Allied ASW operations proved such an operational policy fatal.

As of early March 1945, sixteen German U-boats had sailed as combat cargo transports to the Far East. Only eight boats had actually arrived at Penang or

Jakarta, altogether delivering some 930 tons of cargo. The eight others had in one way or another fallen victim to Allied air and naval forces. The desperate German military situation and shortages in the supply of diesel fuel forced the German Naval Operational Staff on 8 March 1945 to trim immediate transport liaison with Japan to two missions of U-234 and U-876 that were earmarked for taking high-ranking German personnel to various assignments in Japan.[27] The remaining Type IXD2 transports were either redirected to other operational areas or kept in port after the cancellation of their patrols. Ultimately, only U-234 made the trip to Japan, carrying 560 kg of uranium oxide for the Japanese army along with its valuable cargo of raw materials and weapon samples. After the cessation of hostilities the surviving transport boats, including their cargo, were handed over to Allied naval forces.

Even more disappointing were attempts to bring precious raw materials by U-boat from East Asia back to the German realm. Up to the end of 1944, only two U-boats and one Japanese submarine reached France, while no less than nine boats were sunk or forced to return. A final group of four more U-boats departed from the Far East in December 1944 and early January 1945. Although none was lost en route, they nevertheless arrived too late to contribute to the

Table 16.5. Tons of Matériel Transported by Submarine, Europe to Far East, 1944–1945

Matériel	Mercury	Lead	Aluminum	Glass	Steel	Total
Shipped	926.7	860.3	88.0	41.4	153.7	2,070.1
Arrived	396.1	383.1	63.0	12.1	14.7	869.0
Lost	506.5	310.2	25.0	22.7	128.3	992.7
En route	24.1	67.1	—	6.6	10.7	108.5
Turned back	—	100.3	—	—	—	100.3

Table 16.6. Tons of Matériel Transported by Submarine, Far East to Europe, 1944–1945

Matériel	Tin	Rubber	Tungsten	Quinine	Opium	Misc.	Total
Shipped	1,200.8	731.6	595.5	24.8	17.7	35.6	2,606.0
Arrived	327.7	172.4	99.8	5.7	2.2	3.6	611.4
Lost	311.5	219.8	213.0	9.9	7.4	20.6	782.2
En route	116.4	36.3	118.2	0.3	0.2	6.4	277.8
Turned back	445.6	303.1	164.5	8.9	7.9	5.0	935.0

German war effort. Out of a total of 611 tons of raw materials successfully transported by German and Japanese U-boats to Europe by the end of the war, only 434 tons arrived in time to become available for German industry.[28] The use of submarines for importing vital raw materials from the Far East was highly unproductive for the German end.

Taking all surface ship and submarine blockade running operations from the Far East during the period September 1941 to April 1945 into consideration, total German imports of raw materials, foodstuffs, and other commodities amounted to 112,061 tons, comprising 43.5 percent of the total tonnage of 260,228 tons shipped to Europe.[29] Imports of crude rubber and rubber products alone reached 44,560 tons. However, non-vital foodstuffs like edible oil surprisingly constituted more than 40 percent of all cargo shipped.[30] This obvious lack of strategic foresight in German import planning was only recognized at the end of 1942, when the military situation at sea prevented any further steps to correct previous mistakes.

Thus the series of successful blockade-running operations until the winter of 1942 failed to built up sufficient stocks of strategically important raw materials like rubber or high-grade minerals. Consequently, after 1942 German industry suffered from constant shortfalls of these materials. Only strict rationing and increased use of less suitable substitutes, which often reduced the overall quality of the materials produced, were able to buffer the consequences for the German war effort.

In contrast, total Japanese imports from Europe during 1941 to 1945 reached at least 58,356 tons, representing more than 84 percent of all shipments from Europe to the Far East. Unlike their German counterparts, Japanese authorities strictly concentrated shipments on high-tech military equipment and other materials considered important for the Japanese war effort. The abundance of strategic raw materials in the Japanese-controlled hemisphere made Japan less vulnerable to interruptions in the transport link with its European allies. However, the actual amount of high-grade imports from Europe could not compensate for the productive and technological inferiority of the Japanese war industry with respect to the United States, as the leading industrial power of the world.

PART 4

Conclusion

17

Conclusion

In retrospect, the problems inherent in German-Japanese relations between 1934 and 1945 varied with the respective nations' domestic situations and their stance toward naval foreign policy and war planning. In the overall time frame, these varying factors appear to cluster in three distinct periods.

The first period started with the active steps the Japanese navy took to establish closer and special relations with the Reichsmarine and later Kriegsmarine around 1934–35. The second period began in 1938 when, with the Sudeten crisis, first considerations appeared about the respective roles of the partners and the practical extent and handling of support in an assumed armed conflict with the Anglo-Saxon sea powers. These considerations gained special importance with the actual outbreak of war in Europe in 1939. When both navies finally found themselves at war with both the Royal Navy and U.S. Navy in December 1941, the third and final phase was reached.

As for the domestic influences, the German navy's position was weak, relative to the other power centers in Germany, but it had a quite efficient organization, in addition to an officer corps that showed comparatively little internal tension. The Japanese navy, on the other hand, had a strong domestic position but a less efficient organization and strong internal tensions within their officer corps.

The German navy's situation resulted from the consequences of the constitutional shift from monarchy to republic after Germany's defeat in World War I. Once the "favorite pet" of the Kaiser, with extensive rights of direct access to the throne and a large fleet, the German Imperial Navy had been able to exert enormous influence in foreign policy and other matters—much to the annoyance of its powerful rivals, the army and especially the foreign office (*Auswärtiges Amt,* or AA). The AA had been very quick in the twenties to secure itself a dominant position, seeing that the armed forces had discredited themselves through a lost war and mutinies and also had been reduced to practically negligible numbers by the Versailles treaty. From then on, the navy was never again in a position to dominate the decision-making processes on important questions.

One beneficial side effect of their reorganization in the early twenties was, however, that the multitude of high and independent command posts was abolished and the most radical enemies of the Republic were removed from the ranks. This resulted in an officer corps over which, in the thirties, Commander in Chief Raeder could easily rule in an "authoritarian manner" (as he himself put it) but which could, at the same time, readily and uncritically serve as an instrument for Hitler in World War II—although not oriented to national socialist doctrine. Politically, the majority of German naval officers of that time were supporters of an authoritarian state and tended to view the international system as a Darwinian arena.

It seems that similar views in the ranks of the Japanese naval officers caused a certain degree of sympathy on both sides when members of both navies had contacts in the twenties.[1] But unlike the German side, the Japanese navy had not undergone such far-reaching changes and therefore had retained characteristics that sprang from the Prussian features of the Japanese Meiji Constitution, principally the independence of the armed forces from government and parliament. For the navy this also meant the perpetuation of an organization providing for several command posts that at least nominally had the right of direct access to the throne. This system had worked quite well as long as Japan had been under the actual rule of the Genrō (elder statesmen), who exercised rule in the name of the emperor, that is, prepared the decisions that the emperor usually consented to.

The Genrō position had originally been held by the most influential leaders of the clans that had emerged as the winners of the Meiji Restoration in the second half of the nineteenth century. Although the elder statesman role was not formalized by the Meiji Constitution, the constitution basically guaranteed their rule; it provided for the deciding of all important questions by a small circle of a few clan leaders, who usually were well acquainted. But as the Genrō's influence gradually faded, this system became ineffective. Decision-making processes, both on government and internal navy levels, became extremely cumbersome and slow. As a result, factionalism grew strong, and after Katō Tomosaburō's death in 1923 the Japanese navy was practically unable to cure this serious organizational handicap. Moreover, it became difficult to control the younger, more extremist officers, who did not shrink from murder and suicide for political purposes in the factional struggles of the thirties. Such events, of course, made it by no means easier for the Japanese naval leaders to swiftly and effectively formulate naval policy, including relations with the Kriegsmarine.

Actually a victory of the *Kantaiha* (Fleet Faction) over the *Jōyakuha* (Treaty Faction) led to the important decision to leave the Washington and London treaty system and consequently to start the strengthening of ties with the German navy that finally became a formal alliance in World War II.

In the field of foreign policy, the fact that the German navy, after having had its fleet reduced to a *quantité négligeable* by the Versailles treaty, did not appear attractive, even potentially, as an ally in war remained a setback to the Germans until 1935. The main aim of German naval leaders had always been to overcome the limitations of the Versailles treaty and become a full-fledged competitor on the oceans again. But when Hitler started World War II, it was much too early from the Kriegsmarine's point of view. Though it had a few battleships and a sizable U-boat fleet, this situation basically did not change in World War II. There had not been enough time and resources to actually build a fleet strong enough to mount a real challenge toward the Anglo-Saxon supremacy. Lacking a solid contingency plan for a war against the British, the Kriegsmarine had to somehow compensate for its weakness.

On the Japanese side, the fleet since World War I had always been powerful. It was considered a substantial threat in case of war both by the Americans and by the British and their Commonwealth members in the Pacific. The Washington Treaty seemed to settle the naval situation between the potential rivals in the Pacific, but the Japanese navy, formerly an important element in the Anglo-Japanese Alliance, now found itself in a basically isolated position. It had no more allies and found itself stuck with the 5:3 ratio that was considered a violation of the "70 percent principle" advocated by influential naval officers. Compensating for this handicap with the use of modern technology had become difficult because the Anglo-Saxon sources for it had dried up. Thus German sources of technology were eagerly sought.

When Japan finally made the decision to abandon the Washington system, the main points of Japanese naval foreign policy were: (1) To compensate for the precarious raw-materials situation by gaining control of the rich Dutch East Indies (the Southern Advance) but (2) at the same time avoiding an armed clash with the United States, on which Japan was economically dependent, and (3) to secure priority of the so-called Southern Advance policy against the continental plans (the Northern Advance) of the army.

The Japanese navy had carefully devised plans for a war against the U.S. Navy that provided for attrition of the U.S. forces as they approached the western Pacific to retake the Philippines and luring the remainder into a decisive battle. The Royal Navy played only a secondary role here.

With these factors in mind, it seems reasonable to conclude that the origin of the German-Japanese naval alliance developed in 1934. In this year the German navy had just managed, as a consequence of the changed political climate since the Papen and Schleicher cabinets, to reestablish German naval attachés abroad, and the one for Tokyo had just arrived there. He rather soon saw himself presented with unprecedented proposals by the Japanese, peaking in the inspection of Japanese carriers by German experts. Such offers held considerable potential for strengthening a future German fleet that might be able to divert considerable British forces away from the Far East—definitely a positive prospect for Japanese naval planners, who had to face a scenario of growing Anglo-Saxon hostility after the Japanese decision to let the Washington and London treaty expire.

Accordingly, the reintroduction of conscription in Germany and the beginning of rearmament was warmly welcomed on the naval side in Japan, only to be met by rather harsh disappointment because of the German-British naval agreement in London only a short time later. For the German navy, which could represent its position directly at the conference table largely independent of its old rival, the foreign office (AA), these events indicated not only more domestic leeway but, especially, the attainment of the long-desired abolition of the Versailles treaty limitations. The German navy was no longer isolated and, despite its still tiny fleet, had become an interesting partner for some of the big navies.

Completely new, in the Japanese offer of support with carrier technology, was the fact that, after long years of learning from the West, Japan now played the role of the teacher, with one of the Western nations assuming the pupil's position. However, this unprecedented offer was met with mixed reactions on the part of the Kriegsmarine. The head of the construction department (*Hauptamt Kriegsschiffbau*), Admiral Witzell, did not conceal his mistrust, fearing that his department would have to give more than it received. In contrast to the operations department of the Naval War Staff (Skl.), he does not seem to have fully realized the potential of aircraft carriers.[2]

Considered against the background of these governing policy factors, other problems—for instance, differing policies regarding the operational use of submarines—seem less important for the characterization of German-Japanese naval relations. Although the Japanese more than fulfilled their part of the deal, the German side was slow to keep theirs and tried to put it off as long as possible. Apparently private firms, and perhaps not only the navy, were responsible for such reluctance. The German attaché reported signs of annoyance from the Japanese, who were nevertheless unwilling to cut the newly established special relations. Their main emphasis in the association was on what they could gain in the technical field. Oddly—or naturally, depending on how one looks at it—the Japanese always kept silent when the Germans tried to touch upon Japanese tactical or operational experience or Japanese building plans.

From 1936 on, the Kriegsmarine surmised that an armed conflict between the Japanese and the Royal Navy would in the long run be unavoidable. The Tokyo attachés reported to the Berlin naval leaders the main principles of the Japanese navy's foreign policy, with their emphasis on a Southern Advance into the raw-materials-rich region of the southwest Pacific; the necessity of protecting this plan against continental adventures of the army; the precarious economic position of the Island Empire in case of war; and the resulting great caution with regard to the United States.

Berlin also came to understand that the IJN gained prestige at home from its loyal stance, when the young officers' putsch had occurred in February 1936. There had been a lot of sympathy for the putsch in naval ranks, too, though.

When the Washington treaty expired, the German and the Japanese navies found themselves in long-desired positions: The limiting regulations of both treaties devised by the Anglo-Saxon sea powers had been removed. Now, however, the question was how the relations with the United States and Great Britain would develop and what consequences this would have for the two "revisionist" navies and their relations with each other. Although both foresaw the possibility of war with the British, with the war in China and the Sudeten crisis, respectively, neither was ready to devise plans for an effective cooperation. Raeder wanted to support the Chinese and was willing—even in the face of Japanese complaints about German shipping to China—to deceive the Japanese friends; the problem was solved only after Hitler decided to stop support for China and side with Japan. This was also why the Kriegsmarine finally agreed to an intelligence exchange with the Japanese, although it dragged its feet on the matter.

During the Sudeten crisis the Kriegsmarine for the very first time considered the role that the Japanese partner could play in a war with Great Britain. Specifically, the Berlin naval planners hoped for support for their commerce raiders. At the same time they had to realize that, despite the Japanese rapprochement, any guarantees for active help were carefully avoided by the Japanese Navy Ministry, the Kaigunshō. The Japanese Naval General Staff (Gunreibu) showed a little more cooperation in that, behind the Navy Ministry's back, they gave intelligence to the Germans on Allied naval forces.

The Japanese navy's very cautious stance again became clearly visible when war broke out in Europe. Despite considerable hostility, they tried to avoid any confrontation with the British. This even led the Seekriegsleitung to speculations about secret Anglo-Japanese agreements. Only after the German successes of 1940 in Europe did a strictly secret support for the Kriegsmarine's commerce raiders begin.

Meanwhile these German successes were the cause of considerable concern on the part of the Japanese navy, anticipating extremely unwelcome side effects of Germany's European victories on the Dutch East Indies, the main objective of the Southern Advance. These worries were a main reason for the navy's consenting to the Tripartite Pact. But, here again, the chief motivation for their "naval foreign policy" became visible, as they interpreted the pact mainly as an instrument of deterrence against the United States and were unwilling to take any actual risk of being drawn into the European war. A main advantage of the pact, seen from the Japanese navy's point of view, was the immediate possibility of sending a sizable inspection commission to Germany.

From the Kriegsmarine's point of view, participation of the Japanese on the Axis side and a subsequent diversion of British naval forces appeared highly desirable. An unexpected and unique chance to achieve just this seemed to appear for the German naval leaders with the *Automedon* booty. Raeder and his staff seemed to hope for a moment, in December 1940 and January 1941, that at last the situation had come that had been described by Wenneker and Lietzmann repeatedly in their reports from Tokyo since the mid-thirties: namely, that the IJN would seize the opportunity to attack the weak British position in Singapore while British forces were diverted in Europe. Raeder and his comrades even harbored hopes of talking Hitler into giving the global naval perspectives of the Skl. priority over his war of annihilation against the Soviet Union.

But the German naval officers overestimated the role of the Royal Navy in the eyes of their Japanese counterparts as much as they underestimated the threat that the U.S. Navy posed for the Japanese. They also misjudged the level of their Führer's racist determination to fight "his" war against the Soviets. Hitler as well as the Japanese naval leader declined the proposals, and with that, from the viewpoint of the Naval War Staff, a unique chance was lost.

Similar caution was exercised by the Japanese naval leadership when Germany attacked the Soviet Union in June 1941. To participate here in any way would have been a blatant deviation from the policy of giving the Southern Advance priority over continental adventures favored by the Japanese army. Despite a warning received more than two months before, the Japanese took a long time to advise even their own naval representatives in Berlin on their position on this question, which was definitely not what the German side—and in this case the Kriegsmarine, too—had hoped for. In the Skl., the Japanese reaction led to significant bitterness toward the partner who was obviously unwilling to take any clear action in favor of the German ally.

These German reactions revealed that the Skl. had not properly considered the main determinants of the Japanese navy's policy, nor had it factored in the cumbersomeness of the Japanese decision-making process, which had constitutional causes. Unlike Germany, Japan had a constitutional framework that stayed basically intact throughout World War II. That meant that the decision-making process, though slow, always followed the same procedure. In Germany, there was considerable fragmentation in governmental affairs, causing Japanese naval representatives, especially from 1944 on, difficulties in determining who was the really competent partner on many issues.

After its disappointment in the *Automedon* case, the Skl. once more thought it had reason for high hopes regarding cooperation with the Japanese navy. That was shortly after the surprise Japanese attack on Pearl Harbor in December 1941, which also had been a surprise for the Kriegsmarine. During the first months of 1942, German naval planners considered far-reaching plans for coordinated operations with the Japanese, in which the German army would take Suez, the Japanese navy would fight in the northwestern Indian Ocean, and a land corridor between German- and Japanese-controlled areas would be established in the Middle East. Such plans were delusional. Neither did the German navy have enough influence domestically to push its concept through against the OKH and OKW—which would have had to supply the troops for it—nor could Hitler be won over to such an idea. As for the Japanese partner, the German naval planners failed to assess accurately Japan's willingness and ability to support it and the preconditions for doing so. And the decisive events at Midway and the struggle for the Solomons paralyzed the Japanese naval offensive capability from mid-1942 on and made a large-scale operational cooperation impossible.

What now remained of the alliance revolved around submarine activity and the exchange of materials, personnel, and information. The former was reduced to the rather limited and makeshift measure of letting German U-boats operate from Japanese bases in the Indian Ocean. For the Germans, it was in essence a reaction to the fact that the Allied sea lines of communication in the Atlantic were heavily guarded by now and that the U-boats did not meet such heavy defense in the Indian Ocean. There were never enough long-range boats available, though, to really halt Allied sea traffic in an area that the Japanese just could not adequately defend anyway. The other remaining feature, the exchange of materials and personnel by blockade-runners and submarines, was a mere trickle and in no way able to seriously influence the course of the war.

One more thing needs to be assessed here: the influence that cultural differences and perhaps racism had on cooperation. It cannot be denied that they existed and once in a while led to highly unpleasant incidents. German submarine crews at the Japanese bases in East and Southeast Asia often had long stays in port because of lack of spare parts, insufficient or slowly working repair facilities, and problems with provisioning. They were given choice accommodation and recreation facilities that were much better than those provided for their Japanese comrades, who reacted with discontent. German sailors spent considerable time ashore, spending much money, and were sometimes involved in black market activities. As they could usually speak English, they were always popular with girls. These may have been the reasons for occasional brawls and fights between sailors of both navies.[3]

Occasional obstructionism and even sometimes outright hostility were met on both sides. But this can be attributed to German and Japanese propaganda, which were fueling a hatred for anything or anybody of non-Aryan or occidental origin, respectively. Moreover, on the German side, complaints about the Japanese "mentality" can be found relatively often in the records. But even in documents where dissatisfaction and anger about the partner is expressed sharply, any hints as to a racist view are absent.[4] On the contrary, where Germans personally got to know Japanese they often commented quite favorably on their acquaintances, and friendly contact was maintained in many cases even after World War II.[5] That the Japanese actually were often seen as trustworthy and reliable also explains the quite numerous and often well-informed Germans whom they could use as sources of intelligence about their own Axis partners. Thus, in the main, an atmosphere of friendliness and trust on the level of personal contacts seems to have prevailed in both navies.

Why, then, were these allies so reluctant? The answer becomes clear if one reconsiders the above-mentioned domestic and naval foreign policy factors. Seen from the Japanese navy's point of view, the German navy first of all was a potential counterweight against the Royal Navy after the expiration of the Washington and London treaties. To really become a useful ally it first had to build a powerful fleet, and the Japanese tried to promote this by teaching the Germans aircraft carrier technology. But their initial hopes were quickly disappointed by the Anglo-German fleet agreement of 1935, which seemed to make a confrontation improbable.

As war with the British became a growing possibility for both the Japanese and the German navies in the wake of the war in China and the Sudeten crisis, the German position did not reassure the Japanese. The Germans not only initially supported the Chinese, thus making a conclusion of the war more difficult, but also dragged their feet about accelerating the intelligence exchange, which was desired by the Japanese navy. When World War II broke out in Europe, the Germans pushed for Japanese support that would have meant a premature war with both Anglo-Saxon powers and later for a participation or at least support of the German war effort against the Soviet Union. To comply with those requests would have meant sacrificing the principles that formed the basis for the Japanese navy's cherished Southern Advance. And the German navy was simply too weak to offer in exchange anything in the way of support weighty enough to be of any real value to the Japanese in an armed conflict with the United States.

In addition, the Kriegsmarine must have appeared weak on the German home front, as the very different views of Hitler, the OKW, the army, and the air force militated against the Kriegsmarine's opinion in most important questions. The resulting course of German policy and warfare did not fit in with the aims of the Japanese navy, which therefore regarded Germany, as a whole, as a quite fickle ally. The only really constant factor for Japanese naval leaders seems to have been the considerable value of Germany (and by no means only the German navy) as a source of technology. The Japanese interest in this stayed keen from the early twenties until the last days of World War II.

For the Germans it was exactly this high Japanese interest in German technology that created a certain degree of anxiety about ending up on the primarily giving side. This worry can be traced from before the early 1930s at least until late 1944. The Kriegsmarine's priorities until 1938 were the shaking off of the limitations of the Versailles treaty and then the rebuilding of a sizable fleet—a scenario in which the Japanese navy did not play an important role. This changed from 1938 on, when hopes were increasingly placed in this powerful ally, especially since an armed conflict between Japan and the British was considered unavoidable from 1936 on.

But the Kriegsmarine's high hopes were frustrated time and again, and with reason. The Germans failed to realistically assess the importance of the factors lying at the heart of the Japanese navy's Southern Advance policy and the cumbersomeness of the Japanese decision-making processes, as opposed to the Kriegsmarine's requests to attack Singapore or to give priority to operations in the Indian Ocean. It seems that this failure had its roots in the German view of the Japanese role, not as a partner with its own and perhaps "legitimate" interests that had to be accounted for, but only as a means primarily to promote the Kriegsmarine's interests—with practically no consideration given to maintaining a balance of give-and-take so as to make cooperation actually work. It may be indicative for the outlook of German naval planners that, as early as May 1940, Japan was already mentioned as a possible *opponent* in a fight for global predominance to take place after the successful conclusion of the war then in progress.[6]

Considering such a state of mind and the partners' differing objectives, it becomes clear why these allies were very reluctant indeed.

Appendix A

The Tripartite Pact between Germany, Italy, and Japan

The Governments of Germany, Italy, and Japan, considering it as the condition precedent of any lasting peace that all nations of the world be given each its own proper place, have decided to stand by and cooperate with one another in regard to their efforts in Greater East Asia and the regions of Europe, respectively, wherein it is their prime purpose to establish and maintain a new order of things calculated to promote mutual prosperity and welfare of the peoples concerned.

Furthermore, it is the desire of the three governments to extend cooperation to such nations in other spheres of the world as may be inclined to put forth endeavors along lines similar to their own, in order that their ultimate aspirations for world peace may thus be realized. Accordingly, the governments of Germany, Italy, and Japan have agreed as follows:

Article 1
Japan recognizes and respects the leadership of Germany and Italy in the establishment of a new order in Europe.

Article 2
Germany and Italy recognize and respect the leadership of Japan in the establishment of a new order in Greater East Asia.

Article 3

Germany, Italy, and Japan agree to cooperate in their efforts on the aforesaid lines. They further undertake to assist one another with all political, economic, and military means when one of the three contracting parties is attacked by a power at present not involved in the European war or in the Sino-Japanese conflict.

Article 4

With a view to implementing the present Pact, Joint Technical Commissions, the members of which are to be appointed by the respective Governments of Germany, Italy, and Japan, will meet without delay.

Article 5

Germany, Italy, and Japan affirm that the aforesaid terms do not in any way affect the political status that exists at present between each of the three Contracting Parties and Soviet Russia.

Article 6

The present Pact shall come into effect immediately upon signature and shall remain in force for ten years from the date of its coming into force.

At proper time before the expiration of the said term, the High Contracting Parties shall, at the request of any one of them, enter into negotiations for its renewal.

In faith whereof, the undersigned, duly authorized by their respective governments, have signed this Pact and have affixed hereto their Seals.

Done in triplicate at Berlin, the 27th day of September 1940—in the eighteenth year of the Fascist Era—corresponding to the seventeenth day of the ninth month of the fifteenth year of Syowa.

Source: Akten zur Deutschen Auswärtigen Politik (ADAP) Series D, XI.1:175, document 118. Translated by H.-J. Krug.

Extract from Supplementary Note 1 to the Tripartite Pact

[T]he conditions actually prevailing in Greater East Asia and elsewhere do not permit the Japanese Government to rest assured that there is no danger whatever of an armed conflict taking place between Japan and Great Britain, and accordingly they desire to call attention of the German and Italian Governments to such a possibility and to ask whether in such eventuality the Japanese Government may expect assistance and cooperation in every possible form as provided for under Paragraph III of the present Pact *mutatis mutandis.*

Source: Ibid., 106, document 74. Translated by H.-J. Krug.

Extract from Supplementary Note 2 to the Tripartite Pact

[I]nasmuch as the German and Italian Governments recognize and respect the leadership of Japan in regard to the establishment of a new order in Greater East Asia, it is considered highly desirable by this Government that all the former German colonies in the Pacific area should be ceded to Japan, without compensation in the case of the group of islands mandated by Japan and with proper compensation in the case of other mandate islands as well as those actually in British possession.

It is understood as a matter of course that Japan shall accord a specially favorable treatment to the activities of Germany and her nationals in those regions as compared to any other nation and their nationals.

Source: Ibid. Translated by H.-J. Krug.

Appendix B

Secret Supplementary Protocols to the Tripartite Pact

Supplementary Protocol, 27 December 1940

With reference to the Pact signed on this day by the representatives of Germany, Italy, and Japan, the Contracting Parties have arrived at the following understanding:

With a view to determine by consultation with one another the detailed arrangements on the cooperation and mutual assistance between Germany, Italy, and Japan as stipulated in Paragraph III of the Pact, Joint Military and Naval Commissions, preferably one at Tokyo and another at Berlin or Rome, together with a Joint Economic Commission, shall forthwith be organized. The composition of the aforesaid commission(s) shall be determined through consultation by the Governments of Germany, Italy and Japan. The conclusions of the said commissions shall be submitted to the respective Governments for approval in order to be put into force.

Whether or not the Contracting Party or Parties has or have been attacked as stipulated in paragraph III of the Pact, shall be determined by the respective Governments, and, in case the fact of such an attack has been established, the measures of mutual assistance of a political, economic, and military nature to be adopted by the Contracting Parties shall be studied and recommended by the aforesaid Commissions, subject to the approval of the respective Governments.

As the cooperation and mutual assistance stipulated in paragraph III of the Pact have in view as fundamental aims the efforts to establish forthwith a new Order in Greater East Asia and Europe, to eventuate in a new world order, blessing Humanity with a just and equitable peace, Germany and Italy shall, in time of peace as well as war, take all possible measures to restrain a Third Power or Powers on the Atlantic with a view to better enabling Japan, Germany, and Italy to accomplish their common aim of establishing a new order in Greater East Asia and in the Pacific Basin in general. In the event of Japan being attacked by a power or powers not at present involved in either the European war or the Sino-Japanese conflict, Germany and Italy undertake to come to Japan's assistance with all their means and resources.

While Germany and Italy undertake to use their good offices with a view of improving relations between Japan and the USSR, Germany, Italy, and Japan shall make utmost efforts to induce the USSR to act in accord with the main purpose of the present Pact.

The Contracting Parties undertake to exchange from time to time without delay all useful inventions and devices of war and to supply one another with war equipment, such as airplanes, tanks, guns, explosives, etc., which each Party may reasonably spare, together with technical skill and men, should they be required. Furthermore, they are prepared to do their utmost in furnishing one another with and in aiding one another in the efforts to procure minerals as well as machinery for war industries and various requisites for livelihood with machinery of all sorts employed in the production of such requisites.

In conformity with the spirit that prompted the conclusion of the present Pact, the Governments of the Contracting Parties undertake to enter into negotiations without delay, with a view to deciding upon measures of assuring to the other Contracting Parties or their nationals, in the commercial or industrial activities in the regions where the Contracting Parties are respectively recognized to have leadership by virtue of paragraph I and II of the present Pact, a position which is preponderant in comparison to that of any Third Power and its nationals.

The present Protocol shall remain secret and shall not be published.

Source: ADAP Series D, XI.1:108, document 74. Translated by H.-J. Krug.

Secret Supplementary Protocols Exchanged in Tokyo, 27 September 1940

Note: There was strong opposition to the Tripartite Pact in Japan, especially in the navy. To moderate this opposition, Foreign Minister Matsuoka, Special

Delegate Stahmer, and Ambassador Ott exchanged six secret supplementary protocols, to make a definite promise for Japanese special interests in the Greater East Asian Co-Prosperity Sphere, assistance for military technology, and the selling of the former German South Sea islands. But these secret protocols were exchanged without permission from Berlin, and they were not known during the war. According to documents in the Japanese Diplomatic Archives (Nichidokui Dōmeijōyaku Kankei 1 ken [The Tripartite Pact File 3 vol. B.1.0.0.J/X3]), these six secret protocols were all drafted by the Japanese side in English, and Ambassador Ott replied in English to them without changing content. Japanese drafts of these documents were also filed with the documents of the Sanbohonbu (Army General Staff) under the title Sangokujōyaku Kankeitsudzuri, Chuo Sensōshidō (The Tripartite Pact File, Central War Guidance, File No. 1139), now in the Bōeichō Archive, and also printed in Nihon Gaikō Nenpyō narabini Shuyobunsho (Japanese Diplomatic Chronological Table and Fundamental Diplomatic Documents, vol. 2), edited by Gaimushō, Tokyo, 1965. The Tripartite Pact Treaty was also signed on English text.

German Embassy Tokyo, September 27, 1940
No. G.1000
Strictly Confidential

Excellency: At the moment when our conversations on the Tripartite Pact, begun on the 9th of this month in Tokyo, are about to conclude successfully, it is Minister Stahmer's and my sincere desire to express to Your Excellency our deepest appreciation for the decisive part you have played throughout in a most generous and accommodating spirit. We would like also to take this opportunity to state once more in this letter some of the most important points touched upon in our conversation.

The German Government is firmly convinced that the contracting parties are about to enter a new and decisive phase of world history in which it will be their task to assume the leadership in the establishment of a new order in Greater East Asia and Europe, respectively.

The fact that for a long time the interests of the contracting parties will be the same, together with their unlimited confidence in each other, forms the secure foundation for the Pact.

The German Government is firmly convinced that the technical details concerning the execution of the Pact can be settled without difficulties; it would not be in keeping with the far-reaching importance of the Pact, and would also not be practically possible, to try to regulate at the present time all the individual cases which may sometime come up. These questions can only be settled, instance by instance, in a spirit of intimate cooperation.

Conclusions of the Technical Commissions, provided for in article 4 of the Pact, should be submitted to the three governments for approval in order to be put into force. Needless to say, the question whether an attack within the meaning of article 3 of the Pact has taken place must be determined through joint consultation of the three contracting parties.

If Japan, contrary to the peaceful intent of the Pact, be attacked by a power so far not engaged in the European war or the China conflict, Germany will consider it a matter of course to give Japan full support and assist her with all military and economic means.

With regard to the relations between Japan and Soviet Russia, Germany will do everything within her power to promote a friendly understanding and will at any time offer good offices to this end.

Germany will use her industrial strength and her other technical and material resources as far as possible in favor of Japan in order both to facilitate the establishment of a new order in Greater East Asia and to enable her to be better prepared for any emergency. Germany and Japan will further undertake to aid each other in procuring, in every possible way, necessary raw materials and minerals, including oil.

The German Foreign Minister is firmly convinced that, if Italy's assistance and cooperation are sought in reference to the matters above enumerated, she will of course act in concord with Germany and Japan.

I have the honor to submit these statements to your Excellency as the views of the German Foreign Minister conveyed personally by his special delegate, Minister Stahmer, and repeated also in instructions to me from my government. I avail myself of this opportunity to renew to your Excellency the assurance of my highest consideration.

OTT

From Japanese Foreign Minister to German Ambassador in Tokyo
No. 1

Top Secret   **Tokyo, 27 September 1940**

Excellency: I have the honor to acknowledge receipt of Your Excellency's letter No. G.1000 of this date and I feel happy to take note of the contents therein.

I avail myself of this opportunity to renew to Your Excellency the highest consideration.

Matsuoka

From Japanese Foreign Minister to German Ambassador in Tokyo
No. 2

Top Secret   **Tokyo, 27 September 1940**

I have the honor to inform Your Excellency that the Japanese Government earnestly share the hope with the Governments of Germany and Italy that the present European war will remain limited as far as possible in its area and extent and further be terminated as expeditiously as possible.

However, the conditions actually prevailing in Greater East Asia and elsewhere do not permit the Japanese Government to rest assured in the present circumstances that there is no danger whatever of armed conflict taking place between Japan and Great Britain, and accordingly they desire to call the attention of the German Government to such a possibility and to state that they feel confident that Germany will do their utmost to aid Japan in such an eventuality with all means in their power. I hereby pay my respects to Your Excellency once again.

Matsuoka

From German Ambassador in Tokyo to Japanese Foreign Minister
No. 2

G.1001
Top Secret

Excellency: I have the honor to acknowledge receipt of your Excellency's letter No. 133 of this date with contents as follows:

I have the honor to inform Your Excellency that the Japanese government earnestly share the hope with the Governments of Germany and Italy that the present European War will remain limited as far as possible in its sphere and scope and will come to a speedy conclusion and that they shall on their part spare no effort in that direction. However, the conditions actually prevailing in Greater East Asia and elsewhere do not permit the Japanese Government to rest assured in the present circumstances that there is no danger whatever of an armed conflict taking place between Japan and Great Britain, and accordingly they desire to call the attention of the German government to such a possibility and to state that they feel confident that Germany will do their utmost to aid Japan in such eventuality with all means in their power.

I take this occasion to note the contents of Your Excellency's letter. Accept, Mr. Minister, the renewed assurance of my highest consideration.

OTT

From Japanese Foreign Minister to German Ambassador in Tokyo
No. 3

Top Secret **Tokyo, 27 September 1940**

Excellency: I have the honor to ask Your Excellency to confirm the following oral declaration which was made by Your Excellency on behalf of the German Government: The German Government agrees that the former German colonies actually under Japan's mandate in the South Seas shall remain in Japan's possession, it being understood that Germany be in a way compensated therefor.

In regard to other former colonies in the South Seas, they shall be restored automatically to Germany on conclusion of peace ending the present European war.

Afterwards, the German government would be prepared to confer, in an accommodating spirit, with the Japanese government with a view to disposing them as far as possible in Japan's favor against compensation.

I avail myself of this opportunity to renew to Your Excellency the highest consideration.

MATSUOKA

Appendix C

The Führer's Directive No. 24
on Cooperation with Japan

OBERKOMMANDO DER WEHRMACHT W
    F St/Abt.L(I Op)
Nr. 44 282/41 gKdos. Chefs.
Führer Headquarters, 5 March 1941

Directive No. 24: On Cooperation with Japan
The Führer has issued the following directive for
    collaboration with Japan:

1. On the basis of the Three Powers Pact, the object of collaboration must be to induce Japan to undertake positive actions in the Far East as soon as possible. This will tie down strong British forces and the center of gravity of the interests of the U.S.A. will be shifted toward the Pacific.

    The sooner Japan intervenes, the greater will be the prospects for her success in view of the fact that her adversaries have yet to develop their preparations for war. Operation "Barbarossa" will create particularly favorable political and military preconditions for such a step.
2. By way of preparation for this collaboration, it is essential that Japan's war fighting capabilities be increased by all the means available.

To this end, the high commands of the three services are to meet Japanese requests for information about war and battlefield experiences as well as for assistance in military, economic, and technical matters in a comprehensive and generous fashion. Reciprocity is desirable, but this should not inhibit negotiations. Priority should naturally be accorded to those Japanese requests that could have some impact within a short time on the conduct of the war.

In special cases, the Führer reserves the right to take decisions himself.

3. The High Command of the Navy is responsible for the harmonization of operational plans on both sides. This will be subject to the following directives:

   1. The joint objective of strategy to be singled out is the quick defeat of Britain, thereby keeping the U.S.A. out of the war. Apart from this, Germany has no political, military, or economic interests in the Far East that would give rise to any reservations on our part about Japanese intentions.

   2. The considerable success already achieved by Germany in the war on enemy commerce makes it particularly appropriate for strong forces to be committed by the Japanese for the same purpose. Every opportunity is to be seized to exploit the situation in order to support Germany's conduct of war against supply lines.

   3. The raw-materials position of the member states of the Three Powers Pact demands that Japanese acquire control of those areas it requires for the prosecution of the war, especially if the United States intervened. Shipments of rubber must certainly continue after the entry of Japan into the war, as these are of vital importance for Germany.

   4. The capture of Singapore, the key British position in the Far East, would mean a decisive success for the overall conduct of the war by the Three Powers. In addition, attacks are to be made on the other bases of British naval power and of American naval power only if the entry of the United States into the war cannot be prevented—in such a way that the power position of the enemy there is weakened, and substantial forces of all kinds are tied down there, just as they already are by existing attacks on seaborne communications (Australia).

4. Only those questions that are of equal relevance to the three member states are to be discussed in the military committees set up in accordance with the

Threes Powers Pact. In the first instance, these will include economic warfare tasks. The "Main Committee," in conjunction with the High Command of the Armed Forces, is responsible for dealing with specific questions.

5. No indication should be given to the Japanese about Operation "Barbarossa."

The Chief of the High Command of the Armed Forces

KEITEL

Source: Bundesarchiv-Militärachiv, Freiberg im Breisgau (BA-MA), RM 7/970, Weisung Nr. 24 über Zusammenarbeit mit Japan. OKW WFSt/Abt.L (I op.) Nr. 44282/41 gKdos. Chefs., OKM 280/41 gKdos. Chefs. [5 March 1941]. Translated by H.-J. Krug.

Appendix D

Military Agreements Concerning Joint Warfare

Agreement Concerning Joint Warfare, 11 December 1941

With the unshakable resolution not to lay down their weapons until the common war against the United States of America and England will have been fought to its successful end, the parties of this agreement have come to the understanding that:

Article 1

Germany, Italy, and Japan will jointly carry on with the war, forced upon them by the United States of America and England, with all means of power at their disposal until the victorious end.

Article 2

Germany, Italy, and Japan pledge not to contract an armistice or peace with the United States of America or with England without full mutual consent.

Article 3

After the victorious end of the war Germany, Italy, and Japan will continue to most closely collaborate in order to achieve a fair readjustment in the sense of the Tripartite Pact concluded by them on 27 October 1940.

Article 4

The Agreement shall come into effect on signature and shall remain in force as long as the Tripartite Pact.

Source: Rönnefarth, *Konferenzen und Verträge*, 203. Translated by H.-J. Krug.

Military Agreement among Japan, Germany, and Italy, 18 January 1942

Authors' Note: This was a secret record.

The German and Italian armed forces, as well as the Japanese army and navy, hereby conclude, in the spirit of the Three Powers Pact of 27 September 1940 and in connection with the agreement among Germany, Italy, and Japan of 11 December 1941, a Military Agreement in order to ensure operational cooperation among one another and to destroy the fighting capacity of the enemy as quickly as possible.

I. Division of Zones of Operations

The German and Italian armed forces, as well as the Japanese army and navy, will, within the framework of the zones allocated to them hereinafter, carry out the required operations.

1. Japan

   a. The waters to the east of approximately 70 degrees east longitude up to the west coast of the American Continent, as well as the continents and islands located in these waters (Australia, Dutch East Indies, New Zealand, etc.).
   b. The Continent of Asia, east of approximately 70 degrees east longitude.

2. Germany and Italy

   a. The waters to the west of approximately 70 degrees east longitude up to the east coast of the American Continent, as well as the continents and islands located in these waters (Africa, Iceland, etc.)
   b. The Near East, the Middle East, and Europe west of approximately 70 degrees east longitude.

3. In the Indian Ocean, each side may carry out operations across the above-agreed boundary according to the situation.

II. General Plan of Operations

1. Japan
   In collaboration with German and Italian operations against Britain and the United States of America, [Japan] will undertake to carry out operations in the South Seas and the Pacific.

   a. She will eliminate important military bases of Britain, the United States of America, and the Netherlands in Greater East Asia, and will attack and occupy their territories there.
   b. She will strive to eliminate American and British land, sea, and air forces in the Pacific and Indian Oceans in order to achieve command of the sea in the western Pacific.
   c. In the event that the British and American fleets concentrate primarily in the Atlantic, she will step up her war against shipping in the whole of the Pacific and Indian Oceans, as well as sending part of her naval forces into the Atlantic in order to cooperate directly there with the German and Italian navies.

2. Germany and Italy
   In collaboration with Japanese operations in the South Seas and the Pacific, [Germany and Italy] will undertake to carry out operations against Britain and the United States of America.

   a. They will eliminate important bases of Britain and the United States of America in the Near and Middle East, in the Mediterranean and the Atlantic and attack and occupy their territories there.
   b. They will strive to eliminate British and American land, sea, and air forces in the Atlantic and the Mediterranean and to destroy enemy trade.
   c. In the event that the British and American fleets concentrate mainly in the Pacific, Germany and Italy will send part of their naval forces to the Pacific in order to be in a position to cooperate directly there with the Japanese navy.

III. Main Features of Military Cooperation

1. Mutual liaison over the necessary points of operational planning.
2. Cooperation in the area of the war on shipping, including

a. Mutual liaison over planning the war on shipping.

b. Mutual liaison concerning the development of the war on shipping, important information required, and other essential matters.

c. In the event that one party to the Agreement wishes to conduct war on shipping outside its allocated zone of operations, it will inform the other partners about its plans in advance, in order to ensure cooperation and mutual support over the use of operational bases, supply, provisions, rest, repairs, etc.

3. Cooperation concerning the collection and exchange of information essential for operations.

4. Cooperation concerning military psychological warfare.

5. Cooperation to safeguard mutual transmission of military communications.

6. Cooperation to establish a military air link between Japan, Germany, and Italy as long as the technical conditions for the opening of shipping routes and transport by sea across the Indian Ocean are not available.

In faith whereof the Chief of the High Command of the German Armed Forces, the authorized representative of the Italian Armed Forces, and the authorized representative of the Imperial Japanese Navy General Staff have signed this Agreement.

Done in German, Italian, and Japanese original at Berlin, the 18th of January 1942—in the twentieth year of the Fascist Era—corresponding to the eighteenth day of the first month of the seventeenth year of the Syowa Era.

Source: BA-MA, RM 7/253, Militärische Vereinbarung zwischen Deutschland, Italien und Japan. Abschrift Nr. 16, 1204/42 gKdos., [18 January 1942]. Translated by H.-J. Krug.

Appendix E

The *Automedon* Incident

The influence of the *Automedon* Incident on German-Japanese relations has seen varying interpretations. Very careful, for instance, is Rahn, in *Japan und der Krieg in Europa,* who merely ascertained that there were indications that the plan to attack Pearl Harbor had been created only after the evaluation of the documents (149). On the other hand, James Rusbridger comments very decisively on it ("The Sinking of the *Automedon,*" 10f.). He states that the German naval officer, Paul Kamenz, had taken the captured original documents to Berlin, on order of Wenneker, after transmitting a summary there by telegram. On 12 December, in Berlin, according to Rusbridger, the summary was shown to Japanese Naval Attaché Yokoi on the express order of Hitler. Rusbridger goes on to say that when Wenneker, on the same day, made his copies available to the Japanese Navy General Staff, the Gunreibu's deputy head, Kondō Nobutake, had doubted the authenticity of the material and initially considered it to be "play material" that the British had allowed to fall into Axis hands for deceptive purposes. Only after Wenneker had minutely described the capture, says Rusbridger, had Kondō been convinced.

After the Japanese entry into the war Kondō had repeatedly told Wenneker how valuable the material had been for the preparation of the Japanese attacks on Pearl Harbor, the Philippines, and Singapore. Rusbridger concludes from this: "There is no doubt that possession of these documents profoundly affected Japanese war planning in January 1941. . . . It is fair to argue, . . . that the capture of the Chiefs of Staff report from the *Automedon* was the catalyst that sent the Japanese on the path to Pearl Harbor and precipitated the ruinous attack on America's Pacific fleet."

Rusbridger's explanations are, however, imprecise and partly do not concur with the sources, so the suspicion is not unfounded that he did not, or at least not with the proper care, evaluate the original sources. The captured documents could not have been brought to Berlin by Kamenz, because he did not leave Japan until 3 January 1941. Kamenz was a senior lieutenant and had taken the captured documents as prize officer from the *Ole Jacob* to Japan. After that he had promptly left harbor again with the ship and had delivered valuable cargo (aircraft fuel) to a Japanese tanker at an agreed supply dump. Then he returned to Japan on board another ship, arriving in Tokyo on 26 December.[1] In the meantime Wenneker had given the most important documents to couriers who left for Berlin on 6 December.[2] They arrived on 30 December 1940.[3] Obviously Rusbridger had used the war diaries of Lietzmann and Wenneker. These diaries have been translated by John W. M. Chapman, who, for some reason, considerably shortened the entries. For instance, the one of 26 December 1940, which in the original is nearly one and a half pages long, in Chapman's edition is reduced to one sentence.[4] Several details disappeared in the process.

Furthermore, Rusbridger, here, in contrast to all other documents cited in his article, does not mention an archive or summarily mentions "Bundesarchiv" without series or volume numbers. Finding the documents therefore becomes practically impossible, as is also often the case with the works of Chapman. The documents themselves are, however, clearly identified by their "B. Nr." numbers. This makes it possible, with time-consuming research, to identify documents that, despite assurances to the contrary, have thus far (as of 1997) not been given back to the Federal Republic.

For example, Rusbridger mentions a document that contains intelligence of the German Abwehr about the continuing decoding of the German naval code by the Allies and mentions an archive "Bundesarchiv (Freiburg)." The document, which was signed by Dönitz himself, is, however, definitely not present in the BA-MA. Also, certain British authors were not prepared to identify their sources when asked. I thank Mr. Robert Coppock from the Naval Historical Branch of the Ministry of Defence, London, who allowed me to view the original.

Also, Rusbridger's descriptions of Kondō's doubts and Wenneker's subsequent explanation of the capture process find no verification in the sources. The Japanese repeatedly characterized the material as valuable, even on the day of delivery, and Wenneker was ordered by the Skl. to give "Berlin" as the source in order to veil its true origin.[5] That Hitler had ordered the release to Yokoi of the summaries that Wenneker had telegraphed to Berlin on 12 December is also dubious. He himself seems, on 27 December 1940, not yet to have known anything of the capture, when Raeder reported to him about the weakness of the British position at Singapore and proposed, among other things, to discuss "measures" against this base with the Japanese. Hitler appeared skeptical with regard to the proposals of the ObdM that represented the first serious considerations of a coordinated operation with the Japanese navy.[6]

Chapman assumes that the captured documents could have influenced the planning of the Japanese fleet commander, Yamamoto Isoroku, of the attack upon Pearl Harbor and points out that this plan was worked out in December 1940. He does not verify this, however, and bases it instead on a comment of the "well-known Japanese naval historian, Professor Ikeda Kiyoshi," who stated on Japanese television—without giving any precise sources—that the captured material could have been a reason for Yamamoto's plans.[7] There is, however, no evidence that Yamamoto had ever seen the summary that Yokoi had radioed from Berlin. Moreover, Chapman's claim that such material would routinely, automatically have been passed on to the Navy Ministry by the Naval General Staff is not unproblematic. The relationship between them was not always the best, and Yokoi had addressed his radio message not to the deputy head of the Gunreibu, the way it is normally done with secret material, but to the head of the Gunreibu's Third Group (intelligence service).[8] Only documents of general content were simultaneously addressed to the deputies of the Gunreibu and the minister of the navy.

Ikeda Kiyoshi and Ian Nish also discuss the influence of the *Automedon* papers on Japanese planning.[9] While Ikeda pleads a case for the thesis of a decisive influence, Nish is skeptical. The basis of Ikeda's argument is a comparison of two letters of the Japanese fleet commander, Yamamoto Isoroku. The first originates from November 1940 and is meant for Shimada Shigetarō, the head of the China fleet. Yamamoto reports here on map maneuvers that he had played through in the Navy General Staff, together with the staff academy. His purpose had been to demonstrate to the mid-level echelons that were clamoring for a quick military strike against the Dutch East Indies that the Japanese fleet was not strong enough for a war against the united British, Dutch, and American naval forces in the Pacific.[10] In January 1941, however, Yamamoto wrote to Minister of the Navy Oikawa that it was important in a war with the United States to hit the U.S. Navy decisively right at the beginning. Ikeda interpreted this as a change in Yamamoto's position that could be explained by the recently arrived information from the *Automedon* papers. Ikeda does admit, however, that there is no proof that Yamamoto had ever heard of them. Nish, on the other hand, wonders whether the Japanese, even if they had gained information from the papers, would have been able to verify it from other sources and also whether the papers themselves—as situation reports—were not already outdated by November 1940. In addition there had been reason for mistrust on the part of the Japanese, since they had already been pushed by the German side before December 1940 to move militarily against the British in East Asia.

While Nish's speculations cannot be verified in the sources, his observations are at least plausible. Ikeda's interpretation, on the other hand, contradicts one that would reconcile the differing tone of Yamamoto's letters. If one operates from the assumption of a purely military situational evaluation, built on the foundation that Great Britain and the United States were not separable in case of war and that the main enemy of the Japanese fleet would not be the Royal Navy, heavily committed in Europe, but rather the U.S. Navy, then there were certain consequences to be expected from a Japanese attack in the Pacific. It was logical, then, to first reduce the main threat, the U.S. Navy, so that when Japan turned to the weaker enemies, the Netherlands and Great Britain, to take the Dutch East Indies and Singapore, it could hold them practically unthreatened. If the first blows were to fall against these positions, as intended in the German proposals and the plans of the mid-echelons of the Navy General Staff, the main enemy—the U.S. Navy—would still be intact and the retention of the Dutch East Indies and Singapore questionable.

In such a scenario, the information from the *Automedon* papers was practically of no concern, because the commitment of the Royal Navy in Europe and the British inferiority in East Asia were obvious facts. It was more important for the Japanese naval leadership to avoid, if at all possible, a war with the United States, which from their view had to be the reaction to an attack upon Singapore. Neither Nish nor Ikeda consulted the German naval files that reveal those Japanese reactions to the German suggestions. The Japanese response was highly cautious. Even in August 1941 the conquering of Singapore was labeled as a German matter, in a conversation of Groos with Nomura.

Wenneker's Report on the *Automedon* Incident

Authors' note: Telegrams from German naval attaché to German Navy High Command and Naval War Staff, nos. 209 to 212/40, top secret, 7 December 1940.

Of note among materials reaching here on 6 December from Ship 16 is a captured report of the War Cabinet about the situation in the Far East in the event of Japanese intervention against Britain, dated 15 August:

1. In present situation, we [i.e., Britain] are unable to send fleet to Far East.
2. Japan needs Singapore in order to meet its ambitions.
3. Until the situation in Europe clarified itself, open breach between us and America, and Japan improbable.
4. We also must avoid open clash with Japan, gain time and promote military cooperation with Dutch.
5. In absence of fleet, we are unable to prevent damage to our own interests. We should retire to a base from which it will be possible to restore our positions later on.
6. Four possible Japanese attacks:
   a. direct attack,
   b. advance into Indochina or Siam,
   c. attack on Dutch Indies,
   d. attack on Philippines.
7. Japanese first step either Indochina or Siam, then Dutch Indies before Singapore.
8. In current situation, we would put up with Japanese attack on Siam or Indochina without going to war.
9. In event of Japanese attack on Dutch, and they offered no resistance, no war between us and Japan. But if Dutch resist, then they would have our full military support.
10. Hong Kong without any significance and cannot hold out for long even with presence of substantial fleet. However, should be held as long as possible.
11. Strategy in event of war:

a. Impossible to prevent Japanese gaining access to Indian Ocean.

b. We cannot maintain lines of communication with northern Malaya.

c. Hope to maintain bulk of commerce by sea with southern and eastern Australia.

d. Apart from cruiser raids, Japanese attack on Australia improbable without first eliminating Singapore.

e. Japanese occupation of Suwa on Fiji likely in order to use as a base.

f. Need to defend all of Malaya and not only Singapore Island.

g. Holland probably willing to prepare joint plan for defense of Dutch Indies. In view of limited assistance we can give, their help unlikely if British territory attacked. Consequently not desirable to begin general staff talks at this time.

h. As long as no fleet available, forced to turn to air force. This however can only inadequately be provided. Therefore, strong land forces necessary in Malaya. Concentration there a top priority.

i. Borneo indefensible. Very little airpower available for protection of shipping in Indian Ocean.

k. Until situation in Europe improves, Far East gravely threatened, especially if subjected to determined Japanese attacks with heavy naval units.

l. Our construction program never intended to cover war with Germany, Italy and Japan simultaneously. The one hope for providing a fleet for the Far East, based on an early successful action against Italy in the Mediterranean.

12. Objectives we must seek to achieve:

a. Commonwealth must send one division to Malaya.

b. By end of 1940, two fighter squadrons and two squadrons of long-range land aircraft must be sent to Far East.

c. Naval construction program to be accelerated.

d. Withdrawal of garrisons from North China and Hong Kong.

e. New Zealand must send one brigade to Fiji.

f. General staff consultations with Holland, once situation in Malaya improves.

13. Detailed information on the strength of air, sea, and land forces in the Far East.

Note written by German naval attaché:
Request authorization to hand over copy to Japanese Admiralty.

Source: BA-MA, RM 12II/248, fol. 153–55. Translated by H.-J. Krug.

Summary of *Automedon* Papers

Authors' note: This summary was reported to Tokyo by the Japanese naval attaché in Berlin on 12 December 1940.

I received from the GERMAN Navy the minutes of a meeting of the BRITISH Cabinet held on 15 August this year dealing with operations against JAPAN. The document will be sent by the next courier; meanwhile here are the main points:

1. Although JAPAN cherished the ambition of capturing SINGAPORE, the existing situation would not allow BRITAIN to send her fleet to the FAR EAST, and she must defend it by sending Army and Air Force reinforcements.

2. Japan would probably invade FRENCH INDOCHINA or SIAM as a first step, and the NETHERLANDS EAST INDIES and SINGAPORE would follow. However, BRITAIN was not in a position to resort to war in the event of an attack on FRENCH INDOCHINA or SIAM.

3. HONG KONg would be abandoned, but would continue resistance as long as possible.

4. If the operations against the ITALIANS in the MEDITERRANEAN should proceed rapidly and successfully, it could be possible to send a fleet to the FAR EAST.

5. Operations must be conducted jointly with the NETHERLANDS EAST INDIES.

6. Since it was probable that the JAPANESE would occupy SUVA in the FIJI Islands as a base, one brigade must be sent there from NEW ZEALAND.

Source: NARA, RG 457/SRNA 20.

Appendix F

Report from Japanese Naval Attaché
Berlin, 29 June 1941

From: BERLIN, Naval Attaché

Action: TOKYO, Deputy Navy Minister and Deputy Chief of Navy
         General Staff

1600/29 June 1941

49913

1. Time after time we have reported our opinions with those of the Ambassador and Military Attaché regarding the decisions, concerning Japan's attitude, which should have been made immediately, in view of the sudden change in the EUROPEAN, War situation, yet even today, with a full week elapsed since the outbreak of the RUSSO-GERMAN War, nothing definite has been done about JAPAN's attitude. With the deepest regret we have observed that not even her policy has yet been determined. For one thing, the situation in GERMANY is changing with regard to the establishment of a worldwide New Order; if a reply does not come with a clear decision enabling us to surmount this impasse as necessitated by the critical turn of events, ultimately through our hesitancy we will have fruitless [*sic*] abandoned other _____ without establishing anything ourselves. All we ask is that you favor us with a *statement*[?] of your policy. We fear that this unseemly situation will become known. We have already

made efforts with regard to the above opinions in German Serials #492 and in similar dispatches from the Ambassador (Serial #798 in addition to the one mentioned), but the fact that the issue is still undecided we feel to be sound argument and effective proof, so we are making further representations.

2. At the outset of the RUSSO-GERMAN War, Foreign Minister MATSUOKA was under the misapprehension that JAPANESE cooperation was not desired and, although it is well that the misunderstanding in this matter was cleared up later, it is regrettable that at a critical time this misunderstanding existed even temporarily. GERMANY had no reason for requesting cooperation directly of JAPAN since, on the above occasion, there were no restrictions from the point of view of the agreement. Moreover, the taking of SINGAPORE was far more desirable than that. However, after it became apparent, in light of the progress of the JAPANESE-American negotiations, that JAPAN had little or no positive intention of advancing southward, they expressed their desire to receive direct cooperation against RUSSIA if it were possible. The above, however, is limited to a report of the actual state of affairs; our indignation stems from the certainty that, regardless of what GERMANY wants or does not want, we must take resolute action on behalf of the future of EAST ASIA in this time of golden opportunity even though serious difficulties and danger arise. We, here, have no ulterior motives in this matter.

3. The Ambassador had an audience with Foreign Minister VON RIBBENTROP day before yesterday, and when, in accordance with instructions, he brought up the matter of the recognition of the NANKING Government, VON RIBBENTROP promptly gave his consent, immediately upon telephoning Chancellor HITLER at Headquarters and obtaining his consent, he contacted Foreign Minister CIANO by telephone, and within a few minutes the GERMAN-ITALIAN recognition of the NANKING Government was decided. (Our foreign office is said to be adhering to formalities in the above recognition, and, at a time when the RUSSO-GERMAN War is at its height, is making various trifling requests of the GERMAN, ITALIAN, and ROUMANIAN[?] Governments, which are acting in harmony.) Yesterday, Foreign Minister RIBBENTROP went to the headquarters of the Chancellor, and, after learning how the war situation stood, he immediately telephoned the Ambassador to the effect that, "Developments in the war situation are greatly exceeding expectations

and the collapse of RUSSIAN Armies will come within a short time. It is hoped that JAPAN does not miss the opportunity to take action against RUSSIA."

Germany considers it extremely strange that our attitude should still be undetermined today, when we had advance notice in the middle of April.

Source: NARA, RG 457/SRNA 80 to 82.

Appendix G

Chief of Bureau of Military Affairs
to Naval Attaché Berlin, 26 July 1941

Top Secret Ultra RW File [handwritten]
From: Chief of Bureau of Military Affairs, TOKYO.
Action: Naval Attaché in Germany.

07/261900/1941   44013 - 44033

Problems of importance at present arising between JAPAN and GERMANY are threefold:

a. Germany's keen desire that JAPAN should go to war with SOVIET RUSSIA forthwith.

b. GERMAN misgivings regarding a JAPANESE-AMERICAN settlement.

c. JAPAN's declaration of the policy which she will pursue. In the light of Ambassador OOSHIMA's telegrams it is thought that the GERMANS may not be fully conversant with the real circumstances in this country, or may misinterpret them, with the result that needless misconceptions are formed regarding the sincerity of JAPANESE adherence to the Tripartite Pact. The following statement is therefore sent for your guidance and for such use as you may think fit in quarters concerned with GERMAN internal and external affairs.

1. There are two ways of looking at the question of the form which GERMAN-JAPANESE cooperation should take:

a. The view may be held, as it is by the FUEHRER, that the scope of joint action should extend beyond the provisions of the interstate agreements and comprehend (general policy) in its entirety;

b. or it may be considered that action in common by our two countries should be confined strictly within the limits of formal commitments. Where affairs are conducted dictatorially, as by the FUEHRER, the Dictator's individual attitude can find expression unchanged as the national will. Thus national behavior is in no way restricted by the terms of treaties, and action can be taken in accordance with the times freely and independently. The situation in JAPAN is substantially different. The national constitution makes it impossible to organize national policy so simply and arbitrarily as in GERMANY, and decisions upon national policy are therefore unavoidably protracted. But once a decision has been reached, we proceed resolutely to put it into effect. It is a matter of course that this country, in consideration of its national position, should declare that there is no change in its attitude toward the Three Power Pact, which was promulgated by Imperial Rescript and which forms the foundation of our external policy. (There may be great difficulty in convincing the GERMANS of this.)

2. Cooperation between JAPAN and GERMANY being a fundamental condition of *our*[?] Existence, JAPAN's stated intention of establishing the GREATER EAST ASIA Co-Prosperity Sphere, and thereby creating a new and peaceful world order, is entirely in harmony with GERMANY's plans in EUROPE. Both our nations *having a common destiny*[?] and having embarked upon a great and *epoch-making*[?] task, the basic postulates for GERMAN-JAPANESE cooperation are:

a. That both nations maintain and increase their power;

b. That both nations give full play to their own special characteristics in their respective zones of responsibility.

In other words, it is considered that cooperation between JAPAN and GERMANY should go beyond _____ _____ behaving, in every successive situation as it arises, in rigid and automatic adherence to rules.

3. JAPAN has for four years past devoted the whole of her strength in the military and diplomatic spheres to bringing about a solution of the CHINA Incident. Therefore any further extensions of the battlefront are naturally limited and undertaken in a certain order. In this respect JAPANESE policy is in marked contrast to that of GERMANY. For JAPAN the

outcome of the CHINA Incident is the crucial issue, and our (basic policy) must remain, as before, the fulfillment of this purpose. I regret that in our view the proper course is for the settlement of other problems to be undertaken only when we can spare forces (from the main task). The policy which we shall carry out on the above lines consists necessarily in the South in upholding our commercial and political rights and hastening a solution of the CHINA Incident by cutting _____ _____ _____ , while at the same time establishing a self-sufficient and self-contained position such that we cannot be defeated; and in the North the safety of our northern frontiers will be assured by our remaining forces. But needless to say complete preparations will be made for bringing our strength to bear if the need should arise in either region.

4. In the three aspects of our policy as described above there are no grounds whatever for any feeling on the part of GERMANY that our determination is dubious and that it is sitting on the fence. Only JAPAN knows JAPAN's real power. As the GERMANS weigh up GERMANY's own strength and act accordingly, so JAPAN also *must decide the timing*[?] and direction of her actions on the basis of her own power.

Top Secret Ultra
(oh)
From: TOKYO Chief of Office of Naval Communications. 2/10
Action: J.N.A., BERLIN.

07/262300/I 1941   60713-60733

1. Continuation of serial No. 440 from the Bureau of Naval[1] Affairs. As the GERMANS weigh up GERMANY's strength and act accordingly, so JAPAN also decides the direction of her notions, and the occasion on which they are taken, on the basis of her own power.

2. [*sic*] Cooperation between GERMANY and JAPAN is the expression of both the letter and the spirit of the Three Powers Pact. Accordingly, in the attainment of the ultimate aim, each country should plan its own actions, within its own particular sphere of responsibility, while acting in concert with the other on broad issues, in pursuance of the task of restraining and overthrowing enemy countries. Thus it is obvious that if GERMANY attacked EGYPT[?],[2] JAPAN could

not bring about a rapid alteration in the situation by *attacking* RUSSIA[?], or
by attacking SINGAPORE if GERMANY should direct her offensive against EN-
GLAND[?]. And if for instance JAPAN were to ask GERMANY to invade ENGLAND
when the advance to the South is launched (as it duly will be), such request
would serve only to embarrass the GERMANS. In sum, the different measures
and steps necessary for the attainment of the aim will be governed by the
actual strength of each party at the moment concerned. However should both
countries fall into straits where direct and mutual military assistance was a
matter of necessity, the question would call for a different handling.

3. There is no justification for condemning JAPAN on the ground that the negotiations for an adjustment of relations between JAPAN and AMERICA have been
detrimental to GERMANY. In the light of all the preparations now being made
in JAPAN, these negotiations represent a policy the aim of which is to see that
for the time being relations between AMERICA and JAPAN do not reach the ultimate crisis. The hasty commencement of the GERMAN-SOVIET war, due to the
exigencies of GERMANY's prosecution of the war, was made without consideration for the state of JAPAN's preparations, indeed against JAPAN's wishes, and
has placed JAPAN in a disadvantageous position not only as regards the CHINA
Incident but also as regards her affairs north and south. What is worse, whereas
the purpose of the negotiations was to prevent AMERICA from joining in the
war and to find a solution for the CHINA Incident, fresh impetus has been given
to AMERICA's plans for war by GERMANY's action during the negotiations.

4. Faced with a great transformation in the world situation JAPAN is now making rapid strides along the road to the total organization of the country on
a war basis. Until her total organization on a war basis is complete, it is obvious that she cannot, indeed must not, make any more. But it is clear from
the gestures made in the past by the Government that the basic purpose of
the total organization of the country on a war basis is consistent with the
main lines of policy laid down in the Three Powers Pact.

5. For the information of the navy in particular, even if the present conflict
ends in a complete victory for the Axis, due largely to the splendid achievements of the GERMAN army in the fighting on land, great care will be necessary lest the rivalry between JAPAN and the BRITISH and AMERICAN naval
forces, which might still be left impaired by the result in the Far East, should
continue, with JAPAN left to bear the brunt alone.

Source: NARA, RG 457/SRNA 113–115 and 117f.

Appendix H

Report from Japanese Naval Attaché Berlin, 26 May 1944

From: BERLIN

Action: Deputy Navy Minister and Deputy Chief of Naval General Staff, TOKYO

05/262340/1944 98525

I. Repeated Allied air attacks have reduced considerably the efficiency of our office here. Danger to personnel exists in the suburbs of BERLIN to the same degree as within the city proper. Generally speaking, the suburbs lack adequate bunkers and other anti-air installations compared with the city proper of BERLIN. Studies are again being made by German army and navy of methods of constructing bunkers for use by our offices.

II. In the matter of liaison with Supreme Headquarters, our officials as yet have not had an opportunity to visit Supreme Headquarters. The Ambassador, too, has been granted an interview with the foreign office for which no date has been set. Reports from various officials, from the former ambassador and members of the military delegation, seem to indicate that in spite of vigorous attempts to secure action in this matter results have been meager.

With regard to the advisability of moving this office to the suburbs, I have considered this matter carefully since reporting for duty. If one considers only relations with the Operations Department of the GERMAN Navy, a location in the suburbs north of BERLIN seems desirable. From the point of view of the GERMAN officer in charge of dealings with the attachés who are parties in daily dealings with the technical department and other departments, inside the city is preferable; in air force contacts, the Operations Department (Information Division) is in the southwestern part of BERLIN. The technical department is in the city. Our general dealings with the JAPANESE Ambassador and the Embassy are in the city. We have frequent dealings with each of these agencies. A location in the suburbs would inconvenience our communications and traffic with them with the resultant deleterious effect on efficiency. Conditions impose certain limitations, and considered from all points of view, location of the general affairs office inside the city seems advisable. I have taken up residence in the present general affairs office. I have considered the possibility that we might be unable to use the office because of a bombing attack and I am looking for a spare office in the suburbs into which we can move without delay. Warnings are frequent because of raids by enemy planes. They interfere considerably with the efficiency of the office. However, as far as the safety of the personnel is concerned, there is little difference between the suburbs of BERLIN and some place closer in town. In the suburbs, bunkers and other air defense establishments are generally inadequate, but the city proper is comparatively well equipped. We are again negotiating with the GERMAN Navy for the construction of bunkers for the use of the present general affairs office.

In connection with the problem of liaison with Supreme Headquarters, I have not yet been able to get an opportunity for a visit there. Although the Ambassador has made representation endeavoring to get me an interview with the foreign minister, no date has been set as yet. It is my observation, since reporting for duty, that in spite of vigorous efforts on the part of the Ambassador and the various military personnel, this matter of liaison with Supreme Headquarters is a troublesome one.

To wit:

A. The GERMAN philosophy of war has been traditionally concerned with continental warfare. I am inclined to think that while the GERMANS are absorbed

in the conduct of the EUROPEAN war, they feel that there is no direct relationship with the conduct of JAPANESE operations. Consequently, there is
none of the usual liaison between allies. Until the GERMAN plan has been
determined, they are avoiding an exchange of ideas.

B. When they are pressed by us, they do not explain how the conditions with
respect to JAPAN are different. The GERMANS explain only their own side, and
they are not favorably disposed toward discussing the matter.

C. The organization of the machinery for conducting GERMANY's war is itself partially responsible for this situation. The GERMANS are concerned about the
development of this organization, but it is a complex thing. There are many
inconsistencies in the upper strata. As a result of the impact of the personal
ability and political strength of individuals, the center of this organization
shifts. Consequently, there are many persons with whom one must deal.
Moreover, the purpose of negotiations is decided by each man to his own satisfaction. In this situation, it is difficult to know where the center of influence
is. Intercourse and liaison are hampered by the multiplicity of important
offices. In OKW, where the contacts of our military department are principally with Marshall KEITEL, Marshall YODER [person meant is Jodl] has charge
of all the operations except those which are directly concerned with the
Eastern Front. The number of naval officers on the staff of Supreme Headquarters is two, and they are not in the most important places. Since the three
branches of the GERMAN military have High Command offices in various special places, liaison is considerably inconvenienced.

From the standpoint of the navy alone, since the Operations Department
is conveniently located in the suburbs of BERLIN, and, as we often deal
directly with Admiral of the Fleet DOENITZ himself, indirect though it may
be, since, Supreme Headquarters can be contacted through him, the sub-
urban location is satisfactory.

In short, in order to strengthen our relations with Supreme Headquarters,
we must bring about a fundamental change in the attitude of the High
Command. We should tell them JAPAN's situation and plans. At the same
time, even though it is my intention to do my utmost in cooperation with
the Ambassador, military personnel, and military attachés to bring about
this change, it is vital that the central authorities appreciate the real situation and proffer a positive liaison.

Source: NARA, RG457/SRNA 1455–59.

Notes

Authors' Note

To the extent practical, note citations reflect the actual labeling of the archival material, as a researcher at the site would see them. However, we have translated some functional language in the archival material to make it more accessible to readers who are not fluent in German or Japanese. For example, "Attachébericht. Betrifft:" has been translated as "Attaché Report, Re:" and "Nachlass" has been translated as "papers of." The original German terms regarding document security—geheim, gKdos., gKdos. Chefs. (see glossary)—have been retained because they are brief and exact. Page numbers designated "fol." (folios) in archival material refer to stamped numbers, consecutive in any given file, that supersede the document's original typed or handwritten numbers. Original page numbers within individual documents are cited as such when necessary (e.g., "[page] 7 of the report"). Japanese names appear family name first.

Abbreviations Used in References

ADAP	Akten zur Deutschen Auswärtigen Politik 1918–1945 (Archives of the German Foreign Office)
BA-MA	Bundesarchiv-Militärarchiv (Federal German National-German Military Archives), Freiburg im Breisgau
Bl.	Blatt (handwritten page number)
JMSDF	Japanese Maritime Self-Defense Force (Staff College Archives, Yokosuka, Japan)
KTB Skl.	Rahn and Schreiber, *Kriegstagebuch der Seekriegsleitung, 1939–1945* (War journal of the Naval War Staff, 1939–1945)
NARA	National Archives and Records Administration, Washington, D.C.
ONI	Records of the Chief of Naval Operations, Office of Naval Intelligence, Washington, D.C.

PRO   Public Records Office, Kew, U.K.
PAAA   Politisches Archiv des Auswärtigen Amtes
SRGL   Translated Radio Traffic of German Navy Liaison Personnel
SRH   Short Histories of the Naval Security Group
SRMN   OP-20-G Cominch Files Related to U-boat Warfare
SRNA   Translated Radio Traffic of Japanese Naval Attachés in Europe
USNHC   U.S. Naval Historical Center, Operational Archives, Washington, D.C.

Chapter 1. A Short History

1. Sweetman, *American Naval History*, 60ff.
2. Hammitzsch and Brüll, *Japan-Handbuch*, 334.
3. See Schwalbe et al., *Deutsche Botschafter in Japan*, 4 and 6.
4. Steam-corvette *Arcona*, 2,391 tons (Sundewall); sailing-frigate *Thetis*, 1,882 tons (Jachmann); schooner *Frauenlob*, 305 tons.
5. Kerst, *Jacob Meckel*, 33ff.
6. Documented on his departure from Japan by War Minister Ōyama, Duke Katsura, and Colonel Kodama, director of the War College.
7. So said by General Fujii after the battle of the Yalu River and by Field Marshall Kodama after the battle of Mukden.
8. Nohara, *Die "Gelbe Gefahr"* (The yellow peril), 47ff.
9. Sweetman, *American Naval History*, 91.
10. Heavy cruisers *Scharnhorst* and *Gneisenau* (11,600 tons) and light cruisers *Emden, Nuernberg, Leipzig,* and *Dresden* (in 1914).
11. Pauer, *Japan-Deutschland. Wirtschaftsbeziehungen im Wandel*, 11ff.
12. Chapman, "Japan and German Naval Policy," 233.
13. Anglo-Japanese Alliance, 30 January 1902, revised 1905 and 1911, not renewed by Great Britain July 1921.
14. Meurer, *Seekriegsgeschichte*, 465ff.
15. Chapman, "Oil, Deviance and the Traditional World Order: Japanese and German Strategies for Violent Change, 1931–41," 132.
16. Sommer, *Deutschland und Japan zwischen den Mächten*, 43.
17. Ibid., Introduction.
18. Ibid., 2.
19. Stumpf, "Von der Achse Berlin-Rom zum Militärabkommen des Dreierpakts," 132.
20. London Fleet Agreement (22 April 1930) had fixed the relative fleet strengths of the United States, Great Britain, and Japan at 5:5:3 and replaced the former

Washington Agreement (1 January 1922) ratio of USA:UK:Japan:France:Italy = 5:5:3:1.75:1.75.

21. By stopping this arms sale, in 1938 alone Germany lost 181 million marks' worth of urgently needed raw materials.

22. See secret supplementary agreement to Anti-Comintern Pact, Article II: "During the duration of this agreement, the high contracting parties will not contract any political treaties with the USSR that are not in conformance with the spirit of this agreement, without mutual approval." Printed in Rönnefarth and Euler, eds., *Konferenzen und Verträge*, 149.

23. Raeder, *Mein Leben*, 2:182.

24. Sommer, *Deutschland und Japan*, 283.

25. Rahn and Schreiber, *Kriegstagebuch der Seekriegsleitung* (KTB Skl.), 3:71, 10 November 1939.

26. See Krug in Hammitzsch and Brüll, *Japan-Handbuch*, 2001, and Sommer, *Deutschland und Japan*, 354.

27. Sommer, *Deutschland und Japan*, 388.

28. Chapman, "Japan and German Naval Policy," 252.

29. Sommer, *Deutschland und Japan*, 408.

30. German members of the initial Berlin committee were Admiral Dr. Groos (OKW), Major General Becker (air force), Major General Matzky (member of the army general staff, head of attaché department), General Olbrich (air force), Captain Henigst (OKM), Major von Ahlefeld (air force, member of attaché department), and 2d Lieutenant Pabst (secretary). Italian members were General Marras (military attaché), Colonel Teucci (air attaché), Captain De Angelis (naval attaché), Major Casperi (assistant military attaché), and Major Pelesko (assistant air attaché). Representing the Japanese navy were Admiral Nomura (naval head of Japanese inspection commission in Germany), Captain Yokoi (naval attaché), Commander Taniguchi (assistant naval attaché); the army was represented by Lt. General Banzai (army head of above-mentioned inspection commission), Colonel Komatsu (army attaché), and Lieutenant Colonel Nishi (assistant military attaché); Major Endō and Professor Sakata acted as interpreters. The membership seems to have been subject to considerable fluctuation.

31. Nomura, *Hachijū hachinen no kaiko*, 53.

32. Stumpf, "Von der Achse Berlin-Rom," 139.

33. Hirama, "Japanese Naval Preparations for World War II," *Naval War College Review* 44, no. 2 (1991): 66, 70.

34. Ambassador Ōshima was briefed about the impending campaign against the USSR (Operation Barbarossa) only thirteen days ahead of D-Day (see Chapman,

Japan and German Naval Policy, 255). However, the IJN had been informed considerably earlier. See part 2.

35. Sommer, *Deutschland und Japan,* 492.

Chapter 2. Two Navies Prepare for War

1. Lohmann and Hildebrand, *Die deutsche Kriegsmarine, 1939–1945,* pt. 31; Vermehren, *Etappe Ostasien,* pt. 1. Through Göring, the commander in chief of the Luftwaffe became head of the Air Ministry (Reichsluftfahrtsministerium, or RLM) as well.

2. Lohmann and Hildebrand, *Die Deutsche Kriegsmarine,* pts. 32/6 and 261/5.

3. Chapman, *The Price of Admiralty,* 1:xxxi.

4. Freiwald, "German U-boat Activity in the Indian Ocean," Operational Archives, USNHC, Box T66, Essays by German Officers and Intelligence Report ser. 13-C-50, 13 Jan 1950. Published in *ONI Review* 8, no. 8 (Aug 1953): 367. This document will be cited henceforth as the Freiwald report.

5. Boyd and Yoshida, *The Japanese Submarine Force and World War II,* 47–49.

6. Tahira, *Rengō kantai* 1, 112f., 156–73, 195–204, 305–32; Nomura Minoru, *Rekishi no naka Nihon Kaigun,* 28. See also Evans and Peattie, *Kaigun,* 148–50, 174, 197 and 448–49.

7. Ibid., 165.

8. Tsunoda, *Hawai Sakusen,* 38. See also Hirama, "Japanese Naval Preparations."

9. Akasaka, *Kaigun Gunsenbi II,* 163 and 191.

10. *Kokubō Shoyō Heiryoku* (Required forces for defense policy), Teikoku-Kokubō-Hōshin Tzuri (Imperial defense policy file), February to May 1936, Senshibu.

11. Suekuni and Nishimara, *Kaigun Gunsenbi I,* 511–43, 581–83, 542–43.

12. Kaigun Hensan Iinkai, ed., *Kaigun,* vol. 13, *Kaigun kokutai,* 60.

13. Fukui, *Nihon no Gunkan,* 164–68.

14. Tsunoda, *Hawai Sakusen,* 493. Kaigun Hensan Iinkai, ed., *Kaigun,* 4:96–97.

15. Fukui, *Nihon no Gunkan,* 164–68, 170–71; Kishino, *Sensuikanshi,* 33–36.

16. For Admiral Yamamoto's "Comments on Armaments," see Kaigun Suirai Sentai Kankokai, ed., *Kaigun Suiraisentai,* 502–10.

17. "Comments on Armaments" (7 January 1941), Enomoto Shiryō, Rondon-Kaigun Gunshuku-Kaigi Goryoho (London Naval Treaty Conference file, No. 1/2), JMSDF Archives.

18. Tsunoda, *Middouē kaisen,* 17. This quotation is from Yamamoto's speech of late April 1942 to the conference on "Lessons Learned from Pearl Harbor."

Chapter 3. The Axis in Southern Waters

1. Originally designated *Panzerschiff* (armored vessel), then heavy cruiser, twelve thousand tons, eight 9-cylinder diesel motors, 56,809 hp, 28kn, nineteen thousand mi/19kn, six 11-inch guns.

2. Lohmann and Hildebrand, *Die Deutsche Kriegsmarine*, 39–45, pt. 56.

3. BA-MA, RM 12II/248; Rogge and Frank, "*Schiff 16*," Atlantis, 194ff.; Rusbridger, "The Sinking of the *Automedon*," 9ff.; Layton et al., "*And I Was There*," 87–88.

4. BA-MA, RM 12 II/ 248; Chapman, *The Price of Admiralty*, 322ff.

5. For an in-depth discussion of the *Automedon* incident, see appendix E.

6. Chapman,"German Signals Intelligence,"140f.; Tischer, *Die Abenteuer des letzten Kapers*, 53; Rusbridger, "The Sinking of the *Automedon*," 12ff.; Layton et al., "*And I Was There*," 418ff.

7. Vermehren, *Etappe Ostasien*, pt. 1. This is a series of articles Vermehren wrote in the early fifties. They are in BA-MA, RM 12 II/392.

8. Ibid.

9. BA-MA, RM 13/2, B.Nr. 2255/41.

10. Bill of lading of a random blockade-runner: crude rubber, 4,059 tons; tungsten, 48 tons; tin, 116 tons; soy oil, 178 tons; wood oil, 79 tons; coconut oil, 66 tons; tires, 266 tons; leather, 21 tons; intestine hides, 14 tons; hemp, 190 tons; tea, 107 tons; coffee, 24 tons; and egg products, quinine, and sulfates.

11. Vermehren, *Etappe Ostasien*.

12. NARA, RG 457/SRH-008 vol. II, pt. E, chap. XIII, winter 43–44.

13. Fioravanzo, *La Marina dall'8 Settembre 1943 alla Fine del Conflitto*, 87. Commando gruppo sommergibili operanti negli Oceani (Italian oceanic submarine group command CO Ammiraglio Angelo Parona).

14. Rohwer and Hümmelchen, *Chronology of the War at Sea*, 53.

15. Ibid., 38.

16. Dönitz, *Zehn Jahre und zwanzig Tage*, 140.

17. Ibid., 144.

18. Fioravanzo, *La Marina dall'8 Settembre 1943*, 87ff.

19. Convoys HG Gibraltar-England, OG England-Gibraltar; SL Sierra Leone-England, OS England-Sierra Leone.

20. Rohwer and Hümmelchen, *Chronology of the War at Sea*, 167.

Chapter 4. The Japanese in the Indian Ocean

1. Tsunoda, *Rengo kantai* 2, 301–18.

2. Matushita Yoshiō, ed., *Tanaka Sakusen Buchō no Shōgen*, 168.

3. Hattori Takushirō, *Daitōa Sensō Zenshi*, 618–19.

4. Tsunoda, *Rengō kantai* 2, 301–28.

5. Ibid., 126 and 131.

6. Ibid., 285–93.

7. Matome Ugaki, *Fading Victory: The Diary of Admiral Matome Ugaki, 1941–1945,* ed. Goldstein and Dillon, 181. This work is hereafter cited as the "Ugaki diary."

8. Ugaki diary, 79–80.

9. Marder et al., *Old Friends, New Enemies,* 2:131; Tsunoda, *Rengō kantai* 2, 43.

10. Tahira, *Ran'in, Bengaruwan homen kaigun shikkō sakusen,* 622–76; Marder, *Old Friends, New Enemies,* 1:135–36.

11. Churchill, *The Second World War,* 4:159–60.

12. Roskill, *The War at Sea,* 2:30.

13. Nihon Kaigun Sensuikan Shi Hensankai, ed., *Nihon Kaigun Sensuikan Senshi,* 230–33.

14. Tsunoda, *Rengō kantai* 2, 208–9.

15. Kishino, *Sensuikanshi,* 156–58 and 160–61.

16. Nihon Kaigun Sensuikan Shi Hensankai, ed., *Nihon Kaigun Sensuikan Senshi,* 165.

17. Tsunoda, *Rengō kantai* 2, 308.

18. Chapman, *The Price of Admiralty,* 4:735, 767.

19. Ibid., 932. The English translation of the document, originally named "Betrachtung der allgemeinen strategischen Lage nach Kriegseintritt Japan/USA. Vortrag des Chefs der Operationsabteilung bei der ersten gemeinsamen Besprechung der Marine-Verbindungsstäbe," can be found at pages 926–34.

20. Nomura, *Hachijū hachinen no kaiko,* 62–64.

21. Tsunoda, *Rengō kantai* 2, 277–78.

22. Ugaki diary, 170.

23. Sakamoto, *Rengō kantai* 3, 54–56.

24. Ugaki diary, 319.

25. Yoshimatsu, *Rengō kantai* 4, 40–45.

26. Sasaki, *Nansei hōmen kaigun sakusen,* 649–62; Ministry of Defence, *The War with Japan,* 1/2:115.

27. Yoshimatsu, *Rengō kantai* 4, 437–59.

28. Sasaki, *Nansei hōmen kaigun sakusen,* 665–67.

Chapter 5. Axis Submarine Operations in the Indian Ocean

1. Nomura, *Senkan U-511 no unmei* (The fate of U-511), 164ff.

2. U-177 (Gysae), U-178 (Dommes), U-195 (Buchholz), U-196 (Kentrat), U-197 (Barthel), U-198 (Hartmann), U-181 (Lüth).

3. U-168 (Pich), U-183 (Schäfer), U-188 (Lüdden), U-200 (Schonder), U-506 (Würdemann), U-509 (W. Witte), U-514 (Auffermann), U-516 (Wiebe), U-532 (Junker); U-533 (Henning), U-847 (Kuppisch).

4. Operational Archives, USNHC; Report by Commanding Officer of U-188 (Lüdden), "Experiences in Indian Ocean," NID1, ser. 0054 9 Nov 1944 Box T76, TR/PG/7337/1/NID WWII CF individual ships, pt. Erfahrungen und Anregungen. This document will be henceforth cited as the Lüdden report.

5. Lüdden report.

6. Operational Archives, USNHC; War log 4th war patrol USS *Besugo*, FC5-26/A16-3, ser. 01, 1945/05/20.

7. NARA, RG 38/112, Headquarters 441st Counter Intelligence Corps Detachment, Special Operations Section, Admiral Wenneker, "Report about My Stay in Japan," unnumbered, 20 March 1946, 20. This document will be henceforth cited as the "Wenneker report."

8. Brennecke, *Haie im Paradies*, 189.

9. Wenneker report, I, para. 8, and II, para. 3–7.

10. Korv.Kapt. Dommes, former Chef im Südraum, letter to Gr.Adm. Dönitz after release from Spandau Prison, undated. Copy in possession of H.-J. Krug.

11. Lüdden report.

Chapter 6. Practical Cooperation and Exchange of Experience

1. War Log of the Naval Attaché and Military Leader of the *Grossetappe* Japan-China, BA-MA, RM 12 II/248, 159.

2. Wenneker report, II, para. 2; Freiwald report, 363, 367; Lüdden report.

3. Chapman, *The Price of Admiralty*, 2/3: 30.

4. Wenneker war diary, BA-MA, RM 12 II/248, 249.

5. Wenneker report, I, 6.

6. Wenneker report, I, 8.

7. Dommes letter to Gr.Adm Dönitz; see chapter 5, note 10.

8. Lüdden report.

9. See Chapman, "The Origins, and Development of German and Japanese Military Co-operation, 1936–1945."

10. BA-MA, RM 7/253, Skl. an Adm. Groos Betrachtungen zur Frage: Japan im Dreimächtepakt, 46/41 gKdos. Chefs., 14.01.1941.

11. "Shūgiin Sokiroku" (Lower House of Parliament, phase 6), no. 3, *Kanpō-Gōgai* (The government gazette), 22 January 1942, 6; Tsunoda, *Rengō Kantai* 2, 285–93.

12. Ugaki diary, 181.

13. Ibid., 263–64.

14. "Borman's Confidential Instruction on Yellow Peril (5 June 1942)," in Margaret Carlyle, ed., *Documents on International Affairs, 1939–1946*, vol. 2, *Hitler's Europe*, 450.

15. Hauner, *India in Axis Strategy*, 377–420.

16. Hitler, *Hitler's Table Talk*, 263–64.

17. Ibid., 267.

18. Kimata, *Sensuikan Senshi*, 321.

19. Tomi, "Indoyō no Nichidoku Sensuikan Sakusen," 139.

20. Saville, "German Submarines in the Far East," 191–92, and calculated from Roskill, *The War at Sea*.

21. Daitōa Sensō 1 ken: Violation of the laws, Diplomatic Archives.

22. Sugamo Hōmu Iinkai, *Senpan Saiban no Jitssō*, 199–205.

23. Oide, *Raion Kanchō Mayuzumi Haruo*, 107–12; Kimata, *Nihon Sensuikan Senshi*, 539–42.

24. *Kyokutō Kokusai Gunji Saiban Sokkiroku*, vol. 4, no. 151, 60.

25. Kikuchi, "Ei Shōsen Biharu-gō Horyogyakusatu-Jiken no Shinsō," 134–47.

26. Handō, ed. *Yusha no Isho*, 235–36.

27. Padfield, *Dönitz et la Guerre des U-Boote*, 229.

28. Hitler, *Hitler's Table Talk*, 149.

Chapter 7. Building Navies, 1919–1933

1. This applies to the Washington D.C. National Archives and Record Administration (NARA). British materials, especially the German attaché messages code-named "Seahorse Traffic," even after more than fifty years, have not yet been made available at the Public Record Office (PRO) in Kew.

2. For a more complete account, see Sander-Nagashima, "Die deutsch-japanischen Marinebeziehungen 1919 bis 1942," diss., Hamburg 1998.

3. Compare Itō et al., eds. *Katō Kanji Nikki*, 32 and 47.

4. See his report in the presence of the Imperial Family on 29 June 1920, Tahira, *Rengō kantai* 1, 333.

5. See Sander-Nagashima, "Die deutsch-japanischen Marinebeziehungen."

6. BA-MA, RF 04/36172, "Unsere Einstellung zu den Marinen des Auslandes," M I 515/32 gKdos., 01.03.1932.

7. Compare Schreiber, *Revisionismus*, who argues that the idea of England as the main enemy formed an important element of continuity in the thinking of senior German naval officers from the Kaiser's days until the end of World War II.

8. On the conflict of the two Katōs, see Asada, "The Revolt against the Washington Treaty: The Imperial Japanese Navy and Naval Limitation, 1921–1927," *Naval War College Review* 46, no. 3 (1993): 82–97.

9. See Maruyama, *Denken in Japan* (German trans. of *Nihon no shisō*), Frankfurt, 1988.

10. Sander-Nagashima, "Die deutsch-japanischen Marinebeziehungen," 307.

Chapter 8. Rapprochement, 1934–1936

1. Compare Dülffer, *Weimar*, 242.

2. Umbau der Reichsmarine (Rebuilding the Reichsmarine) (signed by Schleicher and Raeder), Mar.B.Nr. 20120/32 gKdos., 15.11.1932, reprinted in Dülffer, *Weimar*, 565f.; also reprinted in Güth, *Marine*, 139f.

3. For the replacement plans and the increased numbers of aircraft carriers and submarines, see Dülffer, Weimar, 251, and Güth, Marine, 158f.

4. For the navy the London negotiations were particularly noteworthy in two respects. First, it gained a position that it had not had since World War I. Mostly independent from the mighty competitors, the Foreign Ministry and the army, and also from Minister von Blomberg, it could develop its position here and also present it directly at the conference table. Ribbentrop was their actual conversation partner on the German side. Compare Dülffer, *Weimar*, 333.

5. Raeder, Guse (of the Navy Command Office), and frontline officers clearly indicated that the treaty could only be temporary. Cf. Dülffer, *Weimar*, 344, 347. Güth, *Marine*, 185, points out that Raeder considered England a potential enemy at that time. Salewski, *Seekriegsleitung*, vol. 1, negates this and presumes that Raeder used the example of England's "heavy ships" to try to get Hitler's permission to build the same. However, Salewski bases his conclusions on Dülffer's interpretation of Guse and not on the handwritten comments and marks in the various versions of this document that clearly show reservations. These reveal the opposite of Salewski's interpretation: They indicate that the final understanding with England was merely an official wording, in no way representing the true view of the navy. In reference to the Fleet Treaty, see also Haraszti, *Treaty-Breakers or "Realpolitiker"?*

6. Guse, in his "Thoughts about the waging of war at sea between France and Germany" in May 1934, opined: "German sea operations against the French troop transports and shipments in the Atlantic are only possible with the use of aircraft, since light reconnaissance forces cannot be taken along because of their limited range. The use of ship-based aircraft finds its limits at sea-swell strength 4. The inclusion of an aircraft carrier is therefore a precondition for a German maritime warfare against the troop transports. . . ." The document is partially reprinted in Güth, *Marine*, 151ff. These comments held true also for other opponents.

7. This also can be gathered from Guse's observations in May 1934. He explained that in a war with France the "main point of emphasis was on the land war." It was also imaginable, however, "that in case of a hardening of the land front, which can happen very early on with strongly fortified border fortifications, sea and air power alone are in the position, with their independent operational abilities, to overcome this hardening and prepare the strategic turning point." Güth,

Marine, 151ff. In view of the experiences of the First World War and the Maginot line it can be assumed that the "hardening" of the land front was not just seen as a mere possibility, but rather as a probability, the significance of the navy thereby presumed by the Marineleitung.

8. Compare the later largely implemented proposals of the Fleet Department in its paper, "Considerations of the Fleet Department about the leadership of a war in the Atlantic" from 1 November 1934. In Güth, *Marine,* at 160ff.

9. In the first half of the thirties, aviation saw, inter alia, the rise of full metal construction, the abandonment of the biplane, retractable landing gear, turbocharged aircraft engines, and variable pitch airscrews.

10. Since this document represents a compromise negotiated between army and navy, it was not very specific and showed few other changes compared to the second revision. The importance of decisive battles very early in a war was emphasized. See Tahira, *Rengō kantai,* pt. 1, 305 and 315, and Lengerer, "Die Bauprogramme der Kaiserlich-japanischen Marine 1937–1945."

11. PAAA, R 33314, note of 10 January 1934, IIM46. The inquiry was answered in such a way that small, hidden quantities, deliverable at a later time, would be accepted.

12. Senshibu, 10 Buōbun S-20/76, Navy Ministry to Naval Attaché in Germany. Response in the matter of the "Marinevereine," 16 February 1934. Chairman of Japanese Naval Society to Navy Ministry regarding German Fleet Society, 19 February 1934, *Übermittlung der Satzung.*

13. Matsushita worked in the armaments bureau during World War I and was a member of the *Kantoku* (a naval organization responsible for collecting technical information and materials for building purposes from abroad) from the summer of 1917 until spring of 1920. In this capacity he was in England from August 1917 until the end of 1919. After that he held influential postings, among others as bureau chief of the minister of the navy. At the time of the *Tōsuiken* (Right of Supreme Command) Debate in 1930, he was the head of the personnel bureau in the ministry, later commander of the naval officer candidate school, and after that commander of the training squadron. After returning from the training cruise of the squadron, he was placed out of the way as head of the small naval stations Maizuru and (later) Sasebo. As an England specialist and enforcer of the personnel policies of Navy Minister Takarabe, he did not seem to be the right man for influential posts in the view of the now strengthened Fleet Faction. He joined the reserves in 1937 and died in 1953. Takarabe himself was virtually thrown out of office by the strong opposition from the Fleet Faction.

14. PAAA, R 85951, RWM (KK Bürkner) to AA, B.Nr. 455 M I, 23.03.1934: Reichskanzlei to AA to RWM 455 M I, Rk. 2914, 26.03.1934, note that Hitler will receive Matsushita. The AA also arranged an additional meeting with the

Reichsaussenminister, ibid.; Japanese Embassy Berlin to AA, note about Matsushita's intentions in Berlin, IV Ja 377, 28.03.1934, and response, ibid.; AA to Imperial Japanese Embassy Berlin; Memo: Matsushita's visit very welcome. Ja 377/34, 06.04.1934.

The visit is also mentioned repeatedly in the works of Chapman, where the interpretations are, however, in error. For example, in Chapman's dissertation, Matsushita is labeled as the head of a technical commission sent in 1934 on the suggestion of Dr. Kaumann, a representative of the German aircraft industry. Chapman, "Origins," 74 (volume 2 continues the pagination from volume 1). Later Chapman claims that Matsushita's squadron visited Germany, whereas the squadron never sailed into German waters. Chapman, "Japan and German Naval Policy," 241.

15. See, PAAA, R 85951, AA to Embassy Tokyo, IV Ja 591, 16.05.1934.

16. PAAA, R 85951, undated draft of a speech of the Reichswehrminister at the dinner in the Japanese embassy in occasion of the visit of Admiral Matsushita, without number, noted on 05.05.1934.

17. PAAA, R 85951, Admiral (Ret.) Behncke speech for the reception for Japanese naval officers on 8 May 1934, no number, 08.05.1934.

18. Ibid.

19. Ibid., 1. Mentioned here is a commission that inspected harbor and dock facilities in Kiel, Flensburg-Mürwik, Hamburg, Cuxhaven, and Wilhelmshaven. The commission consisted of three captains, several commanders, and one lieutenant commander. (See also PAAA, R 85951, *Japanischer Verein in Deutschland*, No. 364, *Der [sic] Offizier-Abordnung des japanischen Schulschiff-Geschwaders*, 25.04.1934.) This is most probably the study commission that received permission from the Marineleitung at the end of May 1935 to inspect a remote-control device for target ships and targets, produced by Siemens in Italy, that was presented in Milan by an Italian firm for demonstration purposes. The device was also to be produced for Italy. Chapman erroneously credits this inspection to the Matsushita mission and claims that it had visited Milan on its way to Germany. See note 14, above. However, the Marineleitung granted permission between 22 and 25 May 1935. This is proven by handwritten comments, on the back of the document, that in turn preclude a visit by the Matsushita mission on the way to Germany. See Chapman, "Origins," 75, note 11, and BA-MA, RM 11/1, Bl. (handwritten page number) 101 and Bl. 102, MAtt to naval attaché [Rome], Re: "Zähringen"-Anlage.

This device was bought the same year by the Japanese and used in trials at Yokosuka. See Itō et al., eds., *Katō Kanji Nikki*, 557, Document 25, Paper from Capt. Yamashita Tomohiko and Lt. Cdr. (E) Waraya Hidehiko, "Views about the cooperation with Germany, 1934" (n.d.). This document, which must originate from the second half of 1934, casts light on the considerations that were the foundation for the rapprochement of the IJN to the Reichsmarine. It strongly emphasizes the need for modern technology for the armaments industry; the Japanese particularly mentioned the "Zähringen" device, the Reichsmarine's gyroscopically based leveling mechanism for gun turrets, fire control devices, diesel motors for water- and aircraft, and optical devices. Ibid., 562f. Yamashita and Waraya were members of the weapons bureau, and at least Yamashita was personally known to Katō. See *Katō Kanji Nikki*, 174, 1 May 1932.

20. PAAA, R 85951, newspaper clippings with reports of the DNB (*Deutsches Nachrichtenbüro*, the German news service) from 7 and 9 May regarding the Matsushita visit: "Reception evening for the Japanese naval officers," 9.05.1934.

21. The newspaper article with Matsushita's speech is not fully preserved in the files. However, it casts an interesting light on differences between the Japanese navy and Foreign Ministry. Ambassador Nagai privately expressed annoyance after Matsushita's speech, "because the parallels drawn therein seemed to him to go too far." PAAA, R 85951, AA to Tokyo Embassy, IV Ja 591, "Information about the Matsushita visit," 16.05.1934.

22. PAAA, R 85951, newspaper clippings, 09.05.1934: "The Japanese naval visitors leave."
    It is noticeable during the visit of Matsushita that the representatives of the *Reichsluftfahrtministerium* (Air Ministry) were not always included into the program. For example, in Behncke's speech, the welcome of the representatives of the RLM is crossed out by hand. Personnel at the Tempelhof airport had not been notified of Matsushita's visit there. See the protest of the RLM against the "unnotified appearance" in BA-MA, RM 11/1, Bl. 104, *Reichsminister der Luftfahrt to Marineleitung*, 1393/34, 8.05.1934.

23. NARA, RG 165, Box 1640, U.S. Army Attaché, Berlin, German-Japanese Relations, 2657-B-763(3), 17.05.1934.

24. These comments that emphasize racial aspects could be explained at least partly as statements made in economic circles with which the Americans seemed to have especially good relations. Unfortunately, the American attaché gives no details about his German conversation partner.

25. Both visits have been covered by Chapman, "Origins," and only the newly discovered aspects of them will be covered here.

26. BA-MA, RM 11/68, Attaché Report, Re: *Ankauf von Luftschiffen durch Japan*, G 53, 09.01.1935. Chapman erroneously considered Breithaupt to be a member of the RLM; he was, in fact, an employee of the German-Manchurian import-export firm. Before his departure he was, however, instructed by the RLM. See Chapman, "Origins," 75.

27. Underlined by hand in the original document and annotated on the left margin with green ink: "The Führer wishes good relations." This proves the strong

interest in Japan on the part of the Nazi government that was already evidenced in May 1934 by the objection of Goebbels and the Foreign Ministry to Count Luckner's mentioning the Japanese naval build-up. The Ministry of Propaganda asked Luckner "to stop such unwise and unnecessary elaborations." See the paper traffic in PAAA, R 85951, IV Ja 873, 28.05.1934 and Luckner's explanation from July 1934, ibid., II 2200/26.7.34, IV Ja 176, 12.02.1935. See also BA-MA, RM 11/68, Attaché Report, 09.01.1935.

28. 41 BA-MA, RM 11/68, handwritten note A IIIc, MAtt 228 geheim, 11.03.1935. "It could be that also here possibilities for counterdemands through the German navy exist." Obviously German naval officers did not want to clear the field for the Luftwaffe.

29. Senshibu, 10 Buōbun, S-20/76, Naval Attaché in Germany (Yokoi) to Deputy Minister of the Navy and Deputy Chief of the Navy General Staff. Report about the deployment of a German flight officer, 14 September 1934. Coeler had entered the navy in 1912 and joined the flight service in 1915 as first lieutenant. During World War I he was stationed with the naval air arm in Zeebrügge, in the Baltic and on reconnaissance aircraft. Accepted into the Reichsmarine, he worked in the *Luftschutzgruppe* on the organizational preparation of the naval air arm, became lieutenant commander in 1929, entered the reserves in 1933, and entered service with the RLM in 1934. During the visit in Japan he carried the title of *Flieger-Vize-Kommodore*. See also Güth, *Marine*, 141.

30. BA-MA, RM 11/68, Attaché Report, Re: Inspection of carrier *Akagi* at 20.01.35, G 71 geheim, 02.02.1935, and Senshibu, 10 Buōbun, S-20, 76, Secretary of Minister of the Navy to Naval Attaché in Germany, Re: Inspection of *Akagi* by Coeler and Wenneker on 21.01.1935 [*sic*], 50 geheim, January 1935 (n.d.). How seriously this report was taken by the RWM is shown by the remark: "has also been seen by the Führer."

31. BA-MA, RM 11/68, Attaché Report, Re: Inspection of battle cruiser *Kongo*, cruiser *Tama* and submarine *J2*, on 10.01.35, G 66 geheim, 24.01.1935. See also PAAA, R 85951, Wenneker and Dirksen to Marineleitung, Nr.2, 07.01.1935, and ibid., Wenneker and Dirksen to Marineleitung, Nr.3, 11.01.1935.

32. BA-MA, RM 11/68, report, 24.01.1935, 2.

33. Ibid., p. 4 of the report. This clue was obviously seen as important in Berlin. The passage in the document is marked "M.P.A.!" (*Marinepersonalamt* or navy personnel office).

34. Ibid., p. 5 of the report. Underlined by hand.

35. Ibid. The craft, all of an older make, had shortly before been refurbished and upgraded and were part of the First Fleet, the mainstay of the Japanese fleet.

36. "I am in doubt if even our level of ten years ago has been reached." Ibid., p. 9 of the report. Underlined by hand.

37. BA-MA, RM 11/68, Attaché Report, Re: Inspection of battle cruiser *Kongo*, etc., G 70 geheim, 04.02.1935.

38. BA-MA, RM 11/68, Wenneker's report, G 71, 02.02.1935. "I could point out, by carefully conveying my impressions about the backwardness of the Japanese fire control systems, what great use the Japanese Navy could gain by a thorough inspection of the *Admiral Scheer*." Namely this last step had particular effect. In view of the without doubt known fact of the great inferiority in the artillery-technical area, it led to the directive that the aircraft carrier should be shown without reservation. Ibid., 4.

   The *Admiral Scheer* was one of the new German Panzerschiffe. The proposal for an inspection did not originate with the German side but was a counterdemand from the Japanese for the permission to inspect an aircraft carrier. Wenneker judged the counterdemand to be "wholly in line with the guideline followed on the Japanese side, namely, to achieve a high [value] for little effort." Ibid., p. 3 of the report. Complaints about "unfair" Japanese practices were already common in the twenties in German naval and industrial circles. Especially in the early twenties, there had been a Japanese "rush" for German armament technology. Considering the rather extraordinary accommodation during the inspection (it was the first inspection of an aircraft carrier through a German naval officer), the appropriateness of Wenneker's judgment is questionable. The inspection is also mentioned in Chapman, "Origins," 78, where the initiative to inspect the carrier is mistakenly attributed to Coeler.

39. BA-MA, RM 11/68, Wenneker's report, G 71, 02.02.1935, 2. Endo was particularly valued by the German side, as Raeder specifically mentioned in a letter to the Minister of the Navy Ōsumi. (Cf. PAAA, R 85951, RWM to AA, Re: Ehrengeschenk an die japan. Marine, Mar. B.Nr. 1053/2 Ang. M, 03.07.1934 and ibid., letter, Raeder to Ōsumi, IV Ja 805, 28.06.1934. Ōsumi's answer in Senshibu, 10 Buōbun, S-20, 76, Secretary of Ōsumi to Naval Attaché in Germany, Re: Brief Adm. Ōsumi Mineos and Adm. Raeder, 25.08.1934.) Endō also stayed in contact after his departure from Germany in the summer of 1934 and wrote, for example, for *Nauticus*. (Cf. BA-MA, RM 11/70, Secretary of Ōsumi to Wenneker, letter and article to be translated and published in *Nauticus*, B.Nr. 3475, 19.08.1935, and ibid., Attaché Report, Re: Contribution of former Japanese attaché in Berlin, Captain Endō, for *Nauticus*, B-Nr. 250, 13.09.1935.) Endō was naval adjutant of the Tennō from 1935 to 1938 and received thereafter a second attaché posting in Germany from 1938 to 1940. After that he became chief of staff of the Yokosuka naval station. He was killed in action in 1944 on

Hollandia bearing the rank of admiral. (Cf. NARA, RG 457, List of Flag Officers of the Japanese Navy Who Have Died During This War, fol. 018, no number, Ultra, 19 June 1945.)

40. "The granting of permission . . . is to be judged as very special. Actually it is incredible, when one knows how persistently and conscientiously they work here to deny foreigners a view into military matters, especially naval matters. This is particularly so for the four aircraft carriers. How great a value the Japanese place on keeping just these ships secret is illustrated by following: The aircraft carriers, even at home port, are placed whenever possible on the outside of the pier, they are never allowed to be visited by the civilian population, Japanese officers and men who are not part of the crew need a special written permission of fleet command, and a few permitted suppliers have to go about their business in a small room situated very close to the gangplank." Wenneker report Nr. G 71, 2f.

41. The question of intervals between landings touched on the area of tactics, in which, next to the area of technology, the Japanese generally behaved most reservedly. Nonetheless, Wenneker and Coeler received so many documents and so much information that "relatively close estimates could be guessed at." Ibid., 5. Shortly before the inspection, Wenneker had received information from the Japanese about tactical matters, including the usage of aircraft carriers. BA-MA, RM 11/68, Attaché Report, Re: Tactical questions, G 64 geheim, 18.01.1935.

42. Ibid., 8.

43. BA-MA, RM 11/1, Bl. 197ff., *Marinewaffenamt to A. Re: Besuch der Japaner auf "Admiral Scheer"*, M.Wa. N. 14093/35 gKdos., 03.05.1935. This is not the actual report of the visit (which does not seem to have been passed down in the files) but only an opinion paper about it.

44. These contacts seem to have been worked on by the Marineleitung in violation of the decrees of the RWM. Defense Minister Blomberg, in September 1934, had issued orders to the heads of the Heer- and Marineleitung, as well as within the RLM, regarding the treatment of inspection and release permits applied for by the attachés of foreign countries. He had divided the permit-seeking countries into two groups. Petitions of the first group could be decided by the heads of the service branches; petitions of the second group, to which Japan belonged, Blomberg had reserved for himself to decide, for foreign policy reasons. The service branches were told not to inform foreign personnel of any matters that were classified as *geheime Kommandosache* (gKdos.) nor to disclose anything that would allow any conclusions about the reforming of the armed forces or violations of the treaty limitations and the *Kriegsgerätegesetz* (regulations concerning armaments security).

In addition, Blomberg ordered that the principle of reciprocity was to be observed and that a list of services and counter-services be maintained for his information. The Marineleitung seems not to have obeyed these orders, because nothing in the files suggests that the Reichswehrminister was in any way informed about the contact with the Japanese, except through the attaché reports. Neither were permissions sought from him. BA-MA, RM 11/1, *Reichsverteidigungsminister to Chef der ML,* 656/34 gKdos., 20.09.1934. Signed by Raeder.

45. Ibid., 197.

46. Ibid., 198. Underlined by hand in the document.

47. The composer of the letter (Rear Admiral Witzell, head of the Weapons Bureau) showed a certain bias. He wrote that the Japanese during the inspection of the carrier *Akagi* "had ruthlessly removed all aircraft and certainly also other things from on board, but then had readily shown everything that was left." With that they had "given away relatively little in terms of factual information, but had achieved the impression of great cooperation." Ibid., Bl. 199. This stands in contradiction to Wenneker's and Coeler's report. According to the usual procedure while lying in harbor, the aircraft had been transferred to the nearby Naval air station at Yokosuka. However, just for the inspection, one fighter plane and one bomber were kept on board. Beyond that, the Germans had the opportunity to view planes of the carrier during a shooting exercise. Wenneker judged the things shown to be of considerable value. See Wenneker's report, BA-MA, RM 11/68, G 71 geheim, 02.02.1935, p. 7 of the report.

48. BA-MA, RM 11/1, Bl.347, note on the information received from RLM, M I 54/35 gKdos., 14.02.1935.

49. Chzech had secretly received training as a pilot. At the time of this consideration he was company commander in Wilhelmshaven.

50. BA-MA, RM 11/1, Bl. 348, note about negotiations between A and K, relating to M I 54/35 gKdos., 16.02.1935 and ibid., Bl.349, A to M, relating to M I 54/35 gKdos., 20.02.1935.

51. BA-MA, RM 11/68, Wenneker to Luftministerium [*sic*] and Marineleitung, MAtt 670 geheim, 08.03.1935, and ibid., Attaché Report, Re: Buying of Heinkel aircraft, G 80 geheim, 15.03.1935. For details regarding Wada, see chapter 11, note 8.

Aichi had originally initiated contact with Heinkel over the firm of Dr. Hack. However, Heinkel hesitated on the question of building instructions. The Japanese were interested in the He 70, which had broken several speed records, and also wanted to purchase the fighter-trainer He 74. Aichi had already purchased the He 65. Faithful to their principle of becoming independent of the supplier as soon as possible, they purchased only a limited number of all the types and developed them further. Out of the He 65 they developed the Japanese improved model Aichi D3A, which was the standard Japanese dive-bomber during the attack upon Pearl Harbor. Cf. Nowarra, *Heinkel,* 86f. Chapman, "Origins," 80, note 22, mistakenly assumes that it was the He 118, Heinkel's new high-performance dive-bomber design, which turned up at Aichi independently of the negotiations mention here. Cf. Nowarra, *Heinkel,* 88.

52. BA-MA, RM 11/68, Attaché Report, Re: 1) Night exercises with submarines. 2) Questions from the Japanese navy, G 81 geheim, 18.03.1935.

53. Compare handwritten remark on demands for counter-services to the questions of the Japanese through the Naval Intelligence Service of the Kommandoamt (A III): "In the answer to M the answering of the questions that were asked by the Japanese navy was not agreed to and therefore no counter-services demanded." BA-MA, RM 11/68, A III to A IV, relating to MAtt 671 geheim, 12.08.1935.

54. BA-MA, RM 11/68, Enclosure 2 to Attaché Report, Re: Aircraft carrier questions, G 91 geheim, 01.04.1935.

55. BA-MA, RM 11/69, Attaché Report, Re: Aircraft carrier questions, G 101 geheim, 26.04.1935.

56. BA-MA, RM 11/69, Attaché Report, Re: Lecture about the German navy. Exchange of experience, G 122 geheim, 04.06.1935.

57. Ibid., 2. Underlined by hand with an exclamation mark of the left margin.

58. PAAA, R 85951, Wenneker and Dirksen to Marineleitung, Nr.70, 06.07.1935.

59. BA-MA, RM 11/70, Attaché Report, Re: Exchange of experience with the Japanese Navy. Recent situation of the matter, G 158 geheim, 26.09.1935. The paper traffic with the head secretary of the Navy Ministry (Commander Tayui) is added to this report.

60. See ibid., added paper traffic with Tayui, 12–15, and PAAA, R 85951, Wenneker and Dirksen to Kriegsmarine, Nr. 112, 26.09.1935.

61. The Kriegsmarine put great emphasis on the fact that the gyroscopically supported gun stabilizers were not included. Withholding them imposed a noticeable limitation on their usefulness, because during high seas the data given by the fire control devices could not effect precise firing because of the instability of the guns.

62. The Japanese, already interested in early 1934, had tried to gain the desired material through direct negotiations with the Krupp, avoiding the Marineleitung (see PAAA, R 33314, 10 January 1934, IIM46). That this did not have the wished-for success was shown by the fact that now they tried the "official" way. Evidently control over the export of naval armaments technology functioned better than it had in the twenties.

63. These negotiations were concluded successfully, and in February 1937 a prototype was shipped to Japan. Heinkel himself commented upon the newly

intensified contacts from 1935 on: "In my factory there now began a new, great phase of technical and aeronautical cooperation with the Japanese that lasted until late in the war." Quoted in Thorwald, ed., *Stürmisches Leben,* 354.

64. The report of the commission, presented on 07.01.1936, is located in BA-MA, RM 8/1600, *Berichterstattung der Japan-Studienkommission Sept.–Dez. 1935.* (Another, identical, copy is in BA-MA, RM 8/1628.)

65. Ibid., 6.

66. Ibid., 7.

67. Ibid., 8.

68. BA-MA, RM 11/70, Attaché Report, Re: a) Preliminary report of the aircraft carrier commission, b) short annotations concerning their stay, 174 geheim, 04.12.1935. Passages underlined by hand in the document.

69. He totally omitted the area of tactics and training, which the Germans would still have had to master after the completion of a carrier.

70. In actuality a previously closed area was newly reopened. The German counterservices were only partly and slowly rendered. The He 118 aircraft was given only after the technical bureau of the Luftwaffe declared it to be inferior to the competing model Ju 87. It was shipped to Japan in the spring of 1937. See note 63.

71. BA-MA, RM 8/1600, Farewell to the German commission (personal notice) of Lieutenant Commander Maeda, 08.11.1935, 87–89.

72. Maeda referred to the legendary founding of the state by Jimmū-Tennō.

73. See Wenneker's exhaustive reporting in BA-MA, RM 11.72, 230 geheim, 06.05.1936. The terms appearing in Maeda's speech about a world of "true peace and true fortune for mankind" that differs from one built on "selfishness" is in need of interpretation. These terms hid the idea of a strictly hierarchical society, structured after Confucian rules, that in essence represented feudalistic viewpoints and were also seen as guiding points for the international system.

Such ideas found their representation in such slogans as "hakkō-ichiu," that is occasionally translated as "universal brotherhood." See Spahn et al., *Japanese Character Dictionary,* 390. The more exact meaning can be deduced by taking notice of the meaning of the written Japanese characters. These literally mean "eight directions—one roof-ridge," which is a metaphor for the world under imperial rule. This state of affairs is characterized as the "true peace" and "true fortune." The hierarchical social structure with the Tennō at its head was, in terms of the inner conditions of the state, named *Kokutai* (literally, "body of the nation," meaning "essence of the nation"). It was the worry of the high military leaders about the preservation of the Kokutai that, in 1945, after the dropping of the A-bomb, delayed the decision to surrender. These connections are analyzed in Maruyama Masao, *Nihon no shisō* (Thought in Japan).

As for the role played by racial considerations in Japanese government circles, see Dower, *War without Mercy*. For the differentiation of the ideology, here necessarily only roughly explained, and its proponents within the inner political constellation in Japan in the second half of the thirties, see Krebs, *Japans Deutschlandpolitik*, 1:306ff.

For the naval officers formed in the German Imperial Navy, the views offered by Maeda must have been received as similar to their own. Compare, for example, the comments of Admiral Groos about his contacts with Japanese naval officers during the civil war–like unrest in Berlin after World War I. BA-MA, (Groos papers), *Manuskript "Seeoffizier in Krieg und Frieden,"* 2. Buch: *In der Republik*, N 165/20, fol. 39f. Groos stated here *expressis verbis* that he felt more closely related to them than to "some German circles" because of the similar views held by the Japanese.

74. PAAA, R 85951, Wenneker and Noebel to Kriegsmarine, Nr. 5, 10.01.1936. The Japanese here asked again that Wenneker offer full support for instruction about the entire production method for armor and test results. In addition a more modest price was requested. Obviously the Germans' inclination to stand by their promises was not particularly strong.

75. BA-MA, RM 11/71, Attaché Report, Re: Thanks of Commander in Chief Kriegsmarine, 190 geheim, 21.01.1936. The thank-you telegram itself was not passed down in the files.

76. Detailed comments on the requests are not possible because the document has apparently not been preserved. It is, however, mentioned in BA-MA, RM 11/72, Attaché Report, Re: Inspection travels of Japanese officers, B.Nr. 224 geheim, 20 April 1936.

77. Wenneker estimated the number of specialists with the Japanese naval attaché in Berlin to be around twenty. BA-MA, RM 11/72, Attaché Report, Re: Inspection travels of Japanese officers, 225 geheim, 24.04.1936.

78. His wish list included in-depth inspections of a cruiser of the *Mogami* or *Atago* class and a modern destroyer; the artillery school in Yokosuka; and the harbor dock and arsenal, aeronautical, and other facilities of Kure naval station; the training facilities of the antiaircraft artillery; and the technical research facilities of the navy and of eight Japanese firms. See BA-MA, RM 11/72, Attaché Report, B.Nr. 224 geheim, 20.04.1936.

79. Ibid.

80. BA-MA, RM 11/72, Secretary of Minister of the Navy (Captain Tayui) to Wenneker, Kambō 1193/2 geheim, 23.04.1936.

81. BA-MA, RM 11/72, Wenneker and Noebel to Marineleitung, Nr. 125, (2. Ausf.), Pol I 495 geheim, 18.06.1936, and BA-MA, RM 11/72, Attaché Report,

Re: Inspections of Japanese ships, schools and docks etc. 237 geheim,
26.06.1936.

82. In the report there is a handwritten remark on the left margin, "Why only halfway?" Ibid.

83. Ibid., p. 2 of the report.

84. "In the SAS (Ships Artillery School) surprisingly one was allowed to view the
artillery command post, as well as a shooting practice room." Ibid., 3.

85. Ibid., 4.

86. Wenneker reported, "It should be particularly noted that the Japanese, when they
wish that something not be understood, use complicated Japanese of the written variety that is not used in colloquial speech." Ibid. Wenneker's knowledge
of the Japanese language consisted solely of self-study and private tutoring. I am
indebted to Frau Ingeborg Krag, Freiburg im Breisgau, one-time secretary of
Wenneker's, for this information.

87. "In view of the practical use that presents itself to us, the result is relatively meager. It has been once again clearly shown that, at least in weapons technical areas,
there is hardly anything to gain from the Japanese navy." Ibid., 3. Underlined by
hand.

88. Ibid., 4f. Underlined by Wenneker himself. The word "England" is additionally
underlined by hand and marked with double lines and exclamation points on
the left margin.

89. The one-time naval attaché in Berlin.

90. BA-MA, RM 11/72, 237 geheim, 26.06.1936, 5.

91. Ibid., 6.

Chapter 9. Cooperation with Caution

1. In October Minister of the Navy Ōsumi had also given the correspondent an interview, in which he indirectly confirmed that the Japanese naval delegation would
advocate at the preconference in London the formula of "mutual tonnage limitations" (the demand for parity with the Anglo-Saxon sea powers). He also drew parallels between Germany and Japan when he responded to Urach's comments on the
frantic modernization efforts of the Japanese Navy, remarking that "being surrounded by resistance and enemies" gives a nation "the necessary tension to truly
achieve great things" and that in the end this "also fits your German people." PAAA,
R 85951, newspaper clipping from the *Völkischen Beobachter*, "Vor dem Beginn der
Londoner Flottenverhandlungen. Japans Marineminister, Admiral Ōsumi, spricht
mit dem *Völkischen Beobachter*," unnumbered, 18.10.1934. The instructions for the
delegation on the preconference led by Rear Admiral Yamamoto Isoroku are located
in Itō et al., eds., *Katō Kanji Nikki*, Document Nr. 29, 571.

2. BA-MA, RM 11/68, Attaché Report, Re: Talks with Admiral Suetsugu, B.Nr 50, 21.12.1934.

3. "[T]he Fleet treaties of Washington and London are rooted deeply into the consciousness of our people. The national sense of justice of our people sees in these treaties a condescending treatment of the Japanese race." BA-MA, RM 11/68, Talks of the *Völkischen Beobachter* correspondent Fürst Urach with Admiral Suetsugu (draft), 19.12.1934. *Anlage* (enclosure) relating to B.Nr. 50.

4. "Without doubt a strong fleet was of prime importance for the foundation of our world power status." Ibid., p. 1 of the report.

5. Ibid, 3.

6. " We have not mixed with the races of foreigners. Hence the belief in the strength and superiority of our race, the belief in our superior privileged statehood position." Ibid., 4.

7. Ibid., 5. Part of the text is underlined.

8. Wenneker here saw confirmed his earlier impressions of the use of submarines by the Japanese, as initially conveyed to him on 10 December 1934 by the commander of the submarine school, Rear Adm. Nomura Naokuni. BA-MA, RM 11/68, Attaché Report, Re: Use of submarines, torpedoes, G 44 geheim, 14.12.1934. In August, Suetsugu had turned down proposals to abolish submarines. Itō et al., eds., *Katō Kanji Nikki,* 544, document 19, Private opinion [offered] to prevent the scrapping of the submarine weapon, 08.08.1934.

9. BA-MA, RM 11/68, Translation of a conversation between Admiral Suetsugu and the naval writer Hirata, January 1935 [n.d.].

10. With that Suetsugu had made public what he had already told the Supreme War Council in the summer of 1934. Compare Itō et al., eds., *Katō Kanji nikki,* 557, document 15, Private opinions regarding armaments limitations, 08.06.1934.

11. A letter from Yamamoto to [Lt. Cdr.] Miwa Yoshitake, 10 November 1934, quoted from Agawa, *Reluctant Admiral,* 37f. The statements are remarkable in several ways. Here the violent conflict with the Anglo-Saxon sea powers is contemplated—of course only after sufficient rearmament, especially concerning airplanes. Yamamoto showed himself optimistic about the outcome. At least in November 1934 the "standard" interpretation, in the literature, of Yamamoto's opposition to a conflict with the United States cannot be correct (as, for example, in Agawa; compare ibid., 32f.). Against his supposed differences with the Fleet Faction there should be considered that he was particularly entrusted with the mission of representing, at the pretalks, the Fleet Faction's main point of emphasis, namely, parity with the United States and England. From Yamamoto's instruction, one can clearly discern that this was *conditio sine qua non* (compare ibid., 34).

Agawa's interpretation, that a previous part in the letter can be construed as critical of these instructions, is not convincing. Yamamoto had mentioned that the superior ranking leaders of the Anglo-Saxon delegations had politely listened to the "foolish views that were presented by a young guy such as myself" (ibid., 37). As Agawa himself explains, this can be taken for the normal Japanese practice of self-disparagement when mentioning one's own opinion or actions. Agawa bases his differing interpretation on the views of Yamamoto's surviving friends after World War II. One must consider, however, that at that time such a view— the admiral showing critical tendencies toward the prewar government— was seen as "politically correct," that let Yamamoto, then, appear favorably. Opposed to that, Yamamoto not only withstood the "cleansing" of the Japanese navy of the members of the Treaty Faction by Minister of the Navy Ōsumi in December 1934, but was promoted during the London preconference to vice admiral. Cf. BA-MA, RM 11/68, Attaché Report, Re: Occurrences in the Japanese and neighboring navies, abgeschl. 10.01.35, G 56 geheim, 15.01.1935; Agawa, *Reluctant Admiral*, 43; and Yamamoto's promotion, ibid., 34. Even the leader of the Fleet Faction, Suetsugu Nobumasa, commented favorably on Yamamoto's exertions for parity in the preconference. Cf. Wenneker's report BA-MA, RM 11/68, B.Nr. G 66, 24.01.1935.

12. Yamamoto seems not to have visited other capitals. Compare Chapman, "Origins," 14, and Agawa, *Reluctant Admiral*, 48f. While Agawa writes without citation that Ribbentrop had sent a secretary to London to get in contact with Yamamoto, Chapman proves that Ribbentrop himself traveled to London. He errs, however, in his assumption that he could not move Yamamoto to visit Berlin. Yamamoto was actually there. Compare PAAA, R 85951, newspaper clippings from *B.Z. am Mittag* with a picture of Yamamoto Isoroku's arrival at Bahnhof Friedrichstrasse Station on 29 January 1935, and Agawa, *Reluctant Admiral*. The picture of the newspaper clipping is identical with one in Mushakōji, *Gaikō urakōji* (Foreign policy behind the scenes), 186, which is, however, dated incorrectly from the end of the twenties. Actually Ribbentrop was in London and also visited Dr. Hack, who had good contacts with the Japanese.

   Chapman bases his assumption on a later letter of Admiral Canaris, in which he reports concerns of the Japanese ambassadors in London and Berlin (Matsudaira and Mushakōji). These did not, however, refer to the visit in general, as Chapman wrongly assumes, but on a meeting, proposed by Ribbentrop, of Yamamoto with Hitler. Compare BA-MA, RM 11/1, Canaris to ObdM. Information from General Ōshima, Abwehr-Abt- Chef 30/35 gKdos., 12.11.1935, and Agawa, *Reluctant Admiral*. Also Krebs, *Japans Deutschlandpolitik*, 1:34, mentions the visit, dating it incorrectly, however, to the beginning of March. From

Agawa and the newspaper clipping, one can gather that Yamamoto arrived on 29 January and stayed for only one or two days in Berlin. Therefore it must have been at the beginning of February.

13. Compare BA-MA, RM 11/68, Attaché Report, Re: Considering the fleet question in Japan, G 87 geheim, 27.03.1935, p. 6 of the report, and Hack papers, note of a talk with Blomberg of 25 September 1935.

14. "Meant is not just the defense of that which Japan already possesses, but also that which it one day hopes to possess, as a colony, as a protectorate or whatever else it may be called . . . . Japan will be the only power factor in this part of the world that guides the destiny of China and other parts of the Far East. That is the goal upon which all else is based, for the achieving of which the Fleet Conference shall become the next step." BA-MA, RM 11/68, Attaché Report, Re: Considering the fleet question in Japan, G 87 geheim, 27.03.1935.

15. BA-MA, RM 11/69, Attaché Report, re: German armament buildup at sea, 204, 02.05.1935.

16. Senshibu, 10 Buōbun, S-20/76, Naval Attaché in Germany to Deputy Minister of the Navy and Deputy Chief of Navy General Staff, 64 strictly secret, May 1935 (n.d.). The instructions were not very detailed.

17. BA-MA, RM 11/69, Wenneker and Dirksen to Marineleitung, 68, 12.06.1935.

18. BA-MA, RM 11/69, Attaché Report, Re: Japan and German fleet rearmament (2. Ausfertigung), G 130 geheim, 21.06.1935. The German rearmament confronted the Japanese navy with the fact that there now existed three branches of service. (Cf. Senshibu, 10 Buōbun, S-20/76, Naval Attaché in Germany to Minister of the Navy, Re: Views about the detachment of an air attaché, 30.05.1935, and Senshibu, 10 Buōbun, S-20/76, Naval Attaché in Germany to Secretary of Minister of the Navy, Re: Air matters, German air force, 04.06.1935. The interests of the German Luftwaffe were temporarily represented in Tokyo by military attaché Ott. Senshibu, 10 Buōbun, S-20/76, Note. Re: Views on the impending arrival of a German air attaché, 07.06.1935.

19. BA-M, RM 11/69, G 130 geheim, 21.06.1935.

20. Ibid., 2.

21. Ibid., 4. Dülffer, *Weimar*, 345, states that Raeder had noted by hand on the first version of the document that German participation at the Fleet Conference was no longer wanted. The first version could not be found in the BA-MA.

22. BA-MA, RM 11/1, Naval Attaché Tokyo to M IV. Report about the capabilities of the Japanese navy, MAtt 207/35 gKdos., to be delivered by safe hand only, 21.06.1935. Further copy in RM 8/1637, fol. 4ff.

23. "Despite greatest effort, I have until now searched in vain for factors that one could truly label as good—except perhaps for a high devotion to duty." Ibid., 20f. of the report.

24. Compare Wenneker's letter accompanying the report, ibid.

25. British crewmembers of submarines that lay in the harbor of Keelung (Taiwan) at the beginning of October were badly maltreated by Japanese police in this incident. The Royal Navy demanded a formal apology from the Japanese navy, which was denied. The relationship between the navies was now heavily burdened.

26. It cannot be considered impossible that the Japanese had noticed the information that the British attachés sometimes gave to Wenneker (the two incidents in which he had been able to photograph the British reports were the most important, but not the only, incidents of this kind).

27. BA-MA, RM 11/72, Attaché Report, Re: Keelung incident, 261 geheim, 24.11.1936. Concerning the maltreatment, Wenneker reported that this was the daily practice of the police, even against Japanese (ibid., 5), and that the press occasionally reported it openly but nothing happened to prevent it (ibid., 4).

28. BA-MA, RM 11/70, Attaché Report, Re: Unchanged Japanese attitude concerning the fleet question, 168 geheim, 21.11.1935.

29. Canaris to Raeder, cf. note 12. Obviously Hack was the middleman here, because his comment from 7 November 1935 is nearly identical with the letter by Canaris. See Hack papers. Krebs, *Japans Deutschlandpolitik*, 2:21, note 96, speculates that perhaps Yamamoto could have paid a second visit but considers that unlikely. Hack's 17 September 1935 comment about a conversation with Ōshima obviously refers to the visit that he made at the end of January 1935; the second proposed visit did not take place.

30. Records of the talks are not available. Merely fragmentary comments about the members are to be found on the back of the letter from Canaris. Here the Japanese ambassador and the attachés, ambassadorial secretary Inoue, Admiral Nagano, special envoy Nagai, Captain Iwashita, and Hack are mentioned.

31. BA-MA, RM 11/71, Attaché Report, Re: Japanese resignation from the fleet conference and the consequences, fol. 78, 191 geheim, 22.01.1936.

32. Ibid., fol. 79. Handwritten remark on the left margin: "For Japan only the combination of England [and] America is of importance, since it is superior to every lone power in the western Pacific even with the keeping of the 5:3 standard."

33. Ibid., fol. 81. This did not concur with other comments, especially concerning the use of submarines, of which Wenneker had already reported in 1934 and 1935: BA-MA, RM 11/68, Attaché Report, Re: Use of submarines, torpedoes, G 44 geheim, 14.12.1934, and BA-MA, RM 20/1756, MAtt to BU, Re: Night exercises with submarines. An extract from Wenneker, G 81 of 18.03.35, MAtt 671 geheim, 27.04.1935. Compare also Nomura Naokuni's comment in his memoirs, that he, when he became rear admiral and commander of the Second U Flotilla in November 1934, had mainly trained in cooperative tactics with the fleet. Nomura, *Hachijū hachinen*, 19.

34. BA-MA, RM 11/71, fol. 83. The numerous question marks on the margin of his report show, however, that the specialists in the Marineleitung were more skeptical than the attaché. To the reporting about the consequences of the fleet conference, compare also BA-MA, RM 11/71, Dirksen to Marineleitung, Relay of a report of the naval attaché about the breaking-off of the fleet conference, 15 geheim, 18.01.1936.

35. BA-MA, RM 11/71, fol. 84. Dirksen similarly judged the Japanese step. He also calculated that the navy would expand and judged the Japanese decision to "shrug off the chains of the Washington treaty" as "a decisive step of Japan on its steeply rising way to becoming the leading greater power of the Far East." BA-MA, RM 11/71, Dirksen to Foreign Office (AA), Relay of Attaché Report Nr. 191 geheim of 22.01.36 including political considerations in that context, 291, 24.01.1936.

Wenneker's observations about the IJN's posture toward the Dutch East Indies were confirmed in April when Nagano, who had just become minister of the navy, presented the Five-Minister Conference (the prime minister, the foreign minister, and the ministers of war, the navy, and finance) the "Outline of National Policy" of the navy. The United States was therein considered to be the main threat, the best outlook for independence regarding raw materials was seen in the development of the South Seas areas, and the Southwest Pacific was considered in every respect the most important region for Japan. The army immediately protested. Cf. Tsunoda, *Gendaishi shiryō*, 8:351–55, and Barnhart, *Japan Prepares*, 44. Also, further army-navy negotiations about future strategic planning in June did not bring about coordination, but rather only a general agreement to strengthen both branches of service.

36. BA-MA, RM 11/71, Attaché Report, Re: Japanese ship building plans, fol. 73, 198 geheim, 07.02.1936.

37. BA-MA, RM 11/71, Attaché Report, Re: New Japanese construction, 207 geheim, 18.03.1936.

38. BA-MA, RM 11/72, Attaché Report, Re: Naval policy matters, 256 geheim, 06.10.1936. Strict secrecy was emphasized at the end of the year, when it was made clear to Wenneker once more that even a partial disclosure of the construction plans was out of the question. BA-MA, RM 11/72, Attaché Report, Re: Naval policy matters, 269 geheim, 31.12.1936. This caused a specialist of the Marineleitung to remark in a handwritten note: "This reminds one of Russia. Where we are such good friends with the Japanese!"

39. BA-MA, RM 11/72, Attaché Report, Re: Leica-Film, 255 geheim, 06.10.1936. The plans were relatively new, so that the Marineleitung could correct its documents. See the respective handwritten commentaries, p. 2 of the report.

40. Cf. BA-MA, RM 11/72, 256 geheim, 06.10.1936, p. 4 of the report. By "southern areas" could only have been meant the Dutch East Indies. Because of its orientation to other areas, the IJN had signaled in the summer of 1936 that it understood German weapons shipments to China. BA-MA, RM 11/72, Attaché Report, Re: General von Reichenau, 240 geheim, 03.07.1936. The representative of the minister of the navy, who had told Wenneker of the resolution to tolerate shipments because of the German lack of hard currency, had merely declared that the Japanese navy, in the interest of maintaining good relations, expected to be informed beforehand. General von Reichenau was traveling in China in connection with the shipments, and the Japanese expressed the hope that he would also come to Japan.

41. He had removed most of the flag officers who belonged to the Treaty Faction from important positions at the end of 1934, parallel to the London preconsultations. Cf. chapter 12, note 35, Wenneker's report G 56 from 15.01.1935.

42. These mostly only had a "semi-active" status anyway— for example, Yamamoto Eisuke, as a member of the Supreme War Council. BA-MA, RM 11/71, Attaché Report, Re: events in the Japanese navy, fol. 156, 314, 25.03.1936.

    Nagano became, in the wake of the February coup attempt of the young army officers that led to the resignation of the government, Ōsumi's successor as minister of the navy. Yamamoto Isoroku became his deputy in December 1936.

43. Prince Fushimi Nomiya, head of the Navy General Staff. His deputy was Shimada Shigetarō. Compare to Fushimi, who was present at the dinner given by Katō Kanji during the first London conference for the German ambassador Voretzsch. PAAA, R 85950, Voretzsch to AA, J.Nr. 669, 24.03.1930.

44. In Japanese literature, the coup is customarily named after the date (26 February) as the "2-26-Incident" (*ni-niroku-jiken*). In the same manner similar occurrences from the 15th of May 1932 are named the "5-15-Incidents" (*go-jūgo-jiken*).

    The "5-15 Incident" of 15 May 1932 was initiated by young naval officers. They murdered Prime Minister Inukai Tsuyoshi and attacked several other high-ranking persons that they considered enemies of their demanded "Shōwa Restoration." This vague phrase basically referred to the abolishment of democratic structures. Although the insurgents did not get the hoped-for support from the army and the public, they were sentenced to light punishments in a public war tribunal, which gave them propaganda opportunities. This coup attempt marked the end of party cabinets in Japan. Cf. Shillony, *Revolt in Japan*, and Storry, *Double Patriots*. Shillony's *Revolt in Japan* should be the standard on the matter.

    In contrast to the May coup, the leaders of the February coup were put on trial in a non-public war tribunal that handed out seventeen death sentences. The army leadership showed itself at first quite hesitant in suppressing the revolt.

Its failure led in the army to the rise in power of the "Tōseiha" (Control Faction) as opposed to the more radical "Kōdōha" (Faction of the Imperial Way). The goal again was a "Showa Restoration." Only under the cabinet of Hiranuma did the "Kōdō Generals" in 1939 gain again more influence. Cf. Krebs, *Japans Deutschlandpolitik*, 312.

45. BA-MA, RM 11/72, Attaché Report, Re: The Japanese navy during and after the occurrences in February, 230 geheim, 06.05.1936. For the occurrences from the view of the German embassy personnel, see the reports of the *Botschaftsrat* Noebel: BA-MA, RM 11/71, fol. 179ff., chronology of events from 26 to 29 February, 867, 03.03.1936.

46. In reality his brother-in-law, who resembled Okada, was murdered. Details of the events can also be found in the reports of the U.S. attachés. See NARA, RG 38, 21950 C-9-c, Report of the U.S. Naval Attaché, Tokyo: The Japanese Army Revolt, 61, 17.03.1936; and NARA, RG 38, 21950 C-9-c, U.S. Naval Attaché, Tokyo. Army Revolt—Japanese Navy's Attitude, 66, 20.03.1936. Regarding the fleet movements during the coup, compare also NARA, RG 38 Box 112, U.S. Naval Attaché, Tokyo. Quarterly Report of Naval Activities, 1 Dec. 1935–29 Feb. 1936, Mar. 1936.

47. See BA-MA, RM 11/72, 230 geheim, 06.05.1936, p. 3 of the report.

48. Ibid., 6.

49. Commander Takada was Wenneker's informant. See chapter 11, note 11, and BA-MA, RM 11/72, 230 geheim, p. 5 of the report.

50. Admiral Katō Kanji is meant here, not to be confused with Vice Admiral Katō Takayoshi, the commander of the Second Fleet, who was the son-in-law and adopted child of Katō Kanji. He also belonged to the Fleet Faction.

51. BA-MA, RM 11/72, 230 geheim, 06.05.1936, 4.

52. Ibid.

53. Ibid., 8.

54. Thus it was Vice Admiral Kobayashi and Rear Admiral Mazaki, a brother of the general with the same name, who were believed to be close to the revolutionaries. Wenneker's reporting is confirmed by the reports of the American naval attaché (NARA, RG 38, 21950 C-9-c, The Japanese Army Revolt, 61, 17.03.1936). The report examines in detail the involvement of young officers with right-wing organizations. His further reporting (NARA, RG 38, 21950 C-9-c, Army Revolt—Japanese Navy's Attitude, 66, 20.03.1936) names additional details about personnel intrigues in the Japanese navy. So Katō Kanji became the "Genrō" of the navy after the death of Grand Admiral Tōgō in 1934. He, as well as Yamamoto Eisuke, were in the running to become prime minister after the resignation of the government. This could have been the reason for Nagano's having Yamamoto removed from the Supreme War Council.

55. The ruling also mandated that only active naval officers could assume the posts of minister of the navy or deputy minister of the navy. Until then reserve officers had been eligible, and, in the absence of the minister, the premier could be the acting minister of the navy. These regulations had long been a point of discontent with the active officers. BA-MA, RM 11/72, Attaché Report, Re: Imperial rescript, concerning appointment of the minister of the navy, 342, 22.05.1936.

56. The talk is of the "committee for the examination of organizational questions and of criteria of national policy." Cf. Tahira, *Rengō kantai,* pt.1, 288ff.

57. See BA-MA 11/72, 230 geheim, 06.05.1936, p. 14 of the report.

58. In this document the German word for "not" is underscored by hand; the word for "forceful" was underscored as Wenneker typed it. See p. 15 of the report.

59. BA-MA, RM 11/72, Attaché Report, Re: Naval policy issues, 249 geheim, 01.09.1936.

60. Obviously a reference to the Abyssinian crisis and to the Spanish Civil War. That the IJN saw a great chance for a forceful southern thrust at the time of the Abyssinian crisis can be seen by comments of Minister of the Navy Yonai from April 1937. In a conversation with Wenneker, Yonai opined that a forceful southward expansion at that time would have been most definitely successful: "No power would have been capable of withstanding Japan. America was too preoccupied with inner difficulties, and England was so weak that it could not even force Italy to submit to its will." Ruefully, Yonai added that this had been a singular chance for Japan and would not return soon. BA-MA, RM 11/73, fol. 81ff., Attaché Report, Re: Naval policy issues, B.Nr. 293 geheim, 29.04.1937. Yonai's observations on the subject can also be found in fol. 90.

Chapter 10. Drawing Closer

1. Senshibu, 10 Buōbun, s-20/76, Secretary of Minister of the Navy to Naval Attaché in Germany, Re: Information on Hashagen, Kambō 3702, 22.08.1934.

2. Ibid. Compare also BA-MA, RM 20/1756, Note relating to MAtt 1333/34, Re: Japan, 26.10.1934. Wenneker's report has not been preserved. It mentioned that the gimbals used on IJN ships came only from the German firm Anschütz, and that in case of war with the United States they planned to use their submarines offensively as destroyers of merchant shipping along the U.S. West Coast. This was exactly congruent with German views.

Chapman, "Japan and German Naval Policy," 238, contradicts this account when, without citation of sources, he attributes to Hashagen and Nomura Naokuni exactly opposite comments. This is only true of Nomura, who in December corrected what Hashagen had reported. Cf. Wenneker's report, BA-MA, RM 11/68, G 44 geheim, 14.12.1934. Hashagen seems to have been busy in Shanghai and came to Germany in November 1934.

3. PAAA, R 85951, *Information No. 455 des Japanischen Vereins in Deutschland*, 20.05.1935; newspaper clipping from *Berliner Börsen-Zeitung*, "Japanischer Offiziersbesuch in Deutschland," unnumbered, 21.05.1935; and *Deutsch-Japanische Nachrichten* 19, "Japanischer Marinebesuch in Deutschland. Ehrung deutscher Seehelden durch japanische Offiziere," unnumbered, 23.05.1935. This mission had left Japan in mid-December 1934 and returned there at the end of August 1935. Its head, Matsunago Sadaichi, was a specialist in artillery and destroyers. He later became vice admiral and held, inter alia, the post of chief of training of the Naval Aviation Department in World War II.

4. More precise details about Okuda could not be found. BA-MA, RM 1169, Attaché Report, Re: Japanese naval officers in Germany, 223, 04.06.1935.

5. Hack papers. Hack's notes at the end of 1935 about his planned trip. He planned to arrive in Tokyo at the beginning of February. Records about this meeting seem not to have been passed down.

6. BA-MA, RM 11/71, fol. 62, Attaché Report, Re: Secondment to Germany (2.Ausf.), 186 geheim, 15.01.1936. The specialists were Captain Fukuda Ryōzō, who later became vice admiral and commander of the China fleet, and Commander Owada, about whom no specific details could be found. They returned to Japan in August 1935.

7. This was correct for the deployment of the naval technicians Sugiyama and Nakamura (BA-MA, RM 11/72, Attaché Report, Re: Events in the Japanese Navy, 348, 09.06.1936.), of Lt. Cdr. Yamashita Kanesumi (engineer) and Senior Lt. Yamazaki Shinji (engineer) (BA-MA, RM 11/72, Attaché Report, Re: Secondment to Germany. [2.Ausf.], 354, 02.07.1936), and of Commander Uchida, an expert for explosives (BA-MA, RM 11/72, Attaché Report, Re: Secondment to Germany, 368, 31.08.1936).

At least some of the officers belonged to the Kantoku; certainly Yamashita and Yamazaki did. Wenneker labeled them as the "supervising officers in weapons construction matters of the ship construction bureau." This also held true for the naval attaché assigned to Berlin in February 1936, Commander Kojima. The Navy Ministry informed Wenneker that Kojima was at the same time appointed "delegate for ship and weapons matters in the ship construction bureau and for weapons matters in the Naval Aviation Department." See BA-MA, RM 11/71, Attaché Report, Re: New naval attaché for Berlin, 294, 06.02.1936.

8. BA-MA, RM 11/72, Attaché Report, Re: Secondments to Germany, 375, 01.09.1936. Wada had early on specialized in aerotechnology, was from 1922 to 1925 at the Kantoku, and had traveled until 1924 through Europe and America for study purposes. He was then instructor at the submarine school and a member of the aviation-technical research department in Hiroshima, before resuming studies in Europe and the United States in 1927, after which he became a member of the

technical section of the Naval Aviation Department. There he was a member and later leader of a special staff, whose apparent mission was to raise the fighting power of naval aviation.

In 1936 he undertook yet another study trip to foreign countries, during which he also visited Germany. He returned in the middle of 1937 and became head of the technical section of the Naval Aviation Department and later head of the aerotechnical arsenal of the navy. Near the end of the World War II he was vice admiral and the head of the Naval Aviation Department. About his companion, Commander Katahira, no further details could be found.

9. BA-MA, RM 11/71, Attaché Report, Re: New naval attaché for Berlin, 294, 06.02.1936.

10. Ibid., p. 2 of the report.

11. Takada Toshitane, an artillery and destroyer specialist, had been in Germany from 1930 to 1932. Subsequently, he taught at the Naval War College and worked for the 3rd Group of the Navy General Staff and the planning committee of the cabinet. At war's end he was a rear admiral. Takada spoke German and took care of Wenneker, who very much regretted his subsequent transfer within the Naval Ministry. BA-MA, RM 11/69, Attaché Report, Re: [Cdr.] Takada, 225, 04.06.1935.

12. PAAA, R 33434, RWM to AA, Re: Training cruises 1935/36, Mar.B.Nr. 58 A Ic geheim, 01.02.1935. Ambassador Dirksen actually emphatically proposed a visit in Japan. PAAA, R 33436, Dirksen to AA, J.Nr. 973, II M 988, 26.03.1935.

13. Here, too, the comparison between the two existing travel plans is interesting. The older version scheduled a stay in Japanese waters of twenty-three days, the longest of the entire trip, including a stay in Miyajima, a harbor on the inland sea where foreigners were only admitted with misgivings. Also notable is that another attempt was made to show the flag in China. For this purpose Nanking and Shanghai were to be visited, for a total of sixteen days—the second longest stay in the waters of a foreign country. The intention of "showing the flag" becomes especially clear considering that, only in these two harbors, among all sixteen, there was to be no training but only, exclusively, representation. BA-MA, RM 6/234, fol. 68, ObdM to Behncke: Plans for cruises abroad 1935–36 of cruisers *Emden* and *Karlsruhe* and the battleship *Schlesien*, OKM 948 A Ic, 23.08.1935. In the final version, both Chinese harbors were deleted, the representation harbors were divided up equally over the whole journey, Miyajima was canceled, and the Japanese stay shortened to sixteen days (the second longest stay of the journey). The *Karlsruhe* now spent nearly a month in U.S. harbors. BA-MA, RM 6/234, fol. 126, Plan of cruise of *Karlsruhe,* enclosure to A IVc 3344/35 geheim, 1935 (n.d.).

14. BA-MA, RM 11/71, fol. 169, Attaché Report, Re: Stay of cruiser *Karlsruhe* in Nagasaki and Kobe, 214 geheim, 25.03.1936. The reports of the ship's captain and the consulate general of Kobe have not been preserved.

15. Compare also PAAA, R 85951, Reports of the Domei Agency, no number, 07.03.1936.

16. BA-MA, RM 11/72, Attaché Report, Re: Events in the Japanese navy, 353, 27.06.1936. Time and composition were frequently changed, for a period of time even canceled altogether. Compare BA-MA, RM 11/72: Attaché Report, Re: Visit of Japanese training squadron in Germany, 391, 04.11.1936, and Attaché Report, Re: Cruise of Japanese training squadron, 412, 30.12.1936. Because of the Keelung incident, which considerably strained Japanese-British relations, it was for a time even doubtful if any Japanese ships would be deployed. Visits of the British Far East Squadron were also delayed. BA-MA, RM 11/72, Attaché Report, Re: Naval policy issues, 269 geheim, 31.12.1936.

17. BA-MA, RM 11/71, fol. 198, A III to M IV to naval attaché Tokyo, Re: Submarines in Vladivostok, 16 A III, 02.01.1936.

18. BA-MA, RM 11/71, fol. 197, Attaché Report, Re: Submarines in Vladivostok, 212 geheim, 24.03.1936.

19. A handwritten remark to a question concerning intelligence trading points to a file that was maintained for this purpose and was entitled, "Intelligence exchange with Japan about Russia." The remark is dated 4 September. The file is seemingly not preserved. BA-MA, RM 11/71, fol. 199, M IV to A III, Re: Intelligence exchange with Japanese navy, MAtt 1049 II.Ang geheim, 28.07.1936.

20. The negotiations had begun without participation of the Japanese navy in the summer of 1935, and they heard of it only at the end of December 1935 through a statement by Hack to the naval attaché in Berlin, Yokoi. During Hack's trip to Japan at the beginning of 1936, he also instructed the secretary of Minister of the Navy Kojima. The naval leadership was skeptical about the treaty, since it saw, in its special emphasis on an anti-Soviet policy, "water on the mills" of its competitor, the army. Compare, Tahira, *Rengō kantai,* pt. 1, 336.

21. BA-MA, RM 11/72, Attaché Report, Re: Naval policy matters, 265 geheim, 01.12.1936. That the Americans no longer had the best sources in Berlin was evident in the report of the U.S. Army attaché that a Japanese admiral had initiated negotiations in Berlin fifteen months before. NARA, RG 165, Box 1640, U.S. Army Attaché, Berlin. The German-Japanese Anti-Bolshevist Agreement, 2657-B-792(1), 30.11.1936. That the negotiations had been kept secret for a long time vis-à-vis the navy can be seen by a note from Hack about the secrecy of the talks from 25 November 1935 (see papers of Friedrich-Wilhelm Hack).

22. See part 1. Concerning Germany's rise to the English position, as main supplier of modern technology for the Japanese navy after the end of the British-Japanese Alliance in December 1921, see also Tahira, *Rengō kantai*, pt. 1, 332.

23. The fact that the Japanese navy could afford to accept Germany's lack of hard currency as a reason of the German armaments shipments to China in the summer of 1936 is explained by the fact that it was primarily a problem for the army, less so for the navy.

24. Whether the Kriegsmarine's final goal was to be recognized as the second-best sea power, equal to or supplanting England, is the subject of the "continuity" debate. While authors such as Salewski and Rahn represent the first thesis, the second thesis has achieved a new foundation through the works of Gerhard Schreiber, who presents a broadened perspective. His interpretation takes into account the attitude of senior officers of the Reichs- and Kriegsmarine who had been socialized in the Imperial German Navy, which in turn had been decisively influenced by Tirpitz.

25. Despite little previous contact, the two navies were similar enough to exchange friendly sentiments such as "Samurai spirit," "Prussianism," "valuing national goods and merits," "national cohesion," or the striving for a "peace of honor, justice, and equality" on ship visits.

26. Idealistic aspects, as evidenced by Maeda, should not be discounted. Their influence is hard to estimate, however, and they were seen by Wenneker very soberly.

27. Compare the observations of Lieutenant Commander Maeda at the farewell of the German commission, chapter 9, note 71.

28. At least one can gather from the above-mentioned conclusions how the third revision of the "Guidelines for the Defense of the Empire," in which the United States, the Soviet Union, China, and England were mentioned as potential enemies, was interpreted by the IJN. The guidelines were decreed in June 1936. In the same month Wenneker gathered, during his conversations with officers, that the anti-British sentiment had become very sharp; that a war with the United States, on the other hand, was considered to be "crazy"; and that war against the Soviet Union was characterized as "national misfortune." China did not count in the overall maritime perspective.

29. One will have to consider that the bureau was overburdened in this time of hectic development. Witzell already seemed to mistrust the Japanese at the time of the report from Coeler and Wenneker about their inspection of the *Akagi*.

30. The role that Reichswehrminister Blomberg played here is not calculable; however, it seems to have been small.

31. BA-MA, RM 11/73, Attaché Report, Re: Visit of Japanese cruiser *Ashigara* in Kiel, 286 geheim, 08.04.1937, fol. 38. This is also the only reference to the visit of the

Emden in Japan in 1937. The reports seem not to be passed down in the naval files or in those of the Foreign Ministry.

32. The *Ashigara* left Yokosuka at the beginning of April and arrived on 9 May 1937 in Portsmouth, where she stayed for nearly two weeks. After that the ship sailed to Kiel and stayed there for a week. Originally her departure from there was planned for 30 May. Since it spent the Japanese Naval Day (27 May, day of the Battle of Tsushima) in Kiel, the Germans suggested that the ship take part in the festivities for the German counterpart (day of the Battle of Jutland, 31 May). The Japanese agreed immediately and stayed a day longer. Ibid., fol. 34 and 36.

33. Ibid., fol. 35. Wenneker reported, notably, that the Japanese wishes were presented in a very demanding way. It was, by the way, not true that all German cruiser commanders were introduced to the Tennō. Kobayashi was probably well informed about this, because the Japanese were in general very aware of etiquette.

Wenneker was apparently irritated by Kobayashi's behavior during a social event, which could explain the somewhat unfavorable undertone of his report. His comments on Kobayashi's person support this speculation: "He is counted as very capable and one predicts a great future for him. This I would like to grant him, if the large quantities of alcohol, which he obviously (and as rumor has it) . . . imbibes, are also in the future not detrimental to his health." (Here the document is marked by the sarcastic handwritten commentary on the left margin, "Prost!") Kobayashi, according to Wenneker, was very popular with the younger officers, since "he has kept himself young, participates in everything and is not a spoilsport."

At Wenneker's teahouse party Kobayashi had suddenly disappeared and then returned a short time later with a white-powdered face, disguised as a geisha, and had performed several dances. In describing the event, Wenneker characterized other officers present as the "best types of Japanese sea officers," obviously praising them in contrast to Kobayashi without expressly saying as much. Cf. ibid., fol. 36. In actuality Kobayashi's behavior was, according to Japanese standards, particularly friendly. Wenneker, at this time not fully acquainted with some Japanese customs, misunderstood it.

34. Maeda had looked after the German aircraft carrier commission in 1935.

35. Among them there were two cameramen who recorded a 45-minute film about the journey, in which the stay in Kiel and the visit of the crew in Berlin were especially emphasized. Also, one of the civilians on board made public speeches about his travel experiences after his return to Japan. About two-thirds of the content dealt with the description of the hearty welcome extended by the German populace. The speaker reported that crewmembers had time and again

come to him with "tears in their eyes" and reported to him the overwhelmingly friendly reception. Wenneker's successor, Lietzmann, considered the film to be the best that he "had ever seen in this area." The propaganda motives of the movie, however, show in the very fact of the mentioned civilians' presence on board. BA-MA, RM 11/73, fol. 307, Attaché Report, Re: Repercussions of the journey of the cruiser *Ashigara* to Europe, 536, 26.10.1937.

36. Cf. BA-MA, RM 11/73, fol. 37.

37. BA-MA, RM 11/73, Attaché Report Re: Naval policy issues, 293 geheim, 29.04.1937, fol. 82.

38. Ibid., fol. 81. Wenneker's observations are confirmed by the reports of his U.S. colleague, who reported that Yonai, answering questions in parliament on 15 February, had carefully pointed out that the budgetary allotment for the navy had to rise in future. The U.S. attaché also had information from a secret meeting of the budget committee of the parliament. According to it, Yonai had declared that although Japan remained committed to the principles of nonthreatening and noninvasion, it still had to maintain an adequate force in the western Pacific. The U.S.-Japan maritime strength ratio was 10:9 at the time of the Shanghai incident and had sunk to 10:8 in the previous year. If this would not be counteracted, then by the end of 1941 a ratio of under 10:6 would be reached.

After the removal of the Washington limitations, Japan was now free in the selection of ship types that were deemed necessary, and there was no reason to join the agreements between Great Britain, the United States, France, and Italy, especially on the question of caliber limitations. These considerations led to the IJN's demands for a higher budget. Despite all assurances that there would be no armaments race, the IJN would build more and bigger ships and stay away from arms limitation treaties. NARA, RG 38, M975, Roll 3, U.S. Naval Attaché, Tokyo. Navy Policy Outlined by Minister in Diet, 46, 27.02.1937.

39. BA-MA, RM 11/73, Attaché Report, Re: Naval policy issues, 293 geheim, 29.04.1937, fol. 84f.

40. Ibid., fol. 82. He heard from Nomura that the question of the fortification of bases was the only exception, in which the Japanese navy thought about agreeing to treaty limitations, since a possible fortification of Manila, Hong Kong, and Singapore gave them headaches (fol. 86).

41. Telegram no. 183 from 21 July 1937. Here he reported from a "solid source" forty-five thousand tons displacement and a main caliber of 40 cm. The document apparently not passed down, is, however, mentioned in a report by Wenneker's successor, Lietzmann: BA-MA, RM 11/3, Bl. 118, Naval Attaché Tokyo to MAtt, Re: Japanese capital ship building, 2/38 gKdos., 10.01.1938.

42. Ibid., Bl. 119. Lietzmann received his data (forty-six thousand tons displacement and forty 6cm guns in triple turrets) from an "Italian, seemingly reliable source."

43. BA-MA, RM 11/73, Attaché Report, Re: Naval policy issues, 293 geheim, 29.04.1937, fol. 89. Compare Wenneker's similarly preferential treatment in comparison with the Soviet attaché in November of the previous year, chapter 10, note 27.

44. BA-MA, RM 11/73, fol. 69, Attaché Report, Re: Detention of SS *Potsdam* in Yokohama, 290 geheim, 22.04.1937.

45. BA-MA, RM 11/73, Attaché Report, Re: Naval policy issues, 293 geheim, 29.04.1937, 6.

46. Ibid.

47. Cf. chapter 10, note 25. The reluctance with which this happened was revealing of Japanese attitudes in the matter. Seemingly only upon the intervention of Prince Chichibu, who was in England for the coronation festivities, was any action taken in the matter. In a letter to the British consul, the governor of Taiwan expressed regret for the incident and explained that the Japanese policemen had been reprimanded for "touching" the British sailors and using "inappropriate" language, which could be traced to their lacking knowledge of English. When the contents of an explanation concerning these matters from the British Foreign Ministry was made known in the lower house in Japan, a storm of indignation rose in the Japanese press. The government was accused of shamefully giving in, since the investigation had concluded that no fault could be found with the Japanese policemen. Wenneker commented: "[This proves a point] that one can make time and again. To admit that one has made a mistake is almost impossible for a Japanese with regard to a 'foreigner.'" BA-MA, RM 11/73, 293 geheim, 29.04.1937, p. 8 of the report.

48. Ibid., 9. It seems that Yonai belonged to that wing of the Japanese navy which in 1937 was not yet convinced that naval aviation had replaced battleships as the main means of warfare on the sea, because he initiated his explanation with the words: "Those of you who time and again see salvation in the airplane state that the worth of the seagoing vessel has considerably lost power against it. This viewpoint is nonsense." The airplane he described as being a "valuable addition."

49. This became clear during secret meetings of the budget committee of the parliament, where Yonai had pointed to the development of the tonnage relationship between the navies of Japan and the United States to justify further resources for fleet armament. British armament seems not to have played a role here. Compare the report of the U.S. naval attaché, paraphrased in note 38.

50. See BA-MA, 11/73, Attaché Report, Re: Naval policy issues, 10. The difference between Yonai's statements and those of other senior naval officers (for example

Nomura Naokuni) is noteworthy. He actually seems to have increasingly stood in opposition with his subordinates in the Navy Ministry on other issues. He himself told Wenneker this shortly after the parliament dissolved. Similar things occurred also in the question of alliance negotiations with Germany a year later. Cf. Krebs, *Japans Deutschlandpolitik,* 1:167.

51. BA-MA, RM 11/73, fol. 92ff., Attaché Report, Re: Repeated political demands by Japanese navy, 295 geheim, 03.05.1937.

52. That Suetsugu—who was, so to speak, the heir of Katō Kanji, the main enemy of the Fleet Treaty in the navy—had an especially strong backing from young officers was already made clear in Wenneker's earlier reports. Compare Suetsugu's characterization as a "demigod of the young officers," in Wenneker's report, G 66 geheim, 24 January 1935, mentioned in note 44 above.

53. Ibid., 4. Compare to this the similar phrasing and tenor of the report of the U.S. naval attaché paraphrased in note 38.

54. Ibid., p. 6 of the report.

55. Ibid.

56. Ibid., 7.

57. BA-MA, RM 11/73, fol. 262f., Attaché Report, Re: Occupation of islands by the Japanese, 323 geheim, 01.11.1937. Haushofer quoted a British cabinet member, who had supposedly explained that a Japanese movement into northern China was for England a step on the little toe; to the Yangtze, a step on the foot; in southern China, however, a kick in the stomach—which the British could not tolerate.

Chapter 11. Bargains and Treaties, 1938–1939

1. BA-MA, RM 8/1637, fol. 26ff., The conflict in East Asia. Report of Haushofer to Raeder. 13.12.37, Enclosure Skl. Ia 1217/38 gKdos., 05.12.1937.

2. Ibid., p. 11 of Haushofer's report.

3. Haushofer here referred to the Japanese air attacks that had in the meantime engulfed all of China and spoke of a "great psychological mishap." In China there occurred, after World War I, the first attempt to wage an air war on a large scale. This was also an object of interest for Western countries because of their war experience with this still relatively young weapons system. Ibid., p. 13 of the report.

4. Ibid., p. 14 of the report.

5. BA-MA, RM 11/73, fol. 518, Attaché Report, Re: Incidents *Panay* and *Ladybird,* 359 geheim, 30.12.1937.

6. "One wants to live in the present and future in a tolerable relationship with the United States. The economic interests form the foundation that has allowed the hostility of yesterday to strongly recede into the background. Different, the attitude toward England." Underlined by hand in the original document. Ibid., p. 2 of the report.

7. Ibid., 3.

8. BA-MA, RM 11/4, Bl. 244ff., Naval Attaché Tokyo to MAtt, Re: Attitude of Japanese navy with regard to England, 36/38 gKdos., 04.08.1938.

9. Ibid., p. 3 of the report. Nomura's confidant was Lieutenant Commander Yoshida. More precise information about this officer could not be found.

10. Ibid.

11. BA-MA, RM 11/4, Naval Attaché Tokyo to MAtt, Re: Attitude of Japanese navy with regard to England, 4.

12. Inagaki Ayao was an artillery specialist and had in 1929–30 traveled through various Western countries for a year. After that he became lecturer at the Naval War College, served in the Navy General Staff, and was plenipotentiary of the IJN at the London Fleet Conference of 1935. As such, he officially represented the final break of Japan with the fleet limitation treaty. That he was selected for this could be a clue to his not very friendly attitude toward the Anglo-Saxon sea powers. After numerous ship postings (as on the aircraft carrier *Kaga*) he became rear admiral and, under Yamamoto Isoroku, head of the general section of the Naval Aviation Department. Later he became, after further postings to the Navy General Staff, commandant of the Naval War College and a member of the supreme technical council of the IJN. He died in 1942.

13. BA-MA, RM 11/4, Naval attaché Tokyo to MAtt, Re: Attitude of Japanese navy with regard to England, 4.

14. Ibid., 5.

15. Ibid.

16. This fact was obviously known to the Kriegsmarine. The weakness of the Royal Navy in the Far East was revealed by investigations at the Marineakademie of the Kriegsmarine in February 1938. The disposition overview of the British fleet showed an aircraft carrier at the China station as the only heavy unit, to which seven cruisers and a few smaller units also belonged. The neighboring Australian, New Zealand, East Indian, and African stations were protected only by a few cruisers and no heavy units. BA-MA, RM 7/1766, *Anlagen zu dem am 16.2.1938 von Korvettenkapitän (E) Gebeschus vor der Marineakademie gehaltene Vortrag über Englands Seerüstung* (Enclosures to the lecture on English armament at sea by Cdr. Gebeschus held at the Naval War College on 16 February 1938, unnumbered, 16.02.1938). See especially Enclosure XI (fol. 23).

17. BA-MA, RM 8/1601, fol. 1ff., *Betrachtungen zum Kriegsfall Japan-England bezw. Japan-anglesächsische Mächte,* B.Nr. 39/38 gKdos., 27.08.1938.

18. Compare Lietzmann's letter to his analysis in BA-MA, RM 8/1601, fol. 17, B. Nr. 452 geheim, 30.08.1938.

19. "The army obviously has a clearer picture about the ties between the Anglo-Saxon powers than the navy does." Ibid.

20. "... unless, if England is decisively tied down elsewhere, the Japanese are forced by fate to take advantage of a chance that might not return again." Ibid.

21. Ibid., 2.

22. "The English rule of the sea, however, lives and dies with the British bases, particularly Singapore." Ibid.

23. Ibid., p. 3 of the report and ibid., 15: "One must at least consider, however, the very grave possibility for Japan of an active military intervention of the U.S.A. in favor of England."

24. Ibid., 4. These observations simply verify facts that had been known to the Kriegsmarine since May 1937. At that time Wenneker had presented a detailed report about the weaknesses of the Japanese armaments industry. See BA-MA, RM 11/73, fol. 107ff., Attaché Report, Re: Japanese wartime economy, 298 geheim, 07.05.1935. In this paper he marked the armaments industrial position of Japan with five theses: "1) The food supply that is fully sufficient during peacetime would be totally inadequate during times of war. 2) The raw materials basis of Japan and especially of the most important armaments industries is very small. 3) Production capacity, especially of the important armaments industries, is still small today. 4) In industry, small and medium production facilities still dominate. 5) Industry is located in areas that are particularly unfavorable for air defense." He detected special weaknesses in the iron and steel industries, the inadequate oil supply, the machine tool industry, and the production of aircraft and diesel motors. Ibid., fol. 108. Pertaining to the last two points Wenneker explained that the creation of precision machine tools had not yet been mastered and that these were mainly imported from the United States and Germany. Ibid., fol. 116f. Concerning the aircraft and diesel motors, the German specialist Dr. Kaumann had pointed out to him that the most efficient and strongest models, which formed the basis for new developments in Japanese firms, all originated from the German firms Daimler-Benz, Junkers, and BMW. British, American, and French firms apparently would not commit their best products to the Japanese. Cf. ibid., fol. 119f. Cooperation in this area between the German and Japanese navies is already provable for 1924. The value of this report is indicated by the handwritten remark of the analyst for the intelligence service in the Skl. (A III): "A welcome addition to the already existing material about this area." Ibid., fol. 107.

25. Probably a reference to the mutinies that occurred in the Royal Navy in the early thirties.

26. BA-MA, RM 8/1601, 27.08.1938, fol. 5f.

27. Ibid., fol. 11.

28. Ibid., fol. 9. The text was underlined by hand.

29. Ibid., fol. 7f.

30. Ibid., fol. 14f.

31. Ibid., fol. 15.

32. "The reasons for eventual Japanese expansion into the south are known. They are given by fate and will unavoidably bring Japan into collision with the British Empire. The British Empire will have to fight for its position. If Japan wants to achieve its war goal—lone preeminence in East Asia, pushing the English out of this area, conquering of *Lebensraum* in the south, together with the sources of raw materials, invasion of New Guinea and Australia, etc.— then it must subdue and destroy British sea power in the East. This will be in the long run only possible through a final and irreversible capturing of Singapore. An attack by Japan upon a British Empire that is not at the same time considerably bound by another conflict means a great risk and is improbable. The leadership of the navy obviously recognizes this, even if within the younger officer corps there are frequently thoughts about a surprise attack. But even against a bound England, an effective movement by the Japanese must be preceded by the creation of full readiness. This demands . . . at least more time." Ibid., fol. 15f.

   As an example for the attitudes of the hawks in the Japanese navy, Lietzmann had reported in November on a presentation by the press officer of the Navy Ministry, Captain Sekine, at the Imperial University Tokyo, in which he, also with force, had advocated achieving Japanese preeminence in Southern China, the South Pacific, and the maritime provinces of the USSR. Lietzmann, however, saw such appearances merely as "propaganda of the radical wing," in which there was hardly any danger for the political or military leadership. BA-MA, RM 11/73, fol. 411ff., Attaché Report, Re: Foreign political objectives of radical wing, 599, 30 November 1937.

33. Compare Wenneker's report about a comment by a representative of the Navy Ministry, B.Nr. 34 geheim, 3 July 1936. See BA-MA, RM 11/72.

34. BA-MA, RM 11/3, Naval Attaché Tokyo to MAtt, Re: Foreign deliveries of war materials to China, 8/37 gKdos., 23.10.1937.

35. Ibid., fol. 59. The actual attitude of the Kriegsmarine regarding the conflict in the Far East is probably shown in a statement to the German warships in deployment to Spain about two months earlier, wherein there was added a comment by hand: "Continuation of economic trade with China is striven for." BA-MA, RM 20/1406, OKM to BdSp, FT 1618 gKdos., 02.09.1937.

36. This seems to be a British attempt, since Great Britain was especially heavily attacked in the Japanese press in connection with shipments to China, to

remove England somewhat from the firing line and perhaps also drive a wedge between Germany and Japan. Compare Lietzmann's B.Nr. 8/37, fol. 58; BA-MA, RM 11/3.

37. Ibid., fol. 60f. Lietzmann's attitude is markedly different from either Wenneker's or Canaris's. While the latter two would clearly disagree with the Japanese in the pursuit of the economic interests of the German Reich (Canaris), or at least insist exactingly upon "counter-services" (Wenneker), Lietzmann here did not even attempt a weighing of interests.

38. BA-MA, RM 11/3, Naval Attaché Tokyo to MAtt relating to Bericht 8/37, Re: Foreign armament shipments to China, 11/37, M 191/37 gKdos., 05.11.1937. Throughout 1938 the Gunreibu supplied lists to Lietzmann (compare his reports B.Nr. 14/38, 28.02.1938 and 21/38 from 23.04.1938 [both BA-MA, RM 11/3], such as 25/38 of 30.05.1938, 27/38 of 16.06.1938, 35/38 of 04.08.1938 and the last, 38/38, of 24.08.1938 [BA-MA, RM 11/4]). The first list alone, covering five months, showed shipments for more than a hundred million rounds of rifle ammunition and twenty thousand crates of bombs and seventy aircraft, as well as diverse light weapons and railroad material. The listed amounts increased with each month.

39. BA-MA, RM 11/3, fol. 77, Note: Result of consultations of ObdM with Reichskriegsminister 12.11.37. Chinese armament orders, M 186/37 gKdos., 16.11.1937. It refers to check number one, the copy that was signed by Raeder and Blomberg.

40. Checks number 9 and 10; the latter is Raeder's personal copy. BA-MA, RM 11/3, fol. 75, and RM 7/1101.

41. Ibid.

42. An addendum to the footnote of the "internal naval" copy of the named document reads: "From this it is further to be concluded that a Chinese building instruction or construction supervision commission is not to be present for longer periods at the docks and factories." BA-MA, RM 7/1101, ObdM to A, Re: Result of consultations ObdM with Reichskriegsminister 12.11.37, M 186/37 II.Ang. gKdos., 19.11.1937.

43. BA-MA, RM 11/73, Attaché Report, Re: Foreign weapons shipments to China, 337 geheim, 26.11.1937. This was only one of many British attempts to drive a wedge between the Japanese navy and the Kriegsmarine by giving the Japanese information about German shipments to China. About a further incident of this nature, Lietzmann reports at the beginning of February 1938 that Captain Kondō named him British figures, according to which in the second half of 1937 62 percent of the China shipments came from Germany, 21 percent from Italy, 11 percent from France, and 3 percent from Great Britain. Kondō requested—even

though there was "no doubt" about the falseness of these numbers—that they nonetheless "be passed along to the OKM for instruction and reverification." BA-MA, RM 11/3, fol. 138, Naval Attaché Tokyo to MAtt, Re: Armament shipments to China, 9/38 gKdos., 07.02.1938.

44. BA-MA, RM 7/1101, fol. 216f., MAtt to Naval Attaché Tokyo, Re: Chinese Armament orders, B.Nr.MAtt 196/37 gKdos., 26.11.1937. A copy is in RM 11/3, fol. 82.

45. Ibid.

46. BA-MA, RM 11/3, fol. 93. Ausl. If to MAtt relating to (with reference to) MAtt 191/37 from 24.11.37 and report, naval attaché Tokyo from 23.10.37, Re: Foreign armament shipments to China, W.A. 663/37 gKdos., 14.12.1937.

47. BA-MA, RM 11/3, fol. 283ff. Canaris to AA relating to Mar.Att. Tokyo 9/38 and 14/38, Re: German armament shipments to China, OKW 464/38 Ausl. If gKdos., 18.06.1938. Compare also BA-MA, RM 11/3, fol. 286, MAtt to T, Comment to naval attaché Tokyo 9/38, 14/38 and 21/38, Re: German armament shipments to China, MAtt 127/38 gKdos., 28.06.1938, and BA-MA, RM 11/4, fol. 110, OKW Ausl If (Bürkner) to MAtt, Comment to naval attaché Tokyo 9/38 and 14/38, Re: German armament shipments to China, OKW 682/38 Ausl. If gKdos., 30.07.1938, as well as BA-MA, RM 11/4, fol. 111, MAtt to Naval Attaché Tokyo, Comment to MAtt 127/38 of 28.6.38, and naval attaché Tokyo 9/38 and 14/38, Re: German armament shipments to China, M 176/38 gKdos., 04.08.1938.

48. Ibid., fol. 285.

49. BA-MA, RM 7/1126, fol. 7ff., A Ic to A Ia, Re: Question of declaration of war of Japan vs. China, 14.01.1938. See fol. 11.

50. BA-MA, RM 11/3, fol. 157ff., Political report of Dirksen to AA, Comment to naval attaché Tokyo 8/38, J 314/38 geheim, 26.01.1938. Especially see fol. 159.

51. BA-MA, RM 11/3, fol. 187ff., Naval Attaché Tokyo to Raeder, 16/38, M 59/38 gKdos., 05.03.1938. Lietzmann sent a report of Noebels in which was stated, among other things, "that according to authentic statements received by members of the embassy from trustworthy sources (particularly from a ship officer on one of the large German fast steamers and a German journalist living in Hong Kong for the time being), enormous amounts of German war material have recently been unloaded in Hong Kong, while Japanese agents stood at the pier and took notes. The consequences we shall soon feel" (fol. 195f.). Passages are underlined by hand in the document. Compare also the explanations of Ernst Heinkel about aircraft (He 111) shipments via ship to China in 1938, beginning an export unprecedented until World War II. The RLM had agreed because of the lack of hard currency. Thorwaldt, *Stürmisches Leben*, 326. The rationale for weapons exports as a method of gaining hard currency can

be verified in the naval files: BA-MA, RM 7/1101, fol. 227f., OKW to OKH, OKM and ObdL, Re: Securing the importation of strategic raw materials by means of export profits, OKW Az. 66f. 21c W Stb W Wi Nr.2023/38 g.K.III gKdos., 13.07.1938 (also RM 11/4, fol. 17f.); as well as BA-MA, RM 7/1101, fol. 229ff., Notes about a conference OKW W.Stb. W.Wi on 15.07.1938 10 Uhr, Re: Securing the importation of important raw materials by export profits; Reference: W Stb. W.Wi 2023/38., B.Nr. B Stat 1216 gKdos. II.Ang. gKdos., 15.07.1938. As to the China shipments, also compare Chapman's clue that the Foreign Ministry in 1937 had knowledge of a spy ring of the Japanese navy that observed the transportation of war materials for China through the Suez Canal. Chapman, "Japan, Germany and the International Political Economy of Intelligence," 40.

52. BA-MA, RM 11/3, fol. 228ff., Naval Attaché Tokyo to MAtt, Re: Issues of steamer *Crefeld* of Norddeutschen Lloyd Bremen, 22/38, M 98/38 gKdos., 19.04.1938.

53. He commented : "It was necessary during the course of these negotiations to clearly point out to the Japanese what the German navy, according to 'German bushido spirit,' would do in the situation, if a ship of the befriended Japanese nation had been forced to stop in a similarly bad condition within German waters." Ibid., p. 2 of the report.

54. Ibid., 3.

55. Letter of Captain Oelrich to Lietzmann, copy, 3f. of the report.

56. Ibid., 4.

57. Ibid., 5.

58. Ibid.

59. Ibid. In the Japanese army, Schubert seemingly received more cooperation. Schubert probably would not have been granted insights by the IJN even without the problem of the German support for China. The Japanese navy, even before the China war, had not tended to divulge information on tactical and operational deployments. Moreover, Schubert was an air force man and thus belonged to a branch of service to whom friendly relations between the navies did not automatically apply.

60. BA-MA, RM 11/4, fol. 25ff., Naval Attaché Tokyo and Deputy Military Attaché to Raeder, 23/38, M 101/38 gKdos., 07.05.1938, Report: "Situation in the Japanese-Chinese conflict, end of April '38." In it they point to the failed Japanese plans, the fact that Japanese forces were insufficient for decisive military operations in China, and the dilemma that no politician or officer in Japan could suggest a peaceful settlement of the China problem without immediately being in danger of assassination attempts by "activist elements."

61. Compare BA-MA, RM 11/4, fol. 87ff., Naval Attaché Tokyo to Raeder, 30/38, J.Nr. 1358/38 gKdos., 06.07.1938. Transmission of a report of Noebel. Lists about the

German shipments were received by Lietzmann from the Japanese Navy General Staff until August. See note 38.

62. Because the sharing of intelligence is already treated by Chapman, "Origins," and also mentioned in "Japan and German Naval Policy," it will be treated here only with the mention of the aspects missing in Chapman.

63. BA-MA, RM 11/73, fol. 99, Attaché Report, Re: Intelligence exchange with Japanese Navy, 296 geheim, 04.05.1937.

64. BA-MA, RM 11/2, fol. 137f., M to A and W.A., M I 88/37 gKdos., 11.05.1937. Kojima appeared on 10 May 1937. Chapman, "Japan and German Naval Policy," 250, dates it to 11 May and does not notice that the step had been already initiated with the conveyance of the material to Wenneker on 4 May.

65. Hack papers, "German-Japanese agreements concerning sharing of intelligence about the Soviet Union" and "German-Japanese agreements concerning undermining of Soviet Union," both of 11 May 1937; see also BA-MA, RM 11/2, fol. 141, A Iii to M relating to M I 88/37, Re: Japanese intelligence exchange. Enclosure: additional agreements on the exchange of intelligence concerning the Soviet Union, A III 3151/37, M 115/37 gKdos., 07.07.1937.

66. BA-MA, RM 20/1637, fol. 9ff., Note A III [about representation of Japanese naval attaché on 10 May 1937], Re: Intelligence exchange about any foreign navies, A III 3012/37 gKdos., 26.05.1937. Handwritten remarks on the document: "1. M is of the opinion that with an intelligence trade in the technical and materiel area between us and Japan, we would, not counting a few special areas, be the giving side. We would, then, only have an interest in cultivating this trade intensively if general strategic and political considerations make it seem worthwhile to make the Japanese fleet as strong as possible and thereby prepare it to be an inhibiting factor to our possible enemies and if it seems improbable that Japan would be on the enemy side in the foreseeable future. A I [first staff officer of the Kommandoamt] does not believe in this. 2. [F]or the time being, an expansion into an exchange about other states does not come into consideration. 3. If for political reasons an intelligence trade cannot be avoided, then it would have to be planned similarly to the recent German-Italian one."

67. BA-MA, RM 11/2, fol. 142ff., M to A III. Note on renewed representation of the Japanese naval attaché, M I 115/37, relating to 113/37, 88/37, M I 2210/37 gKdos., 10.07.1937. Kojima had presented the new suggestions on 8 July. Wenneker had already on 25 June 1937 (with report number 147) announced the forthcoming presentation of new suggestions of the Japanese and had asked that his successor, Captain Lietzmann (who was already preparing to depart as Wenneker's replacement), bring with him the response of the Kriegsmarine. The report itself is seemingly not preserved, but can without doubt be inferred from BA-MA, RM

20/1637, fol. 97, M I (Kiderlen) to A III. Mitteilung Meldung Mar.Att. Tokio, M 2210 geheim, 28.06.1937, in connection with the mentioned material in BA-MA, RM 11/2, fol. 159, MAtt to naval attaché Tokyo, Re: Exchanging intelligence with Japan, MAtt 132/37 gKdos., 18.09.1937.

68. Ibid., back of fol. 142. The Japanese suggestion was kept noticeably general: "1. Imperial Japanese Navy will be prepared, if the German Kriegsmarine is of the same opinion, to give reciprocal aid for the heightening of the battle readiness of the fleet. 2. Imperial Japanese Navy wishes, in this vein, to make technical (weapons and equipment) as well as tactical (training) exchanges with the German Kriegsmarine. 3. Objects for the exchange and details are to be discussed later."

The thesis held by Krebs, *Japans Deutschlandpolitik*, 1:152, that by this agreement with the navy the Western powers were also incorporated into the intelligence trade, is based on Kojima's imprecise remembrances and is false (cf. Tahira, *Rengō kantai*, pt. 1, 340f.). It is also false that the texts of the agreements with the navy and the German documents with the wording of the agreement with Ōshima are not preserved. They are to be found in BA-MA, RM 20/1637, fol. 142–51. Compare Krebs, *Japans Deutschlandpolitik*, 2:70.

69. "The starting of such an exchange will be judged mainly under political viewpoints. . . . A reason to especially push the issue from the German side should not be present." BA-MA, RM 11/2, fol. 152f., A III to M I relating to A III 3012 of 26.05.37, and opinion of A I, Re: Intelligence exchange with Japan., A III 3186/37 gKdos., 14.07.1937. Further copy in RM 20/1637, fol. 93f.

70. BA-MA, RM 11/2, fol. 154f., M to A III. Re: Intelligence exchange with Japan, 120/37 gKdos., 15.07.1937. It was explained here that the development of a trustworthy cooperation of both navies lay "in the interests of the current German politics" and that the actual extent could be easily controlled by the Kriegsmarine.

71. BA-MA, RM 11/2, Fol. 155f., M Wa I to M. Re: Intelligence exchange with Japan, M Wa I 2988/37 gKdos., 02.08.1937. Other copies in RM 20/1482, fol. 24f., and RM 20/1637, fol. 98f. He had already shown a similarly critical attitude, namely, in connection with the aircraft carrier instructions obtained through the Japanese navy, even though the Germans had been the "takers" in that case.

72. BA-MA, RM 11/2, MAtt to Naval Attaché Tokyo, Re: Intelligence exchange with Japan, MAtt 132/37 gKdos., 18.09.1937.

73. Compare BA-MA, RM 11/3, fol. 57, Naval Attaché Tokyo to MAtt, Re: Intelligence exchange with Japan., 251/37 gKdos., 15.11.1937, as well as Lietzmann's letters, 3/38 and 4/38, from 12.01.1938, ibid., fol. 120 and 176, and his reports 345/37 of 14 December 1937 in BA-MA, RM 11/73, fol. 449.

74. BA-MA, RM 11/3, Bl. 179f., A III to Naval Attaché Tokyo, A III 3819/38 gKdos., 18.03.1938.

75. Ibid. In the text a handwritten "1.11" is included as the date for the corresponding explanation of the attaché Kojima. That Maeda, who worked for the Gunreibu, had made differing comments could be a clue to the different attitudes between the Kaigunshō and the more strongly pro-German Gunreibu.

76. Ibid., fol. 180.

77. BA-MA, RM 11/3, fol. 201f., A III to M annotations of ObdM on report of naval attaché Tokyo (M 37/38 gKdos.), A III FM 3736, M 69/38 gKdos., 04.04.1938. Enclosure.

78. It is interesting that Ōshima received instructions from the Army General Staff in Tokyo in July 1938 to sound out the possibility of an alliance with Germany. Compare Krebs, *Japans Deutschlandpolitik,* 1:162f.

79. BA-MA, RM 20/1637, fol. 199ff., 3.Skl. to OKW (Abw.), Re: Intelligence exchange with Japan, 3.Skl. 4228 gKdos., 28.07.1938.

80. Ibid., fol. 200.

81. Ibid., fol. 200f.

82. Cf. BA-MA, RM 11/4, fol. 143, M to 3.Skl., Re: Naval attaché Tokyo 37/38 of 10.08.38, M 210/38 gKdos., 06.09.1938, and ibid., 30.09.1938, as well as the reference from 4 October 1938. These dealt with the statements of the Soviet defector Ljuschkow that the Japanese had passed on to Lietzmann.

83. Remarks about a signed agreement from Kojima on 7 July 1938 in Chapman, "Japan and German Naval Policy," 253, are false. On that date the Japanese spoke to the OKM and informed it about Ōshima's statements. Cf. BA-MA, RM 20/1637, fol. 199ff., 3.Skl. [intelligence] to OKW, 28 July 1938. The signing on 7 October 1938 is mentioned in a report from Commander Menzel, who apparently traveled to Tokyo upon prompting of the OKM. BA-MA, RM 7/1100, fol. 62ff., 3.Skl. to 1.Skl., Re: Japan-Exchange. Report IV and V. *Auszug aus Bericht dem Freg.Kpt. Menzel über Konsultationen mit der japanischen Marine in Tokio* (Extract from Cdr. Menzel's report about consultations with the IJN in Tokyo), 3.Skl. 3739/39 gKdos., 25.05.1939.

84. BA-MA, RM 6/58, fol. 233ff., SIGIN, organization, possibilities, and results. Lecture given at the end of Kriegsspiel (map exercise and war game) A 1938/39, gKdos., 03.1939 (n.d.). As to states with whom the Kriegsmarine cooperated on this area, only Italy and Finland are named.

85. See Menzel's report, fol. 64. Source same as note 83.

86. Ibid., fol. 63.

87. Ibid., fol. 64.

88. Ibid.

89. Maeda had been in Germany before, on board the *Ashigara,* and had in 1935 escorted the German aircraft carrier commission. He and Adm. Nomura

Naokuni seemed to be the officers in the Gunreibu who were responsible for the maintaining of relations with the Kriegsmarine, if necessary even without consultations with the Navy Ministry.

90. BA-MA, RM 11/3, Fol. 138f., Naval Attaché Tokyo to MAtt, Re: Political suggestions of the Japanese navy, 1/38 gKdos., 10.01.1938.

91. Ibid. This show how far the IJN also acted independently on foreign political issues. This proposal was probably not even coordinated with the Navy Ministry. Lietzmann, however, took it seriously and considered it to have special meaning "in view of the known influence of the army and navy upon Japanese politics." Ibid., fol. 139. The observations about the South Seas mandate areas carry the handwritten remark: "Upon the wish of the Foreign Minister this step will be temporarily held back." Ibid. The lack of coordination within the Japanese navy on this question is apparent in a further report by Lietzmann from the end of January. Here, on order of the German ambassador, he mentioned the matter to Admiral Nomura in the Navy General Staff and at the same time asked the Japanese naval attaché in Berlin, who reported to the Navy Ministry, not to mention Maeda's proposal. Nomura informed him that this question would be debated in a cabinet meeting. BA-MA, RM 11/3, fol. 144f., Naval attaché Tokyo to MAtt, Re: *Südseemandate*, 6/38 gKdos., 28.01.1938.

92. Disinterest in the former German South Sea colonies was soon proclaimed by the Foreign Ministry. Chapman, "Origins," 272, n.78. There were still thoughts in the Skl. on the colonies in the autumn of 1939 (in actuality first considerations are already provable for January 1939) that also incorporated the "return" of parts of New Guinea, the Bismarck Archipelago, the northern Solomons, Nauru, and parts of Samoa. BA-MA, RM 7/1107, fol. 8, A Iik to 1.Skl., A Iik 2330/39 gKdos., 14.10.1939. These were at first put in the background during talks with the head of the Skl. and the ObdM, where the African colonies were given priority. The analyst thought, however, that the incorporation of the Pacific areas, because of their "high economic value," should be considered and remarked: "For the takeover and protection, only the navy would at first be in position to do this." At the same time he thought that the "German possessions lying north of the Equator are left out because of our relations to Japan." The operational department of the Skl. took up a contrary position: "The German legal claim incorporates all colonies." However, it pointed to the "missing power foundations" and therefore saw such plans as a "splintering of forces, that is not permissible for a long time in view of the other duties of the navy." BA-MA, RM 7/1107, fol. 9, 1.Skl. to A II., Re: *Deutsche Kolonien im Stillen Ozean*, 2237/39 gKdos., 21.10.1939. Such remarks show that promoting German "legal claims" in the Pacific was not considered impossible after the creation of the "power founda-

tions." Other voices, as from the Allgemeinen Marineamt, stated this: "Claims as to the incorporation of the German possessions in the Pacific Ocean into the colonial planning are fully endorsed by the B Wi." BA-MA, RM 7/1107, fol. 11, B Wi to A II, Re: *Rückgabe der Kolonien,* B Wi II 9765/39 gKdos., 20.10.1939.

Chapter 12. Japan's Response to the Outbreak of War

1. BA-MA, RM 48/28, fol. 46ff. *Politischer Ausblick auf Grund der Unterrichtung des Amtschefs A am 12.7.1938, Äusserungen des Führers auf "Grille" und des Feldmarschalls Göring auf "Herrmann Schoemann" am 22.7.* (unnumbered) gKdos. Chefs.

The document is unreadably dated by hand, with the note: "One copy of it is in Berlin." (For the copy see BA-MA, RM 20/1138, *Beitrag I E relating to den "Schlussbetrachtungen" des Oberkommandos der Kriegsmarine relating to den Kriegsspielen 1937/38, gKdos., gez. am 17.09.1938.*) It goes on: "For the preparations from a military standpoint one cannot assume the best case situation, but a worst-case scenario has to be considered as possible." Both in the best- as well in the worst-case scenarios, England was given first place among the enemy powers (BA-MA, RM 48/28, fol. 48). Italy was seen as an ally in the best-case scenario. Japan appeared in the plans of Fleet Command as a power from which no current help was to be expected from an operational standpoint, even indirectly:

> 1.) A successful waging of war in the North Sea is not possible in view of the enemy superiority of surface forces. 2.) For a protection of the Atlantic imports, our maritime forces are not sufficient. The imports will come to a halt, unless they can be led into the North and Baltic Seas under neutral flags via neutral neighboring countries, or led under the protection of a neutral great power directly into our harbors. The latter will probably not be achieved, since the only greater power that comes to mind—Japan—will be otherwise occupied.

Ibid., fol. 49. These explanations were nothing other than a declaration of bankruptcy for the concept of protection of imports from the Atlantic, which had been seen as war-deciding since the times of Zenker (commander in chief of the Reichsmarine in the twenties) and had provided the navy the right to exist as an independent branch of service.

Salewski, in *Seekriegsleitung,* 1:40ff., supposes that Germany accepted the risk of war against England "only during and after the Sudeten crisis," on the basis of a memo presented by Cdr. Hellmut Heye (1.Skl.) entitled "Maritime Warfare against England and Resulting Demands for Strategic Goal Setting and Buildup of the Kriegsmarine" on 25 October 1938. The documents cited here apparently became accessible after Salewski's evaluation of the record.

2. BA-MA, RM 11/4, fol. 181ff., 1.Skl. to M, 1.Skl. Ic 1209/38 gKdos., 18.08.1938.

3. Ibid. The agreement of Hitler is remarked in fol. 183 by hand: "Führer has given his agreement to Italy + Japan."

4. BA-MA, RM 11/4, fol. 190, MAtt to Naval Attachés Tokyo and Rome, M 245/38 gKdos., 13.09.1938.

5. BA-MA, RM 11/4, fol. 191, Note without volume number, gKdos., 15.09.1938.

6. BA-MA, RM 11/4, fol. 192, MAtt to Naval Attaché Tokyo, Re: Cooperation with Japanese Navy, M 291/38 gKdos., 29.09.1938.

7. BA-MA, RM 11/4, fol. 194, 3.Skl. to MAtt, Re: Cooperation with Japanese Navy, 3.Skl. 4654/38 gKdos., 14.10.1938.

8. BA-MA, RM 20/1138, fol. 210ff., *1. Ausgabe* (First draft) of a compilation: "Operational considerations," 1938. With addendum: "General political situation," gKdos. The "operational thoughts" are marked with "5 September." The addendum touches on Japan's role: "USA will support our enemies immediately with all methods, even without entry into the war. Should Japan actively participate on our side, it could create a certain balance for us against the USA and . . . act in a hemming manner on America" (fol. 213). "A noticeable betterment of the German economic warfare could be achieved by using Italian or Japanese harbors and bases in Africa and in the Pacific" (fol. 214).

9. BA-MA, RM 6/58, fol. 33ff., "Organization and tasks of the *Etappen*" (experiences from the time of tension, oil supply), gKdos., January 1939 (n.d.). The author pointed out, however, that there was an oil shortage in Japan and that they too were dependent upon the great oil companies dominated by the Anglo-Saxons (e.g., Standard Oil). Compare also U.S. Navy Operational Archives, Washington, T 91 TR 29, ONI 6/47, "The setting-up of the *Etappe*," conclusion of a speech held on 16 February 1938 at the *Marineakademie*.

10. These consisted mainly in the increase of his staff by Germans, conscripted during peacetime, working with civilian firms in the area, so that the organization of the German shipping traffic and possible supply measures could be secured. The KTB (war journal) that he had written from 20 September to 1 October 1938 is in BA-MA, RM 11/74, fol. 6ff., Naval Attaché Tokyo to OKM, Chief of Staff, and Canaris, 40/38 gKdos., 06.10.1938.

11. BA-MA, RM 11/74, fol. 24f., Naval Attaché Tokyo to MAtt, 42 gKdos., 07.10.1938.

12. See BA-MA, RM 11/74, 40/38 gKdos., 06.10.1938, fol. 17.

13. Cf. Kojima, *Deutschland und ich*, pt. 1, 13.

14. With that, Yonai stood opposed to the majority of department and section leaders of his own ministry and to prevailing opinion in the fleet and the Navy General Staff (Gunreibu), which favored a closer cooperation with Germany and

a harder course against Great Britain. Yonai's conduct was extraordinary for a Japanese; he often could push through his policies only by not informing his own subordinates about his intentions and by not mentioning their proposals at the numerous conferences of the inner cabinet (the so-called Five-Minister Conference, composed of the prime minister, the foreign minister, and the ministers of finance, navy, and war) that dealt with the question of alliance with Germany. The divergent attitude of the Gunreibu is noticeable in the increasing negotiations and agreements made with the German side without informing the ministry. The alliance negotiations are precisely recounted in Krebs, *Japans Deutschlandpolitik*, 227ff.

15. Ibid., 283. Resistance in naval circles also becomes clear from reports of the U.S. naval attaché in Tokyo, which state that Yonai himself mentioned the skeptical attitude of the Japanese navy to the U.S. ambassador on the evening of the 19 April 1939. NARA, RG 38, M975 Roll 3, U.S. naval attaché Tokyo. German-Italian-Japanese Military Alliance, Serial No. 94, 27 April 1939. See also NARA, RG 38, M975, Roll 3, the verification in a report about the German-Italian treaty conclusion, U.S. naval attaché, Tokyo. Japan and the German-Italian Military Alliance. Serial No. 116, 24 May 1939.

16. Krebs, *Japans Deutschlandpolitik*, 304.

17. BA-MA, RM 12 II/247, fol. 4, 26.08.1939.

18. BA-MA, RM 12 II/247, fol. 8, 26.08.1939.

19. Kojima, *Deutschland und ich*, pt. 1, 11.

20. This he commented upon bitterly: "After I had repeatedly explained to the Navy Ministry that the guests of honor sent by the Japanese navy should now, after repeated invitations from the head of the German Empire, please attend, and after also obviously Admiral Förster has personally engaged himself in this direction, I consider the bailing out of Admiral Ōsumi, with or without orders from Tokyo, a pitiable demonstration of shameful character." BA-MA, RM 12 II/247, fol. 68, 19.09.1939. Originally he had heard on the evening of 1 September that Ōsumi had received orders from the Navy Ministry to go to Berlin despite his initial hesitation. On the evening of the first day of war, Lietzmann had been invited by officers of the Navy Ministry and the Gunreibu, who assured him of unofficial support. Lietzmann especially pointed out the "extraordinarily friendly and comradely" nature of the conversation and particularly remarked, "Of a disgruntlement in the navy about the German rapprochement to Russia I have up until now not noticed anything, anywhere." BA-MA, RM 12 II/247, fol. 22, 02.09.1939.

Förster, former commander in chief of the Fleet, now retired and chairman of the German-Japanese society, had traveled to Italy, where the Japanese guests had in the meantime arrived by ship, and had met there with Kojima, Ōsumi, and Terauchi. See Kojima, *Deutschland und ich,* pt. 1, 12. Chapman, "Japan and German Naval Policy," 240 and 252, has made an error here. He states that Förster had made presentations in Tokyo and erroneously suggests that Förster was sent there in order to persuade the Japanese navy to give up their resistance to an alliance with Germany. Lietzmann had, according to Chapman, not possessed a high enough rank or enough influence. Also, Chapman's observation that Canaris, Fricke, Bürkner, and even Göring had put pressure on the naval attaché Endō in this matter is highly questionable. Göring was in no way a friend of the idea of an alliance with Japan. Even a leaning of the Kriegsmarine toward the creation of an alliance with Japan cannot be proven.

From mentions in Lietzmann's war journals one can only gather that Förster pushed for Ōsumi's visit, but not, however, where this happened. This is made clear from Kojima's report. In the English translation of the Lietzmann/Wenneker war journals published by Chapman, the above event is only given in shortened form and one day earlier. Compare Chapman, *The Price of Admiralty,* 1:26, in which the entry for 19 September 1939 is completely missing.

21. Cf. Krebs, *Japans Deutschlandpolitik,* 379. For this a completely new method was created, namely, a questioning of the elder statesmen (*jūshin*). This referred to the former prime ministers, but the architects of the plan had made sure that "unwanted" members of this circle were not included and had, moreover, gotten the help of Admiral Okada, who was now inactive and could in the end convince Yonai.

22. KTB Skl., 1:64, 13 September 1939. However, on the day of the outbreak of war the Gunreibu had immediately started transmitting the positions of warships of the Western powers to the German naval attaché. BA-MA, RM II/247, fol. 19, Lietzmann, 2 September 1939.

23. KTB Skl., 1:90, 16 July 1939, and 1:95, 17 July 1939. "An event of greatest significance . . . . The possible consequences . . . can be estimated as quite substantial and as very favorable for Germany. Its assessment . . . must, beyond that, consider the very substantial difficulties that the events cause the Western powers."

24. KTB Skl., 1:164, 25 September 1939. At this time the pocket battleships *Graf Spee* and *Deutschland* stood in the Atlantic as commerce raiders. The commander of the *Deutschland* was Wenneker, who had returned from Japan. Kojima reported a meeting in the North Atlantic of the German pocket battleship, under the command of his friend, with the Japanese steamer *Hakone Maru,* on which Ōsumi and Kojima were returning to Japan. Kojima, *Deutschland und ich,* pt. 1, 12. The meeting occurred on 11 October. Compare also Wenneker's entry in his war journal. BA-MA, RM 12 II/247, fol. 354, 9 April 1940.

25. KTB Skl., 2:56f., 6 October 1939. A further clue to the very cooperative attitude of the Soviet side was the hint of the German naval attaché in Moscow that German merchant ships that were in East Asia could return to Europe via the North Siberian route in the summer of 1940. Such an undertaking meant that high security against the British threat was only possible, however, with Soviet help.

26. KTB Skl., 2:89, 10 October 1939, and 2:123, 16 November 1939. The reporting of German ship movements seems, however, to have been stopped a short time later upon German request. The Skl. itself tended to pursue a "pragmatic" attitude even toward friendly neutrals, by commenting, "The current order . . . not to stop Italian, Spanish, Russian and Japanese ships can only have validity so long as these powers do not turn deaf ears to our requests" (KTB Skl., 2:79, 9 October 1939). In reality this was not put into effect; on the contrary, the Japanese tankers (just as the American, Soviet, Italian, and Spanish ones) were exempted from the order for the German submarines to immediately attack such ships within the American war zone (KTB Skl., 3:190, 23 November 1939), and the Japanese naval attaché Endō received a secure route from the Kriegsmarine for Japanese merchant ships that led from Rotterdam along the German coastline (KTB Skl., 4:6, 1 December 1939).

27. Wagner, *Lagevorträge*, 44. Presentation on 10 November 1939, as well as KTB Skl., 3:71, 10 November 1939.

28. KTB Skl., 3:96, 14 November 1939.

29. See BA-MA, RM 11/4, fol. 192, M 291/38, 29.09.1938. This also included that the territorial waters of the neutral countries, in this case Japan, be allowed to be used for supply ships. The agreement formed the foundation for the use of remote South Sea islands as supply dumps for German auxiliary cruisers. One must here contradict Krebs, *Japans Deutschlandpolitik,* 343, who believes that it merely dealt with the exchange of intelligence. Compare also Tahira, *Rengō kantai,* pt. 1, 426. Also Krebs's cynical evaluation of the Japanese suggestion that the Kriegsmarine should serve itself from Soviet boats in the Far East does not seem quite accurate, since the Kriegsmarine's relations with the Soviet Union at this point were even better than its relations with the IJN. In actuality not just Raeder, but also the head of the OKW, endorsed the shipment of Soviet submarines to Germany, which Hitler, however, refused. Wagner, *Lagevorträge,* 47, presentation of ObdM to Hitler on 22 November 1939 and KTB Skl., 3:174, 22 November 1939.

30. KTB Skl., 3:109, 15 November 1939.

31. Near the end of October 1939. Compare Tahira, *Rengō kantai* 1, 387f. Minister of the Navy Yoshida agreed to the study of the Gunreibu.

32. Ibid., 431.

33. Krebs, *Japans Deutschlandpolitik,* 377f.
34. KTB Skl., 3:224, 27 November 1939.
35. KTB Skl., 4:2, 1 December 1939.
36. KTB Skl., 4:14, 3 December 1939.
37. KTB Skl., 4:74, 11 December 1939.
38. KTB Skl., 5:16, 3 January 1940. "According to official Japanese sources the unhindered shipping of German export products to Japan was achieved on a Japanese steamer sailing from Genoa. There are further negotiations between Tokyo and London in order to achieve England's general agreement for the shipping of German goods to Japan."

   The Japanese demands are listed in BA-MA, RM 7/1294, fol. 87ff., *Bericht deutsche Gesandtschaft Den Haag Re: Englisch-japanische Verhandlungen über die Ausfuhr deutscher Waren nach Japan,* [unnumbered], 12.01.1940. Here the caution practiced by the British side in this matter was also noticeable: Of the four ships that had left Germany with German goods bound for Japan in December 1939, three were inspected by the British in the Downs. The inspections had been short and "not seriously meant." For another ship, whose sailing for Japan through the North Sea had been planned near the end of January, the Japanese side had already gained the assurance that "one did not plan to make difficulties this time either." Furthermore the Japanese planned in future to route German goods via Trieste and Genoa. Compare, also from the same source, reports about the preferential treatment of the Japanese ship *Sanyo Maru,* ibid., fol. 70 and 71f., 22 and 27 December 1939.

   By December the German Foreign Ministry, noting the complaints of the Japanese, commented mildly: "It now seems that, despite the sharpness of the protests, Japan is striving for British concessions on the path of negotiations and its measures will depend upon the British handling of the trade barriers." BA-MA, RM 7/1294, AA to OKM. *Übersicht über Reaktionen der neutralen Regierungen auf Sperre deutscher Ausfuhren durch Feindmächte,* 23276 geheim, 10.12.1939. The Skl. had in addition asked the AA to ask the befriended powers to stop the trade of contraband with Germany's enemies. In its answer the AA thought that the talks with Japan would be the "most difficult" but agreed to instruct the embassy accordingly. No answer from the Japanese side seems to have been passed down in the naval files.
39. KTB Skl., 5:169, 21 January 1940, and BA-MA, RM 12 II/247, fol. 278ff., same date.
40. BA-MA, RM 12 II/247, fol. 29, 5 September 1939. In the literature published up until now, the "warning" of the Kriegsmarine in this matter has been overlooked. The registered number of the KTB of Lietzmann (854/39) shows that the KTB had to have arrived at the Skl. in 1939, which is also verified through parallel

entries in the war diary of the Etappen organization of the Kriegsmarine (*Marine-Sonderdienst*). The Etappen organization was responsible for supplying German maritime forces in extraterritorial water and harbors. It also gathered intelligence. Even at the beginning of the tensions, before the outbreak of war, the German naval attaché in Japan, in his function as head of the Grossetappe Japan/China, was at the same time an organ of the Etappen organization. In actuality the greater part of his workforce was absorbed by Etappen matters. See BA-MA, RM 13/1, fol. 277, *Stand der Etappenorganisation der Kriegsmarine am 10.12.39*, [unnumbered], 10.12.1939.

41. KTB Skl., 5:174, 22 January 1940, and 5:205, 25 January 1940.

42. Ibid., 5:174.

43. On 24 January 1940 a Japanese gunboat stopped a British steamer near the Chinese coast but just checked the papers. The Skl. commented: "The Japanese actions seem to have been very careful." KTB Skl., 5:225, 31 January 1940.

44. KTB Skl., 5:253, 31 January 1940.

45. KTB Skl., 6:45, 6 February 1940; 6:90, 12 February 1940.

46. KTB Skl., 6:113, 15 February 1940. Here the Japanese were even suspected of having made "certain promises to England in secret."

47. KTB Skl., 7:198, 27 March 1940. At the end of January the Skl. had noted in its war diary the main reason for the IJN's caution in view of the possibility of an armed conflict with the U.S.A. At the time the American-Japanese economic treaty was discontinued on 26 January 1940, the Skl. noted, 34 percent of all goods imported to Japan originated from the United States and 18 percent of Japanese exports went there. Fifty-six percent of the needs for heavy industry were imported from the U.S.A.

The KTB-keeper commented, "The numbers show the great dependence of Japan on the economic trade with America and its resulting unfavorable political position versus the USA." Thus Japan's disadvantage—not only political, but also economic and with that strategic—seems not to have been duly considered in plans on the German side (especially by Ribbentrop) to use an alliance with Japan as a deterrent against the USA. KTB Skl., 5:213, 26 January 1940. The mentioned strategic disadvantage was a main topic of Japanese naval studies. Cf. Tahira, *Rengō kantai*, pt. 1, 387ff.

48. Ibid., 440f. Study from 30 January 1940.

49. KTB Skl., 5:51, 8 January 1940. At the beginning of October 1939 the German naval attaché in Moscow had pointed out that at least thirty-five of the ships in East Asia could be brought back via the North Siberian route. KTB Skl., 2:74, 8 October 1939.

50. KTB Skl., 5:82, 12 January 1940, and ibid., 6:49, 6 February 1940.

51. KTB Skl., 8:5f., 1 April 1940.

52. KTB Skl., 11:112f., 10 July 1940. The Skl. celebrated the arrival in the Pacific as a unique event in the history of maritime warfare. KTB Skl., 13:156, 161, 12 September 1940.

53. KTB Skl., 10:104, 10 June 1940.

54. KTB Skl., 5:120ff., 16 January 1940.

55. KTB Skl., 7:142, 23 March 1940.

56. KTB Skl., 7:198f., 27 March 1940.

57. KTB Skl., 9:12f., 314f., 2 and 31 May 1940.

58. BA-MA, RM 12 II/247, fol. 350, 3 April 1940. The deputy head of the Navy General Staff, Vice Adm. Kondō Nobutake, had invited Wenneker into a teahouse for a private conversation and mentioned during the talks that the United States was not in a position to turn to "two sides." Sinkings of British ships in East Asian waters would increase the standing of the German Empire and would without doubt cause great enthusiasm with the Japanese people. In Berlin the Skl. commented: "Opinion of the Navy General Staff, but hardly of the Navy Ministry." KTB Skl., 8:61, 8 April 1940. Obviously the Navy General Staff judged additional military pressure on Great Britain to be favorable for the Japanese position in the question of southern expansion.

59. Cf. Shimanuki, *Shōwa 16-nen*, 40; Hara, "Daihonei rikugunbu," pt. 1, 29, and Tahira, *Rengō kantai*, pt. 1, 442ff. The thoughts found their way onto paper in the naval study, "Measures against the Dutch East Indies in the case of violation of Dutch neutrality."

60. Tahira, *Rengō kantai*, pt. 1, 442ff.

61. Ibid., 447.

62. KTB Skl., 9:128, 13 May 1940.

63. KTB Skl., 9:159, 16 May 1940, and 9:234, 23 May 1940. In order to calm the Japanese regarding possible German claims, Foreign Minister von Ribbentrop at the end of May saw himself forced to proclaim the lack of German interest in the Netherlands' Pacific colonies, which was greeted enthusiastically in Japan. Ibid., 9:252, 25 May 1940. That did not close the subject for the German foreign office, however. In the middle of September the Skl. noted that the AA's observations regarding the future of the Dutch East Indies amounted to a statement that, however it might look, Germany would definitely "claim its right of copartnership." KTB Skl., 13:141, 11 September 1940.

64. KTB Skl., 10:2, 1 June 1940.

65. KTB Skl., 10:86, 8 June 1940.

66. KTB Skl., 11:295f., 25 July 1940.

67. KTB Skl., 16:89, 7 December 1940. Six of the seven auxiliary cruisers were planned for these areas. The trade war with surface forces reached its high point in the winter of 1940 to 1941.

68. This was the highest level of priority for the allocation of raw materials and workforces. "The incorporation of the auxiliary cruisers as one of the most valuable weapons for the trade war in supplementation of the submarine war in the *Sonderstufe* must be pushed through and will be mentioned in the presentation by the head of the Skl. in the next meeting with the Führer." KTB Skl., 16:111, 9 December 1940. This, however, did not happen. Raeder merely mentioned an increase in the production of submarines during his presentation of 27 December 1940 and mentioned "grave doubts" about "Barbarossa" before a victory over Great Britain, whereupon he ran up against a stone wall, since Hitler was already certain of his course. Then Raeder had seemingly dropped the demand of the navy to incorporate the auxiliary cruisers into the *Sonderstufe*. Compare Wagner, *Lagevorträge*, 173f.

69. This was the case in the beginning of December 1940, when the captured tanker *Ole Jacob* made for Kobe from auxiliary cruiser "Ship 16." The ship had been ordered by the Skl. to go to one of the remote supply dumps, and the Japanese, shortly before its arrival in Kobe, had urgently asked that this not be done. The tanker, however, had very important captured documents on board that "Ship 16" had captured from the British steamer *Automedon*. The commander of "Ship 16," Captain Rogge, wanted to give this material into the hands of the German naval attaché, Wenneker, as fast as possible. But *Ole Jacob* in the meantime had to leave port again within twenty-four hours. KTB Skl., 16:162, 13 December 1940, and RM II/248, fol.143–149. For the significance and consequences of the captured documents, see below.

70. The transports through the Soviet Union were camouflaged, that is, declared falsely. Upon request of the Foreign Ministry, however, a shipment of airplanes and aircraft parts for the auxiliary cruisers was openly admitted to the Soviet side in December 1940. They thereupon declared that the transport was not in agreement with Soviet neutrality—in marked contrast to the friendly attitude taken, shortly before, toward agreements about bases for German ships. KTB Skl., 16:74, 14 December 1940.

71. KTB Skl., 19:330, 24 March 1941.

72. KTB Skl., 16:342, 31 December 1940; ibid., 17:36, 3 January 1941; and RM 12 II/248, fol. 176, 30 December 1940.

73. "The excellent successes of both ships in the Pacific Ocean are fully recognized by the Skl. They far surpass the expectations placed in the operational area. Skl. congratulates the ships on their successes." KTB Skl., 17:19, 2 January 1941. To the

Allies' special measures due to the activities of the German auxiliary cruisers, compare KTB Skl., 17:151f., 12 January 1941.

74. KTB Skl., 20:355f., 25 April 1941.

75. KTB Skl., 20:322, 390, 22 and 27 April 1941.

76. The statement found in Hara, "Daihonei rikugunbu, kaisen keii," pt. 1, 90f., that Wenneker had encouraged a Japanese move against Indochina in June, does not find verification in his war diary. Instead, one can gather from this that the Japanese leaned toward caution: "Admiral Kondō explained to me that there was great interest in French Indochina on the part of the Japanese armed forces, [but] averred that one could currently not decide on moving more actively because of the unavoidable [provocation] of the Western powers and America." BA-MA, RM 12 II/247, fol. 410, 18 June 1940. Kojima had already informed Wenneker that, in the event of a U.S. embargo on machine tools, the situation would become "very serious" if the embargo were also extended to oil and scrap metal. In this case the only option that remained would be the forceful capturing of the Dutch oil fields in the Dutch East Indies. Ibid., fol. 403, 11 June 1940. The typical naval tendency to remain "short of war," despite all desire for expansion to the south, was evidently still dominant in June.

77. KTB Skl., 10:220, 21 June 1940, and ibid., 11:39, 4 July 1940, and 11:199f., 18 July 1940. Weapons shipments to China through France and Great Britain could be stopped with Japanese influence—in the case of England, only for a short period of time.

78. Nihon Kokusai Seiji Gakkai, ed., *Taiheiyō sensō e no michi* (The way to the Pacific war), 4:20. As to delaying a confrontation with the United States, compare Hara, "Daihonei rikugunbu," pt. 1, 447.

79. Tsunoda Jun, ed., *Gendaishi shiryō*, 10:369.

80. Tahira, *Rengō kantai*, pt. 1, 485.

81. Ibid., 457. Compare also the explanations of Kojima in a conversation with Wenneker in BA-MA, RM 12 II/248, fol. 46ff., 13 September 1940. The replacement of the Japanese naval attaché in Germany, Endō, by Yokoi Tadao seems to be related to personnel changes in the Navy Ministry. Compare Wenneker's remarks to the "known Anglophile tendencies" of Endō, ibid., fol. 50, 17 September 1940. In the German naval files the name of the removed attaché is mostly given as "Yendo" (which spelling is also possible). The spelling of "Endō" is, however, more common and is therefore given preference here.

Also, in a conversation with the now inactive Admiral Suetsugu Nobumasa, one of the sharpest hawks in the IJN, Wenneker could gather that "with the new minister a considerable change in the navy's position relative to the Axis had occurred, and the alliance that was now in the works would not be sabotaged by the navy." BA-MA, RM 12 II/248, fol. 65, 21 September 1940.

82. Compare the explanations of Krebs in *Japans Deutschlandpolitik,* 471.

83. Compare Tahira, *Rengō kantai,* pt. 1, 458, to the conclusions of the most important Naval officers. The now-outmaneuvered main enemy of an alliance with Germany, Yamamoto Isoroku, had no option left but to accept the inevitable and, at least in light of the conflict with the United States that he now expected, to demand a doubling of the strength of the naval air arm.

84. Ibid. The original German proposal had defined the activating condition of the alliance as an attack by a power not involved in the conflicts in Europe and China.

85. KTB Skl., 13:316, 24 September 1940.

86. BA-MA, RM 12 II/248, fol. 67, 25 September 1940. This attitude was shared by the Kriegsmarine. Compare KTB Skl., 13:363, 27 September 1940. The text of the pact can be found in ADAP, Series D, XI, Document No. 188.

87. Ibid., fol. 74 and 75, entries of 28 and 30 September 1940. Also, at the reception for the Italian embassy, Oikawa only sent his deputy, Vice Admiral Toyoda. Ibid., fol. 76, 2 October 1940.

88. Ibid., fol. 79, 3 October 1940.

89. KTB Skl., 13:375, 28 September 1940, and 14:13, 2 October 1940.

90. KTB Skl., 13:387, 29 September 1940.

91. KTB Skl., 14:2, 1 October 1940.

Chapter 13. Intelligence Exchange

1. Compare, generally, as to the relations, especially: Rahn, "Japan and Germany, 1941–1943"; "Der Krieg im Pazifik"; "Japan und der Krieg in Europa"; and "Kriegswende im Pazifik 1942," as well as Krebs, *Japans Deutschlandpolitik;* "Deutschland und Pearl Harbor"; and "Japan und der deutsch-sowjetische Krieg." Additionally (even if partly obsolete and with only negligible viewing of the maritime aspects studied here) Chapman, "Origins," and Martin, "Deutschland und Japan"; "Die Militärische Vereinbarung zwischen Deutschland," "Italien und Japan vom 18. Januar 1942"; "Japans Weg in den Krieg"; "Das deutsch-japanische Bündnis"; "Japans Weltmachtstreben 1939–1941"; "Japan im Krieg 1941–1945"; "Zur Vorgeschichte des deutsch-japanischen Kriegsbündnisses"; and "Die deutsch-japanischen Beziehungen während des Dritten Reiches."

2. Until now the current literature has overlooked the possibility that the capture of the *Automedon* was made possible by the Kriegsmarine's cracking of a British radio code. It is nevertheless provable that the Kriegsmarine could read British radio communications about the movement of merchant ships in the Indian Ocean in the autumn of 1940. The war diary of the naval intelligence service records that, for the beginning of October, the original codes were available for

important British operations. Among them was the Government Telegraph Code, about which the KTB explains: "3.) Government-Telegraph Code (original code available): The code is solved on a running basis. Approximately 10 days after each change the radio communications can be partly read and after 20 days constantly read. Generally the code is kept for two months. Mainly ship movements with important destination points are radioed. (Mainly in the south Atlantic and the Indian Ocean)." BA-MA, RM 7/103, fol. 154f., *Stand der englischen Entzifferung,* 2458/40 gKdos. Chefs., 08.10.1940. In view of this state of affairs, a planned interception of the *Automedon* by using its radio traffic is probable. The Kriegsmarine's striving to keep this valuable source a secret from the Japanese would also explain the orders of the Skl. to Wenneker to label Berlin as the source of the gained information. Compare BA-MA, RM 12 II/248, fol. 162, MAtt 3205, 10.12.1940.

3. The original documents were captured by the Allies at war's end in Germany, together with the Naval files. They were taken to Great Britain and had not, as of 1997, been released in the PRO. The copies given to the Japanese seem to have been destroyed. Direct information about the contents of the papers is provided by the short summaries that the Japanese naval attaché in Berlin, Yokoi, had sent to the Third Group of the Navy General Staff in Tokyo. His radio report was decoded and translated by the Americans. The translation occurred only after war's end, on 18 August 1945. NARA, RG 457/SRNA 20, Japanese naval attaché Berlin to Head 3.Sect. Navy General Staff, 739, 12.12.1940. Compare also Chapman, *The Price of Admiralty,* 2/3:338. The wording of this important document is found in the annex. Wenneker's more exhaustive summary is found in his KTB: BA-MA, RM 12 II/248, fol. 153ff., 7 December 1940.

4. The tanker entered the harbor only to deliver the secret documents and against the orders of the Skl., which, however, did not yet know anything about the loot. BA-MA, RM 12 II/248, fol. 143, 4 December 1940. The news created "noticeable dismay" at the Navy Ministry, where Wenneker went immediately. Ibid., fol. 144, 149.

5. Ibid., fol.162. The permission was granted the day before. The deputy head of the Navy General Staff, Kondō Nobutake, repeatedly verified to Wenneker how valuable the handed-over material was to the Japanese navy. Compare also the presentation in Rahn, "Japan und der Krieg in Europa," 148ff.

6. For an in-depth discussion, see appendix E.

7. KTB Skl., vol. 16, Bl. 234 to 239, 20 December 1940. Here one can find very bitter words (for example, "Insufficient buildup of U-boat weapon is seen by Skl. as a crime against the future of the German people") that were later erased or reworded by Fricke by hand. Compare also ibid., Bl. 270, 24 December 1940. Substantial extracts from the KTB entry of 20 December 1940 can be found in

the protocol of the Raeder presentation before Hitler on 27 December, of course without the sharp barbs of the war diary keeper. See Wagner, *Lagevorträge*, 171ff.

8. Wagner, *Lagevorträge*, 173f.

9. KTB Skl., vol. 16, Bl. 326.

10. That no such entries can be found in Wenneker's war diaries is not yet solid proof that such an order was not given. Not all telegrams and radio messages that arrived at the attaché in Tokyo are listed. Replies to missing documents are present (e.g., Wenneker's agreement to the prevention of an "intellectual sell-out" to the Japanese, BA-MA, RM 12 II/248, fol. 249, 13 March 1941, further copy in BA-MA, RM 7/1233, Mar.Att. Tokio 97 geh. to Kriegsmarine Berlin auf MAtt 2223g [Skl. 5359 geh.] 10759/41 geheim, 13.03.1941), and even correspondence of the highest secrecy (Chefsache) is missing or noted only partially. Wenneker often made the war diary entries for several days at a time and, because of the heavy workload, obviously might not always note even important proceedings. Questions about the supply and repair of German merchant ships in Japan, which for the duration of the war were subordinate to the attaché as head of the Grossetappe China-Japan, were moved more and more into the foreground. This tendency increased at least until 1943 and led to the comment in the last parts of the war diary that managed to get to Germany (covering the period from mid-February through the end of March 1943): "The war diary of the naval attaché Tokyo contains only pure logistics that have no worth anymore for the 3.Skl." BA-MA, RM 12 II/252, *Vortragsnotiz für C/3.Skl.* 3821/44, 11.04.1944.

An important conclusion as to the worth of the Wenneker war diary as a source is that it must be evaluated together with the other files of the Skl.

11. BA-MA, RM 7/253, fol. 2ff., Skl. to Adm. Groos. *Betrachtungen zur Frage: Japan im Dreimächtepakt*, 46/41 gKdos. Chefs., 14.01.1941.

12. Compare ibid., fol. 18. "The current weakness of England in Asia–Far East is a temptation to attack Singapore."

13. Ibid., fol. 11. "Strong vulnerability of USA-sea routes in the Pacific . . . lessens relief of British tonnage according to new facts." Compare also fol. 13f.: "An energetic attack upon the enemy tonnage from advantageous strategic positions in the Indian Ocean and Pacific through Japan will hardly allow America to use large parts of its cargo space on the England route." An attack upon Singapore ranged behind the shipping war (fol. 18), that was the mission in war (fol. 16).

14. Compare note 7. Here the basic idea for the "Great Plan," so called by Salewski, was born. One must contradict Salewski, who sees this only from February 1942 onward. Compare Salewski, *Seekriegsleitung*, 2:83. He seems not to have been aware of the *Automedon* incident and therefore overlooks the hopes of the Skl. that it raised. See also Krebs, *Japans Deutschlandpolitik*.

15. See Lietzmann's letter in BA-MA, RM 8/1601, fol. 17, B. Nr. 452 geheim, 30.08.1938 and chapter 12, note 20. Raeder had received a copy of this for his personal instruction from Ambassador Ott. Also Wenneker had made similar reports in 1936. See BA-MA, RM 11/72, 230 geheim, 06.05.1936. The chance seemed to present itself here to "activate" long-latent leanings in the Japanese navy.

16. Compare BA-MA, RM 7/1110, fol. 183, Skl. to HSK "Schiff 16" und alle ausserheimisch, relating to Kriegstagebuch "Schiff 16," unnumbered, 27.02.1941. Here the Skl. stated that the captured material, including the "Report [to the] War Cabinet," had been received and saw itself, after consideration of all reports and experiences, affirmed in their view "that the Japanese are prepared for any support, [but] are, however, striving to keep face and to seem outwardly neutral." The Japanese had therefore been assured that a "certain pause" would set in, in the supply activities of the logistics branch. None of this spoke to any conviction that the Japanese navy would offer stronger support for the Axis than it already had, or that the IJN had any immediate intention to enter the war on the Axis side.

17. ADAP D XII, Document No. 100, Telegramm Ribbentrop-Ott.

18. On 5 March Ott held a confidential conversation with the deputy head of the Navy General Staff, Kondō, that was followed by another conversation "under four eyes" (confidential, between two persons) on 8 March, this time between Kondō and Wenneker. BA-MA, RM 7/253, fol. 40ff., Mar.Att. Tokio to OKM/MAtt, Re: *Japans Beteiligung an europäischen Krieg.* 174/41 gKdos., 13.03.1941. Excerpts from the Japanese protocols of these talks can be found in Hara, "Daihonei rikugunbu, kaisen keii 3," 375ff. Wenneker's war diary should contain a special report identical to BA-MA, RM 12 II/248, 174/41 gKdos., fol. 244, 08.03.1940, but he only mentions it.

19. BA-MA, RM 7/253, fol. 25ff., Mar.Att. Tokio to OKM/MAtt, Re: *Der Eintritt Japans in den europäischen Krieg. Möglichkeiten und Auswirkungen.* Enclosure: *Zusammenstellung über die Streitkräfte Japans und seiner Gegner,* 75/41, gKdos., 03.02.1941.

20. Ibid., fol. 29.

21. Ibid., fol. 33. This document contradicts Martin's interpretation that Wenneker, with this study and his report from 13 March 1941, had wanted to warn Berlin, before the talks with Kondō, against wishfully thinking that the United States would not take action. The opposite is true: Wenneker supported just this thesis. Compare Martin, "Deutschland und Japan," 33, note 40.

22. Admiral (Ret.) Sekkine.

23. Wenneker report, BA-MA, RM 7/253, fol. 40ff., 174/41 gKdos., 13.03.1941.

24. At the same time Wenneker had been told of specific strategic aspects of importance to the Japanese. The dependency on importing raw materials, as well as the

U.S. submarine threat to Japanese sea routes, was decisively important in the outbreak and course of the Pacific war.

25. See Wagner, *Lagevorträge*, 173f. This was also reflected in Hitler's directive from the beginning of March. BA-MA, fol. 31ff., RM 7/970, *Weisung* (Order) *Nr. 24 über Zusammenarbeit mit Japan.* (OKW WFSt/Abt.L (I op.) Nr. 44282/41 gKdos. Chefs., 05.03.1941. Here the goal, pursuant to the Tripartite Pact, was to move Japan to act in the Far East as fast as possible, and the possible takeover of Singapore was characterized as a "decisive victory." That German statements relating to "coordination of operational plans" were hollow was exposed, however, by the fact that no time was set for "operational consultations" to implement "coordination of operational plans of both sides." Furthermore, "About operation Barbarossa no references are to be made to the Japanese" (ibid.). Explanations of running or planned operations were exempted by the naval leadership a few days later. KTB Skl., vol. 13, Bl. 183, 13 March 1941. The directive is reprinted in appendix C.

At the beginning of 1941 a Japanese naval commission under Nomura Naokuni arrived in Germany. It had no orders to coordinate warfare. This can already be seen by their official title: *Kaigun kendoku gunji shisatsudan* (Naval Inspection Group assigned to Germany). Nomura's report about the visit is preserved in Japanese archives and deals exclusively with technical and organizational matters. It lies in the Military History Department (Senshibu) of the National Institute for Defense Studies in Tokyo. 1 Zenpan 242, Shōwa ichijūroku. Kaigun kendoku gunji shisatsudan hokoku. Kaigun kendoku shisatsudanchō Nomura Naokuni.

From the German navy files, the reluctance of the Skl. to inform the Japanese about operational intentions and the disinterest of the Japanese in coordinating operations is clearly recognizable. The Skl. ordered headquarters that were supposed to be visited by the Japanese commission not to mention any current or planned operations. By earlier operations a "prevention of too strong an interest in certain questions" was to be maintained. Especially, no facts were to be given about sections and strength in connection with the invasion in England; even though those preparations were made only for deceptive purposes. At the same time the Skl. demanded reports about the preferred questions of the Japanese in order to receive "a certain additional view into the operational viewpoints of the Japanese navy that are in general strongly veiled." BA-MA, RM 7/253, fol. 38f., Io to Gruppen West und Nord, BdU op, Admiral Frankreich. Re: Behandlung operativer Fragen gegenüber japanischer Marinekommission, 4951/41 gKdos., 13.03.1941. From the answers the purely technical interest of the Japanese was noticeable. BA-MA, RM 7/1233, fol. 192, Telegramm BdU op 570 gKdos. to 1.Skl., 24.03.1941. Compare also the statements of Commander Falcks, note 38, below.

26. Even in April Kondo expressly emphasized to Wenneker that the possession of Singapore would not change anything in the Japanese dependency on U.S. imports. BA-MA, RM 11/77, 017, Attaché Report, Re: *Unterhaltung mit dem Vizechef des Admiralstabes, Vizeadmiral Kondo,* 279 gKdos., 17.04.1941. Near the end of May Wenneker was informed by Kondō "that the attack upon Singapore is not even debated anymore in government circles." BA-MA, RM 12 II/249, fol. 21, 05.23.1941.

27. Except by Chapman, this source (NARA, RG 457/SRNA) seems to have been ignored in the literature. Chapman does, however, mention the "K" Operation, but confuses it with an exchange of information about aircraft torpedoes. Compare Chapman, "Signals Intelligence Collaboration," 238f. and 251, note 17. He describes it partly in a very detailed manner, but does not name any sources. Some of the wording is taken almost word for word from the SRNA.

28. NARA, RG 457/SRNA 1, Head 3rd Sect. Navy General Staff, to Japanese Naval Attaché, Washington, 016, 01.05.1940.

29. NARA, RG 457/SRNA 6, Head 3rd Sect. Navy General Staff to Japanese Nav.Att. Berlin, 742, 29.08.1940.

30. NARA, RG 457/SRNA 7, Head 3rd Sect. Navy General Staff to Japanese naval attaché Berlin., 780, 02.09.1940, and ibid., SRNA 8, Head 3rd Sect. Navy General Staff to Japanese naval attaché Washington, 786, 03.09.1940. The name of the German contacted, who was supposed to initiate contact on 20 September 1941, was given as "Mand" (probably Abwehragent Gustav Mand). Compare Chapman, "Signals Intelligence Collaboration," 251.

31. NARA, RG 457/SRNA 9, Japanese Naval Attaché Washington to Head, 3rd Sect. Navy General Staff, 177, 21.09.1940 and Ibid., SRNA 148 as well as ibid., SRNA 10, Japanese Naval Attaché Berlin to Head 3rd Sect. Navy General Staff, 653, 21.10.1940.

32. NARA, SRNA 13 and SRNA 167, Japanese Naval Attaché Washington to Head 3rd Sect. Navy General Staff, relating to 245, 09.11.1940; SRNA 14, Head 3. Sect. Navy General Staff to Japanese naval attaché Berlin, 046, 12.11.1940; and SRNA 15, Japanese naval attaché Berlin to Head 3rd Sect. Navy General Staff, 709, 13.11.1940. Here Yokoi mentions that he had made direct contact with the Abwehr in Berlin in this matter.

33. NARA, RG 457/SRNA 5311, Head 3rd Sect. Navy General Staff to Japanese naval attaché Berlin, 421, 13.03.1941. This was Lieutenant Commander Fukushima.

34. Compare Yokoi's report in SRNA 28 of 10 March 1941.

35. NARA, RG 457/SRNA 30, Japanese Naval Attaché Berlin to Head 3rd Sect. Navy General Staff, unnumbered, 18.04.1941. The Abwehr agent was named "Grosskopp"

here. Chapman, "Signals Intelligence Collaboration," 251, writes without sources in connection with this matter of Lieutenant Colonel Grosskopf, who was the head of the technical Luftwaffensection of the Abwehr (Abwehr I T/Lw).

36. NARA, RG 457/SRNA 44, Head 3rd Sect. Navy General Staff to Japanese naval attaché Berlin, unnumbered, 03.05.1941.

37. Ibid.

38. NARA, RG 457/SRNA 45, Japanese Naval Attaché Berlin to Head 3rd Sect. Navy General Staff and Captain Ōtani, unnumbered, 03.05.1941. Here is probably meant Lieutenant Commander Ōtani, who worked with the KO Shanghai and is mentioned in Wenneker's war diary as a contact with the representatives of the Abwehr there, mainly Theodor Siefken. Siefken was responsible for SIGINT in Shanghai. Compare BA-MA, RM 12 II/250, fol.108f., 22 October 1941. That Ōtani was informed about the "K" Operation hints that it actually was a cooperative SIGINT operation. Obviously the Abwehr wanted to keep these activities of its emissary secret, even from the German ambassador in Tokyo ("because of the nature of his duties and the need for keeping them as secret as possible among the GERMANS in TOKYO.") The Ōtani mentioned here is not to be confused with the naval engineer, Ōtani Buntarō, who was a member of the Japanese Naval Inspection Commission in Germany, where he stayed until war's end. Chapman's remarks on this in "Signals Intelligence Collaboration," 251, are speculative in nature and without a listing of sources. Cf. NARA, RG 38/13, Report: Cooperation of the German and Japanese Navies, without number and undated. The report can be found in the files about the interrogation of the crew of the German submarine U-234 that was on its way to Japan with a few high-ranking specialists and a cargo of uranium at the time of the German capitulation. One of them was Cdr. Gerhard Falck, who was one of the most senior specialists of Japan in the Kriegsmarine and immediately took care of the Japanese inspection commission after their arrival. He obviously wrote the report, which is in German. Falck was supposed to become Wenneker's technical consultant. Compare NARA, RG 457/SRNA 3349, Japanese naval attaché Berlin to Head, Equipment Bureau, 746, 30.11.1944. In the files that Falck had with him there was, among other things, a list of the commission members (NARA, RG 38/13, *Liste der Marinebesichtigungskommission, M Wa Stb 386/41 geh.*, n.d.) and he could give information about the whereabouts of the members (NARA, RG 165/466, *Liste der Angehörigen des japanischen Marineattachéstabes in Deutschland und ihr vermuteter Verbleib*, unnumbered, n.d.).

39. NARA, RG 457/SRNA 60, 63, 64, 87, 93 and 103. The messages mainly deal with recruitment of coworkers and the financial arrangements for it.

40. NARA, RG 457/SRNA 55, Japanese Naval Attaché Washington to Head 3rd Sect. Navy General Staff, 286, 23.05.1941.

41. NARA, RG 457/SRNA 56, Japanese naval attaché Washington to Head 3rd Sect. Navy General Staff, 291, 28.05.1941.

42. NARA, RG 457/SRNA 131, Head 3rd Sect. Navy General Staff to Japanese Naval Attaché Berlin, Nachricht für "G", unnumbered, 16.08.1941.

43. NARA, RG 457/SRNA 57, Head 3rd Sect. Navy General Staff to Japanese Naval Attaché Washington, unnumbered, 17.06.1941.

44. NARA, RG 457/SRNA 85, Head 3rd Sect. Navy General Staff to Japanese Naval Attaché Berlin, 498, 10.07.1941.

45. NARA, RG 457/SRNA 144, Japanese Naval Attaché Washington to Head of Bureau for Naval Affairs and Head 3rd Sect. of Navy General Staff, 578, 31.09.1941. The document proves that the "K" Operation was actually SIGINT against the U.S. Navy. In the area of SIGINT, a close cooperation of the Japanese navy was already present in 1941 with the German side, which is has until now been overlooked in the literature (e.g., in Chapman, "Signals Intelligence Collaboration"). However, the cooperation partner was not the Kriegsmarine but rather the Abwehr. This explains the noticeable disinterest of the Japanese on this topic during the visit of the inspection commission in Germany. Their need was already covered from this side.

46. For example Martin, "Deutschland und Japan," 97, note 13, with further references.

47. NARA, RG 457/SRNA 80–82, Japanese Naval Attaché Berlin to Deputy Minister of the Navy and Deputy Chief of Navy General Staff, 499, 29.06.1941. This document is reprinted in appendix F.

48. "We must take resolute action on behalf of the future of EAST ASIA, in this time of golden opportunity." NARA, RG 457/SRNA 81.

49. "Our foreign office is said to be adhering to formalities in the above recognition, and, at a time when the RUSSO-GERMAN War is at its height, is making various trifling requests of the GERMAN, ITALIAN and ROMANIAN Governments, which are acting in harmony." NARA, RG 457/SRNA 82.

50. Ibid.

51. NARA, RG 457/SRNA 113–15 and 117, Chief of Bureau for Military Affairs to Japanese Naval Attaché Berlin. 440, 26.07.1941. This document is printed in appendix G.

52. "[I]t is thought that the GERMANS may not be fully conversant with the real circumstances in this country . . . The situation in JAPAN is substantially different. The national constitution makes it impossible to organize national policy so simply and arbitrarily as in GERMANY, and decisions upon national policy are therefore unavoidably protracted. . . . There may be great difficulty in convincing the GERMANS of this." Ibid., SRNA 113f.

53. Ibid., SRNA 114. This was even given as "basic postulate" of cooperation: "that both nations give full play to their own special characteristics in their respective zones of responsibility."

54. Compare ibid., SRNA 115.

55. "Each country should plan its own actions, within its own particular sphere of responsibility, while acting in concert with the other on the broad issues." Ibid., SRNA 117.

56. "However, should both countries fall into straits where direct and mutual military assistance was a matter of necessity, the question would call for different handling." Ibid. This passage clearly shows that such mutual support was not considered necessary by the Japanese navy at that point in time.

57. Ibid., SRNA 118.

58. Ibid.: "Even if the present conflict ends in a complete victory for the Axis, due largely to the splendid achievements of the GERMAN Army in the fighting on land, great care will be necessary lest the rivalry between JAPAN and the BRITISH and AMERICAN Naval forces, which might still be left impaired by the result in the Far East, should continue, with JAPAN left to bear the brunt alone."

59. Compare Kondō's explanation about dependency on raw materials and the vulnerability of the Japanese sea routes, in note 23.

60. BA-MA, RM 7/94, fol. 407–12, Re: Conversation with Vice Admiral Nomura on 06.08.1941, relating to 17934/41 gKdos.

61. Ibid., fol. 407.

62. The document is printed in Sander-Nagashima, "Deutsch-japanische Marine-beziehungen," 614–22. Fricke commented on Nomura's statements by using, inter alia, such expressions as "an old dirty trick again," "nonsense," and "is this now stupid or outrageous."

63. BA-MA, RM 7/253, fol. 124, Mar.Att. Tokio to OKM und OKW, Mar.Att. 1088 gKdos., 05.11.1941.

64. KTB Skl., vol. 27, Bl. 110, November 1941.

65. Ike, ed., "Japan's Decision for War," 262.

66. BA-MA, N 165/21, fol. 122.

67. In the decoded Japanese attaché radio traffic there can be found no messages to or from Berlin for the time shortly before Pearl Harbor, but the order to the attaché in Washington to destroy the cipher machine is preserved. This does not yet mean, however, that there were no messages between Berlin and Tokyo, since the collection of messages is not complete. A fragment of a report can be found about a conversation between Nomura and Groos from 22 November during which the German seemingly asks the question about military cooperation in case of Japanese entry into the war. NARA, RG 457/SRNA 178, Nomura to Deputy Minister of the Navy and Deputy Chief of Navy General Staff, 806, N 35, 22.11.1941.

68. NARA, RG 457/SRNA 203f., Japanese Naval Attaché Berlin to Deputy Chief of Navy General Staff, 087, 24.01.1942.

69. Details of the planning and financial arrangements for Mann and other agents can be found in NARA, RG 457/SRNA 5323, Japanese Naval Attaché Berlin to Head 3rd Sect. Navy General Staff, 171, 18.02.1942, and ibid., SRNA 209, Head 3rd Sect. Navy General Staff to Japanese Naval Attaché Berlin, 200, 21.02.1942. Mann could be the former business partner of Commander (Ret.) von Knorr, who had been naval attaché in Tokyo before World War I and had after war's end founded a firm there. Mann had been his partner there and had worked under cover for the Marineleitung at the beginning of the twenties. The likelihood of his being the same person gains from the Japanese practice of using contacts made at that time. Another contact was the engineer Dr. Techel, who had played a key role in the camouflaged submarine construction of the Reichsmarine. In 1924, after his trip to Japan, Canaris had warned that the Japanese had wanted to exploit him for their purposes.

    During the decoding of the radio messages the Americans seem not to have recognized the connections. On a message with orders to the Japanese naval attaché to gain the technical specifications of Dutch submarines in the Dutch East Indies by Techel ("Please take steps, such as using 'Techel,' to investigate the principal details, performance, etc., of DUTCH submarines"), one can find the commentary: "Meaning unknown." NARA, RG 457/SRNA 11, Head 3rd Sect. Navy General Staff to Japanese Naval Attaché Berlin, 027, 05.11.1940. This happened before the Japanese officially asked for the plans of the Dutch submarines at the Kriegsmarine. Cf. KTB Skl., vol. 17, Bl. 309, 23 January 1941.

70. NARA, RG 457/SRNA 239, Japanese Naval Attaché Berlin to Head 3rd Sect. Navy General Staff, 482, 04.06.1942. That Mann was left in the belief that his work for the Japanese remained unknown to the German side, can be seen from the Japanese report about Mann's information about a German deserter. Mann had first met the *Funkbootsmann* (radio operator) in February 1942 in Madrid. Yokoi reported about this to Tokyo: "He informed us here, enabling the Germans to make immediate disposition of the case, as a result of which the OKW expressed their thanks to us. (The fact that we are cooperating with the OKW is being kept strictly secret from him.)" NARA, RG 457/SRNA 240, Japanese Naval Attaché Berlin to Head 3rd Sect. Navy General Staff, 483, 04.06.1942. One can assume that the radio operator was murdered or abducted into the German sphere of influence, which in essence would be the same. It is possible that the Japanese saw in this a potential threat to the willingness of Mann to cooperate.

71. NARA, RG 457/SRNA 250, Head 3rd Sect. Navy General Staff to Japanese Naval Attaché Berlin, 076, 21.06.1942.

72. This radio message is illuminating in that the code names of sources of the attaché are revealed. Yokoi reported to the Head of the Naval Intelligence Service in May

1942 that his sources, "P," "O," "S," "L," and "X" must be especially protected against being compromised with respect to the Germans. "P" was a submariner from World War I. He belonged to the NCO branch and knew Dönitz; his reports were trustworthy. The last was also true for "O," a technician in the Headquarters of the Luftwaffe. Details to "S," "L," and "X" Yokoi did not give. In the SRNA files there can be found multiple reports about "S" that identify him as a highly placed source in the Italian Foreign Ministry. Compare SRNA 5310, 62, 65, and 104.

Chapter 14. Intentions and Evasions

1. Cf. Martin, "Deutschland und Japan," 59.
2. BA-MA, RM 7/253, fol. 205f., Militärische Vereinbarung zwischen Deutschland, Italien und Japan. Abschrift Nr. 16, 1204/42 gKdos., 18.01.1942. Another copy can be found in RM 7/1063, fol. 62–64, Anlage (enclosure) relating to 1.Skl. 1204/42. Martin, "Deutschland und Japan," 232ff. contains a reprint of the document out of the files of the PAAA. BA-MA, RM 7/253, fol. 196–97, Re: *Zusammenarbeit mit Japan*, 29715/41 gKdos., 31.12.1941.
3. BA-MA, RM 7/253, fol. 208–16, Denkschrift I opa (Rost), unnumbered, 12.02.1942.
4. BA-MA, RM 7/253, fol. 226-229, note by Ib (plan) (Assmann), unnumbered, gKdos. Chefs., 21.03.1942.
5. Ibid., fol. 227.
6. Ibid.
7. "Since the OKW/WFSt obviously does not plan to hold such an instruction, I consider it necessary to hand in a petition to the Wehrmachtführungsstab, since the Skl. is probably the only post that can fully appreciate the changing consequences of the Japanese and German land and sea operations in their full meaning." Ibid., fol. 228f.
8. BA-MA, RM 7/253, fol. 390-394, *Besprechung Chef WFSt, General d. Art. Jodl, mit japanischem Vizeadmiral Nomura und japanischem Generallt. Bansai im FHQu am 5.8.1942*, 1581/42 gKdos. Chefs., dated from 8 August 1942.
9. Ibid., fol. 391. This passage was promptly underlined and annotated with a question mark by a reader in the Skl.
10. Ibid., fol. 393.
11. Wenneker stated later that he had only heard of the complete scope of the Japanese losses at the battle of Midway around 1943–44. NARA, RG 38/112, Headquarters 441st Counter Intelligence Corps Detachment. Special Operations Section. Admiral Wenneker. *Report about My Stay in Japan*, without number, 20.03.1946; 6 of this report.
12. BA-MA, RG 7/253, fol. 512f., Mar.Att. Tokio to OKW, Skl. und MAtt (Mar.Att.2683 gKdos.), *Lagebeurteilung zu Jahresende*, ObdM 2723/42 gKdos.

Chefs., 17.12.1942. Another copy in RM 7/1063, fol. 211ff. Cf. Rahn, "Japan und der Krieg in Europa," 163f.

13. BA-MA, RM 7/253 fol. 514, Keitel to Wenneker (OKW/WFSt/O552243/42 gKdos. Chefs.), Reply to Mar.Att. Tokio 2683 gKdos., ObdM 2788/42 gKdos. Chefs., 24.12.1942. Another copy in RM 7/1063, fol. 215f.

14. Wenneker was ordered in March 1943: "Skl. puts great value on reporting of proven method. For reports to the OKW use Chefs. OKW/WFSt 552243/42 from 24 December." This was nothing other than the order to report to the OKW what they wanted to hear, but to report the facts to the Skl. BA-MA, RM 7/1064, I OPA to Mar.Att. Tokio, 6423/43 gKdos., 03.03.1943.

15. NARA, RG 457/SRNA 113–15 and 117, Head of Bureau for Naval Matters to Japanese Naval Attaché Berlin. 440, 26.07.1941.

16. NARA, RG 457/NR 877 CBCB34 19460000, Box 187, 190/37/11/1, "The German Navy and Japan." S-45.224, top secret. The study originates from 1946 and was only declassified in the spring of 1996.

   Besides the captured German naval files, the results of the relevant interrogations of POWs and the American and British decoding of the signal traffic were also used, including the still-classified "Seahorse Traffic" (German attaché signal traffic, Berlin-Tokyo). The following observations rely heavily on this important document.

17. NARA, RG 457/SRNA 4796f., Chief of Staff for Military Matters, Head 3rd Sect. of the Navy General Staff, Minister of the Navy and Chief of Navy General Staff to Abe, 291, 28.04.1945. The Japanese actually believed for a time that the Skl. had agreed. In actuality their proposal was denied on 27 April at the latest. Compare the handwritten commentary, ibid. That behind this Japanese proposal stood the agreements of the "No separate peace treaty" is possible but is not apparent in the sources.

18. Ibid., 8f.

19. Ibid., 9.

20. Details on the chartering are found in BA-MA, RM 12 II/278, 281, 294, 304, 309, 310.

21. The newest and most extensive work on blockade running is Brice, *Blockadebrecher*. As to the transported goods and quantities, see part 3, below.

22. Allied successes against the blockade-runners were mostly based on breaking the German naval codes. Normally the blockade-runners kept strict radio silence. However, the German submarines operating in sea areas where the Skl. presumed friendly merchantmen to be sailing to and from East Asia were not allowed to attack lone merchant ships. These messages were also read by the Allies and gave valuable starting points for the hunt on blockade-runners. For details about oper-

ations of the Allies in order to finally suppress the blockade-runner traffic around the years 1943–44, see NARA, RG 457/SRH 260, Narrative of Anti-Blockade Runner Operations South Atlantic, 1 December 1943–8 January 1944 (OPPLAN BR), with message from Com. 4th Fleet (Ingram) to CinC U.S. Fleet via CinC U.S. Atlantic Fleet, dated from 14 February 1944, [no number], Secret, 15 January 1944.

23. Seahorse Traffic, ZTPGU 23903, 04.04.1944, quoted from "German Navy and Japan," 11.

24. Seahorse Traffic, ZTPGU 24323, 18.04.1944, ibid.

25. Seahorse Traffic, ZTPGU 26660, 19.06.1944, ibid.

26. Seahorse Traffic, PPA 14, 22.09.1944, ibid., 12.

27. NARA, RG 457/SRNA 428, Abe to Tokyo, 494, N 170, 21.05.1943.

28. "German Navy and Japan," 13; NARA, RG 457/SRNA 426f., Japanese Naval Attaché Berlin to Deputy Minister of the Navy and Deputy Head of the Navy General Staff, 487, 17.05.1943.

29. NARA, RG 457/SRNA 110f., Berlin to Tokyo. Travel route "Satsuki 2," 808, 01.04.1944. Since this information was known to the U.S. Navy by 10 April 1944, it is probable that it was used for the hunt for the submarine.

30. "German Navy and Japan," 14. Even in 1944 Hitler had to make clear to the Kriegsmarine that both of the boats were presents. NARA, RG 457/SRNA 1194f., Japanese Naval Attaché Berlin to Deputy Minister of the Navy and Deputy Chief of the Navy General Staff, 867, 21.04.1944.

31. NARA, RG 457/SRNA 477-479, Tokyo to Japanese Naval Attaché Berlin, 429, 04.07.1943. Notification of the inspections on 16 July.

32. Ibid., 16.

33. This conclusion is drawn in a study called "German Signals Intelligence," chapter 4 of which is devoted to German-Japanese cooperation in this area. It does not seem to have been made accessible to the public yet. It is, however, mentioned in the conclusion of "The German Navy and Japan," 16.

34. The submarines were of the types XXI and XXIII, with new propulsion, whose high speeds underwater founded Dönitz's hope on a "new submarine war."

35. How seldom one received precise information is illustrated by Wenneker's commentary to one of the few Japanese reports about this topic: BA-MA, RM 12 II/252 fol. 307, 19 March 1943. "Finally the Japanese navy is giving me a halfway complete compilation of Russian shipping in the previous year." Underlined by author.

36. "The Germans gave more than they received, both in intelligence about themselves and in intelligence about the enemy." "German Navy and Japan," 17.

37. In June Yokoi had imparted to the Skl. that the Japanese navy wanted to continue such deployments into the Indian Ocean until end of 1942. He had not, however, been able to give strength estimates about the forces earmarked for this. BA-MA,

RM 7/253, fol. 365f., *Aktenvermerk*, 15784/42 gKdos., 30.06.1942. In August the Japanese still claimed all African coastal waters in the Indian Ocean as their operational area. Cf. Tokyo to Japanese Naval Attaché Berlin and Rome, 692, 12.08.1942, and Tokyo to Naval Attaché Berlin, 064, 24.08.1942. Quoted from "German Navy and Japan," 21.

38. Yokoi to Tokyo, 915, 13.10.1942, ibid., 22.

39. Compare BA-MA, RM 7/253, fol. 445f., Skl. to Mar.Att. Tokio, 85 gKdos., 11.11.1942. Another copy in RM 7/1089, fol. 602f.

40. BA-MA, RM 7/253, fol. 447, Note on report of Japanese liaison officer, 2342/42 gKdos. Chefs., 12.11.1942.

41. Tokyo to Mar.Att. Berlin, 751, 11.11.1942. Quoted from "German Navy and Japan," 22.

42. BA-MA, RM 7/253, fol. 470, Note on report of Japanese Liaison Officer Taniguchi, 2486/42 gKdos. Chefs., 24.11.1942.

43. BA-MA, RM 7/253, fol. 473, Note on report of Japanese liaison officer, 2598/42 gKdos. Chefs., 03.12.1942.

44. Ibid. The commentator was Rost.

45. BA-MA, RM 7/253, fol. 475–79, note: betr. Einsatz der japanischen Ubootswaffe, 2625/42 gKdos. Chefs., 06.12.1942.

46. Japanese Mar. Att. Berlin to Tokyo, SJA 527, 01.07.1943. Quoted from "German Navy and Japan," 26.

47. Japanese Mar. Att. Berlin to Tokyo, SJA 316, 09.08.1943. Quoted from "German Navy and Japan," 26.

48. BA-MA, RM 12 II/252, fol. 313, 22.03.1943.

49. Abe to Tokyo, SJA 450, 16.08.1943, "German Navy and Japan," 24.

50. BA-MA, RM 7/254, fol. 168–70, Niederschrift über die Besprechung + 1/Skl. (i.V. C./Skl) mit Vizeadmiral Abe am 24.8.1943, 2517/43 gKdos. Chefs., 25.08.1943, and NARA, RG 457/SRNA 537-540, Abe an stellv. Minister of the Navy und stellv. Chef Admiralstab., 947, N186, 28.08.1943.

51. Abe to Tokyo, SJA 496 (N192), 16.09.1943. Quoted from "German Navy and Japan," 27.

52. NARA, RG 457/SRNA 577-579, Tokyo to Abe, 802, 22.09.1943.

53. "German Navy and Japan," 27.

54. "German Navy and Japan," 25.

55. Cf. note 22.

56. See also part 1 and compare to this Saville, "German Submarines in the Far East," U.S. Naval Institute *Proceedings* 87 (1961), no. 8: 80–92. This version suffers from lack of analysis, and Saville could at that time not yet prove the connection with Ultra. Further information to this can be found in NARA, RG 457/SRMN-054, OP-20-GI Special Studies Relating to U-Boat Activity, 1943–1945; RG 457/SRMN-

051A, OP-20-GI Memoranda to COMINCH F21 on German U-Boat Activities Oct. 1943–Sept. 1944; RG 457/SRMN-037, COMINCH File: U-Boat Intelligence Summaries January 1943–May 1945; RG 457/SRMN-068, OP-20-GI Memoranda to COMINCH F21 on German U-boats east of Capetown; RG 457/ SRH-232, U.S. Navy COMINCH Radio Intelligence Appreciations Concerning German U-boat Activity in the Far East (January–April 1945); RG 457/SRH-142, Ultra and the Campaigns against the U-boats in World War II; RG 457/SRH-008, Battle of the Atlantic, vol II, U-boat Operations.

57. "German Navy and Japan," 29.

58. Ibid., 31.

59. NARA, RG 457/SRNA 2602-2604, Abe to Tokyo. Report about a conversation with Dönitz in Quarters "Koralle" on 26 September 1944, N 256, 27.09.1944. The conversation was unfavorably influenced by the news, during the talks, of the sinking of U-859 off Penang by an Allied submarine. The difficulties that the Japanese were having in supplying adequate ASW capabilities in the zone around the base, and with that to secure a precondition for submarine operations, could not have been illuminated more clearly.

60. NARA, RG 457/SRNA 3553f. and 3567, Tokyo to Japanese Naval Attaché Berlin and Abe, 061, 18.12.1944.

61. "German Navy and Japan," 39.

62. NARA, RG 457/SRGL 1301-1303, Skl. to Wenneker, 16 and 17.08.1944.

63. NARA, RG 457/SRGL 2141, Wenneker to Kriegsmarine Berlin, 106, 21.12.1944.

64. Cf. NARA, RG 457/SRNA 1455–1459, Japanese Naval Attaché Berlin to Deputy Minister of the Navy and Deputy Chief of the Navy General Staff, 985, 26.05.1944. This important document is reprinted in appendix H.

65. NARA, RG 457/SRNA 4243f. Abe and Kojima to Deputy Minister of the Navy and Deputy Chief of the Navy General Staff, 035, N 299, 01.03.1945. Both naval officers explained here that even the Japanese army could better instruct the Germans than they could.

66. NARA, RG 457/SRNA 3261, Japanese Naval Attaché Sweden to Head 3rd Sect. of the Navy General Staff and Japanese Naval Attaché in Germany, 585, 20.11.1944.

67. NARA, RG 457/SRNA 3325, Abe and Kojima to Japanese Naval Attaché Sweden, 737, N 272, 27.11.1944.

68. NARA, RG 457/SRNA 3385, Head 3. Sect. of the Navy General Staff to Japanese Naval Attaché Berlin, 040, 05.12.1944.

69. NARA, RG 457/SRNA 3401, Japanese Naval Attaché Sweden to Head 3rd Sect. of Navy General Staff, Army and Vice-Admiral Abe, 627, 05.12.1944.

70. NARA, RG 457/SRNA 603-606, Abe to Deputy Minister of the Navy and Deputy Chief of the Navy General Staff, 162, N 197, 15.10.1943.

71. NARA, RG 457/SRNA 753f., Chief of the Bureau for Military Affairs to Japanese Naval Attaché Berlin, 144, 08.01.1944. This was the cargo manifest of "Matsu" (pine tree), which was the code name for I-29. The tungsten was the main part of the cargo.

72. NARA, RG 457/SRNA 968f., Abe to Minister of the Navy and Head of the Navy General Staff, 226, 12.03.1944.

73. NARA, RG 457/SRNA 1259–1269, Japanese Naval Attaché Berlin to Minister of the Navy. Inspection report, channel fortifications, 888, 04.05.1944. This and other radio messages were known to the Allies on 8 May 1944. Compare also conclusions of Boyd from his analysis of the Allied decoding of the radio traffic of Ambassador Ōshima. Boyd, *Hitler's Japanese Confidant*, 105.

74. Such as in the case of I-52, which received under the code name "Momi" (fir tree) on 9 June 1944 instructions from Kojima about a meeting with a German submarine on 22 June. The instructions also included the measures that were to be enacted in case of failure. The boat was to surface, for the first two nights, during the first ten minutes of each hour at the ordered meeting place, with an east-west course. Kojima's orders were already known to the Allies on 13 June. I-52 was destroyed on 24 June by Allied ASW forces, who were obviously waiting for it at the meeting place. NARA, RG 457/SRNA 1571f., Japanese Naval Attaché Berlin to Commander "Momi," 055, 09.06.1944.

75. NARA, RG 457/SRGL 1561, Skl. to Wenneker, MAtt 1550 gKdos., 20.10.1944. The cooperation with Kojima in Berlin was praised here. "Judging by what the Skl. now knows, one now has the impression there, that, in contrast to earlier differing opinions, the Japanese navy could give various information of great interest and worth." Wenneker was instructed to test the readiness of Japanese posts for close cooperation.

76. NARA, RG 457/SRGL 2141, 106, 21.12.1944.

77. BA-MA, RM 7/189, fol. 307, Niederschriften über die Besprechung des ObdM mit dem Führer am 3.12.1944, 3648/44 gKdos. Chefs., 03.12.1944. Ten days later the request of Kojima was presented: BA-MA, RM 7/254, fol. 257 and 260f. Aktennotiz, [no number], 13.12.1944. Abe and Kojima supported the German wish: NARA, RG 457/SRNA 3520–3523, Abe to [Deputy] Minister of the Navy and [Deputy] Chief of Navy General Staff, 798, N 276, 15.12.1944; RG 467/SRNA 3743ff. Abe to [Deputy] Minister of the Navy and [Deputy] Chief of Navy General Staff, 859, N 280, 05.01.1945.

78. NARA, RG 457/SRNA 3742, [Deputy] Minister of the Navy and [Deputy] Chief of Navy General Staff to Japanese Naval Attaché Berlin, 089, 05.01.1945.

79. NARA, RG 38, Box 4, Marinesonderdienst Zweigstelle Heimat to Marinesonderdienst Ostasien, Tokio. Betr. Ladungs- und Nachschublisten "U.234," B.Nr. 227/45 gKdos., 18.03.1945.

80. "Atombomben Heisse Ladung," *Der Spiegel*, no. 2, 8 January 1996, 148f. Suggestions proposed here state that the captured uranium oxide could have been used for the U.S. atomic weapons that were used against Hiroshima and Nagasaki.

81. Short characterizations of the ten German passengers can be found in NARA, RG 38, Box 4, Op-16-Z to Op-16-PT. "Passengers on U-234, now prisoners of war, available for interrogation," [no number], 29 May 1945.

82. NARA, RG 165, Box 466, protocol of the overhearing [by hidden microphones] of [POWs Fehler, Bode, and Bernadelli], 3966, 29.05.1945.

83. See NARA, RG 38, Box 4, Op-16-Z to Op-16-PT, [no number], 29 May 1945.

84. Colonel von Sandrart, former head of the Bremen air defenses, who was informed about the newest tests of antiaircraft weapons of the Luftwaffe, and Senior Lieutenant Menzel, who had been deployed at the Wernichen test center near Berlin. Ibid.

85. The engineer August Bringewald and technician Franz Ruf. Bringewald were considered by the Americans to be "the top engineer[s] of the Messerschmidt factory." Ibid.

86. These were Senior Lieutenants Hellendoorn (antiaircraft specialist) and Bulla (naval aviator).

87. Lieutenant Commander Schlicke was an engineer with three doctorates whom the Americans considered to be "Germany's top ranking specialist in research and testing of radar, infra-red and D/F." Commander Falck was a naval officer as well as engineer and shipbuilding specialist. In addition he possessed lengthy experience in negotiations with the Japanese. He had been responsible for the Japanese inspection commission in 1941.

88. Geschwaderrichter (Magistrate) Nieschling. Termed a "100 percent Nazi" by his U.S. interrogators, he could claim that he had arrested Lieutenant Commander Kranzfelder, the only naval officer involved directly in the incidents of 20 July 1944, ibid. For Nieschling's observations about Kranzfelder, see NARA, RG 165, Box 522, Protocol of overhearing of Humann-Nieschling, 4068 secret, 13.06.1945.

89. Among the blockade-runners captured by Allied naval forces in January 1944 was also the German ship *Burgenland*. Prisoners on board were either murdered or not let out of their cells before the scuttling of the ship. This incident was part of a judicial proceeding against Wenneker in the sixties.

90. NARA, RG 457, SRH-075, Japanese reaction to German defeat, 5. Compare also, Spector, *Listening to the Enemy*. From the BdU Wenneker had received orders that one boat should return to Europe. NARA, RG 457/SRGL 2944 and 2946, BdU op to Wenneker and Head of Southern Area, [no number], 07.05.1945. The last date can be traced back to a writing error during the translation of the message, because Wenneker's answer, that the boats were not seaworthy and therefore

could not return, is dated from 5 May 1945. Ibid., SRGL 2958, Wenneker to Dönitz, *Chefsache* 87, 05.05.1945. On the same day he had also reported that the Navy General Staff had advised him that large parts of the Japanese forces were considering capitulation "as far as the conditions are somewhat honorable." NARA, RG 457/SRGL 2956, *Chefsache* 82, 05.05.1945. This message was also read by the Allies and deemed so important that it was presented to the highest decision makers (e.g., Churchill). PRO, HW 1/3770, ULTRA/ZIP/ZGA/140, Wenneker to Dönitz, *Chefsache* 82, top secret "U", 05.05.1945. The document seems also to have been relayed on 14 May 1945 to U.S. posts.

91. NARA, RG 457/SRNA 2783f. Deputy Minister of the Navy, Tokyo, to Abe and Japanese Naval Attaché Berlin, 913, 08.10.1944.

92. NARA, RG 457, SRH-075, 2.

93. Compare the paper traffic in BA-MA, RM 12 II, vols. 294, 306, 316, 346, 356, and 388.

94. Compare also BA-MA, RM 12 II/392 OKM. KTB Captain Paul Werner Vermehren, Assistant of the Naval Attaché Tokyo, 18 May 1945–8 January 1947.

Chapter 15. Exchange of Personnel

1. MS *Asaka Maru*, 7,399 GRT, Nippon Yusen KK, Tokyo.

2. Cf. BA-MA, RM 12 II/248, fol. 254 and 265, 17.03.1941 and 28.03.1941.

3. The German naval attaché Tokyo informed the German naval staff on 26 February 1943 that Captain Onoda would leave for Berlin via Siberia in early March. BA-MA, RM 12 II/252, fol. 285, MAtt 580, 06.03.1943. Likewise some members of the Japanese naval commission of 1941 returned to Japan in 1943 via Siberia. Obviously the Trans-Siberian route was closed by the Russians later on in 1943, so Japanese officials preferred to go by submarine to Europe thereafter.

4. KTB Skl., 50:620, 29 October 1943.

5. Personal information from Dr. Sönke Neitzel, 24 April 1999.

6. NARA, RG 457/SRNA 4667ff., Japanese Naval and Military Attachés of the Naval and Military Mission, Germany, to Navy and Army Vice Ministers and Vice Chiefs of Naval and Army General Staffs, 15115–16155, 12.04.1945. According to this message, Generaloberst Köller, chief of the air force staff, suggested on 9 April 1945 the advance air transport to Japan of Major General Wild and another officer from the staff of the designated air force attaché, General Kessler, to speed up the exchange of experience gained in warfare with new weapons.

7. NARA, Microfilm Publ. T1022, roll 1770, KTB Skl. CIX, *Beitrag 1/Skl. Ig zum Kriegstagebuch des ObdM Monat Mai*, 6, 1.Skl. Ig 1196/42 gKdos. Chefs. 19.06.42.

8. Cf. BA-MA, RM 12 II/252, fol. 304, 17.03.1943.

9. German Mar.Att. Tokyo to OKM/Skl. Ausl. III 0195 gKdos., 25.12.1943, KTB 1.Skl. Iu, PG 33335; NARA Microfilm Publ. T1022, roll 2063. BA-MA, RM 7/122, fol. 410–11, *Vermerk: betr. Einholen japanischen Ubootes "Kiefer,"* 1.Skl. Ik 8166/44 gKdos., 16.03.1944.

10. KTB of U-180, 9 February 1943–3 July 1943, PG 30167; ONI roll T-93-E, NARA. Microfilm Publ. T1022, roll 2836; RG 242. See also NARA, RG 457/SRNA 439, Head 3rd Sect. Naval General Staff to Naval Attaché Berlin, 18600, 20.05.1943 For details see BA-MA, RM 7/1067.

11. The two Japanese officers were Cdr. Emi Tetsushi, a former U-boat commander, and Lt. Cdr. (E) Tomonaga Hideo, formerly serving with the Submarine Testing Command.

12. Nomura, *Senkan U-511 Go no Unmei* (Fate of U-boat U-511), 164ff.

13. PRO, ADM 223/51, German-Japanese interchange of technical information.

14. PRO, ADM 223/622, fol. 246f., German U-boats of Capetown, 1.–4. offensive, translated Italian report on Italian submarine specialists in Pasir Panjang. See also NARA, RG 457/SRH 019, Blockade-running between Europe and the Far East by submarine, 1942–1944.

15. NARA, RG 457/SRNA 426, Japanese Naval Attaché Berlin to Navy Vice Minister and Vice Chief of Naval General Staff, 17.05.1943. Designated Japanese commander of U-1224 was Lt.Cdr. Norita Sadatoshi.

16. NARA, RG 457/SRH 019, Blockade-running between Europe and the Far East by submarine 1942–1944.

17. Details on personnel assigned to the various stations is given in NARA, RG 457/SRNA 554, Tokyo to Japanese Naval Attaché in Germany, 10.09.1943.

18. Names of the passengers and type of cargo aboard the I-29 are given in NARA, RG 457/SRNA 753, Chief of Bureau of Military Affairs, Tokyo, to Japanese Naval Attaché in Germany, 08.01.1944.

19. For the role of signal intelligence in the sinking of I-52, see chapter 17, note 74. Likewise, the routes and approximate positions followed by RO-501 and I-29 became known to the Allies by the messages given in NARA, RG 457/SRNA 1096, Japanese Naval Attaché in Germany to Chief of Office of Naval Command, 01.04.1944, and SRNA 1218, Commander I-29 to CINC 6th Fleet, 25.04.1944. The loss of I-52 and the rediscovery of its wreck by a private treasure hunter group in 1995, in order to salvage its load of two tons of gold, is described by David Miller, "The Mystery of the Last Voyage of Japanese Submarine I-52," *Warship* 1996, 25–30, and Carl Boyd, "U.S. Navy Radio Intelligence during the Second World War and the Sinking of the Japanese Submarine I-52," *Journal of Military History* 63(2): 339–54.

20. NARA, RG 457/SRNA 1256, Japanese Naval Attaché to Navy Vice Minister and Vice Chief of Naval General Staff, 3 May 1944.

21. 1.Skl. IE 26858/44 gKdos., *Niederschrift der Besprechung der Japanischen Marine-Kommission beim Chef der Seekriegsleitung, Admiral Meisel, am 29.08.1944, PG 33862*; NARA Microfilm Publ. T1022, roll 2135.

22. Mar.Att. Tokyo to BdU and Skl. E 1047 gKdos., 26.04.1944, KTB 1.Skl. CIX, PG 33861, and Skl. to Mar.Att. Tokyo, 1.Skl. Ic 13292 gKdos. 01.05.1944, PG 33861, NARA Microfilm Publ. T1022, roll 2135.

23. NARA, RG 457/SRNA 2167, Japanese Naval Attaché Berlin to Bureau of Military Affairs 328, contained in NARA, RG 457/SRNA 2395, Navy Vice Minister and Vice Chief of Naval General Staff to Japanese Naval Attaché in Germany, 9 September 1944. German approval for the transport of up to three passengers is noted in NARA, RG 457/SRNA 2238, Japanese Naval Attaché in Germany to Navy Vice Minister and Vice Chief of Naval General Staff 358, 27.08.1944.

24. Previously only three German naval officers (Lt. Cdr. Hoppe, Lt. Schrein, and Midshipman Rudolf as interpreter), who had reached Japan as part of the crew of the ill-fated armed merchant cruiser HSK 10 (*Thor*) were given the opportunity to stay for some weeks on the Japanese aircraft carrier *Zuikaku* during a workup period in Japanese home waters in April/May 1943.

25. NARA, RG 457/SRGL 1794f., Skl. to German Mar.Att Tokyo 119, 25.11.1944.

26. See chapter 15, note 77. The names of nine officers are given in NARA, RG 457/SRGL 2222, Skl. to German Mar.Att Tokyo 72, 15.01.1945.

27. NARA, RG 457/SRNA 3607/3609, Japanese Naval Attaché to Navy Vice Minister and Vice Chief of Naval General Staff 823, 23.12.1944.

28. NARA, RG 457/SRNA 3604f., Japanese Naval Attaché Germany to Navy Vice Minister and Vice Chief of Naval General Staff 821, 22.12.1944, and NARA, RG 457/SRNA 3697, Japanese Naval Attaché Germany to Navy Vice Minister and Vice Chief of Naval General Staff 848, 30.12.1944, contain details about the schedule for departures of the individual U-boats and their respective passengers selected by the Japanese for transfer to Japan.

29. NARA, RG 457/SRGL 2494, Skl. to German Mar.Att Tokyo 191, 15.02.1945. PRO, DEFE 3/742, 538f., ZIP/ZTPGU 37471, Commander in Chief U-boats to Commander U-boats Far East, 08.03.1945.

30. NARA, RG 457/SRNA 4908ff., Vice Admiral Abe, from Sweden, to Navy Minister and Chief of Naval General Staff 342, 28.05.1945 explains the background for the suicide of Technical Commanders Shōji and Tomonaga aboard U-234. The war patrol of U-234 and the circumstances of the surrender are described in Hirschfeld, *Feindfahrten*, 362–67.

Chapter 16. Transport of Materials

1. BA-MA, RM 12/II 249, 28.06.1941, 30.06.1941, 02.07.1941.

2. NARA Microfilm Publ. T1022, roll 1770, KTB Skl. CIX, *Beitrag 1/Skl. Ig zum Kriegstagebuch des Ob.d.M. Monat Mai*, 7, 1.Skl. Ig 1196/42 gKdos. Chefs.

19.06.1942. Compare also KTB German Nav. Att. Tokyo, BA-MA, RM 12 II/248, fol. 115 and 232f., 07.11.1941 and 20.02.1941.

3. Vermehren, *Etappe Ostasien.*

4. NARA Microfilm Publ. T1022, roll 1770, KTB Skl. C IX, *Beitrag 1/Skl. Ig zum Kriegstagebuch des Ob.d.M. Monat Mai,* 8ff., 1.Skl. Ig 1196/42 gKdos. Chefs. 19.06.1942. See also Dinklage and Witthöft, *Die deutsche Handelsflotte 1939–1945,* 2:48ff.

5. KTB Skl., 20:50, 04 April 1941.

6. KTB German Nav.Att. Tokyo, BA-MA, RM 12 II/249, fol. 72, 21.07.1940.

7. See KTB Skl., 28:368, 24 December 1941, and 28:378, 25 December 1941.

8. KTB German Nav.Att. Tokyo, BA-MA, RM 12 II/250, fol. 40, 24.09.1941.

9. NARA Microfilm Publ. T1022, roll 1770, KTB Skl. C IX, *Auszug aus Bericht über die Durchführung des Blockadebruchs 1941/1942 (OKM 1015/42 Chefs.) L 6 HWK Nr. 041/42 Chefs., Anlage 2 zum Beitrag 1. Skl. Ig zum KTB des OBdM Monat Mai,* 1 Skl. Ig 1196/42 gKdos. Chefs., 19.06.1942.

10. NARA Microfilm Publ. T1022, roll 1770, KTB Skl. C IX, Naval Staff to OKW-WFSt betr. *Blockadebrecherreisen 1942/43,* 1.Skl. 753/43 gKdos., 13.01.1943.

11. BA-MA, RM 13/2, *KTB der Etappenorganisation der Kriegsmarine (Marine-Sonderdienst),* 4:209ff., *Einsatz von Etappen-V-Schiffen zur Durchführung von Blockadebrecheraufgaben,* 10.07.1942. See also NARA Microfilm Publ. T1022, roll 1770, KTB Skl. C IX, Beitrag 1.Skl. Ig zum KTB des OBdM Monat Juni, 1.Skl. Ig 1413/42 gKdos., 21.07.1942 for details on cargo carried to Japan by M/V *Dresden.*

12. BA-MA RM 7/224, *OKW Sonderstab HWK zu Chef OKW betr. Bericht über die Durchführung des Blockadebruches 1942/43, HWK 0117/43,* gKdos. Chefs., 05.06.1943.

13. NARA Microfilm Publ. T1022, roll 1770, *KTB Skl. C IX, Beitrag 1.Skl. Ig zum KTB des OBdM Monat November [1942],* 1.Skl. Ig 242/43 gKdos., 19.01.1943.

14. KTB Skl., 40:350, 16 December 1942.

15. NARA Microfilm Publ. T1022, roll 1770, *KTB Skl. C IX, Aktenvermerk betr. Planungen für den Blockadebruch 1943/44,* 1.Skl. Ig 1667/43 gKdos. Chefs. 02.06.43. For details see NARA Microfilm Publ. T1022, roll 1770, KTB Skl. C IX, *Beitrag 1.Skl. Ig zum KTB des OBdM Monate Oktober–Dezember (1943),* 1.Skl. Ig 838/44 gkdos., 09.03.1944.

16. NARA, RG 457/SRH 260, United States Atlantic Fleet, HQ Cdr. Fourth Fleet, Narrative of Anti-Blockade Runner Operations South Atlantic, December 1, 1943–January 8, 1944, A16-1(2)/A16-3, serial no. 0025, 15 January 1944.

17. KTB Skl., 53:310, 18 January 1944. NARA Microfilm Publ. T1022, roll 1770, *KTB Skl. C IX, Beitrag 1.Skl. Ig zum KTB des OBdM Monat Mai 1944,* 1.Skl. Ig 2189/44 gKdos., 11.07.1944.

18. BA-MA RM 7/224, *OKW Sonderstab HWK to Chef OKW betr. Bericht über die Durchführung des Blockadebruches 1942/43, HWK 0117/43,* gKdos. Chefs., 05.06.1943.

19. NARA Microfilm Publ. T1022, roll 1770, *KTB Skl. C IX, OKW Sonderstab HWK to Chef OKW betr. Blockadebrecher, L 23 HWK Nr. 113/43,* gKdos., 23.01.1943.

20. The majority of the cargo load was lost on 13 October 42 when I-30 sank off Singapore after hitting a mine during its final transfer passage to Japan.

21. BA-MA RM7/224, Skl. to Abt. Ausland IV for German Mar.Att. Tokyo, on details of 115 t[on]s of German cargo requested for transport on I-30, 1.Skl. I Op a 7500/42 gKdos., 30.03.1942, and German Mar.Att. Tokyo to OKW-Ausl. IV for Skl., on Japanese refusal, Mar.Att. 635 of 02.04.42. The Japanese navy offered transportation for only three tons of cargo load because only about five tons load capacity was expected for the return trip to Japan.

22. Fioravanzo, *La Marina dall'8 Settembre 1943 alla Fine del Conflitto,* 87ff.

23. NARA Microfilm Publ. T1022, roll 1770, KTB Skl. C IX, Naval Staff to Japanese Nav. Att. VAdm. Abe on request for Japanese transport U-boats, 1.Skl. I Op a 1771/43 gKdos. Chefs., 24.06.1943; and 1.Skl. Ik/I Op a 2051/43 gKdos. Chefs., 21.07.1943. The Japanese first turned down the German request, but later agreed to sent two U-boats to Europe; see KTB Skl., vol. 47, 16 July 1943, and NARA Microfilm Publ. T1022, roll 1770, KTB Skl. C IX, Naval Staff to German Nav. Att. Tokyo, 1.Skl. Iop a 2585/43 gKdos. Chefs., of 29.08.1943.

24. NARA, RG 226, Translation of Chef HWK an Chef OKW, Bericht Blockadebruch nach Japan, 05.01.45, B.Nr. XL 15492, 13.07.45. See also Niestlé, *German U-Boat Losses,* 185f.

25. Ibid.

26. NARA Microfilm Publ. T1022, roll 1770, KTB Skl. C IX, *Einsatz Uboote zur Einfuhr aus Ostasien, Mar.Rüst/M Rü Iib 2262/44 gKdos. vom 19.07.1944, Anlage 3,* (enclosure 3) relating to 1.Skl. Ig 22894/44 gKdos.

27. PRO, DEFE 3/742, 538f., ZIP/ZTPGU 37471, Commander in Chief U-boats to Commander U-boats Far East, 08.03.1945. At that time only five long-range cargo transports (U-873 through U-876 of Type IXD2, and the Type XB boat U-234) were operational in German home waters, with two Type IXD42 (U-883 and U-884) in the final stage of completion.

28. NARA, RG 226, 05.01.45, B.Nr. XL 15492, 13.07.45. See also Niestlé, *German U-Boat Losses,* 185f.

29. NARA, RG 38/112, Headquarters 441st Counter Intelligence Corps Detachment. Special Operations Section. Admiral Wenneker, *Report about My Stay in Japan,* [no number], 20.03.1946, 20, gives slightly different figures by

omitting those blockade-runners that were prematurely recalled or returned from other causes.

30. BA-MA RM7/225, *Aktenvermerk Abschliessende Betrachtung über den Blockadebruch mit Überwasserschiffen 1941/1944*, 1.Skl. Ig 672/44 gKdos., 02.03.1944. Incomplete data on material transport by submarines is given in NARA, RG 226, translation of *Chef HWK an Chef OKW, Bericht Blockadebruch nach Japan, 05.01.45*, B.Nr. XL 15492, 13.07.45.

Chapter 17. Conclusion

1. See Sander-Nagashima, "Die deutsch-japanischen Marinebeziehungen, 1919 bis 1942," chaps. 2 and 3.

2. The potential that lay here might be imagined if one thinks of operations like "Rheinübung" (battleship *Bismarck*'s Atlantic operation) as the operations of a carrier group. The threat to Allied SLOCs would have taken on a different dimension.

3. Charles Dana Gibson even reports about a hanging of a German sailor by the heels in Singapore. Evidence of this from the records could not be established, though. Charles Dana Gibson, "The Far East Odyssey of the UIT-24," *Naval History* (Winter 1990): 19–23.

4. See, for instance, Admiral Fricke's scathing remarks on the margin of Groos's report on his talk with Nomura on 6 August 1941. BA-MA, RM 7/94, 407–12.

5. Indication of this can be found in personal effects of deceased former German naval officers, such as admirals Behncke, Groos, and Wenneker. See also parts of Cdr. Falck's report mentioned above.

6. BA-MA, RM 7/263, memo, "Betrachtungen über die Grundlage des Flottenaufbaues," [no number], Chefs., 01.05.1949, 66.

Appendix E: The *Automedon* Incident

1. BA-MA, RM 12 II/248, fol. 173f., 26 December 1940.

2. Ibid., fol. 149, 5 and 6 December 1940.

3. KTB Skl., 16:342, 31 December 1940.

4. Cf. Chapman, *The Price of Admiralty,* 2/3:343.

5. BA-MA, RM 12 II/248, fol. 162, 11 and 12 December 1940.

6. Cf. Presentation of the ObdM to the Führer on 27 December 1940, 1600 hours. Iop 2/41, reproduced in Wagner, *Lagevorträge,* 173.

7. Cf. Chapman, "Japanese Intelligence," 162.

8. See NARA, RG 457/SRNA 20.

9. See Ikeda and Nish, "Germany and the Capture of the *Automedon* Documents—I. A Japanese Appreciation," and Nish, "Germany and the Capture of the *Automedon* Documents—II. A British Appreciation," both in *German-Japanese Relations in the 1930s.*

10. Compare Ikeda, op. cit., 42f.

Appendix G: Chief of Bureau of Military Affairs to Naval Attaché Berlin, 26 July 1941

1. Crossed out by hand and changed to "Military."
2. Crossed out by hand and changed to "Russia."

Glossary

German Terms

Admiral Ostasien	admiral, East Asia, and German naval attaché, Tokyo
Auswärtiges Amt (AA)	foreign office
Befehlshaber der Unterseeboote (BdU)	commander in chief, submarine force
Bundesarchiv (BA)	Federal German National Archives
Chef im Südraum (CiS)	commander, southern area
"Eisbär"	"Polar Bear," code name for submarine task group at Cape of Good Hope.
Etappendienst der Kriegsmarine	Naval Supply Service
Flottenkommando	Fleet Command
Fregattenkapitän (F.Kapt.)	commander, senior rank
geheim (G)	secret
geheime Kommandosache (gKdos.)	higher than top secret; on need-to-know basis
geheime Kommando- sache Chefsache (gKdos. Chefs.)	highest degree of secrecy in the Wehrmacht

Grossadmiral (G. Adm.)	admiral of the fleet, grand admiral
Grossetappe Japan-China	Naval Supply Service, East Asia
Hilfskreuzer	auxiliary merchant cruisers (AMC)
Kapitän zur See (Kapt.z.S.)	captain (navy)
Korvettenkapitän (K.Kapt.)	commander, lower rank
Kriegsmarine	German navy (from 1935)
Kriegstagebuch (KTB)	war journal
Marinekommandoamt	Navy Command Office (later Quartiermeisteramt [Skl/QuA])
Marineleitung	Navy High Command (from 1919)
Marinesonderdienst (MSD)	Naval Special Service
Militärabkommen	military agreement
Militärarchiv (MA)	military archives
"Monsun"	"Monsoon," code name for submarine task groups in Indian Ocean
NSDAP	National Socialist Democratic Workers' Party
Oberbefehlshaber der Luftwaffe (OBdL)	commander in chief, air force
Oberbefehlshaber der Marine (OBdM)	commander in chief, navy
Oberkommando der Kriegsmarine (OKM)	Navy High Command (from 1935)
Oberkommando der Wehrmacht (OKW)	Armed Forces High Command (from 1938)
Oberkommando des Heeres (OKH)	Army High Command
Oberleutnant (Oblt.)	first lieutenant
OKW Amt Ausland	Armed Forces Foreign Section

OKW Amt Ausland Abwehr	Secret Military Intelligence Service
OKW Sonderstab HWK (Handelskrieg und wirtschaftliche Kampfmassnahmen)	Special Staff for Economic Warfare (from Oct. 1939)
OKW/Wehrmacht Führungsstab (OKW/WFSt)	Armed Forces Command Staff (from 1942)
Operationsabteilung (1/Skl)	Operations Division
Panzerschiffe	armored ships
Reichsaussenminister	foreign minister
Reichskriegsminister	war minister
Reichskriegs- ministerium (RKM)	War Ministry
Reichsluftfahrts- ministerium (RLM)	Air Ministry
Reichsmarine	German navy (from 1919)
Reichsverkehrs- ministerium (RVM)	Transport Ministry
Reichswehr- ministerium (RWM)	Defense Ministry
"Seehund"	"Seal," code name for submarine task group off South Africa
Seekriegsleitung (Skl)	Naval War Staff
Unterseeboots- führungsabteilung (2/Skl BdU op)	submarine operations division
Vizeadmiral (V.Adm.)	vice admiral

Japanese terms

Gaimushō	Foreign Ministry
Genrō	elder statesmen or oligarchs
Gozen-kaĭgi	Imperial Conference

Gunreibu	Navy General Staff
Jōyakuha	Treaty Faction
Kaigunshō	Navy Ministry
Kantaiha	Fleet Faction
Kantoku	Naval organization that collects technical information and building materials for construction projects abroad
Kokubō hoshin	"Guidelines for Defense of the Empire," national defense policy
Rengō kantai	Combined Fleet
Tennō	emperor

Bibliography

Note: The titles of published works in Japanese have been translated or paraphrased. The names of Japanese authors appear surname first according to Japanese custom.

Unpublished Sources

Papers of Friedrich-Wilhelm Hack.
Unpublished material in the possession of Prof. Dr. Bernd Martin and Dr. Gerhard Krebs.

Bundesarchiv-Militärarchiv, Freiburg im Breisgau (BA-MA)

MS #P-108. Studies of Historical Division, Headquarters United States Army, Europe. Foreign Military Studies Branch.

N165. Papers of Admiral [Ret.] Dr. h.c. Otto Groos.

N391. Papers of Grossadmiral Erich Raeder.

N565/14. Papers of Admiral Bürkner, Korrespondenz mit amerikanischen Historikern.

N565/32. Papers of Admiral Bürkner, Deutsch-Japanische Gesellschaft.

RF 04/36172. Untitled, filmed material of the former Zwischenarchiv Potsdam.

RH 8/v.3606. Untitled.

RM 6/22. Flottenfragen verschiedener Länder.

RM 6/31. Grossadmiral Raeder, Handmaterial. Deutsche Marinepolitik, 5 January 1932–27 May 1944.

RM 6/45. Vorbesprechungen zur Flottenkonferenz 1935. Hinweise auf Attaché-Berichte.

RM 6/58. Anlagenheft zur Schlussbesprechung Kriegsspiel A 1938/39 in Oberhof.

RM 6/77. Oberkommando der Kriegsmarine. ObdM Persönlich. Grossadmiral Raeder. 8 November 1942–23 Januar 1943.

RM 6/81. Handmaterial ObdM Kriegsfragen, 8 März 1939–1 März 1943.

RM 6/382. Attaché- Verwaltungs- und Personalangelegenheiten. November 1930–Dezember 1933, M I-3.

RM 7/85. 1.Skl. Teil B I. Überblick über die Lage Atlantik. Überblick über die Ausserheimische Kriegsführung. 31 Dezember 1940–31 März 1944.

RM 7/86. 1.Skl. Teil B II. Lageübersicht Westraum/Nordsee (15 Oktober 1941–31 Dezember 1943).

RM 7/94. KTB Skl, 1.Skl, Teil B V, Anlagen verschiedenen Inhalts, Januar 1941–Dezember 1941, vol. 4.

RM 7/96. KTB Skl, 1.Skl, Teil B V, Anlagen verschiedenen Inhalts, August 1942–Dezember 1942, vol. 6.

RM 7/98. KTB Skl, 1.Skl, Teil B V, Anlagen allgemeinen Inhalts, Juni 1943–Dezember 1943, vol. 8.

RM 7/103. KTB Skl, 2.Skl, September 1939–16 Februar 1940, 15 März 1940–6 Dezember 1940.

RM 7/104. KTB Skl, 3.Skl, B-Dienst, 1 Januar 1941–31 Dezember 1941.

RM 7/105. KTB Skl, 1.Skl, Teil B VI, Nachrichtendienst, B-Dienst, 1 Januar 1942–31 Dezember 1942.

RM 7/106. KTB Skl, 1.Skl, Teil B VI, Nachrichtendienst, B-Dienst, 1 Januar–15 Juni 1943, 1 Juli–31 August 1943, 1 November–4 Dezember 1943.

RM 7/108. KTB Skl, 1.Skl, Teil B VI, Nachrichtendienst, B-Dienst, 5 Dezember 1943–31 Oktober 1944, 16 Februar–28 Februar 1945, 16 März–10 Mai 1945.

RM 7/109. KTB Skl, 1.Skl, Teil B VII, Handelsschiffahrt, September 1939–Dezember 1941.

RM 7/110. KTB Skl, 1.Skl, Teil B VII, Handelsschiffahrt, Januar 1942–Oktober 1944.

RM 7/117. KTB Skl, 1.Skl, Teil B X, Lageübersicht Ostasien, Seekrieg im Stillen und Indischen Ozean, Dezember 1941–Juli 1944.

RM 7/119. KTB Skl, 1.Skl, Teil C I, Kreuzerkrieg ausserheimische Gewässer 1939/40.

RM 7/120. KTB Skl, 1.Skl, Teil C I, Kreuzerkrieg ausserheimische Gewässer 1941.

RM 7/121. KTB Skl, 1.Skl, Teil C I, Kreuzerkrieg ausserheimische Gewässer 1942.

RM 7/122. KTB Skl, 1.Skl, Teil C I, Kreuzerkrieg ausserheimischen Gewässer, 2 Januar 1943–2 Juli 1945.

RM 7/134. KTB Skl, 1.Skl, Teil C IIb, Westraum-Atlantikküste-Flottenoperationen, vol. 3, 3 Januar 1943–13 Mai 1944.

RM 7/171. KTB Skl, 1.Skl, Teil C V, Luftkrieg, vol. 3, 14 November 1941–7 Januar 1945.

RM 7/175. KTB Skl, 1.Skl, Anlage zum KTB Teil C VI und XV: Januar bis 3 April 1945.

RM 7/189. KTB Skl, 1.Skl, Teil C VIII, Überlegungen des Chefs der Skl. und Niederschriften über Vorträge beim Führer. Vom: Januar 1943 bis: Dezember 1944.

RM 7/222. KTB Skl, 1.Skl, Teil C IX, Versorgungsfragen. Undated.

RM 7/223. KTB Skl, 1.Skl, Teil C IX, Versorgungsfragen, Januar 1942–Dezember 1943.

RM 7/224. KTB Skl, 1.Skl, Teil C IX, Versorgungsfragen. Undated.

RM 7/225. KTB Skl, 1.Skl, Teil C IX, Versorgungsfragen, Januar 1944–Dezember 1944.

RM 7/229. KTB Skl, 1.Skl, Teil C XI, Handelsschiffahrt, Januar 1942–Dezember 1942.

RM 7/232. KTB Skl, 1.Skl, Teil C XII, Wirtschaftskriegführung, März 1939–November 1943.

RM 7/253. KTB Skl, 1.Skl, Teil C XV, Zusammenarbeit mit Japan, Januar 1941–Dezember 1942.

RM 7/254. KTB Skl, 1.Skl, Teil C XV, Zusammenarbeit mit Japan, Januar 1943–Dezember 1944.

RM 7/259. 1.Skl. Teil Ca. Grundlegende Fragen der Kriegführung. Januar 1942–Januar 1943.

RM 7/260. 1.Skl. Teil Ca. Grundlegende Fragen der Kriegführung. Januar 1943–Dezember 1943.

RM 7/263. KTB Skl, 1.Skl, Teil C, Flottenaufbau nach dem Kriege, Juli 1940–November 1943.

RM 7/277. KTB Skl, 1.Skl, Teil D, Lageberichte ausserheimische Gewässer, 1 Juli 1941–9 November 1943.

RM 7/309. KTB Skl, 1.Skl, Teil D, Lageberichte Ostasien. 7 Dezember 1941–9 Dezember 1944.

RM 7/310. KTB 1.Skl., Teil D, Lage: Handelsschiffahrt. 23 August 1939–3 September 1940.

RM 7/360. Marineattaché Tokio G 46 G 9a Ausweiche Kaihin–Hotel Kamakura (1944).

RM 7/703. 3.Skl. Material zur Feindlage. Pazifik 07.12.1942–01.01.1943.

RM 7/703. 3.Skl. Material zu Feindlage. Grossbritannien und Nordirland 23.9.1942–12.11.1942, Vereinigte Staaten von Amerika 23.9.1942–7.1.1943, Mittelmeer 7.10.1942–10.5.1943, Pazifik 7.12.1942–1.2.1943.

RM 7/706. 3.Skl. Material zur Feindlage. Dezember 1944–April 1945.

RM 7/707. 1.Skl. Handakte zum KTB Teil C. Feindlageberichte 3.Skl. 30 Dezember 1942–21 Dezember 1944.

RM 7/792. 3.Skl. B. (X)-B.-Meldungen und (X)-B.-Lageberichte. 22 Oktober 1941–31 Dezember 1941.

RM 7/794. OKM Abtlg. Funkaufklärung. (X)-B.-Lageberichte. 1 Juli 1942–31 Dezember 1942.

RM 7/846. KTB Skl, 1.Skl, C IV, KTB U-Bootskriegführung, 1942.

RM 7/847. KTB Skl, 1.Skl, C IV, KTB U-Bootskriegführung, Januar 1943–März 1944.

RM 7/848. KTB Skl, 1.Skl, C IV, KTB U-Bootskriegführung, März 1944–Januar 1945.

RM 7/849. KTB Skl, 1.Skl, C IV, U-Bootskriegführung, Dezember 1944–April 1945.

RM 7/854. KTB Skl, 1.Skl. Teil D, Verschiedenes aus den letzten Tagen des Krieges, 1 Mai 1935–31 Mai 1945.

RM 7/883. KTB Skl, 1.Skl, Seekrieg 1939, Akte Weisungen der Seekriegsleitung an die Gruppen.

RM 7/887. KTB Skl, 1.Skl, Seekrieg 1941, Heft 2b-2, Weisungen und Berichte der Gruppe West, Januar 1941–Mai 1942.

RM 7/970. Naval Führer Directives, 10 January 1941–25 April 1941.

RM 7/1063. Zusammenarbeit Deutschland-Japan, Akte: X,1 vom 21.11.1941 bis 6.5.1943 Band 1.

RM 7/1064. Meldungen und Berichte aus Tokio. (in 1.Linie: deutsch. u. jap. Mar.Att.) Rückfragen der Skl. Aktz.: X,5 vom: 10.12.41 bis: 16.4.43 Band 1.

RM 7/1066, 1067. Akte X,9. Fahrt japanischen U-Boots nach Deutschland (Kirschblüte). Februar 1942–November 1942. Akte X,10. Deutsch-japanisches U-Treffen. Januar 1943–September 1943.

RM 7/1067. KTB Skl, 1.Skl, Deutsch-japanisches U-Treffen, Akte X, 10, Band 1, vom 2.1.43 bis 4.9.43.

RM 7/1071. Kriegswissenschaftliche Abteilung. Deutsche Allgemeine Zeitung. Zeitungsausschnitte und -auszüge. Japanisches KTB Teil VII, 1.9.1944–18.2.1945.

RM 7/1072. Untitled.

RM 7/1076. 1.Skl, Lagezimmer. Attaché-Meldungen. 28 September 1939–28 Dezember 1941.

RM 7/1088. KTB Skl, 1.Skl, Lagezimmer. Funksprüche an "Ausserheimische" Akte Nr.7, Band 1, 30 Dezember 1941–15 August 1942.

RM 7/1089. KTB Skl, 1.Skl, Lagezimmer. Funksprüche an "Ausserheimische" Akte Nr.7, Band 2, 16 August 1942–31 Dezember 1942.

RM 7/1099. KTB Skl, 1.Skl, Teil B V, Anlagen verschiedenen Inhalts, Januar 1944–Juli 1944.

RM 7/1100. Marinepolitische Angelegenheiten, 25.11.1938–15.6.1940.

RM 7/1101. 1.Skl. Ic. Ic 5–1 und 5-2 Verschiedenes, 3 August 1933–29 Juni 1940.

RM 7/1102. 1.Skl. Ic. 5-2 Verschiedenes, 27 Februar 1939–29 Juni 1940.

RM 7/1107. 1.Skl. Ic. 9-1 Deutsche Kolonien. Oktober 1939–November 1939.

RM 7/1110. 1.Skl. Ic. Politische Unterrichtung der ausserheimischen Streitkräfte (Funksprüche), August 1939–September 1943.

RM 7/1126. V, 2, Kriegserklärung.

RM 7/1233. 1.Skl. III.a. Berichterstattung der deutschen Japan-Kommission. Japan Kommission Januar 1941–Juli 1941.

RM 7/1257. GKdos-Akte Gen.Ref.III a24, vol.1. Schiffstypen (U-Boote).

RM 7/1294. 1.Skl. IC: II. Führung des Wirtschaftskrieges durch den Gegner. 4. Beschlagnahmen deutscher Ausfuhren vom: November 1939 bis: August 1940.

RM 7/1462. Untitled.

RM 7/1574. 1.Skl. Lagezimmer, Verschiedenes, 7 Januar–8 August 1941, Band 2.

RM 7/1575. 1.Skl. Lagezimmer, Verschiedenes, 15 Juli–28 Dezember 1941, Band 3.

RM 7/1576. 1.Skl. Lagezimmer, Verschiedenes, 6 Mai–3 September 1942, 18-1.

RM 7/1577. 1.Skl. Lagezimmer, Verschiedenes.

RM 7/1580. Untitled.

RM 7/1588. Unterlagen für russ. Kontrollkommission. 26.5.1945. Akte I,5, Band 2.

RM 7/1589. Unterlagen für Brit./Amerik. Kontrollkommission. 11.5.1945. Akte: I,6, Band 1.

RM 7/1590. OKM/1.Skl. Unterlagen für die Alliierten.

RM 7/1592. 1.Skl. Ia Handakte Number [sic] 4. Überwasserkriegführung. Juni 1941–Dezember 1941.

RM 7/1595. 1.Skl. Ia HStabschef-Besprechung. 4–5 Dezember 1941.

RM 7/1693. Die Seekriegsleitung und die Vorgeschichte des Feldzuges gegen Russland.

RM 7/1741. Oberkommando der Kriegsmarine, Handakte Registratur Ib, 1941–1943, Band 1, Teil II.

RM 7/1742. Oberkommando der Kriegsmarine, Handakte Registratur Ib, 1943–1944, Band 2.

RM 7/1749. Oberkommando der Kriegsmarine, Handakte Ib 1.Skl. Feindliche Absichten (Allgemein).

RM 7/1750. Oberkommando der Kriegsmarine, Handakte Ib 1.Skl. Allgemeines. Berichte und Erfahrungen.

RM 7/1765. Verschiedene Unterlagen (Heft 2) K.Kapt. Assmann. 1929–1939.

RM 7/1766. 1.Skl.–Korv.Kapt. Assmann. Sammlung 1. Allgemeine Gedanken u. Erfahrungen 1937–1938.

RM 7/1771. 1.Skl. Handakten. Korv.Kapt. Assmann. Sammlung 6. Denkschriften und allgemeine Gedanken zur Kriegführung. Juli 1940–Juli 1942.

RM 7/1786. Vortrag des Chefs des Stabes der Skl. bei der Besprechung der Oberbefehlshaber in "Koralle" am 15.2.1944.

RM 7/2443. 1.Skl. Ik Wichtige Angaben aus der Hilfskreuzerkriegführung 20. März 1943. Blockadebrecher–Allgemeines–August 1939–Mai 1940. Fahrbefehle für Hilfsschiffe 11 Februar 1942–29. März 1944.

RM 8/1600. Berichterstattung der Japan-Studienkommission Sept.-Dez. 1935.

RM 8/1601. OKM Seekriegsleitung. Betrachtungen zum Kriegsfall Japan-England bezw. Japan-angelsächsische Mächte.

RM 8/1617. OKM Seekriegsleitung. Betrachtungen zur Lage Japans, von 1.Skl. Ib.

RM 8/1628. Berichterstattung der Japan-Studienkommission Sept.–Dez. 1935.

RM 8/1633. OKM Seekriegsleitung. Vortrag des Chefs des Stabes der Skl. bei der Besprechung der Oberbefehlshaber in "Koralle" 15 Februar 1944.

RM 8/1637. OKM Seekriegsleitung. Japan, Sammelband.

RM 8/1707. Skl/KA Handelsschiffahrt. Vernehmungen von Besatzungsangehörigen deutscher Handelsschiffe, die aus der Internierung nach Deutschland zurückgekehrt sind. August 1939–November 1944.

RM 11/1. Attaché- und Auslandsangelegenheiten. M IV-1. 1.1.1934 bis 18.8.1936.

RM 11/2. Attaché- und Auslandsangelegenheiten. M IV-2. 19.8.1936 bis 28.9.1937.

RM 11/3. Attaché- und Auslandsangelegenheiten. M IV-3. 1.10.1937 bis 11.7.1938.

RM 11/4. Attaché- und Auslandsangelegenheiten. M IV-4. 23.9.1937 bis 1.11.1938.

RM 11/61. M.Att. Italien -Land-. 7.5.41 bis 29.10.42.

RM 11/68. Berichte des Marine-Attachés Tokio, 1935, Band 1, 14 Dezember 1934–28 August 1935, Teil 1.

RM 11/69. Berichte des Marine-Attachés Tokio, 1935, Band 1, 14 Dezember 1934–28 August 1935, Teil 2.

RM 11/70. Berichte des Marine-Attachés Tokio, 1935, Band 2, 8 August 1935–17 Dezember 1935.

RM 11/71. Berichte des Marine-Attachés Tokio, 1936, Teil 1, 26 Februar 1935–31 Dezember 1936.

RM 11/72. Berichte des Marine-Attachés Tokio, 1936, Teil 2, 26 Februar 1935–31 Dezember 1936.

RM 11/73. Berichte des Marine-Attachés Tokio, 1937, 8 Januar 1937–30 Dezember 1937.

RM 11/74. Oberkommando der Kriegsmarine, MAtt., Japan, Mob., Band 1, 6 September 1938–3 Juli 1940.

RM 11/75. Oberkommando der Kriegsmarine, MAtt., Japan, Mob., Band 2, 9 Juli 1940–19 Dezember 1940.

RM 11/77. Oberkommando der Kriegsmarine, MAtt., Japan, Mob., Band 4, 8 April 1941–24 Dezember 1941.

RM 11/78. Oberkommando der Kriegsmarine, MAtt., Japan, Mob., Band 5, 26. Oktober 1941–24 März 1942.

RM 12 II/186. Berichte des Marineattaché Rom. Undated.

RM 12 II/192. Berichte des Marineattaché Rom. Undated.

RM 12 II/198. Berichte des Marineattachés in Italien 1939. 14 August 1939–29 Dezember 1939. Band 2.

RM 12 II/247–52. KTB des Marine-Attachés und militärischen Leiters der Grossetappe Japan-China, Bände 1–6.

RM 12 II/253. KTB des Chefs des Marinesonderdienstes beim Mar.-Att., Tokyo. Teil 1 vom 1.4.–30.4.1943.

RM 12 II/278. Marinestützpunkt Yokohama: Charterverhandlungen (Herr Winter), 20.6.–15.12.1944.

RM 12 II/281. Mar.Att. Tokio (Mar. Etappe Yokohama): Charterangelegenheiten betr. M/S "Lilly," M/S "Bogota," M/S "Quito," M/S "Spreewald," D "R. C. Rickmers," T. D. "Winnetou," (19.6.1941–6.9.1944).

RM 12 II/294. Marinestützpunkt Yokohama: Akte betr. Charterverträge 4.1.–10.10.1945.

RM 12 II/304. Neue Charter. Mosel, Winnetou, Bogota, Quito.

RM 12 II/306. Dt. Marineattaché Tokio. Forderungen für Transporthilfe der ehemals dt. Handelsschiffe in den Jahren 1944/45.

RM 12 II/309. Ch.2, Charterangelegenheiten, Charterverträge 1943.

RM 12 II/310. Ch.2, Charterangelegenheiten, Charterverträge 1943.

RM 12 II/313. Marinestützpunkt Yokohama: H1 Handelsschiffe: D "Havenstein" (="Teisho Maru"), 24.9.1939–29.1.1945.

RM 12 II/314. Marinestützpunk Yokohama: H1 Handelsschiffe: S/S (D) "Mosel," 17.4.1941–1.6.1945.

RM 12 II/315. Marineattaché Tokio: Marinestützpunk Yokohama: H 2 Handelsschiffe: M/s "Quito," 25.5.1943–5.5.1945.

RM 12 II/316. Marineattaché Tokio: Marinestützpunkt Yokohama: H 3 Handelsschiffe: M/S "Bogota," 15.6.1941–25.9.1945 mit KTB v. 16.12.1943–17.1.1944.

RM 12 II/323. Marineattaché Tokio: L 13 Zubringerfrachten (Verwaltungsakten betr. Versorgungsgüter) 24.4.1944–24.7.1945.

RM 12 II/346. Untitled. Undated.

RM 12 II/350. Untitled. Undated.

RM 12 II/356. Untitled. Undated.

RM 12 II/357. Mar. Attaché Tokio: G 1 b Verkaufsverhandlungen über das Elektro-Turbinenschiff (Schnelldampfer) "Scharnhorst" mit den Japanern, 24.2.1942–17.10.1945.

RM 12 II/358. Mar. Attaché Tokio: G 43 Kommssionen 1943/44.

RM 12 II/360. Mar. Attaché Tokio: G 46 G9a Ausweiche Kaihin-Hotel Kamakura (1944).

RM 12 II/362. Marineattaché Tokio G 9b.

RM 12 II/364. Marineattaché Tokio G 46 10a Lieferungen und Leistungen an die Japaner 1943–1945.

RM 12 II/365. Marineattaché Tokio G 46 10b (1944).

RM 12 II/376. Marineattaché Tokio: A 35 Internierungslager Hakone, Schriftverkehr mit Amerikanern, 4.9.1945–24.5.1947.

RM 12 II/388. Marineattaché Tokio: Internierungslager Hakone, Schriftverkehr mit Amerikanern, 18.5.1945–10.12.1946.

RM 12 II/392. OKM. KTB Kapt. Paul Werner Vermehren. Gehilfe zum Mar. Att. Tokyo. 18.5.1945–8.1.1947.

RM 13/1. Oberkommando der Wehrmacht (O.K.W.)/Abteilung Ausland Gruppe IV. Kriegstagebuch der Etappenorganisation der Kriegsmarine (Marine-Sonderdienst). Band I, 22 August 1939–30 November 1939. Band II, 1 Dezember 1939–30 September 1940.

RM 13/2. Oberkommando der Wehrmacht (O.K.W.)/Abteilung Ausland Gruppe IV. Kriegstagebuch der Etappenorganisation der Kriegsmarine (Marine-Sonderdienst). Band III, 1 Oktober 1940–30 Juni 1941. Band IV, 1 Juli 1941–31 Januar 1942.

RM 13/3. Oberkommando der Wehrmacht (O.K.W.)/Abteilung Ausland Gruppe IV. Kriegstagebuch der Etappenorganisation der Kriegsmarine (Marine-Sonderdienst). Band V, Band VI.

RM 20/380. 1.Skl. Ic 2-1 Attaché-Angelegenheiten. 16 Januar 1923–26 August 1933.

RM 20/1095. Kriegsspiel A 1938. Vortragssammlung über die während des Kriegsspiels in Krummhübel gehaltenen Vorträge. Beilage 2 zu 103-9-1.

RM 20/1138. A Ia-120-1/1.Skl. Ia-120-1 Verwendung der Marine im Kriegsfalle (a) Organisatorische Vorarbeiten und Überlegungen (b) Operative Vorarbeiten, Vorträge usw. vom 28.5.1936 bis 18.8.1939.

RM 20/1406. Zusammenfassende Aufstellungen der politischen Lage durch A Ic vom: 16.10.1936 bis: 11.4.1939.

RM 20/1482. A IV Allgemeines. Vom 13.3.1937 bis 14.5.1942.

RM 20/1635. A IIc I Heft 1.

RM 20/1636. 1.Skl. Ic 1-2 Marinepolitische Angelegenheiten. 20 November 1929–27 Juli 1935.

RM 20/1637. 1.Skl. Ic 1-3 Marinepolitische Angelegenheiten. 21 Januar 1936–20 Februar 1939.

RM 20/1639. 1.Skl. Ic 2-2 Attaché-Angelegenheiten. 4 Dezember 1933–11 Dezember 1933.

RM 20/1706. ML/BU Umbau vol. II.

RM 20/1710. 1/Skl. Iu. 2–1. AUSBILDUNG. Oktober 1921–April 1927.

RM 20/1717. ML/Bu Jan. 1932 und Okt. 1933.

RM 20/1756. ML/BU. Sammlung Japan, vol. 1. 1930–1935.

RM 48/28. Flottenkommando. (1) Stellungnahme Admiral Carls zur Entwurfstudie Seekriegführung gegen England. (2) Politischer Ausblick auf Grund der Unterrichtung des Amtschefs A am 12.7.1938.

National Archives and Records Administration, Washington, D.C. (NARA)

RG 38. Records of the Chief of Naval Operations, Office of Naval Intelligence
RG 165. Records of the War Department
RG 226. Records of the Office of Strategic Services (OSS)

RG 242. German Navy Records Related to U-Boat Warfare

RG 319. Records of the [U.S.] Army Staff

RG 457. Records of the National Security Agency

RG 457/NR 877 CBCB34 3735A, Box 187, 190/37/11/1. The German Navy and Japan.

RG 457/SRGL. Translations of intercepted Berlin/Tokyo radio messages between German navy liaison personnel, June 1942–May 1945.

RG 457/SRH-008. Battle of the Atlantic. Vol. II. U-Boat Operations.

RG 457/SRH-009. Battle of the Atlantic. Vol. I. Allied Communications Intelligence.

RG 457/SRH-019. Blockade-running between Europe and the Far East by Submarines, 1942–1944.

RG 457/SRH-020. The Role of COMINT in the Battle of Midway.

RG 457/SRH-075. Japanese Reaction to German Defeat.

RG 457/SRH-102. Identifications, Locations and Command Functions of Significant Japanese Army/Navy Personnel.

RG 457/SRH-111. Magic Reports for the Attention of the President 1943–1944.

RG 457/SRH-142. Ultra and the Campaigns against the U-Boats in World War II.

RG 457/SRH-152. Historical Review of OP-20-G.

RG 457/SRH-158. A List of Japanese Merchant Ships. 2d ed. PSIS 100–101. 1 February 1945.

RG 457/SRH-199. Japanese Army Shipping Organization.

RG 457/SRH-232. U.S. Navy COMINCH Radio Intelligence Appreciations Concerning German U-Boat Activity in the Far East (January–April 1945).

RG 457/SRH-260. OP-20-G File of Memoranda. Reports and Messages on German Blockade Runners (World War II, 1943–1944).

RG 457/SRMN-037. COMINCH File. U-Boat Intelligence Summaries, January 1943–May 1945.

RG 457/SRMN-051A. OP-20-GI Memoranda to COMINCH F21 on German U-Boat Activities, Oct. 1943–May 1945.

RG 457/SRMN-054. OP-20-GI Special Studies Relating to U-Boat Activity, 1943–1945.

RG 457/SRMN-068. Untitled.

RG 457/SRNA. Translation Reports of Intercepted Japanese Naval Attaché Messages, 1942–1946.

U.S. Naval Historical Center, Operational Archives, Washington, D.C.

War Log 4th War Patrol USS *Besugo*, FC5-26/A16-3, serial 01, 1945/05/20.

T66. Essays by German Officers and Intelligence Report ser. 13-C-50, 13 Jan. 1950. Essay Capt. Freiwald, "German U-boat activity in the Indian Ocean." *ONI Review* 8, no. 8 (Aug. 1953): 362–70.

T76. TR/PG/7337/1/NID WWII CF individual ships. Report by Commanding Officer of U-188 (Lüdden), Experiences in Indian Ocean, NID1, ser. 0054, 9 Nov. 1944.

T91 TR 29, ONI 6/47, The Setting-up of the Etappe.

Gaiko Shiryokan, Tokyo

A7-9-14. Nichidokui Taibeisen Suikō Tandokufukōwa oyobi Shin Chitsujo Kensetsu kyōryoku ni kansuru kyōtei Kankei.

A7-9-37. Daitōa Sensō Kankei 1 Ken kokusaiho Ihankoi Kankei.

A7-9-49. Kaisen ni Chokusetsu Kankei aru Jōyakokusaku Kettei.

A7-9-52. Sensōchū no Jōyakukokusaku Kettei Bunsho Shō.

B1.0.0.J/X3. Nichidokui Domeijōyaku 1 Ken.

Bōeichō Kenkyūjo Senshibu, Tokyo

1/Zenpan/242. Showa ichijūroku. Kaigun kendoku gunji shisatsudan hokoku. Kaigun kendoku shisatsudanchō nomura naokuni.

10/Buobun/S-3/58. Kaigundaijin Kambo Kiroku. Showa Ninen. Honpo chuto Taikoshikan tsuki bukan Ofuku bunsho ichi.

10/Buōbun/S-4/59. Shōwa Sannendo. Honpō chūtō Taikōshikan tsuki Bukan Ōfuku bunsho. Fu-, I-, So-, Haku-, sonotakoku.

10/Buōbun/S-8/64. Shōwa Yonnen. Honpō chūtō Taikōshikan tsuki Bukan Ōfuku bunsho. I-, Haku-, Sosu,- Pō-, Doku-, Ran-, Bakkoku.

10/Buōbun/S-9/65. Kaigunshō Fukukan. Shōwa Gonen. Zaigai Taikōshikan tsuki bukan Ōfuku bunsho.

10/Buōbun/S-14/70. Kaigunshō Fukukan. Shōwa Rokunen. Zaigai Taikōshikan tsuki bukan Ōfuku bunsho ichi.

10/Buōbun/S-20/76. Jishōwa kyūnen shishōwajūnen. Zaigai Taikōshikan tsuki Bukan Ōfuku Bunsho.

10/Buōbun/T-13/35. Hi. Furansu, Shina, Oranda, Burashirukoku oyobi kakoku zatsu taikōshikanfubukan ōfukubunsho. Taishō kyūnen. Kaigunshō fukukan.

10/Buōbun/T-17/39. Eikoku, Beikoku, Furansukoku, Ikoku, Sorenkoku, Supein zatsu taikōshikanfubukan ōfukubunsho. Taishō jūnen. Kaigunshō fukukan.

10/Buōbun/T-18/40. Hi.Taisho jūichinen. Kaigunshō fukukan. Taikōshikanfubukan ōfukubunsho. Ikoku no bu. Supein no bu sono hoka.

Chōdoku Rikugun Bukan Denpō Tsuzuri.

Daihonei Sensōshidōhan Kimitsu Senso Nikki.

[No registry number]. Indoyō no nichidoku sensuikan sakusen.

Kaigunshō/Kōbun bikō/S 3-71/3701. Shōwa Sannen, Kōbun Bikō, Maki Rokujūhachi.

Kansen Go, Gaikoku Gunkan no Nihon Ryōkai Deiri Torishimari, Hōki Nyushuhō ni kansuru Ken, Gaikoku Gunkan Raihō, Eikoku, Beikoku, Furansukoku, Dokkoku. Kaigunshō/Kōbun bikō/S Moto-49/3402. Taishō Jūgonen Shōwa Gannen, Kōbun Bikō, Maki Kan Jūsan. Dokkoku Benke Taishō Raihō Ikken.

Kasumigasekishiryō daiichigo.

Moto Kaigun Taishō Nomura Naokuni Danwa Shuroku.

Moto Kaigun Taishō Nomura Naokuni Memo.

Nichidokui Kyōtei Mondai Keii.

Nichidokui Sangoku Jōyaku Kankei Tsuzuri.

Shōwa 14nen Bokyukotei Kaigunshosiryō.

Teikoku Kokubō Hōshin Tuzuri.

Japan Maritime Self-Defense Force (JMSDF) Staff College Archives, Yokosuka

Enomoto Shiryō Gohoroku.

Public Records Office (PRO), Kew, U.K.

ADM 199/549. Eastern Command, War Diaries

ADM 223. Admiralty Intelligence Papers

HW 1. Daily ULTRA—Notes to the Attention of the Prime Minister

DEFE. Ministry of Defence

Literature and Published Sources

Abshagen, Karl Heinz. *Canaris. Patriot und Weltbürger.* Stuttgart, 1959.

ADAP. See *Akten zur Deutschen Auswärtigen Politik.*

Agawa Hiroyuki. *The Reluctant Admiral. Yamamoto and the Imperial Navy.* Tokyo, 1979.

———. *Yonai Mitsumasa.* 2 vols. Tokyo, 1979.

Aizawa Jun. "Nihon Kaigun no senryaku to Sankoku Dōmei mondai" (The strategy of the Japanese navy and the problem of the Tripartite Pact). In *Nihon no kiro to Matsuoka gaiko, 1940–41 nen,* edited by Miwa Kimitada and Tobe Ryōichi, 39–54. Tokyo, 1994.

Akasaka Sachiharu. *Kaigun gunsenbi, Kaisen igo* (The armament of the navy after the outbreak of war). Senshi Sōsho (War history series), edited by Bōei Kenshūjo Senshi Shitsu, vol. 88. Tokyo, 1975.

———. *Kaigun kōkū gaishi* (History of naval aviation). Senshi Sōsho (War history series), edited by Bōei Kenshūjo Senshi Shitsu, vol. 95. Tokyo, 1976.

Akten zur Deutschen Auswärtigen Politik 1918–1945 (ADAP, Archives of the German foreign office). Series C: 1933–1937, 6 vols., Göttingen, 1971–1981. Series D: 1937–1945, 13 vols., Baden-Baden, 1950–1970. Series E: 1941–1945, 8 vols., Göttingen, 1969–1979.

Alden, John D. "Japanese Submarine Losses in World War II." *Warship International* 22, no. 1 (1985): 12–31.

Altrichter, Helmut, and J. Becker, eds. *Kriegsausbruch 1939: Beteiligte, Betroffene, Neutrale.* Munich, 1989.

Amamiya Shōichi. "Kindai Nihon no sensō shidō no kōzō to tenkai: Seiryaku to senryaku tono kankei o chūshin to shite" (Warfare in modern Japan: Structure and development), *Ibaragi daigaku kyōyōbu kiyō*, no. 7 (April 1975): 21–71; no. 8 (April 1976): 57–111.

Andrade, Ernest, Jr. "The Cruiser Controversy in Naval Limitations Negotiations, 1922–1936." *Military Affairs* 48, no. 3 (1984): 113–20.

Andrew, Christopher, and David Dilks, eds. *The Missing Dimension: Governments and Intelligence Communities in the 20th Century.* London, 1985.

Andrew, Christopher, and Jeremy Noakes, eds. *Intelligence and International Relations, 1900–1945.* Exeter, 1987.

Arai Tatsuo. *Katō Tomosaburō.* Tokyo, 1958.

Aritake Shūji, ed. *Okada Keisuke.* Tokyo, 1956.

Asada Sadao. "Japanese Admirals and the Politics of Naval Limitation: Katō Tomosaburo vs. Katō Kanji." In *Naval Warfare in the Twentieth Century,* edited by Gerald Jordan, 141–66. London, 1977.

———. "The Japanese Navy and the United States." In *Pearl Harbor as History,* ed. Dorothy Borg and Shumpei Okamoto, 225–59. New York, 1973.

———. "Nihon kaigun to tai-Bei seisaku oyobi senryaku" (The Japanese navy and its policy and strategy versus the U.S.A.). In *Nichi-Bei kankeishi,* edited by Hosoya Chihiro et al., vol. 2, 87–149. Tokyo, 1971.

———. "The Revolt against the Washington Treaty: The Imperial Japanese Navy and Naval Limitation, 1921–1927." *Naval War College Review* 46, no. 3 (1993): 82–97.

———. "Washinton kaigi o meguru Nichi-Bei seisaku kettei katei no hikaku: Hito to kikō" (Comparative study of the Japanese and U.S. decision-making processes at the Washington conference: People and mechanisms). In *Taigai seisaku kettei katei no Nichi-Bei hikaku,* edited by Hosoya Chihiro and Watanuki Joji, 419ff. Tokyo, 1977.

Ashi Hideo. Kairō doitsu sensuikan no hatōroku (1). Kyūnihonkaigun no "Ro 500 sen" no kotonado (1) (From the log of the German U-boat *Seawolf.* About submarine RO-500 of the old Japanese navy (1)). In *Suikō* 6-5 (1994): 24–27.

———. Kairō doitsu sensuikan no hatōroku (2). Kyūnihonkaigun no "Ro 500 sen" no kotonado (2) (From the log of the German U-boat *Seawolf.* About submarine RO-500 of the old Japanese navy (2)). In: *Suiko* 6-6 (1994): 17–19.

———. Kairō doitsu sensuikan no hatōroku (3). Kyūnihonkaigun no "Ro 500 sen" no kotonado (3) (From the log of the German U-boat *Seawolf.* About submarine RO-500 of the old Japanese navy (3)). In *Suikō* 6-7 (1994): 13–15.

Baring, Arnulf et al., eds. *Zwei zaghafte Riesen: Deutschland und Japan seit 1945.* Stuttgart, 1977.

Barnhart, Michael A. *Japan Prepares for Total War: The Search for Economic Security,* *1919–1941.* Ithaca, 1987.

———. "Japan's Economic Security and the Origins of the Pacific War." *The Journal of Strategic Studies* 4, no. 2 (1981): 105–24.

———. "Planning the Pearl Harbor Attack: A Study in Military Politics." *Aerospace Historian* 49, no. 4 (1982): 246–52.

Barth, Johannes. *Als deutscher Kaufmann in Fernost. Bremen-Tsingtau-Tokyo,* *1891–1981.* Berlin, 1984.

Beesly, Patrik. *Very Special Intelligence. Geheimdienstkrieg der britischen Admiralität* *1939–1945.* Frankfurt am Main, 1978.

Bendix, R. "Preconditions of Development: A Comparison of Japan and Germany." In *Aspects of Social Change in Japan,* edited by Ronald P. Dore, 27–70. Princeton, N.J., 1973.

Benett, Ralph. "Intelligence and Strategy in World War II." In *British and American Approaches to Intelligence,* edited by Ken G. Robertson, 130–52. New York, 1987.

Bensel, Rolf. "Die deutsche Flottenpolitik von 1933 bis 1939. Eine Studie über die Rolle des Flottenbaus in Hitlers Aussenpolitik." (Supplement) 3, *Marine Rundschau,* April 1958.

Berghahn, Volker R. *Rüstung und Machtpolitik: Zur Anatomie des "Kalten Krieges" vor* *1914.* Düsseldorf, 1973.

———. *Der Tirpitzplan. Genesis und Verfall einer innenpolitischen Krisenstrategie unter Wilhelm II.* Düsseldorf, 1971.

Bernstein, Barton J. "Seizing the Contested Terrain of Early Nuclear History: Stimson, Conant, and Their Allies Explain the Decision to Use the Atomic Bomb." *Diplomatic History* 17, no. 1 (1993): 35–72.

Bird, Keith W. *German Naval History: A Guide to the Literature.* New York, 1985.

———. "The German Navy in World War II" (no. 92). In *Reevaluating Major Naval Combatants of World War II: Contributions in Military Studies,* edited by James J. Sadkovich, 99–127. Westport, Conn., 1990.

Bloss, Hartmut. "Die Abberufung der Beraterschaft (April-Juli 1938)." In *Die deutsche Beraterschaft in China 1927–1938: Militär, Wirtschaft, Aussenpolitik,* edited by Bernd Martin (with Militärgeschichtliches Forschungsamt [Military History Research Institute]), 249–71. Düsseldorf, 1981.

Böddeker, Günter. *Die Boote im Netz. Der dramatische Bericht über Karl Dönitz und das Schicksal der deutschen U-Boot Waffe.* Bergisch Gladbach, 1981.

Bōei Kenshūjo Senshi Shitsu, ed. *Daihon'ei kaigunbu. Daitōa senso kaisen keii* (Imperial Headquarters, Navy Department: Prologue to the outbreak of the Pacific war), pt. 1. Senshi Sosho (War history series), vol. 100. Tokyo, 1979.

———. *Daihon'ei kaigunbu. Daitōa sensō kaisen keii.* (Imperial Headquarters, Navy Department. Prologue to the outbreak of the Pacific war), pt. 2. Senshi Sōsho (War history series), vol. 101. Tokyo, 1979.

Bōei Kenshūjo Senshi Shitsu, ed. *Rikukaigun nenpyō. Fuheigo yōgo no kaisetsu* (Chronology of army and navy. Annex: Explanation of military and naval terms). Senshi Sōsho (War history series), vol. 102. Tokyo, 1980.

Bonatz, Heinz. *Die Deutsche Marine-Funkaufklärung 1914–1945.* Darmstadt, 1970.

Boog, Horst. "'Baedecker-Angriffe' und Fernstflugzeugprojekte 1942: Die strategische Ohnmacht der Luftwaffe." *Militärgeschichtliches Beiheft zur Europäischen Wehrkunde/Wehrwissenschaftlichen Rundschau* 5, no. 4 (1990): 1–18.

———. *The Conduct of the Air War in the Second World War: An International Comparison.* Studies in Military History, vol. 2. New York, 1991.

———. "German Air Intelligence in World War II." *Aerospace Historian* 33 (1986): 121–29.

———, ed. *Luftkriegführung im Zweiten Weltkrieg: Ein internationaler Vergleich.* Herford, 1990.

Booth, K. *Navies and Foreign Policy.* London, 1979.

Borg, Dorothy, and Shumpei Okamoto, eds. *Pearl Harbor as History: Japanese-American Relations 1931–1941.* New York, 1973.

Böttcher, S. "Die Japaner denken und handeln anders." *Aus Politik und Zeitgeschichte* 19 (1981): 35–38.

Boyce, Robert, and Esmonde M. Robertson, eds. *Paths to War: New Essays on the Origin of the Second World War.* New York, 1989.

Boyd, Carl. *Hitler's Japanese Confidant: General Ōshima Hiroshi and MAGIC Intelligence, 1941–1945.* Lawrence, Kans., 1993.

———. "The Japanese Submarine Force and the Legacy of Strategic and Operational Doctrine Developed between the World Wars." In *Selected Papers from the Citadel Conference on War and Diplomacy, 1978,* edited by L. H. Addington et al., 27–40. Charleston, S.C., 1979.

———. "U.S. Navy Radio Intelligence during the Second World War and the Sinking of the Japanese Submarine I-52." *Journal of Military History* 63, no. 2: 339–54.

Boyd, Carl, and Akihiko Yoshida. *The Japanese Submarine Force and World War II.* Annapolis, Md., 1995.

Boyle, John Hunter. *China and Japan at War, 1937–1945: The Politics of Collaboration.* Stanford, Calif., 1972.

Bracher, Karl Dietrich, ed. *Deutschland zwischen Krieg und Frieden. Beiträge zur Politik und Kultur im 20.Jahrhundert.* Volume commemorating Hans-Adolph Jacobsen. Düsseldorf, 1991.

Bradley, John Hunter, and Jack W. Dice. *The Second World War: Asia and the Pacific.* Wayne, N.J., 1984.

Bragadin, Marc Antonio. *The Italian Navy in World War II.* Annapolis, Md., 1957.

Braun, Hans-Joachim. "Technologietransfer im Flugzeugbau zwischen Deutschland und Japan 1936–1945." In *Deutschland-Japan in der Zwischenkriegszeit,* edited by

Josef Kreiner und Regine Mathias, 325–40. Bonn, 1990.

Breit, Gotthard. *Das Staats- und Gesellschaftsbild deutscher Generale beider Weltkriege im Spiegel ihrer Memoiren.* Boppard am Rhein, 1973.

Brennecke, Jochen. *Das grosse Abenteuer–Deutsche Hilfskreuzer 1939–1945.* Biberach, 1959.

———. *Haie im Paradies.* Preetz, 1961.

———. *Die Wende im U-Boot Krieg. Ursachen und Folgen 1939–1943.* Herford, 1984.

Brice, Martin. *Blockadebrecher: Der Durchbruch von Handelsschiffen der Achsenmächte durch die alliierten Sperrgürtel im 2. Weltkrieg.* Stuttgart, 1984.

Carlyle, Margaret, ed. *Documents on International Affairs, 1939–46.* Vol. 2, *Hitler's Europe.* London, 1954.

Carsten, F. L. *Reichswehr und Politik 1918–1933.* Cologne, 1964.

Caspary, Sigrun. "Die japanische militärische Luftfahrtindustrie im Spannungsfeld zwischen Technologietransfer und Autarkiestreben." Master's thesis, University of Bonn, 1992.

———. "Rikukaigun Kōkūshi to Dokuni Gijutsu Kōryū" (History of the army, air force, and naval air arm and the German-Japanese exchange of technology). *Gunji Shigaku* 124 (vol. 31, no. 4) March 1996, 37–51.

Chapman, John W. M. "Commander Ross R.N. and the Ending of Anglo-Japanese Friendship, 1933–1936." *International Studies 1985/II.* Sheffield, 1977.

———. "A Dance on Eggs: Intelligence and the 'Anti-Comintern.'" *Journal of Contemporary History* 22, no. 2 (1987): 333–72.

———. "The Far East in German Peacetime Planning for Crises, 1925–1939." *Proceedings of the British Association for Japanese Studies* 6, no. 1 (1981): 50–71.

———. "German Signals Intelligence and the Pacific War." *Proceedings of the British Association for Japanese Studies* 4 (1979): 131–49.

———. "The 'Have-Nots' Go To War: The Economic & Technological Basis of the German Alliance with Japan." In *International Studies 1984/III, The Tripartite Pact of 1940: Japan, Germany and Italy,* edited by Ian Nish, 25–73. Papers by John W. M. Chapman, Jost Dülffer, and Ernest Bramsted published by the International Centre for Economics and Related Disciplines, London School of Economics. London, 1984.

———. "The Imperial Japanese Navy and the North-South Dilemma." In *Barbarossa: The Axis and the Allies,* edited by John Erickson and David Dilks. Edinburgh 1994.

———. "Japan and German Naval Policy, 1919–1945." In *Deutschland-Japan. Historische Kontakte,* edited by Josef Kreiner, 211–64. Bonn, 1984.

———. "Japanese Intelligence, 1919–1945: A Suitable Case for Treatment." In *Intelligence and International Relations, 1900–1945,* edited by Christopher Andrew and Jeremy Naokes, 145–90. Exeter, 1987.

———. "Japan, Germany and the International Political Economy of Intelligence." In *Deutschland-Japan in der Zwischenkriegszeit,* edited by Josef Kreiner and Regine Mathias, 27–60. Bonn, 1990.

———. "Japan in German Aviation Policies of the Weimar Period." In *Japan und die Mittelmächte im Ersten Weltkrieg und in den zwanziger Jahren,* edited by Josef Kreiner, 155–73. Bonn, 1986.

———. "Oil, Deviance and the Traditional World Order—Japanese and German Strategies for Violent Change 1931–41." In *Tradition and Modern Japan,* edited by P. G. O'Neill, 130–39. Tenterden, Kent, 1981.

———. "The Origins and Development of German and Japanese Military Co-operation, 1936–1945." 2 vols. Ph.D. diss., Oxford University, 1967.

——— "Pearl Harbor: The Anglo-Australian Dimension." *Intelligence and National Security* 4, no. 3 (1989): 451–60.

———. "The Polish Connection." In *Proceedings of the British Association of Japanese Studies II/1,* edited by G. Daniels and P. Lowe, 57–78. Sheffield, 1977.

———. "The Polish Labyrinth and the Soviet Maze—Japan and the Floating World of Signals Intelligence 1919–1939." In *International Studies 1982/II, Some Aspects of Soviet-Japanese Relations in the 1930s,* edited by Ian Nish, 66–87. London: London School of Economics, International Centre, 1982.

———. "Signals Intelligence Collaboration among the Tripartite Pact States on the Eve of Pearl Harbor." *Japan Forum* 3, no. 2 (1991): 231–56.

———. "The Transfer of German Underwater Weapons Technology to Japan." In *European Studies of Japan,* edited by C. T. Dunn and Ian Nish, 165–71. London, 1976.

———, ed. and trans. *The Price of Admiralty: The War Diary of the German Naval Attaché in Japan, 1939–1943.* 4 vols. Sussex, U.K., 1982–89.

Churchill, Winston S. *The Second World War.* 6 vols. Harmondsworth, 1989.

Coox, Alvin D. *The Anatomy of a Small War: The Soviet-Japanese Struggle for Changkufeng/Khasan, 1939.* Contributions in Military History, no. 13. Westport, Conn.: Greenwood, 1977.

———. "Effects of Attrition on National War Effort: The Japanese Army Experience in China, 1937–38." *Military Affairs* 32 (1968): 57–62.

———. "The Japanese Army Experience." In *New Dimensions in Military History: An Anthology,* edited by Russell F. Weigley, 125–51. San Rafael, Calif., 1975.

———. *Nomonhan: Japan against Russia, 1939.* 2 vols. Stanford, Calif., 1985.

———. "Repulsing the Pearl Harbor Revisionists: The State of Present Literature on the Debacle." *Military Affairs* 50 (1986): 29–31.

———. "The Rise and Fall of the Imperial Japanese Air Forces." *Aerospace Historian* 27, no. 2 (1980): 74–86.

Corbett, Julian S. *Die Seekriegsführung Gross-Britanniens.* Berlin, 1939.

Costello, John E. *The Pacific War*. London, 1981.

Crowley, James B. *Japan's Quest for Autonomy: National Security and Foreign Policy 1930–1938*. Princeton, N.J., 1966.

———. "A New Asian Order. Some Notes on Prewar Japanese Nationalism." In *Japan in Crisis: Essays on Taisho Democracy*, edited by Bernard S. Silberman and Harry D. Harootian, 270–98. Princeton, N.J., 1974.

Daniels, G., and P. Lowe, eds. *Proceedings of the British Association of Japanese Studies II/1*. Sheffield, 1977.

Deist, Wilhelm, ed. *The German Military in the Age of Total War*. Leamington Spa, 1985.

———, ed. "Militär und Innenpolitik." In *Quellen zur Geschichte des Parlamentarismus und der politischen Parteien, 2.Reihe*, edited by Erich Matthias and Hans Meier-Welcker. Düsseldorf, 1971.

Detwiler, Donald S., and Charles B. Burdick, eds. *War in Asia and the Pacific 1937–1949*. 15 vols. New York, 1980.

Deutsches Marine Institut et al., eds. *Die deutsche Marine: Historisches Selbstverständnis und Standortbestimmung*. Herford, 1983.

———, eds. *Marine-Flieger: von der Marineluftschiffabteilung zur Marinefliegerdivision*. Bonn, 1988.

Dinklage, Ludwig, and Hans Jürgen Witthöft. *Die deutsche Handelsflotte 1939–1945: unter besonderer Berücksichtigung der Blockadebrecher*. Göttingen, 1971.

Dirksen, Herbert von. *Moskau, Tokio, London. Erinnerungen und Betrachtungen zu 20 Jahren deutscher Aussenpolitik, 1919–1939*. Stuttgart, 1949.

Doi Akira et al., eds. *Shōwa shakai keizai shiryō shusei: Kaigunshō shiryō* (Collection of sources of the social and economic history of the Shōwa period: The records of the Navy Ministry). 20 vols. Tokyo, 1978–1999.

Dönitz, Karl. *Zehn Jahre und zwanzig Tage* (Memoirs: Ten years and twenty days). Bonn, 1963; reprint, London, 1990.

Dore, Ronald P., ed. *Aspects of Social Change in Japan*. Princeton, N.J., 1973.

Dower, John W. *Japan in War and Peace: Selected Essays*. New York, 1993.

———. "The Useful War." *Daedalus* 119, no. 3 (1990): 49–70.

———. *War without Mercy: Race and Power in the Pacific War*. New York, 1986.

Doyle, Michael K. "The United States Navy—Strategy and Far Eastern Foreign Policy, 1931–1941." *Naval War College Review* 29, no. 3 (1977): 52–60.

———. "The U.S. Navy and War Plan Orange, 1933–1940: Making Necessity a Virtue." *Naval War College Review* 33, no. 3 (1980): 49–63.

Drechsler, Karl. *Deutschland-China-Japan. Das Dilemma der deutschen Fernostpolitik*. East Berlin, 1964.

Dülffer, Jost. "Aufrüstung zur Weltmacht: Die deutsche Marinepolitik, 1919–41." *Revue internationale d'histoire militaire*, no. 73 (1991): 101–18.

————. "Determinanten der deutschen Marine-Entwicklung in der Zwischenkriegszeit (1920–39)." *Marine Rundschau* 72, no. 1 (1975): 8–19.

————. "Determinants of German Naval Policy, 1920–1939." In *The German Military in the Age of Total War*, edited by Wilhelm Deist, 152–70. Leamington Spa, 1985.

————. "Politik zum Kriege: Das Dritte Reich und die Mächte auf dem Weg in den Zweiten Weltkrieg." *Neue politische Literatur* 26, no. 1 (1981): 42–58.

————. "Die Reichs- und Kriegsmarine 1918–1939." In *Handbuch zur deutschen Militärgeschichte 1648–1939*, edited by Militärgeschichtlichens Forschungsamt, vol. 5, 337–488. Munich, 1983.

————. "The Tripartite Pact of 27 September 1940: Fascist Alliance or Propaganda Trick?" *International Studies 1984/III, The Tripartite Pact of 1940: Japan, Germany and Italy*, edited by Ian Nish, 1–24. Papers by Jost Dülffer, John Chapman, and Ernest Bramsted, published by the International Centre for Economics and Related Disciplines, London School of Economics. London, 1984.

————. *Weimar, Hitler und die Marine: Reichspolitik und Flottenbau 1920 bis 1939.* Düsseldorf, 1973.

Dülffer, Jost, Bernd Martin, and Günter Wollstein, eds. *Deutschland in Europa. Gedenkschrift für Andreas Hillgruber.* Berlin, 1990.

Dull, Paul S. *Die kaiserlich japanische Marine, 1941–1945.* Stuttgart, 1980.

Dunn, C. T., and Ian Nish, eds. *European Studies of Japan.* London, 1976.

Duppler, Jörg. "Aufbau und Entwicklung der deutschen Marineflieger 1913 bis 1958." In *Marineflieger. Von der Marineluftschiffabteilung zur Marinefliegerdivision*, edited by Deutschen Marine Institut, 14–61. Herford, 1988.

————. *35. Historisch-Taktische Tagung der Flotte. Führung und Einsatz von Seestreitkräften bei Operationen im Zusammenwirken mit anderen Teilstreitkräften.* Herford 1995.

————. *Der Juniorpartner. England und die Entwicklung der Deutschen Marine 1848–1890.* Herford, 1985.

Erickson, John, and David Dilks, eds. *Barbarossa: The Axis and the Allies.* Edinburgh, 1994.

Evans, David C. *The Japanese Navy in World War II: In the Words of Former Japanese Naval Officers.* Annapolis, Md., 1969.

Evans, David C., and Mark Peattie. *Kaigun: Strategy, Tactics, and Technology in the Imperial Japanese Navy.* Annapolis, Md.: Naval Institute Press, 1997.

Ferris, John. "A British 'Unofficial' Aviation Mission and Japanese Naval Developments, 1919–1929." *Journal of Strategic Studies* 5, no. 3 (1982): 416–39.

Fioravanzo, Giuseppe. *La Marina Dall' 8 Settembre 1943 alla fine del conflitto. La Marina Italiana nella Seconda Guerra Mondiale.* Vol. 15. Rome, 1971.

Forndran, Erhard, et al., eds. *Innen- und Aussenpolitik unter nationalsozialistischer Bedrohung. Determinanten internationaler Beziehungen in historischen Fallstudien.* Opladen, 1977.

Förster, Jürgen. "Strategische Überlegungen des Wehrmachtführungsstabes für das Jahr 1943." *Militärgeschichtliche Mitteilungen* 13, no. 1 (1973): 95–106.

Fox, John P. "The Formulation of Germany's Far Eastern Policy, 1933–1936." Ph.D. diss., London School of Economics, 1972.

———. "Japan als Machtfaktor in Deutschlands Europa- und Fernostpolitik von Versailles bis Locarno." In *Deutschland-Japan in der Zwischenkriegszeit,* edited by Josef Kreiner and Regine Mathias, 61–90. Bonn, 1990.

Frieser, Karl-Heinz. *Blitzkrieg-Legende. Der Westfeldzug 1940.* Munich, 1995.

Fujii Yoshie, Takahashi Tadayoshi, and Ishibashi Takahisa. "Zadankai: Shōwashi no gunbu o megutte: Baden-Baden kara Ni-Ni-Roku made" (Round-table talk: The military in the Shōwa period: From Baden-Baden to the 2-26 Incident. Presenter: Hata Ikuhiko). In *Shōwashi no gunbu to seiji,* edited by Miyake Masaki, vol. 1, 275–304. N.p., 1983.

Fujiwara Akira. "Kokubō kokusaku no meguru riku-kaigun no tairitsu" (The conflict between army and navy about national defense policy). In *Ronshū: Nihon Gendaishi,* edited by Akira Fujiwara and Matsuo Takayoshi, 337–60. Tokyo, 1976.

———. *Nihon gunjishi* (Japanese military history). 2 vols. Tokyo, 1987.

———. *Strategy and Politics of Japan during the Second World War: Politics and Strategy in the Second World War. Germany, Great Britain, Japan, the Soviet Union and the United States.* San Francisco, 1975.

Fujiwara Akira and Matsuo Takayoshi, eds. *Ronshū: Nihon gendaishi* (A collection of essays on contemporary Japanese history). Tokyo, 1976.

Fukui Shizuo. *Nihon no Gunkan* (Japanese naval ships). Tokyo, 1956.

Fuller, Richard. *Shōkan—Hirohito's Samurai: Leaders of the Japanese Armed Forces 1926–1945.* London, 1992.

Funke, Manfred, ed. *Hitler, Deutschland und die Mächte. Materialien zur Aussenpolitik des Dritten Reiches.* Bonner Schriften zur Politik und Zeitgeschichte, vol. 12. Düsseldorf, 1976.

Fuwa Hiroshi. *Marē shinkō sakusen* (The attack operations against Malaya). Senshi Sōsho (War history series), edited by Bōei Kenshūjo Senshi Shitsu, vol. 1. Tokyo, 1966.

Gaimushō. *Nihon gaikō bunsho: 1930-nen Rondon kaigun kaigi* (The London Naval Treaty of 1930). 2 vols. Tokyo, 1983–84.

———. *Nihon gaikō bunsho: Rondon kaigun kaigi keika gaiyō* (Summary of the developments during the London Naval Conference). Tokyo, 1979.

———. *Nihon gaikō bunsho: Taishō 5 Nen* (Japanese diplomatic documents of 1917). Tokyo, 1967.

———, ed. *Nihon Gaikō Nenpyō narabini Shuyō Bunsho* (Chronological table of Japanese diplomatic history and essential diplomatic documents). Tokyo, 1966.

Gibson, Charles Dana. "The Far East Odyssey of the UIT-24." *Naval History* 4, no. 1

(Winter 1990): 19–23.

Goldstein, Donald M., and Katherine V. Dillon, eds. *Fading Victory: The Diary of Admiral Matome Ugaki, 1941–1945.* Pittsburgh, Pa., 1991.

Gray, Edwyn. *Operation Pacific: The Royal Navy's War against Japan, 1941–1945.* Annapolis, Md., 1991.

Gronau, Wolfgang von Weltflieger. *Erinnerungen 1926–1947* (Memoirs 1926–1947). Stuttgart, 1955.

Groos, Otto. *Seekriegslehren im Lichte des Weltkrieges.* Berlin, 1929.

Gunjishigakkai. Daihonei Sensō Shidōhan Kimitsu Nikki (Secret diary of General Headquarters War Guidance Section). Tokyo, 1998.

————, ed. *Dainijisekaitaisen* (The Second World War). Vol. 1, *Hassei to kakudai* (Origin and spread). Tokyo, 1990.

————, ed. *Dainijisekaitaisen (Ni)* (The Second World War). Vol. 2, *Shinjuwan zengo* (The time around Pearl Harbor). Tokyo, 1991.

Gunton, Dennis. *The Penang Submarines: Penang and Submarine Operations, 1942–45.* Penang, Malaysia, 1970.

Güth, Rolf. "Vor 40 Jahren: Grossadmiral Raeder nimmt seinen Abschied." *Marine Forum* 58 (1983): 23–26.

————. *Die Marine des Deutschen Reiches 1919–1939.* Frankfurt am Main, 1972.

————. "Organisation der deutschen Marine in Krieg und Frieden, 1913–1933." In *Handbuch zur deutschen Militärgeschichte,* edited by Militärgeschichtlichen Forschungsamt, vol. 5, 263–336. Munich, 1983.

Haasch, Günther, ed. *Die Deutsch-Japanischen Gesellschaften von 1888–1996.* Berlin, 1996.

Hagan, Kenneth J., ed. *In Peace and War: Interpretations of American Naval History, 1775–1984.* Westport, Conn., 1984.

Halder, Generaloberst [Franz]. *Kriegstagebuch. Tägliche Aufzeichnungen des Chefs des Generalstabes des Heeres, 1939–1942.* 3 vols. Edited by Hans-Adolf Jacobsen. Stuttgart, 1962–64.

————. *Selection and Training of German Officers for Military Attaché Duty.* Königstein, 1951.

Hammitzsch, Horst, and Lydia Brüll, eds. *Japan-Handbuch.* Stuttgart, 1984.

Handō Kazutoshi. *Senshi no Isho: Taiheiyō Sensō ni chitta yushatachi no sakebi.* Tokyo, 1995.

————, ed. *Yusha no Isho* (A warrior's testament). Tokyo, 1995.

Hansen, Ernst Willi. *Reichswehr und Industrie: Rüstungswirtschaftliche Zusammenarbeit und wirtschaftliche Mobilmachungsvorbereitungen 1923–1932.* Boppard am Rhein, 1978.

Hara Shirō. "Daihonei rikugunbu: Daitōa sensō kaisen keii" (Imperial Headquarters, Army Department: The circumstances of the outbreak of the Pacific war), pt.

1. Senshi Soshō (War history series), edited by Bōei Kenshūjo Senshi Shitsu, vol. 65. Tokyo, 1973.

———. "Daihonei rikugunbu: Daitōa sensō kaisen keii" (Imperial Headquarters, Army Department: The circumstances of the outbreak of the Pacific war), pt. 3. Senshi Sōsho (War history series), edited by Bōei Kenshūjo Senshi Shitsu, vol. 69. Tokyo, 1973.

———. "Daihonei rikugunbu: Daitōa sensō kaisen keii" (Imperial Headquarters, Army Department. The circumstances of the outbreak of the Pacific war), pt. 4. Senshi Sōsho (War history series), edited by Bōei Kenshūjo Senshi Shitsu, vol. 70. Tokyo, 1974.

Harada Kumao. *Fragile Victory: Prince Saionji and the London Naval Treaty Issue, from the Memoirs of Baron Harada Kumao.* Detroit, 1968.

———. *The Saionji-Harada Memoirs, 1930–1940.* Washington, D.C., 1978.

———. *Saionjikō to seikyoku* (Prince Saionji and politics). 8 vols. and 1 *Zusatzband* (supplementary volume). Tokyo, 1950–52.

Haraszti, Eva H. *Treaty-Breakers or "Realpolitiker"? The Anglo-German Naval Agreement of June 1935.* Boppard am Rhein, 1974.

Hashimoto Mochitsura. *Sunk: The Story of the Japanese Submarine Fleet 1942–1945.* London, 1954.

Hata Ikuhiko. "Kantaiha to jōyakuha: Kaigun no habatsu keifu" (Fleet faction and treaty faction: Genealogy of factional strife in the navy). In *Shōwashi no gunbu to seiji,* edited by Miyake Masaki et al., vol. 1, 193–232. Tokyo, 1983.

———, ed. *Nihon Rikukaigun sōgō jiten* (Comprehensive handbook of the army and navy). Tokyo, 1991.

Hatano Sumio and Asada Sadao. "The Japanese Decision to Move South." In *Paths to War,* edited by Robert Boyce and Esmonde M. Robertson, 383–407. New York, 1989.

Hattori Takushirō. *Daitōa Sensō Zenshi* (Prologue of the Pacific war). Tokyo, 1956.

———. "Japans Operationsplan für den Beginn des Pazifischen Krieges." *Wehrwissenschaftliche Rundschau* 7, no. 5 (1957): 247–74.

Hauner, Milan. *India in Axis Strategy: Germany, Japan, and Indian Nationalists in the Second World War.* Stuttgart, 1981.

Haupt, Bernhard. "Die japanische Seemacht im Zweiten Weltkrieg: Die Ursachen des Zusammenbruchs (I–II)." *Marine Forum* 51, no. 3 (1976): 56–59 and 51, no. 4 (1976): 93–97.

Hauser, Oswald, ed. *Weltpolitik II.* Fourteen lectures. Göttingen, 1975.

Haushofer, Karl. *Alt-Japan: Werdegang von der Urzeit bis zur Grossmacht-Schwelle (1868-Meiji).* Berlin, 1938.

Hayashi Kentarō. "Japan and Germany in the Interwar Period." In *Dilemmas of Growth in Prewar Japan,* edited by James W. Morley, 461–88. Princeton, N.J., 1974.

Henke, Josef. *England in Hitlers politischem Kalkül 1935–1939.* Boppard am Rhein, 1973.

Henny, Sue, and Jean-Pierre Lehmann, eds. *Themes and Theories in Modern Japanese History.* London, 1988.

Hentschel, Volker. *Wirtschaftsgeschichte des modernen Japan.* 2 vols. Stuttgart, 1986.

Hildebrand, Klaus. *Deutsche Aussenpolitik 1933–1945: Kalkül oder Dogma?* Stuttgart, 1980.

———. *Das Dritte Reich.* Munich, 1980.

———. "Hitlers 'Programm' und seine Realisierung 1939–1942" In *Hitler, Deutschland und die Mächte. Materialien zur Aussenpolitik des Dritten Reiches,* edited by Manfred Funke, 63–93. Düsseldorf, 1976.

———. *Das vergangene Reich. Deutsche Aussenpolitik von Bismarck bis Hitler 1871–1945.* Stuttgart, 1995.

Hillgruber, Andreas. "Die 'Hitler Koalition': Eine Skizze zur Geschichte und Struktur des 'Weltpolitischen Dreiecks' Berlin-Rom-Tokyo, 1933–1945." In *Vom Staat des Ancien Régime zum modernen Parteienstaat: Festschrift für Theodor Schieder zu seinem 70. Geburtstag,* edited by Helmut Berding et al. Munich; Vienna, 1978.

———. *Hitlers Strategie, Politik und Kriegführung 1940–1945.* Frankfurt am Main, 1965.

———. "Japan und der Fall 'Barbarossa.'" In *Wehrwissenschaftliche Rundschau* 18 (1968): 312–36.

———, ed. *Probleme des Zweiten Weltkrieges.* Cologne, 1967.

Hillgruber, Andreas, and Jost Dülffer, eds. *Ploetz: Geschichte der Weltkriege. Mächte, Ereignisse, Entwicklungen 1900–1945.* Freiburg, 1981.

Hinsley, F. H. *British Intelligence in the Second World War.* Vol. 3, pt. 1. London, 1984.

Hirama Yōichi. "Dainiji taisenchu no nidoku kaigun (1). Doitsu no kaisen to nihon kaigun" (The German and Japanese navies in World War II (1). The German war at sea and the Japanese navy). *Bōeidaigakkōkiyō dairokujūsanshū,* no. 63 (September 1991): 57–89.

———. "Dainiji taisenchū no nidoku kaigun (sononi). Nihon kaigun no indoyo sakusen" (The German and Japanese navies in World War II (2). Operations of the Japanese navy in the Indian Ocean). *Boeidaigakkokiyo dairokujūgoshū,* no. 65, (September 1992): 1–33.

———. "Dainiji taisenchū no nidoku kaigun (3). Nihon kaigun to nidokuso kankei" (The German and Japanese navies in World War II (3). The Japanese navy and Japanese-German-Soviet relations). *Bōeidaigakkōkiyō dairokujūgoshū.* Betsuzu. Heisei rokunen sangatsu. No. 68 (March 1994): 111–62.

———. "Dainiji taisenchū no nidoku kaigun (4). Nidoku gijutsu koryu" (The German and Japanese navies in World War II (4). Technical exchange between

Japan and Germany). *Bōeidaigakkōkiyō (Shakaikagakuhen) dairokujūgoshū. (nanakyū).* Betsuzu. XXX. No. 71 (September 1995): 1–37.

———. "Dainiji taisenchū no nidoku kaigun (5). Nidoku jinbutsu koryu" (The German and Japanese navies in World War II (5). Exchange of personnel between Japan and Germany). *Bōeidaigakkōkiyō (Shakaikagakuhen) dairokujūgoshū. (kyūsan).* Betsuzu. No. 74 (March 1997): 1–34.

———. "Dainiji taisenchū no nidoku kaigun (6). Nidoku keizai kankei" (The German and Japanese navies in World War II (6). Japanese-German economic relations). *Bōeidaigakkōkiyō (Shakaikagakuhen) dairokujūgoshū. (jūsan).* Bessatsu (special issue). No. 76 (March 1998): 1–3.

———. "Dainiji taisenchū no nidoku kaigun (7). Dokui kaigun no indoyō sakusen" (The German and Japanese Navies in World War II (7). Operations of the German and Italian navies in the Indian Ocean). *Bōeidaigakkōkiyō (Shakaikagakuhen) dainanajūhachishū. (jūichisan).* Betsuzu. No. 78 (March 1999): 23–50.

———. "Doitsu no Haisen to Nichidoku Kaigun" (German defeat and the Japanese and German navies). In *Dainiji Sekaitaisen no Shūen* (The termination of World War II), edited by Gunjishigakkai, 300–317. Tokyo, 1995.

———. "Japanese Naval Preparations for World War II." *Naval War College Review* 44, no. 2 (1991): 63–81.

Hirschfeld, Wolfgang. *Feindfahrten: Das Logbuch eines U-Boot-Funkers.* Vienna, 1982.

Hitler, Adolf. *Hitler's Secret Conversations, 1941–1944.* With an introductory essay by H. R. Trevor-Roper. New York, 1981.

———. *Hitler's Table Talk, 1941–1944.* Translated by Norman Cameron and R. H. Stevens, with introduction and preface by H. R. Trevor-Roper. London, 1973.

Hoffmann, Peter. "The Gulf Region in German Strategy Projections, 1940–1942." *Militärgeschichtliche Mitteilungen* 44, no. 2 (1988): 61–73.

Höhne, Heinz. *Canaris. Patriot im Zwielicht.* Munich, 1976.

Hone, Thomas C., and M. D. Mandeles. "Interwar Innovation in Three Navies: U.S. Navy, Royal Navy, Imperial Japanese Navy." *Naval War College Review* 40, no. 2 (1987): 63–83.

Hosoya Chihirō. "Sangoku dōmei to Nissho chūritsu jōyaku" (The Tripartite Pact and the neutrality agreement between Japan and the Soviet Union). In *Taiheiyō sensō e no michi,* edited by the Nihon Kokusai Seiji Gakkai, vol. 5, 159–331. Tokyo, 1988.

———. "The Tripartite Pact, 1939–1940." In *Deterrent Diplomacy,* edited by James W. Morley, 191–257. New York, 1976.

———, ed. *Nichi-Ei kankeishi, 1917–1949* (History of Japanese-British relations 1917–1949). Tokyo, 1982.

Hosoya Chihirō and Saitō Makoto, eds. *Washinton taisei to Nichi-Bei kankei* (The Washington system and U.S.-Japanese relations). Tokyo, 1978.

Hosoya Chihirō and Watanuki Jōji, eds. *Taigai seisaku kettei katei no Nichi-Bei hikaku* (A comparison of the foreign policy decision-making process in the U.S.A and Japan). Tokyo, 1977.

Hosoya Chihirō et al., eds. *Nichi-Bei kankeishi: Kaisen ni itaru 10-nen, 1931–1941* (History of U.S.-Japanese relations: The decade before the outbreak of war, 1931–1941). 4 vols. Tokyo, 1978.

Huan, C. "La collaboration entre l'Allemange et le Japon durant la seconde Guerre Mondiale." *Revue historique des armées*, no. 1 (1991): 71–82.

Ike Nobutaka, ed. "Japan's Decision for War." Records of the 1941 Policy Conferences. Stanford, Calif., 1967.

Ikeda Hisao. *Raion Kanchō Ayuzumi Haruo* (Lion Captain: Ayuzumi Haruo). Tokyo, 1988.

Ikeda Kiyoshi. "The Douglas Mission and British Influence on the Japanese Navy." In *Themes and Theories in Modern Japanese History*, edited by Sue Henny and Jean-Pierre Lehman, 179. London, 1988.

———. "Japanese Strategy and the Pacific War, 1941–1945." In *Anglo-Japanese Alienation 1919–1952*, edited by Ian Nish, 177–98. Cambridge, 1982.

———. *Kaigun to Nihon* (The navy and Japan). Tokyo, 1981.

———. *Nihon no kaigun* (Japan's navy). 2 vols. Tokyo, 1966

———. "Nihon no sensō shidō keikaku" (Japan's plans for warfare). *Hōgaku* Zasshi 43, no. 2 (July 1979): 1–34.

———. "Rondon kaigun jōyaku hiroku: Ko kaigun taishō Katō Kanji ikō, Shōwa 13-nen" (Katō Kanji's "secret memoirs" about the London Naval Treaty). *Hōgaku Zasshi* 16, no. 1 (August 1969): 123–42.

———. "Rondon kaigun jōyaku to tōsuiken mondai" (The London Naval Treaty and the problem of Imperial Supreme Command authority). *Hōgaku Zasshi* 15, no. 2 (1968): 1–35.

Ikeda Kiyoshi, ed. "Rondon kaigun jōyaku ni kansuru gunreibu gawa no shiryō 3-pen" (The London Naval Treaty and the Japanese navy: Materials of the navy general staff). *Hōgaku Zasshi* 15, no. 4 (March 1969): 102–26.

Ikeda Kiyoshi and Ian Nish. "Germany and the Capture of the *Automedon* Documents. I—A Japanese Appreciation." In *German-Japanese Relations in the 1930s*, edited by Ian Nish, 38–44. London, 1986.

Iklé, Frank W. *German-Japanese Relations, 1936–1940*. New York, 1956.

Inoue Shigeyoshi. *Omoide no ki* (Memories of an age). 2 pts. Tokyo, 1956.

Ishikawa Shingo. *Shinjuwan made no Keii. Kaisen no Shinsō* (The circumstances leading to Pearl Harbor: The truth about the outbreak of war). Tokyo, 1960.

Itani Jirō, Rehm-Takahara Tomoko, and Hans Lengerer. "Japanese Special Attack Weapons." *Warship* 765 (1992): 170–84.

Itō Kōbun. "Seitōseiji no suitai to tōsuiken" (The decline of party politics and Imperial Supreme Command). In *Shōwashi no gunbu to seiji*, vol. 1, edited by Miyake Masaki, 41–79.

Itō Takashi. "Doitsu e no senko ichimangosenkairi. Sensōmakki busshiyusō to jōhokōkan no tame doitsu e muke shuppatsushi buji tōchaku shita saigo no sensuikan tōjōki" (A journey of 15,000 miles by submarine to Germany. War diary of the last submarine to sail for the purposes of transport and exchange of information that arrived without incident). *Rekishi to Jinbutsu*, no. 8 (August 1977): 64–73.

———. *Shōwa shoki seijishi kenkyū: Rondon kaigun gunshuku mondai o meguru sho seiji shūdan no taikō to teikei* (A study of diplomatic history in the early Shōwa Period: Conflict and cooperation of political groups in the controversy about the London Naval Treaty). Tokyo, 1969.

Itō Takashi, Nomura Minoru, and Sawamoto Tsuneo. "Sawamoto Yorio kaigunjikan nikki. Nichibei kaisen zenya" (Diary of Deputy Chief of Navy General Staff Sawamoto Yorio. The eve of the outbreak of war between Japan and the U.S.A.) In *Chūō kōron*, no. 1 (1988): 434–80.

Itō Takashi and Sasaki Takashi, eds. *Mazaki Jinzaburō nikki* (Diary of Mazaki Jinzaburō). 6 vols. Tokyo, 1982–87.

Itō Takashi et al., eds. *Honjō Shigeru nikki* (Diary of Honjō Shigeru). 5 vols. Tokyo, 1982.

———, eds. *Zoku Gendaishi Shiryō 4. Rikugun. Hata Shunroku nikki* (Series of sources on contemporary history, vol. 4. Army. Diary of Hata Shunroku). Tokyo, 1983.

———, eds. *Zoku Gendaishi Shiryō 5. Kaigun. Katō Kanji nikki* (Series of sources on contemporary history, vol. 5. Navy. Diary of Katō Kanji). Tokyo, 1994.

Iura Jōjirō. *Sensuikantai* (The submarine fleet). Tokyo, 1953.

Jäckel, Eberhard. *Hitlers Weltanschauung. Entwurf einer Herrschaft.* Tübingen, 1969.

———. "Der Weg Japans in den Zweiten Weltkrieg." In *Kriegsausbruch 1939*, edited by Helmut Altrichter and J. Becker, 247–61. Munich, 1989.

Jacobsen, Hans-Adolf. *Nationalsozialistische Aussenpolitik 1933–1938.* Frankfurt am Main, 1968.

James, D. Clayton. "American and Japanese Strategies in the Pacific War." In *Makers of Modern Strategy: From Machiavelli to the Nuclear Age*, edited by Peter Paret with Gordon A. Craig and Felix Gilbert, 703–32. Princeton, N.J., 1986.

Jane, F. T. *The Imperial Japanese Navy.* 1904. Reprint, London, 1984.

Jenkins, David. *Battle Surface: Japan's Submarine War against Australia 1942–1944.* Sydney, 1992.

Jentschura, Hansgeorg, et al. *Die japanischen Kriegsschiffe 1869–1945.* Munich, 1970.

Jordan, Gerald, ed. *Naval Warfare in the Twentieth Century.* London, 1977.

Kaigun daijin kanbō, ed. *Kaigun kankei giji sokkiroku* (Notes of parliamentary sessions related to naval matters). 10 vols. Tokyo, 1984.

Kaigun Hensan Iinkai, ed. *Kaigun* (Navy) 13 vols. Tokyo, 1981.

Kaigun Rekishi Hozonkai, ed. *Nihon Kaigunshi* (Japanese naval history). 11 vols. Tokyo, 1995.

Kaigun Suirai Sentai Kankokai, ed. *Kaigun Suiraisentai* (The navy's torpedo squadron). Tokyo, 1979.

Kandeler, Hermann. "1943: Djakarta—deutscher Marinestützpunkt. *Marine Forum* 49, nos. 6–7 (1974): 206–8.

Kanpō-Gōgai (The government gazette) 22 January 1942 (Shūgiin Sokkiroku, no. 3).

Kármán, Theodore von. *Die Wirbelstrasse: Mein Leben für die Luftfahrt.* Hamburg, 1968.

Katō Yōko. "'Churitsu' Amerika o meguru kōbō. Bōkyō kyōteikyōka kōshō to kokusai kankyō" (Attack and defense versus the "neutral" U.S.A. Talks about the strengthening of the common German-Japanese Italian defense agreement and the international situation). *Kindai Nihon Kenkyū* 11 (1989): 120–46.

Kawabata Masahisa, ed. *1940-nendai no sekai seiji* (Global policy in the 1940s). Kyoto, 1988.

Kehr, Eckhart. *Schlachtflottenbau und Parteipolitik, 1894–1901.* Berlin, 1930.

Kehrig, Manfred. *Die Wiedereinrichtung des deutschen militärischen Attachédienstes nach dem Ersten Weltkrieg (1919–1933).* Boppard am Rhein, 1966.

Kennedy, Paul. "Japanese Strategic Decisions, 1939–1945." In *Makers of Modern Strategy,* edited by Peter Paret et al., 199–218. Princeton, N.J., 1986.

Kennedy, Paul M. *Aufstieg und Verfall der britischen Seemacht.* Bonn, 1978.

Kerst, Georg. *Jacob Meckel: Sein Leben, sein Wirken in Deutschland und Japan.* Göttingen, 1970.

Kido Kōichi Nikki Kenkyūkai, ed. *Kido Kōichi nikki* (Diary of Kido Kōichi). 2 vols. Tokyo, 1967.

Kikuchi Seigo. "Ei Shōsen Biharu-gō Horyogyakusatu-Jiken no Shinsō" (The truth about the slaughter of the crew of SS *Bihar*). *Maru,* Bessatsu (special issue), July 1986, 134–47.

Kimata Jirō. *Nihon Sensuikan Senshi* (History of Japanese submarines operations). Tokyo, 1993.

Kisaka Jun'ichirō. "Ajia-Taiheiyō sensōron—sensō no koshō to seikaku o megutte" (About the Asiatic-Pacific War—its name and characteristics). In *1940-nendai no sekai seiji,* edited by Kawabata Masahisa, 366–86. Kyoto, 1988.

———. "Recent Japanese Research on the Second World War." In *Neue Forschungen zum Zweiten Weltkrieg,* edited by Jürgen Rohwer and H. Müller, 239–55. Koblenz, 1990.

Kishino Hiromitsu. *Kaijō goeisen* (The convoy war). Senshi Sōsho (War history series), edited by Bōei Kenshūjo Senshi Shitsu, vol. 46. Tokyo, 1971.

———. *Sensuikanshi* (History of the submarine war). Senshi Sōsho (War history series), edited by Boei Kenshūjo Senshi Shitsu, vol. 98. Tokyo, 1979.

Kitano Tamiyo, ed. *Zoku Gendaishi shiryō* (Series of sources on contemporary history). 12 vols. Tokyo, 1982–96.

Knipping, Franz, and Klaus-Jürgen Müller, eds. *Machtbewusstsein in Deutschland am Vorabend des Zweiten Weltkrieges*. Paderborn, 1984.

Kobayashi Tatsuo. "Kaigun gunshuku jōyaku (1921–1936-nen)" (Naval treaties, 1921–1936). In *Taiheiyō sensō e no michi*, vol. 1, edited by Nihon Kokusai Seiji Gakkai, 3–160. Tokyo, 1963.

———. "The London Naval Treaty, 1930." In *Japan Erupts*, edited by James W. Morley, 11–117. New York, 1984.

Koda Yoji. "Commander's Dilemma: Admiral Yamamoto and the Gradual Attrition Strategy." *Naval War College Review* 46, no. 4 (1993): 63–74.

Kojima Hideo. "Deutschland und ich. Pt. I, Nichidoku Geppō." *Monatsberichte (monthly report) der Japanisch-Deutschen Gesellschaft, no. 274* (September 1976): 8–14; pt. II, no. 275 (October 1976): 6–10.

———. "Doitsu zaikin bukkan no kaisō" (Memories of the time as an attaché in Germany). In *Kaiso no nihonkaigun*, 153–68. Tokyo, 1985.

———, ed. *Gendai Shiryo* (Contemporary historical documents). Vols. 1–3. Tokyo, 1987.

———. "Die militärische Zusammenarbeit zwischen Deutschland und Japan im Raume des Indischen Ozeans sowie die Verbindung beider Länder mit U-Booten im Zweiten Weltkrieg." Undated manuscript in possession of the Berthold J. Sander-Nagashima.

Krebs, Gerhard. "Admiral Yonai Mitsumasa as Navy Minister (1937–39)—Dove or Hawk?" In *Western Interactions with Japan: Expansion, the Armed Forces and Readjustment 1859–1956*, edited by Peter Lowe and Herman Moeshart, 74–83. Sandgate, Folkestone, Kent, 1990.

———. "Deutschland und Pearl Harbor." *Historische Zeitschrift* 253 (1991): 313–69.

———. "The Japanese Air Forces." In *The Conduct of the Air War in the Second World War*, edited by Horst Boog, 228–34. New York, 1991.

———. "Die japanischen Luftstreitkräfte." In *Luftkriegführung im Zweiten Weltkrieg. Ein internationaler Vergleich* (The conduct of the air war in the Second World War: An international comparison). Edited by Horst Boog, 269–75. Herford, 1993.

———. *Japans Deutschlandpolitik 1935–1941. Eine Studie zur Vorgeschichte des Pazifischen Krieges*. 2 vols. Hamburg, 1984.

———. "Japan und der deutsch-sowjetische Krieg 1941." In *Zwei Wege nach Moskau. Vom Hitler-Stalin-Pakt bis zum "Unternehmen Barbarossa,"* edited by Bernd Wegner, 564–83. Munich, 1991.

Krebs, Gerhard, and Bernd Martin, eds. *Formierung und Fall der Achse Berlin Tokyo.* Vol. 8 of *Monographien aus dem Deutschen Institut für Japanstudien der Philip-Franz-von-Siebold-Stiftung.* Munich, 1994.

Kreiner, Josef, ed. *Deutschland-Japan. Historische Kontakte.* Studium Universale [series], vol. 3. Bonn, 1984.

——, ed. *Japan und die Mittelmächte im Ersten Weltkrieg und in den zwanziger Jahren.* Bonn, 1986.

Kreiner, Josef, and Regine Mathias, eds. *Deutschland-Japan in der Zwischenkriegszeit.* Studium Universale [series], vol. 12. Bonn, 1990.

Kudō Michihiro. *Nihon kaigun to Taiheiyō sensō* (The Japanese navy and the Pacific war). 2 vols. Tokyo, 1982.

Kurono Taeru. "Teikoku Kokubō Hōshin Senryaku Sakusenyōheiko" (Strategy and tactics and the "Guidelines for the defense of the empire"). *Gunji Shigaku* (124) 31, no. 4 (March 1996): 37–51.

Kusaka Ryūnosuke. *Kaigunshikan no Hanshōki* (Notes from one-half of the life of a naval officer). Tokyo, 1973.

Kyokutō Kokusai Gunji Saiban Sokkikiroku (Proceedings of the International Military Tribunal for the Far East), vol. 5. Tokyo, 1968.

Layton, Edwin T., Roger Pineau, and John Costello. *"And I Was There": Pearl Harbor and Midway—Breaking the Secrets.* New York, 1985.

——. "24 Sentai, Japan's Commerce Raiders." U.S. Naval Institute *Proceedings,* June 1976, 53–61.

Leasor, James. *Geheimkommando. Deutsche Schiffe im Indischen Ozean.* Vienna, 1978.

Lebra, Joyce C., ed. *Japan's Greater East Asia Co-Prosperity Sphere in World War II: Selected Readings and Documents.* Kuala Lumpur, 1975.

Legahn, Ernst. *Meuterei in der Kaiserlichen Marine. Ursachen und Folgen.* Herford, 1970.

Lengerer, Hans. "Die Bauprogramme der Kaiserlich-japanischen Marine 1937–1945." *Marine Rundschau* 85 (1988): 35–41, 101–7, 165–70, 231–37, 295–99.

——. "Strategie und Taktik des Flugzeugträger-Einsatzes bei der Kaiserlich Japanischen Marine." *Marine Forum* 63 (1988): 107–13.

Lengerer, Hans, and Sumie Kobler-Edamatsu. *Pearl Harbor 1941: Der Paukenschlag im Pazifik nach japanischen Dokumenten.* Friedberg, 1982.

Lengerer, Hans, et al. "Vor 40 Jahren: Die Entstehung des Operationsplanes für den Angriff auf die US-Pazifikflotte in Pearl Harbor." *Marine Rundschau* 78, no. 12 (1981): 645–55.

Lengerer, Hans, Sumie Kobler-Edamatsu, and Tomoko Rehm-Takahara. "Strategische und taktische Planung der kaiserlich-japanischen Marine für die Entscheidungsschlacht gegen die amerikanische Marine." *Marine Forum* 1/2 (1985): 17–26.

Lewin, Ronald. *The Other Ultra*. London, 1982.

Libal, Michael. *Japans Weg in den Krieg. Die Aussenpolitik der Kabinette Konoye, 1940–41*. Düsseldorf, 1971.

Lohmann, Walter, and Hans H. Hildebrand. *Die deutsche Kriegsmarine 1939–1945: Gliederung, Einsatz, Stellenbesetzung*. 3 vols. Bad Nauheim, 1956–64.

Lowe, Peter, and Herman Moeshart, eds. *Western Interactions with Japan: Expansion, the Armed Forces, and Readjustment, 1859–1956*. Sandgate, Folkestone, Kent, 1990.

Lüddecke, Werner Jörg. *Morituri*. Stuttgart, 1963.

Luttwak, E. N. *The Political Uses of Seapower*. Baltimore, 1974.

Maichi Shinbunsha, ed. *Tōkyō Saiban Hanketsu* (The judgment of the Tokyo war criminal court). Tokyo, 1949.

Major, John. "The Naval Plans for War, 1937–1941." In *In Peace and War*, edited by Kenneth J. Hagan, 237–62. Westport, 1984.

Marder, Arthur, J. Jacobsen, and John Horsfield. *Old Friends, New Enemies: The Royal Navy and the Imperial Japanese Navy*. 2 vols. New York, 1981–90.

Martin, Bernd. "Das deutsch-japanische Bündnis im Zweiten Weltkrieg." In *Der Zweite Weltkrieg*, edited by Wolfgang Michalka, 120–37. [Edited on behalf of] Militärgeschichtlichen Forschungsamtes. Munich, 1989.

———. "Die deutsch-japanischen Beziehungen während des Dritten Reiches." In *Hitler, Deutschland und die Mächte*, edited by Manfred Funke, 454–70. Düsseldorf 1976.

———. "Deutschland und Japan im Zweiten Weltkrieg. Vom Angriff auf Pearl Harbor bis zur deutschen Kapitulation." In *Studien und Dokumente zur Geschichte des Zweiten Weltkrieges*, edited bu Hans Adolf Jacobsen, vol. 2. Göttingen, 1969.

———. "Die Einschätzung der Lage Deutschlands aus japanischer Sicht: Japans Abkehr vom Bündnis und seine Hinwendung auf Ostasien, 1943–1945." In *Die Zukunft des Reiches, Gegner, Verbündete und Neutrale, 1943–1945*, edited by Manfred Messerschmidt and Ekkehart Guth, 127–46. Herford, 1990.

———. "Faschistisch-militaristische Grossmachtpolitik." In *Zwei zaghafte Riesen*, edited by Arnulf Baring, 93–126. Stuttgart, 1977.

———. "Japan im Krieg 1941–1945." In *Weltpolitik II*, edited by Oswald Hauser, 131–52. Göttingen, 1975.

———. "Japans Weg in den Krieg: Bemerkungen über Forschungsstand und Literatur zur japanischen Zeitgeschichte." In *Militärgeschichtliche Mitteilungen* 23, no. 1 (1978): 183–209.

———. "Japans Weltmachtstreben 1939–1941." In *Weltpolitik II*, edited by Oswald Hauser, 98–130. Göttingen 1975.

———. "Japan und der Krieg in Ostasien. Kommentierender Bericht über das Schrifttum." In *Literaturbericht zur Geschichte China und zur japanischen Zeitgeschichte,* edited by Rolf Tranzettel and Bernd Martin, 79–220. Munich, 1980.

———. "Japan—Zur Rezeption und wechselseitigen Beeinflussung von Herrschaftspraktiken und Weltmachtbestrebungen." In *Innen- und Aussenpolitik unter nationalsozialistischer Bedrohung,* edited by Erhard Forndran et al., 87–109. Opladen, 1977.

———. "Die 'Militärische Vereinbarung zwischen Deutschland, Italien und Japan' vom 18 Januar 1942." In *Probleme des Zweiten Weltkrieges,* edited by Andreas Hillgruber, 134–44. Cologne, 1967.

———. "Verhängnisvolle Wahlverwandtschaft—Deutsche Einflüsse auf die Entstehung des modernen Japan." In *Deutschland in Europa,* edited by Jost Dülffer, Bernd Martin, and Günter Wollstein, 97–116. Gedenkschrift für Andreas Hillgruber. Berlin, 1990.

———. "Zur Vorgeschichte des deutsch-japanischen Kriegsbündnisses." *Geschichte in Wissenschaft und Unterricht* 21 (1970): 606–15.

Martin, Bernd, with Militärgeschichtlichen Forschungsamt, eds. *Die deutsche Beraterschaft in China 1927–1938: Militär, Wirtschaft, Aussenpolitik.* Düsseldorf, 1981.

Maruyama Masao. *Denken in Japan.* Frankfurt am Main, 1988.

———. *Nihon no Shisō* (Thought in Japan). Tokyo, 1967.

Masland, John W. "Japanese-German Naval Collaboration in World War II." U.S. Naval Institute *Proceedings* 75, no. 2 (1949): 178–87.

Matloff, Maurice. *Strategic Planning for Coalition Warfare, 1943–1944.* Washington, D.C., 1959.

Matloff, Maurice, and Edwin M. Snell. *Strategic Planning for Coalition Warfare, 1941–1942.* Washington, D.C., 1953.

Matsushita Yoshio, ed. *Tanaka Sakusen Buchō no Shōgen* (The testimony of the head of the operations department, Tanaka). Tokyo, 1978.

Mattesini, Francesco. *Betasom: la guerra negli oceani, 1940–1943.* Rome, 1993.

May, Ernest R., ed. *Knowing One's Enemies: Intelligence Assessments before the Two World Wars.* Princeton, N.J., 1984.

Meissner, Kurt. *Deutsche in Japan 1639–1939: Dreihundert Jahre Arbeit für Wirtsland und Vaterland.* Stuttgart, 1940.

Meskill, Johanna Menzel. *Hitler and Japan: The Hollow Alliance.* New York, 1966.

Messerschmidt, Manfred, and Ekkehart Guth, eds. *Die Zukunft des Reiches: Gegner, Verbündete und Neutrale, 1943–1945.* Herford, 1990.

Meurer, Alexander. *Seekriegsgeschichte in Umrissen: Seemacht und Seekriege vornehml. vom 16. Jh. ab* (Sea power and wars at sea from the 16th century on). Leipzig, 1943.

Michalka, Wolfgang, ed. *Der Zweite Weltkrieg: Analysen, Grundzüge, Forschungsbilanz.* Munich and Zürich, 1989.

Michaux, Theo. "Rohstoffe aus Ostasien. Die Fahrten der Blockadebrecher." *Wehrwissenschaftliche Rundschau* 5, no. 11 (1955): 485–507.

Mikesh, Robert C. *Japanese Aircraft: Code Names & Designations*. Atglen, Pa., 1993.

Militärgeschichtliches Forschungsamt, ed. *Deutsche Militärgeschichte 1648–1939*. 6 vols. Munich, 1983.

———. *Der globale Krieg: Die Ausweitung zum Weltkrieg und der Wechsel der Initiative 1941–1943*. Das Deutsche Reich und der Zweite Weltkrieg [series], vol. 6. Stuttgart, 1990.

———. *Militärgeschichte: Probleme—Thesen—Wege*. Stuttgart, 1982.

———. *Die operative Idee und ihre Grundlagen: Ausgewählte Operationen des Zweiten Weltkrieges*. Vorträge zur Militärgeschichte [series], vol. 10. Herford, 1989.

Military Intelligence Division, U.S. War Department. *German Military Intelligence, 1939–1945*. Frederick, Md., 1984.

Miller, David. "The Mystery of the Last Voyage of Japanese Submarine *I-52*." *Warship* 1996: 25–30.

Ministry of Defence (Navy). *The U-Boat War in the Atlantic*. Vols. 1–3. London, 1989.

Ministry of Defence, ed. *The War with Japan*. 5 vols. London, 1995–97.

Miwa Kimitada, ed. *Sekai no naka no Nihon* (Japan in the world). Sōgō kōza Nihon no shakai bunkashi (Series on Japanese social and cultural history), vol. 7. Tokyo, 1974.

Miwa Kimitada and Tobe Ryoichi, eds. *Nihon gaiko no kiro to Matsuoka gaiko, 1940–41nen* (Japan's crucial foreign policy decisions and Matsuoka's foreign policy, 1940–41). Tokyo, 1994.

Miyake Masaki. "Die Achse Berlin-Rom-Tokyo im Spiegel der japanischen Quellen." *Mitteilungen des Östrreichschen Staatsarchivs* 21 (1968): 408–45.

———. *Nichi-Doku-I sangoku dōmei no kenkyū* (A study of the Tripartite Pact). Tokyo, 1975.

———. "Nichi-Doku kankei no rekishiteki tenkai to Soren" (The historical development of Japanese-German relations and the Soviet Union). In *Sōgō kōza Nihon no shakai bunkashi*, vol. 7, edited by Miwa Kimitada, 362–431. Tokyo, 1974.

Miyake Masaki et al., eds. *Shōwashi no gunbu to seiji* (The military in the Shōwa period and politics). 5 vols. Tokyo, 1983.

Morley, James W. *The China Quagmire: Japan's Expansion on the Asian Continent, 1935–1941*. New York, 1983.

———. *Deterrent Diplomacy: Japan, Germany and the USSR, 1935–1940*. New York, 1976.

———. *The Fateful Choice. Japan's Advance into Southeast Asia, 1939–1941*. New York, 1980.

———. *Japan Erupts. The London Naval Conference and the Manchurian Incident, 1928–1932*. New York, 1984.

Morley, James W., ed. *Dilemmas of Growth in Prewar Japan*. Princeton, N.J., 1974.

Muggenthaler, August K. *Das waren die deutschen Hilfskreuzer 1939–1945: bwaffnete Handelsschiffe im Einsatz*. Stuttgart, 1981.

Müller, Klaus-Jürgen. "Military and Diplomacy in France and Germany in the inter-war Period." Undated manuscript in the possession of the authors.

———. "The Military, Politics and Society in France and Germany." Undated manuscript in the possession of the authors.

———. "Revision, Aufrüstung und nationale Sicherheit. Der Grundsatzkonflikt zwischen Militär und Diplomatie in Deutschland 1933–1935." In *Deutschland zwischen Krieg und Frieden*, edited by Karl Dietrich Bracher, 19–30. Düsseldorf, 1991.

Müller, Klaus-Jürgen, and Eckardt Opitz, eds. *Militär und Militarismus in der Weimarer Republik*. Beiträge eines internationalen Symposium an der Hochschule der Bundeswehr Hamburg, 5–6 May 1977. Düsseldorf, 1978.

Mushakōji Kintomo. *Gaikō urakōji* (Foreign policy behind the scenes). Tokyo, 1952.

Nakamura Takafusa. *Economic Growth in Prewar Japan*. New Haven, Conn., 1983.

Niestlé, Axel. *German U-Boat Losses during World War II: Details of Destruction*. London, 1998.

Nihon Kaigun Sensuikan Shi Hensankai, ed. *Nihon Kaigun Sensuikan Senshi* (War history of the Japanese navy's submarines). Tokyo, 1979.

Nihon Kindai Shiryō Kenkyūkai, ed. *Nihon Rikukaigun no Seido Soshiki Jinji* (Organization, posts and personnel of the Japanese army and navy). Tokyo, 1971.

Nihon Kokusai Seiji Gakkai, ed. *Taiheiyō sensō e no michi* (The path to the Pacific war). 7 vols. Supplement 1, 1962–63. Tokyo, 1987–88.

Nish, Ian. *Alliance in Decline*. London, 1972.

———. "German-Japanese Relations in the 1930s." Papers by Nobutoshi Hagihara, Erich Pauer, Kiyoshi Ikeda, and Ian Nish. *International Centre for Economics and Related Disciplines, London School of Economics: International Studies, 1986/III*. London, 1986.

———. "Germany and the Capture of the *Automedon* Documents. II—A British Appreciation." In *German-Japanese Relations in the 1930s*, edited by Ian Nish, 45–49. London, 1986.

———. "Some Aspects of Soviet-Japanese Relations in the 1930s." *International Centre for Economics and Related Disciplines, London School of Economics: International Studies 1982/II*. London, 1982.

———, ed. "Anglo-Japanese Alienation 1919–1952." *Papers of the Anglo-Japanese Conference on the History of the Second World War*. Cambridge, 1982.

———, ed. "The Tripartite Pact of 1940: Japan, Germany and Italy." Papers by Jost Dülffer, John Chapman, and Ernest Bramsted. *International Centre for Economics and Related Disciplines, London School of Economics: International Studies 1984/III.* London, 1984.

Nohara Komakichi. *Die "Gelbe Gefahr": Japan und die Erhebung der farbigen Völker.* Stuttgart, 1938.

Nomura Minoru. "Daihon'ei kaigunbu, Rengo kantai. Dai Sandan sakusen zenki" (Imperial Headquarters, Navy Department. Combined Fleet: The beginning period of third stage operations), pt. 6. Senshi Sōsho (War history series), edited by Boei Kenshūjo Senshi Shitsu, vol. 45. Tokyo, 1971.

———. "Daihon'ei kaigunbu, Rengō kantai. Sensō saishūki" (Imperial Headquarters, Navy Department Combined Fleet. The end of the war), pt. 7. Senshi Sōsho (War history series), edited by Bōei Kenshujō Senshi Shitsu, vol. 93. Tokyo, 1976.

———. "Military Policy-makers behind Japanese Strategy against Britain." In *Anglo-Japanese Alienation 1919–1952*, edited by Ian Nish, 147–56. Cambridge, 1982.

———. *Rekishi no naka no Nihon kaigun* (The Japanese navy in history). Tokyo, 1980.

———. "Sangoku dōmei teiketsu to kaigun: Oikawa Koshiro to Yamamoto Isoroku" (The Japanese navy and the conclusion of the Tripartite Pact: Navy Minister Oikawa Koshiro and Admiral Yamamoto Isoroku). *Nihon Rekishi*, no. 362 (July 1978): 67–75.

———. "Taiheiyō sensō no Nihon no sensō shidō" (Japanese warfare in the Pacific war). *Nenpō kindai Nihon kenkyū*, no. 4 (n.d.): 29–50.

———. "Taiheiyō sensō to Nihon no senryaku" (The Pacific war and Japanese strategy)." In *Nichi-Be: Kankeishi: Kaisen ni itaru 10-nen, 1931–1941*, edited by Hosoya Chihirō, 105–13. Tokyo, 1982.

———, ed. *Jijū Bukan Jō Eiichirō Nikki* (Diary of the aide-de-camp to the Emperor Jō Eiichirō). Tokyo, 1987.

———, ed. *Jō eiichirō nikki* (Diary of Jō Eiichirō). Tokyo, 1982.

Nomura Minoru and Itō Takashi, eds. *Kaigun taishō Kobayashi Seizō oboegaki* (The memos of Admiral Kobayashi Seizō). Tokyo, 1981.

Nomura Naokuni. *Hachijū hachinen no kaiko* (Looking back at eighty-eight years). Tokyo, 1974.

———. *Senkan U-511 Go no Unmei: Hiroku Nichi Doku I kyōdō sakusen.* (The fate of U-boat U-511. The combined German-Italian-Japanese operations). Tokyo, 1956.

Nowarra, Heinz. *Heinkel und seine Flugzeuge.* Friedberg, 1975.

———. *Die verbotenen Flugzeuge 1921–1935.* Stuttgart, 1980.

Nozawa Tadashi. Nihon kōkūki sōshū (Encyclopedia of Japanese aircraft). Vol. 6, Yunyūkihen (Imported aircraft). Tokyo, 1972.

Oberkommando der Kriegsmarine. *Operationen und Taktik, MDv. 601.* Heft 5, *Die Fahrt des Hilfskreuzers Schiff 16 (Atlantis).* Berlin, 1943.

———. *Operationen und Taktik. MDv. 601.* Heft 6, *Die Fahrt des Hilfskreuzers Schiff 33 (Pinguin).* Berlin 1943.

———. *Operationen und Taktik. MDv. 601.* Heft 7, *Die erste Fahrt des Hilfskreuzers Schiff 10 (Thor).* Berlin, 1943.

———. *Operationen und Taktik, MDv. 601.* Heft 10, *Die Fahrt des Hilfskreuzers Schiff 41 (Kormoran).* Berlin, 1943.

———. *Operationen und Taktik. MDv. 601.* Heft 14, *Die erste Fahrt des Hilfskreuzers Schiff 49 ("Komet").* Berlin, 1944.

———. *Operationen und Taktik. MDv. 601.* Heft 15, *Die Fahrt des Hilfskreuzers Schiff 36 (Orion).* Berlin 1944.

Ohmae Toshikazu. "Die japanischen Operationen im Bereich des Indischen Ozeans." *Marine Rundschau* 55, no. 2 (1958): 49–54.

Oide Hisahi. *Raion Kanchō Mayuzumi Haruo* (Lion Captain Mayuzumi Haruo). Tokyo, 1995.

Okada Tadahiro, ed. *Okada Keisuke Kaikoroku: Rondon gunshuku mondai nikki.* (Okada Keisuke's Memoirs: Diary of the problems at the London Naval Armament Limitation Conference). Tokyo, 1950.

Ōkubo Tatsuya, ed. *Shōwa Shakai keizai shiryō Shūsei: Kaigunshō Shiryō* (Collection of sources on the social and economic history of the Showa period: The records of the Navy Ministry). 20 vols. Tokyo, 1978–1999.

Okumiya Masatake and Hirokoshi Jiro. *Zero! The Story of the Japanese Navy Air Force 1937–1945.* London, 1959.

Okumiya Masatake, Jirō Horikoshi, with Martin Caidin. *Zero! The Air War in the Pacific during World War II from the Japanese Viewpoint.* Washington, 1979.

O'Neill, P. G., ed. *Tradition and Modern Japan.* Tenterden, Kent, 1981.

Ooe Shinobu. *Tōsuiken* (Imperial Supreme Command authority). Tokyo, 1983.

Osterfeld, Wilhelm. *Wer knackte den Schlüssel "M"?: Eine Zusammenstellung gelesener Fakten, erinnerter Einzelheiten und erdachter Zusammenhänge.* Lübbecke/Westf., 1985.

Ozawa teitoku denki henshū iinkai, ed. *Teitoku Ozawa Jisaburō den* (Biography of Admiral Ozawa Jisaburō). Tokyo, 1969.

Padfield, Peter. *Dönitz et la Guerre des U-Boote.* Paris, 1986.

Pantzer, Peter. "Deutschland und Japan vom Ersten Weltkrieg bis zum Austritt aus dem Völkerbund (1914–1933)." In *Deutschland-Japan. Historische Kontakte,* edited by Josef Kreiner, 141–60. Bonn, 1984.

———. "Japan und Österreich zwischen beiden Kriegen." In *Japan und die Mittelmächte im Ersten Weltkrieg und in den zwanziger Jahren,* edited by Josef Kreiner, 175–232. Bonn, 1986.

Paret, Peter, et al., eds. *Makers of Modern Strategy: From Machiavelli to the Nuclear Age.* Princeton, N.J., 1986.

Parillo, Mark P. "The Imperial Japanese Navy in World War II." In *Reevaluating Major Naval Combatants of World War II*, edited by James J. Sadkovich, 61–77. Westport, Conn., 1990.

———. "The Japanese Merchant Marine in World War II." Diss., Ohio State University, 1987.

Pauer, Erich. "Deutsche Ingenieure in Japan, japanische Ingenieure in Deutschland in der Zwischenkriegszeit." In *Deutschland-Japan. Historische Kontakte,* edited by Josef Kreiner, 289–324. Bonn, 1984.

———. *Japan-Deutschland. Wirtschaft und Wirtschaftsbeziehungen im Wandel.* Japanwirtschaft [series], edited by the Deutsch-japanischen Wirtschaftsförderungsbüro, no. 19. Düsseldorf, 1985.

Peattie, Mark R. "Akiyama Saneyuki and the Emergence of Modern Japanese Naval Doctrine." U.S. Naval Institute *Proceedings* 103, no. 1 (1977): 60–69.

Pelz, Stephen E. *Race to Pearl Harbor: The Failure of the Second London Naval Conference and the Onset of World War II.* Harvard Studies in American-East Asian Relations, vol. 5. Cambridge, Mass., 1974.

Pfitzmann, Martin. *U-Bootgruppe Eisbär: Einsatz vor Kapstadt.* Rastatt, 1986.

Pike, David Wingeate, ed. *The Opening of the Second World War: Proceedings of the Second International Conference on International Relations, held at the American University of Paris, 26–30 September, 1989.* New York, 1991.

Potter, Elmar B., Chester W. Nimitz, and Jürgen Rohwer, eds. *Seemacht: Eine Seekriegsgeschichte von der Antike bis zur Gegenwart.* Herrsching, 1982.

Presseisen, Ernst L. *Germany and Japan: A Study in Totalitarian Diplomacy.* The Hague, 1958.

Raeder, Erich *Mein Leben.* 2 vols. Tübingen, 1956–57.

Rahn, Werner. "Einsatzbereitschaft und Kampfkraft deutscher U-Boote 1942. Eine Dokumentation zu den materiellen Voraussetzungen und Problemen des U-Boot-Krieges nach dem Kriegeintritt der U.S.A." (Combat readiness and fighting power of 1942 German submarines. Documentation on the material preconditions and problems of U-boat warfare after the U.S. entered the war). *Militärgeschichtliche Mitteilungen* 47 (1990): 73–132.

———. "Japan and Germany, 1941–1943: No Common Objective, No Common Plans, No Basis of Trust." *Naval War College Review* 46, no. 3 (1993): 47–68.

———. "Japan und der Krieg in Europa." In *Der globale Krieg,* edited by Militärgeschichtlichen Forschungsamt, 143–70. Stuttgart, 1990.

———. "Korreferat II: Reichsmarine und Weltmachtstreben." In *Militär und Militarismus in der Weimarer Republik,* edited by Klaus-Jürgen Müller and Eckart Opitz, 183–88. Düsseldorf, 1978.

———. "Der Krieg im Pazifik." In *Der globale Krieg,* edited by Militärgeschichtlichen Forschungsamt, 171–271. Stuttgart, 1990.

———. "Kriegswende im Pazifik 1942." *Truppendienst* 21, no. 5 (1982): 456–63.

———. "Weiträumige deutsche U-Boot-Operationen 1942/43 und ihre logistische Unterstützung durch U-Tanker." In *Die operative Idee und ihre Grundlagen. Ausgewählte Operationen des 2.Weltkrieges*, edited by Militärgeschichtlichen Forschungsamt, 79–97. Herford, 1989.

Rahn, Werner, and Gerhard Schreiber. *Kriegstagebuch der Seekriegsleitung, 1939–1945*. Edited by Hansjoseph Maierhöfer. Herford, Ger., 1988.

Ratenhof, Udo. *Die Chinapolitik des Deutschen Reiches 1871–1945: Wirtschaft, Rüstung, Militär*. Boppard am Rhein, 1987.

Robertson, Ken G., ed. *British and American Approaches to Intelligence*. New York, 1987.

Rohwer, Jürgen. *Axis Submarine Successes, 1939–1945*. Annapolis, Md., 1983.

———. "Literatur zum Thema: Funkaufklärung im Zweiten Weltkrieg." *Marine Rundschau* 77, no. 10 (1980): 638–40.

———. "Der Seekrieg im Indischen Ozean 1941–1945." In *Seemacht: Eine Seekriegsgeschichte von der Antike bis zur Gegenwart*, edited by Elmar B. Potter, Chester Nimitz, and Jürgen Rohwer. Herrsching, 1982.

Rohwer, Jürgen, and Gerhard Hümmelchen. *Chronology of the War at Sea, 1939–1945*. Oldenburg, 1968.

Rohwer, Jürgen, and Eberhard Jäckel, eds. *Die Funkaufklärung und ihre Rolle im Zweiten Weltkrieg*. Stuttgart 1979.

Rohwer, Jürgen, and H. Müller, eds. *Neue Forschungen zum Zweiten Weltkrieg. Literaturberichte und Bibliographien aus 67 Ländern*. Koblenz, 1990.

Rohwer, Jürgen et al., eds. *Kriegswende Dezember 1941*. Koblenz, 1984.

Role, Maurice. "La stratégie navale japonaise dans l'Océan Indien au printemps 1942." *Guerres mondiales et conflits contemporains* 40, no. 159 (1990): 53–71.

Röling, B. V. A., and C. F. Rüter, eds. *The Tokyo Judgement The International Military Tribunal for the Far East (I.M.T.F.E.), 29 April 1946–12 November 1948*. 3 vols. Amsterdam, 1977.

Rönnefarth, Helmut K. G., and Heinrich Euler, eds. *Konferenzen und Verträge. Vertrags-Ploetz*. Pt. 2, vol. 4, *Neueste Zeit 1914–1959*. Würzburg, 1959.

Roskill, Stephen W. *The War at Sea, 1939–1943*. 4 vols. London, 1954–61.

Rössler, Eberhard. *Die Geschichte des deutschen U-Bootbaus*. Munich, 1975.

Ruge, Friedrich. *Entscheidung im Pazifik: Die Ereignisse im Stillen Ozean, 1941–1945*. 3rd ed. Hamburg, 1961.

———. *Der Seekrieg, 1939–1945*. Stuttgart, 1954.

———. *In vier Marinen: Lebenserinnerungen als Beitrag zur Zeitgeschichte*. Munich, 1979.

Rusbridger, James. "The Sinking of the *Automedon*, the Capture of the *Nankin*: New Light on Two Intelligence Disasters in World War II." *Encounter* 64, no. 5 (May 1985): 8–14.

Sadkovich, James J., ed. *Reevaluating Major Naval Combatants of World War II.* Military Studies, no. 92. Westport, Conn., 1990.

Sagan, Scott D. "The Origins of the Pacific War." *Journal of International History* 18, no. 4 (1988): 893–922.

Sakamoto Kanami. *Daihon'ei kaigunbu, Rengō kantai.* "Shōwa 18-nen 2-gatsu made" (Imperial Headquarters, Navy Department. Combined Fleet: Development until June 1943), pt. 3. Senshi Sōsho (War history series), edited by Bōei Kenshūjo Senshi Shitsu, vol. 77. Tokyo, 1974.

———. *Nihon Sensuikan Senshi* (The combat history of the Japanese submarines). Tokyo, 1979.

Salewski, Michael. *Die deutsche Seekriegsleitung, 1935–1945.* Vol. 1, *1935–1941.* Frankfurt am Main, 1970; vol. 2, *1942–1945.* Munich, 1975; vol. 3, *Denkschriften und Lagebetrachtungen, 1938–1944.* Frankfurt am Main, 1973.

———. *Entwaffnung und Militärkontrolle in Deutschland, 1919–1927.* Munich, 1966.

———. "Korreferat I: Reichsmarine und Weltmachtstreben." In *Militär und Militarismus in der Weimarer Republik,* edited by Klaus-Jürgen Müller and Eckhart Opitz, 177–82. Düsseldorf, 1978.

———. *Tirpitz: Aufstieg—Macht—Scheitern.* Göttingen, 1979.

———. "Die Washingtoner Abrüstungskonferenz von 1922." *Marine Rundschau* 70 (1973): 33–50.

Sambō Honbu, ed. *Haisen no kiroku* (Record of defeat). Tokyo, 1979.

———, ed. *Sugiyama memo. Daihon'ei, seifu renrakukaigi tō hitsuki* (Notes of General Sugiyama on the conferences between Imperial Headquarters and the government). 2 vols. Tokyo, 1967.

Samuels, Richard J. "Reinventing Security: Japan Since Meiji." *Daedalus* 120, no. 4 (1991): 47–68.

Sander-Nagashima, Berthold. "Die deutsch-japanischen Marinebeziehungen, 1919 bis 1942." Ph.D. diss., University of Hamburg, 1998.

Sandhofer, Gert. "Das Panzerschiff 'A' und die Vorentwürfe von 1920 bis 1928. *Militärgeschichtliche Mitteilungen* 1 (1967): 35–62.

Sanematsu Yuzuru. *Saigo no toride: Teitoku Yoshida Zengo no shōgai* (The last fortress: The life of Admiral Yoshida Zengo). Tokyo, 1974.

Santoni, Alberto. *Ultra siegt im Mittelmeer: Die entscheidende Rolle der britischen Funkaufklärung beim Kampf um den Nachschub für Nordafrika vom Juni 1940 bis Mai 1943.* Koblenz, 1985.

Sasaki Masao. *Nansei hōmen kaigun sakusen* (The naval operations in the southwestern area). Senshi Sōsho (War history series), edited by Bōei Kenshūjo Senshi Shitsu, vol. 54. Tokyo, 1972.

Satō Haykutarō. *Chūbu Taiheiyō hōmen kaigun sakusen* (1). "Shōwa jūshichi nen gogatsu made" (Naval operations in the Central Pacific. Pt. 1: until May 1942). Senshi Sōsho (War history series), edited by Bōei Kenshūjo Senshi Shitsu, vol. 38. Tokyo, 1970.

Saunders, H. H. *Duell im Pazifik. Von Pearl Harbor bis Hiroshima: Der Zweite Weltkrieg in Ostasien, 1941–1945.* Leoni, Switzerland, 1982.

Saville, Allison W. "German Submarines in the Far East." U.S. Naval Institute *Proceedings* 87, no. 8 (1961): 80–92.

Schildt, Axel. *Militärdiktatur mit Massenbasis? Die Querfrontkonzeption der Reichswehrführung um General von Schleicher am Ende der Weimarer Republik.* Frankfurt am Main, 1981.

Schmalenbach, Paul. *Die deutschen Hilfskreuzer, 1895–1945.* Oldenburg, 1977.

Schreiber, Gerhard. "Reichsmarine, Revisionismus und Weltmachtstreben." In *Militär und Militarismus in der Weimarer Republik,* edited by Klaus-Jürgen Müller and Eckart Opitz, 149–76. Düsseldorf 1978.

———. *Revisionismus und Weltmachtstreben: Marineführung und deutsch-italienische Beziehungen, 1919 bis 1944.* Stuttgart, 1978.

———. "Thesen zur ideologischen Kontinuität in den machtpolitischen Zielsetzungen der deutschen Marineführung 1897 bis 1945." In *Militärgeschichte. Probleme—Thesen—Wege,* [edited on behalf of] Militärgeschichtlichen Forschungsamtes by Manfred Messerschmidt, Klaus A. Maier, Werner Rahn, and Bruno Thoss, 260–80. Stuttgart, 1982.

Schröder, Klaus. "Zur Entstehung der strategischen Konzeption Grossadmiral Raeders." *MOV-Nachrichten* 46 (1971): 14–18, 45–48.

Schroeder, Paul W. *The Axis Alliance and Japanese-American Relations, 1941.* Ithaca, N.Y., 1958.

Schulze, Henrik. *Die Militärstadt Jüterbog in alten Ansichten.* Zaltbommel, Netherlands, [no year].

Schwalbe, Hans, et al., eds. *Deutsche Botschafter in Japan, 1860–1973.* Tokyo, 1974,

Seno Sadao. "A Chess Game with No Checkmate: Admiral Inoue and the Pacific War." *Naval War College Review* 26, no. 4 (1974): 26–39.

Senshi Sōsho Shiryōshū, ed. *Kaigun nendo sakusen keikaku (Shōwa 11-nen–Shōwa 16-en)* (The yearly operational plans of the navy, 1936–1941). Tokyo, 1986.

Shibata Shin'ichi. "Nichidokui sankokukan tandoku fukōwa kyōtei teiketsu mondai" (The problem of the agreement between Germany, Italy and Japan not to conclude a separate peace treaty). *Kokugakuin daigaku nihonbunka kenkyūjo kiyō,* no. 73 (1994): 26–42.

Shillony, Ben-Ami. *Revolt in Japan: The Young Officers and the February 26, 1936, Incident.* Princeton, N.J., 1973.

Shimanuki Takeharu. *Daihon'ei rikugunbu. Shōwa 15-nen gogatsu made* (Imperial Headquarters, Army Department development until May 1940). Senshi Sōsho (War history series), edited by Bōei Kenshūjo Senshi Shitsu, vol. 8. Tokyo, 1967.

———. *Daihon'ei rikugunbu. Shōwa 16-nen 12-gatsu made* (Imperial Headquarters, Army Department development until December 1941). Senshi Sōsho (War history series), edited by Bōei Kenshūjo Senshi Shitsu, vol. 20. Tokyo, 1968.

———. "Daiichiji sekai sensō ogo no kokubo hōshin, shoyō heiryoku, yōhei kōryo no hensen" (The guidelines for the defense of the empire after World War I: The change in the force levels deemed necessary and in the tactical concept). *Gunji shigaku* 9, no. 1 (1973): 65ff.

Shinmin, Yukihiko. "Jōyaku kaigun jidai no hōkai" (The collapse of the age of naval agreements). *Kokugakuin daigaku hōken ronsō*, no. 10 (March 1983): 78–118.

Shinmyō, Takeo, ed. *Kaigun sensō kentō kaigi kiroku: Taiheiyō sensō kaisen no keii* (Notes of the discussion about the navy and the Pacific war: The circumstances that led to its outbreak). Tokyo, 1976.

Shinohara, Yūkō, et al. *Rengō kantai kansen gaido, 1872–1945* (A guide to warships of the Combined Fleet, 1872–1945). Tokyo, 1994.

"Shōwa Tennō no Dokuhaku 8 Jikan" (The Shōwa Tennō's eight-hour monologue). *Bungei Shunju* 68, no. 13 (1990): 68.

Silberman, Bernard S., and Harry D. Harootian, eds. *Japan in Crisis: Essay on Taisho Democracy.* Princeton, N.J., 1974.

Sommer, Theo. *Deutschland und Japan zwischen den Mächten, 1935–1940. Vom Antikomiternpakt zum Dreimächtepakt. Eine Studie zur diplomatischen Vorgeschichte des Zweiten Weltkrieges.* Tübingen, 1962.

Spahn, Mark, Wolfgang Hadami, and Kimiko Winter. *Japanese Character Dictionary.* Berlin 1989.

Stegemann, Bernd. *Hitlers "Stufenplan" und die Marine. Historische Studien zu Politik, Verfassung und Gesellschaft.* Festschrift for Richard Dietrich on his 65th birthday. Bern, 1976.

Storry, R. *The Double Patriots.* London, 1957.

———. *Japan and the Decline of the West in Asia, 1894–1943.* London, 1979.

Stumpf, Reinhard. "Von der Achse Berlin-Rom zum Militärabkommen des Dreierpakts." In *Der globale Krieg,* edited by Militärgeschichtlichen Forschungsamt, 127–43. Stuttgart, 1990.

———. *Die Wehrmacht-Elite. Rang- und Herkunftsstruktur der deutschen Generale und Admirale 1933–1945.* Boppard, 1982.

Suekuni Masao and Nishimura Kunigoro. *Kaigun gunsenbi, Shōwa 16-nen 11-gatsu made* (Naval armament until November 1941). Senshi Sōsho (War history series), edited by Bōei Kenshūjo Senshi Shitsu, vol. 31. Tokyo, 1969.

Sugamo Hōmu Iinkai, ed. *Senpan Saiban no Jissō* (Truth of the war crimes tribunal). Tokyo, 1952.

Suikōsha, ed. *Kaisō no nihonkaigun* (Remembering the Japanese navy). Tokyo, 1985.

Sweetman, Jack. *American Naval History: An Illustrated Chronology of the U.S. Navy and Marine Corps, 1775–present.* Annapolis, Md., 1991.

Symonds, Craig L., et al., ed. *New Aspects of Naval History: Selected papers presented at the Fourth Naval History Symposium, United States Naval Academy, 25–26 October 1979.* Annapolis, Md., 1981.

Taguchi Hiroshi. Untitled. *Kaigun kikan gakkō daiyonjūgo* (August 1960): 48–52.

Tahira Nagayoshi. *Daihon'ei kaigunbu, Rengō kantai. Kaisen made* (Imperial Headquarters, Navy Department. The Combined Fleet until the outbreak of war), pt. 1. Senshi Sōsho (War history series), edited by Bōei Kenshūjo Senshi Shitsu, vol. 91. Tokyo, 1975.

———. *Nachizumu Kyokutō Senryaku* (The Nazi Far Eastern policy). Tokyo 1997.

———. *Ran'in, Bengaruwan hōmen kaigun shikkō sakusen* (Naval attack operations in the waters around the Dutch colonies and in the Bay of Bengal). Senshi Sōsho (War history series), edited by Bōei Kenshūjo Senshi Shitsu, vol 26. Tokyo, 1969.

Tajima Nobuo. "Nichidoku bōkyō kyōtei zō no saikōsei (1). Doitsugawa no seijikatei o chūshin ni" (The Tripartite Pact reconsidered [1]. The political events on the German side as a guideline). *Seijō Hōgaku* 24 (June 1987): 139–88.

———. "Nichidoku bōkyō kyōtei zō no saikōsei (2). Doitsugawa no seijikatei o chūshin ni (The Tripartite Pact reconsidered (2). The political events on the German side as a guideline). *Seijō Hōgaku* 25 (July 1987): 105–42.

———. *Nachisumugaikō to "Manshūkoku"* (Nazi foreign policy and "Manchukuo"). Tokyo, 1992.

Tajima Nobuo and Sanematsu Yuzuru, eds. *Kaigun taishō Yonai Mitsumasa oboegaki* (The memos of Admiral Yonai Mitsumasa). Tokyo 1978.

Takagi Sōkichi. *Shikan Taiheiyō sensō* (Opinions on the Pacific war). Tokyo, 1969.

———. *Taiheiyō sensō to riku-kaigun no koso* (The Pacific war and the rivalry between army and navy). Tokyo, 1967.

———. *Takagi kaigun shōshō oboegaki* (The memos of Admiral Takagi). Tokyo, 1979.

———. *Takagi Sōkichi nikki* (Diaries of Takagi Sōkichi). Tokyo, 1985.

Tanemura Suketaka, ed. *Daihon'ei kimitsu nisshi* (The secret diaries of Imperial Headquarters). Tokyo, 1952.

Thies, J. *Architekt der Weltherrschaft. Die "Endziele" Hitlers.* Düsseldorf 1976.

Thomer, Egbert. *Unter Nippons Sonne: Deutsche U-Boote, Blockadebrecher und Basen in*

Fernost. Based on notes of Fregattenkapitän Oskar Herwartz. Minden, Westf., 1959.

Thomsen, Karl-August. "Marine-Stützpunkt Penang." *Köhlers Flotten-Kalender* 48 (1960): 146–56.

Thorwald, Jürgen, ed. *Ernst Heinkel. Stürmisches Leben.* Stuttgart, 1953.

Tischer, Heinz. *Die Abenteuer des letzten Kapers: Hilfskreuzer Thors Reise in die Katastrophe.* Grosshansdorf, 1983.

Tobe Ryōichi et al., eds. *Shippai no honshitsu—Nihongun no soshikoronteki kenkyū* (The essence of failure—An organizational analysis of the Japanese forces). Tokyo, 1984.

Tōgō Shigenori. *Jidai no ichimen* (One side of an age). Tokyo, 1952.

Tomi Ichirō. "Indoyō no Nichidoku Sensuikan Sakusen" (Japanese-German submarine operations in the Indian Ocean). *Hatō* (November 1989–June 1990), 85: 95–107; 86: 75–90; 87: 72–83; 88: 135, 145–88.

Toyama Saburō. *Ikari to pain. Nihon Kaigun sokumenshi* (Anchor and flagstaff. A historical profile of the Japanese navy). Tokyo, 1983.

————. "Die japanischen Planungen für den Grossostasienkrieg 1941." In *Kriegswende Dezember 1941,* edited by Jürgen Rohwer et al., 17–34. Koblenz, 1984.

————. *Nihon kaigunshi* (Japanese naval history). Tokyo, 1980.

————. "Years of Transition: Japan's Naval Strategy from 1894 to 1945." *Revue Internationale d'Historie Militaire,* no. 38 (1978): 162–82.

Trauzettel, Rolf, and Bernd Martin. "Kriegsziele." *Vierteljahreshefte für Zeitgeschichte* 8 (1960): 121–33.

————. *Literaturbericht zur Geschichte China und zur japanischen Zeitgeschichte.* Munich, 1980.

Tsunoda Hitoshi. *Hawai sakusen* (The Hawaii operation). *Senshi Sōsho* (War history series), edited by Bōei Kenshūjo Senshi Shitsu, vol. 10. Tokyo 1967.

————. *Middouē kaisen* (The Midway sea battle). *Senshi Sōsho* (War history series), edited by Bōei Kenshūjo Senshi Shitsu, vol. 14. Tokyo, 1971.

Tsunoda Jun. "Die amtliche japanische Kriegsgeschichtsschreibung über den Zweiten Weltkrieg in Ostasien und im Pazifik." In *Jahresbibliographie der Bibliothek für Zeitgeschichte* 45 (1973): 393–405.

————. "The Navy's Role in the Southern Strategy." In *The Fateful Choice,* edited by James W. Morley, 241–95. New York, 1980.

Tsunoda Jun, ed. *Gendaishi shiryō* (Materials on contemporary history). 45 vols. Tokyo, 1962–80.

————, ed. *Ugaki Kazushige nikki* (Diary of Ugaki Kazushige). 3 vols. Tokyo, 1968–71.

Tsunoda Jun and Uchida Kazutomi. "The Pearl Harbor Attack: Admiral Yamamoto's Fundamental Concept." *Naval War College Review* 31, no. 2 (1978): 83–88.

Tsunoda Kyuji. "Daihon'ei kaigunbu, Rengō kantai. Shōwa 17-nen 6-gatsu made" (Imperial Headquarters, Navy Department, the Combined Fleet until June 1942), pt. 2. *Senshi Sōsho* (War history series), edited by Bōei Kenshūjo Senshi Shitsu, vol. 80. Tokyo, 1975.

Turner, L. C. F., et al. *War in the Southern Oceans.* London, 1961.

Ugaki Matome. *Fading Victory: The Diary of Admiral Matome Ugaki, 1941–1945.* Pittsburgh, Pa., 1991.

United States Government Printing Office et al. *Documents on German Foreign Policy, 1918–1945,* Series D (1937–1945). Washington, D.C., 1949–64.

Vermehren, Paul. *Etappe Ostasien.* Unpublished. BA-MA, RM 12 II/392.

Vietsch, Eberhard von. *Wilhelm Solf: Botschafter zwischen den Zeiten.* Tübingen, 1961.

Vlahos, Michael. "The Naval War College and the Origins of War-Planning against Japan." *Naval War College Review* 33, no. 4 (1980): 23–41.

Wagner, Gerhard, ed. *Fuehrer Conferences on Naval Affairs, 1939–1945.* Annapolis, Md., 1990.

———. *Lagevorträge des Oberbefehlshabers der Kriegsmarine vor Hitler, 1939–1945.* Munich, 1972.

Wagner, Wieland. *Japans Aussenpolitik in der frühen Meiji-Zeit (1868–1894): Die ideologische und politische Grundlegung des japanischen Führungsanspruchs in Ostasien.* Stuttgart, 1990.

Wegner, Bernd, ed. *Zwei Wege nach Moskau. Vom Hitler-Stalin-Pakt bis zum "Unternehmen Barbarossa."* Munich, 1991.

Wehler, Hans-Ulrich, ed. *Der Primat der Innenpolitik.* Berlin, 1965.

Weigley, Russel F., ed. *New Dimensions in Military History: An Anthology.* San Rafael, Calif., 1975.

Weinberg, Gerhard L. "Globaler Krieg: Die Beziehungen zwischen dem europäischen und pazifischen Kampfraum während des Zweiten Welktkrieges." In *Deutschland zwischen Krieg und Frieden,* edited by Karl Dietrich Bracher et al., 89–98. Bonn, 1990.

———. *A World at Arms: A Global History of World War II.* Cambridge, 1994.

Winton, John. *Ultra at Sea.* New York, 1989.

Yamamoto Chikao. "Daihon'ei kaigunbu, Rengō kantai. Dai Sandan sakusen chūki" (Imperial Headquarters, Navy Department. Combined Fleet. The mid-period of third-stage operations), pt. 5. *Senshi Sōsho* (War history series), edited by Bōei Kenshūjo Senshi Shitsu, vol. 71. Tokyo, 1974.

Yomiuri Shimbunsha. *Showashi no Tenno* (The Tenno in the Showa period). 30 vols. Tokyo, 1969–76.

Yoshii Hiroshi. "The Imperial Japanese Navy and the Three Nations Pact." *Folia Humanistica* no. 207 (1980):157–70.

———. "Die Kaiserlich-japanische Kriegsmarine und der Dreimächtepakt." In *Deutschland-Japan. Historische Kontakte,* edited by Josef Kreiner, 223–38. Bonn, 1984.

Yoshimatsu Yoshihiko. "Daihon'ei kaigunbu, Rengō kantai. Dai Sandan sakusen zenki" (Imperial Headquarters, Navy Department. Combined Fleet. The beginning of third-stage operations), pt. 4. *Senshi Soshō* (War history series), edited by Bōei Kenshūjo Senshi Shitsu, vol. 39. Tokyo, 1970.

Zetzsche, Hans-Jürgen. "Logistik und Operationen: Die Mineralölversorgung der Kriegsmarine im Zweiten Weltkrieg." Ph.D. diss., University of Kiel, 1986.

Index

About the Authors

Capt. Hans-Joachim Krug, GN (Ret.), joined the German navy in 1938 and served during World War II in U-boats in the Indian Ocean and in Southeast Asia. At the end of the war, he was the executive officer of U-219. After re-enlisting in the German navy in 1956, Krug served on the staff of the German military representative to NATO in Washington, D.C., and later became department head for the German Fleet Radar School. From 1969 to 1973, he was the military attaché to the German embassy in Tokyo, after which he served in the German Intelligence Service until he retired in 1978. Capt. Krug came out of retirement a short time later to work as the technical adviser for Wolfgang Petersen's film *Das Boot*. He lives in Wolfratshausen, Germany.

Rear Adm. Hirama Yōichi, JMSDF (Ret.), joined the Japan Maritime Self Defense Force (JMSDF) in 1954. After graduating from the National Defense Academy of Japan in 1957, Admiral Hirama served in the JMSDF for thirty-one years, including service as a deck officer and as commander of the destroyer *Chitose*. He retired in 1988. After retirement he taught military history for ten years at the National Defense Academy, and he is currently a lecturer at the National Defense Institute, JMSDF Staff College, Tsukuba University, and Tokiwa University. He received a doctorate in history from Keio University in 1997. Admiral Hirama has written numerous books and articles on military history, including *World War and the Japanese Navy* and *The Anglo-Japanese Alliance*, both in Japanese. He lives in Chiba City, Japan.

Cdr. Berthold J. Sander-Nagashima, GN, joined the Federal German Navy in 1977, where he specialized in antisubmarine warfare and served aboard fast patrol boats (FPBs) and frigates. He was promoted to officer in 1980. Along with his German navy training, Cdr. Sander-Nagashima has received flight-officer training from the U.S. Navy, and he holds a degree in pedagogy from German Armed Forces University and a doctorate in history from Hamburg University. His book *Die deutsch-japanischen Marinebeziehungen 1919–1942* (German-Japanese Naval Relations) was published in 1998. Cdr. Sander-Nagashima currently serves as staff officer and naval historian for *Militärgeschichtliches Forschungsamt* (German Armed Forces Military Research Office), and as a lecturer in Japanese studies at Freie Universität Berlin. He lives in Berlin.

Axel Niestlé has been a private researcher of World War II military history for almost twenty years, focusing on the Battle of the Atlantic and the operation and technical history of German U-boats. His previous publications include illustrated technical monographs on the famous German World War II Type VII C and Type IX C U-boats, and the book *German U-boat Losses during World War II: Details of Destruction,* the latter published by the Naval Institute Press. After an early career as a scientific assistant at the Technical University of Berlin, he now owns a planning office that specializes in the rehabilitation of polluted areas and waste disposal sites. He lives in Dabendorf, Germany.

The Naval Institute Press is the book-publishing arm of the U.S. Naval Institute, a private, nonprofit, membership society for sea service professionals and others who share an interest in naval and maritime affairs. Established in 1873 at the U.S. Naval Academy in Annapolis, Maryland, where its offices remain today, the Naval Institute has members worldwide.

Members of the Naval Institute support the education programs of the society and receive the influential monthly magazine *Proceedings* and discounts on fine nautical prints and on ship and aircraft photos. They also have access to the transcripts of the Institute's Oral History Program and get discounted admission to any of the Institute-sponsored seminars offered around the country.

The Naval Institute also publishes *Naval History* magazine. This colorful bimonthly is filled with entertaining and thought-provoking articles, first-person reminiscences, and dramatic art and photography. Members receive a discount on *Naval History* subscriptions.

The Naval Institute's book-publishing program, begun in 1898 with basic guides to naval practices, has broadened its scope to include books of more general interest. Now the Naval Institute Press publishes about one hundred titles each year, ranging from how-to books on boating and navigation to battle histories, biographies, ship and aircraft guides, and novels. Institute members receive significant discounts on the Press's more than eight hundred books in print.

Full-time students are eligible for special half-price membership rates. Life memberships are also available.

For a free catalog describing Naval Institute Press books currently available, and for further information about subscribing to *Naval History* magazine or about joining the U.S. Naval Institute, please write to:

Membership Department
U.S. Naval Institute
291 Wood Road
Annapolis, MD 21402-5034
Telephone: (800) 233-8764
Fax: (410) 269-7940
Web address: www.navalinstitute.org